INDIA

PATRICK FRENCH

INDIA

A Portrait

ALFRED A. KNOPF · NEW YORK · 2011

THIS IS A BORZOI BOOK
PUBLISHED BY ALFRED A. KNOPF

Originally published in Great Britain by Allen Lane, an imprint of the
Penguin Group, a division of Penguin Books Ltd., London.

Library of Congress Cataloging-in-Publication Data
French, Patrick, [date]
India : a portrait / Patrick French.—1st U.S. ed.
p. cm.
Includes bibliographical references and index.
ISBN 978-0-307-27243-0
1. India—History—1947– 2. India—Politics and government—1947– 3. India—
Economic conditions—1947– 4. India—Social conditions—1947– I. Title.
DS480.84.F75 2011
954.04–dc22   2011003921

Jacket design by Carol Devine Carson

Manufactured in the United States of America
First United States Edition

MG

CONTENTS

INTRODUCTION

In 1997 I wrote *Liberty or Death*, an account of Indian independence and partition. Almost as soon as it was out, I wanted to do a sequel which looked at India in a new way, for what it was becoming rather than for what others wanted it to be. Some sort of unleashing was taking place, the effects of which were not yet clear, and the country appeared to be passing through epic and long-awaited changes. I was diverted by a biography, though even while I was writing it I was noticing the little revolutions in India, and the historical impulses that lay behind them.

Nearly everyone has a reaction to India, even if they have never been there. They hate it or love it, think it mystical or profane; find it extravagant or ascetic; consider the food the best or the worst in the world. For East Asians, it is a competitor and a source of some of their own spiritual traditions. For Americans, it is a challenge, a potential hub of cooperation or economic rivalry—both countries are diverse and hulking, their national identities strong and to an extent constructed, their populations loquacious and outgoing and admiring of entrepreneurial success. For many Europeans, India is a religious place with a special, undefined message. For the British, it is a link to old prestige, a land interesting mainly in the past tense. For the Pakistanis—the estranged siblings of the Indians—it is a site of threat and fascination.

Public discourse about India is caught in these old ways of looking. Inside the country itself, responses to recent economic progress are often pinned either to earlier socialist instincts against capital and globalization, or on seeing it as a triumphant riposte to past humiliations. The postcolonial outlook—vital in the early years of freedom as a means to take the nation forward, and as an antidote to constant Western assumptions about the restricted destiny of former colonies—has become an intellectual straitjacket which limits fresh thought at a time when something new is happening.

In *India* I have tried to write about the country both from the inside and from the outside—or from a distance. The information passes through three different prisms. The first is political, the second economic and the third social. The individual stories, calamities, aspirations and triumphs of many people are at the heart of the narrative. Each of the three sections— *Rashtra* or nation, *Lakshmi* or wealth, *Samaj* or society—seeks to answer, in an indirect way, the question: why is India like it is today?

Rashtra is about the birth of a nation. For any country, the moment of conception or formation is vital in explaining what happens later (think of Israel or the United States). In those early days, India was a beacon to Asian and African peoples who were seeking freedom from foreign rule. The dream turned stagnant, as a controlled, statist mindset took over. India was nominally not aligned in the Cold War and the Soviet Union was its friend—but many Indians wished to go West to seek their fortune. New political leaders arose, powered by caste, religion or regional affinity, and politics in India changed, following its own unique conventions and traditions. A handful of families became ever more important; the final chapter in *Rashtra* looks at how Indian democracy really works, and at the triumph of nepotism.

In *Lakshmi*, recent economic liberalization is placed in a deeper historical context. Why was international trade rejected with such force and certainty after independence? What makes a new nation prosperous? Why did people raised on a diet of socialism become robustly and even rapaciously capitalist, embracing the idea of economic creativity? Who becomes super-rich, who gets by and who remains super-poor? The rapid growth of the Indian economy was sparked by a near calamity in 1991, when the remnants of the country's gold reserves had to be sent to Switzerland in a bid to raise cash. There was nothing inevitable about India's rise, and *Lakshmi* uses the personal tales of the poor and the rich to explain how it happened.

The third section, *Samaj*, is more nebulous: it is about broad social patterns, and the characteristics that make India itself. The narrative shows things that might be taken for granted in India—the fact the "untouchable" father of the constitution was not allowed to sit in a classroom, the misconduct of the police and bureaucracy, the role of servants, the genetics of caste, the importance of India's many Muslims and their loyalty to the national ideal, and the deep and enduring influence of forms of faith. Through looking at the past, and sometimes at quite distant moments in history, the apparent peculiarities and continuing problems of the present can be revealed.

Globally, India is now sometimes portrayed as having a competitive edge over more sluggish developed countries that have abandoned thrift, given up on saving and refused to postpone gratification. Values that are embedded in an Indian way of life appear to have an unexpected relevance. A friend, Niranjan, forwarded me an email. It caught the idea that people like himself had a distinctive way of operating, and their lateral approach presented them with a new advantage. Like other Indians, Niranjan was taking pleasure in the possibility that the citizens of his country were highly motivated, and no longer perceived only as the victims of famine or superstition:

An Indian man walks into a bank in New York City and asks for the loan officer. He tells the loan officer that he is going to India on business for two weeks and needs to borrow $5,000. The bank officer tells him that the bank will need some form of security for the loan, so the Indian man hands over the keys of a new Ferrari parked on the street in front of the bank. He produces the title and everything checks out. The loan officer agrees to accept the car as collateral for the loan.

The bank's president and its officers all enjoy a good laugh at the Indian for using a $250,000 Ferrari as collateral against a $5,000 loan. An employee of the bank then drives the Ferrari into the bank's underground garage and parks it there. Two weeks later, the Indian returns, repays the $5,000 and the interest, which comes to $15.41.

The loan officer says, "Sir, we are very happy to have had your business, and this transaction has worked out very nicely, but we are a little puzzled. While you were away, we checked you out and found that you are a multimillionaire. What puzzles us is, why would you bother to borrow $5,000?"

The Indian replies: "Where else in New York City can I park my car for two weeks for only $15.41 and expect it to be there when I return?"

Ah, the mind of the Indian!

With its overlap of extreme wealth and lavish poverty, its mix of the educated and the ignorant, its competing ideologies, its lack of uniformity, its kindness and profound cruelty, its complex relationships with religion, its parallel realities and the rapid speed of social change—India is a macrocosm, and may be the world's default setting for the future.

PART I

RASHTRA · NATION

I

ACCELERATED HISTORY

IN LADAKH the air is thin and dry, and it is cold even when the sunlight burns you. Tashi Norbu could remember how, in 1948, Buddhist monks in their dark red robes had built an improvised, rocky airstrip near the monastery in Leh. Out of the sky came a buzzing metal shape, a Dakota aeroplane carrying India's new prime minister, Jawaharlal Nehru. It landed in a cloud of dust.

"We had never seen a car or a motor vehicle at that time," Tashi Norbu said, sitting above his apricot orchard, speaking in a Tibetan dialect. He was an old man, an expert in medicinal herbs, water diversion and the correct way to shoot a bow and arrow. He wore a long brown robe secured with a lime-coloured sash, and on his head he had wedged a homburg.

"There were no roads in Ladakh. A plane lands from the sky, you can't imagine . . . All the local people put their hands together and prayed to the plane, we were all praying."

Ladakh is a mountainous region by the borders of Tibet, China and Pakistan. In the rush of history, it might have ended up on the wrong side of the line; but it is in India. It feels like the remoter parts of Tibet, though without the Chinese influence. By a quirk of history, Ladakhis follow Tibetan Buddhism, having avoided the waves of Muslim invasions that changed the traditions of their neighbours. Geographically inaccessible, the region preserves an ancient way of living. The present, powerless King of Ladakh's lineage dates back an incredible thirty-eight generations to 975. His family lost their influence more than a century ago, and he lives in a little hilltop palace.

Tashi Norbu thought of himself as a Ladakhi above all else. "As children, we hadn't heard about India. We didn't know who the Indians were. We knew they were 'gyagarpa,' people who came from the plains, but it was not until I grew older and saw a map that I understood how big India was. Some things changed after independence: a politician came to visit us from Srinagar in Kashmir, but we didn't know what that meant, whether he was a religious leader or a king, or what.

"I can remember when I first saw the Indian army using kerosene! I couldn't believe the flames, how easily they could make them. They told us we could buy kerosene in Leh if we sold eggs. We would take the eggs, carry them like a baby while crossing the [Indus] river, sell them to a trader, buy the kerosene, and carry the kerosene back to the village.

"Pandit Nehru told the chief lama he should become a leader, and the lama said since we were in a mountain region he would rather be a worker. He handed a shovel to Nehru, who began digging! They took some photographs of it. Yes, I am content to be with India. We would never have got along with Pakistan, because they are Mohammedans and follow different customs. As for China, it is communist; you have to take permission for everything you want to do, and you can't speak your mind. In India you can speak your mind, so I'm happy to be with them."[1]

Ladakh is about as far north as you can get in India. The modern nation created after independence was implacably diverse, culturally and geographically.

Tamil Nadu is more than 1,500 miles south of Ladakh. It is a different kind of world. While Ladakhis are wiry, with narrow facial apertures—a small nose, mouth and ears and slit eyes, perhaps in response to the icy, windy climate—Tamils usually have a wide sprawl of a face, in keeping with the southern lushness. The land is rich with vegetation, paddy fields and mango trees, and the view from the coast is filled with fishing boats, long painted skiffs with curved prows, catching kingfish. Young men dive low for stone fruit—giant blue-green mussels, which they pluck off the rocks.

When the Indian national flag was chosen at independence, a tricolour of saffron, white and green, Ashoka's wheel of dharma, or law, was placed at its centre. The emperor Ashoka had united the subcontinent before the birth of Christ, but even his kingdom stopped advancing when it reached the south. The southern tip of India, perhaps more than any other place on earth, has an unbroken chain to the ancient past. There have been caste wars, the usual comings and goings of power, with one imperial dynasty replacing another in earlier times, but no invasion. European traders—British, Dutch, Portuguese and French—had all pursued their interests forcefully over the centuries, but the society had retained its own earlier forms. It would be as if the religion or culture at the time of the pharaoh Amenhotep III, who ruled Egypt in the fourteenth century BCE, had survived in snatches in the everyday life of modern Egyptians.

The noise of central and northern India can at times drown out the subtlety of the south, which has been so vital in determining the country's present status. On the edge of Chennai or Madras, it can be so luxuriant and humid and quiet that you feel as if you are in another land; but it is just another face of India, with the tinkle of bicycle bells and the echoes of a temple the only distraction. Saravankumar, a professor, described it to me this way: "The identity we have here goes right back to the first century, to the Tamil poem *Puram 183*. I would say my Tamilness comes from the language."[2] I could understand what he meant, and could see—or hear, on the street and in the home—how the high-speed, bubbling Tamil tongue was part of the environment. So while the north had its upheavals, the south went on forever.

The nation can be triangulated in many ways: it is all India. Far across to the east, about 1,750 miles from Chennai and the same distance from Ladakh—up near Burma, Bhutan and Bangladesh—lies Meghalaya. It is a hilly and rainy state, a kingdom with rushing waterfalls, tropical forests and unexpectedly successful rock groups. The people look different from Tamils or Ladakhis, and follow their own traditions.

Take just one tribe in Meghalaya as an example, the Khasi people, who are more than a million strong. Their language bears some connection to Khmer, which is spoken in Cambodia. They are a matrilineal society: their family name comes from the mother's side, and the last daughter in the family to leave the family home is the custodian of all ancestral property. The Khasi religion is not connected to any other faith and emphasizes a belief in one supreme god, U Blei. In their creation myth, the Moon (which is male) and the Sun (which is female) stand symbolically for the divine presence. The Khasis have a covenant with their deity—who is the dispenser, the maker, the giver, the creator, the divine law. They believe in the concept of "iapan," or pleading with god for everything they need, and are very sure about how they came to be on earth—by descending a golden ladder from the mount of heaven's navel. What they are not sure about is how exactly man came to be created by god.

As Kynpham Sing Nongkynrih, a Khasi, explained to me in perfect English: "Although we believe we were created by god, we also think that it is not the business of humans to know exactly how. As I said, the Khasis believe in one supreme god, who is formless, or rather whose form man cannot even begin to imagine, for that is forbidden. A Khasi does not believe in idol worship, since he must not conceive the appearance of god. We do not have a place of worship since our religion is private and familial. True worship takes place in one's heart, or at one's family's hearth. Because of this, the Khasi religion remains largely unorganized, and it is completely lacking in missionary tendencies. This is because a Khasi believes his god is also the god of the Hindu, the Muslim, the Christian, and of all other people. His motto is, therefore, 'Ieit la ka jong, burom ia kiwei'—'Love one's own, and respect others.' As for me, I will always prefer my own religion to any other because it's the only religion that I know which does not believe in hell's damnation. The Khasi universe is two-tier—heaven and earth—and there is no room for hell."[3]

Each of these disparate places was part of the nation that was born in 1947.

When the British gained control of the subcontinent in the eighteenth and nineteenth centuries, they often preferred to rule through a local potentate. They did not make a lot of converts to Christianity. By propping up client rulers and giving them imperial baubles and titles, they could secure influence at minimum cost. This strategy of containment succeeded until the early twentieth century, when a new class of Indian nationalists, stirred by ideals of liberty and democracy, used peaceful mass resistance to campaign for an end to foreign rule. The Indian National Congress had been established in 1885 by English-speaking professionals who wanted a greater involvement in government. Under the creative guidance of Mohandas Gandhi—the Mahatma, or "great soul"—the Congress became a popular movement of liberation from the British empire.

While this new political force challenged imperial control and promoted itself as the true voice of India, many Muslims, who made up nearly a quarter of the population, felt excluded by the largely Hindu idiom in which it operated. The Muslim elite, which still retained much of its influence after the decline of the Mughals and the rise of the European powers, was not attracted by what Gandhi represented. Many felt that for all the talk of inclusiveness, the Congress leadership was made up largely of Hindus from the higher end of the caste system who would, if India became independent, undermine the security and status of Muslims. With their homespun khadi clothing, their emphasis on Hindi rather than Urdu as the national language of India, their big rallies and their belief in profound social reform, the Congress leaders seemed like a threat. The Congress-run provincial governments which took office in parts of India in the 1930s were presented as the heralds of a new "Hindu Raj."

When political uncertainty grew during the Second World War, large numbers of Muslims turned to Mohammad Ali Jinnah, who wanted to establish a homeland or a place of safety for their community in parts of north India where Muslims were in a majority. The Indian National Congress failed to acknowledge the gravity of this demand. As late as 1946, Jinnah's Muslim League was willing to accept a federation in which defence, foreign policy and communications remained under common control, rather than a fully independent Pakistan. During the final negotiations, Jinnah was boxed in by a triumphalist Congress and British incompetence: the result was the bloody and disastrous partition of the Indian empire into two dominions, Pakistan and India.

It was a time of accelerated history, when a political leader's decisions might have enormous and fateful consequences. In the largest mass migration in history, Hindus and Sikhs escaped to India and Muslims escaped to Pakistan. Even setting aside the vast, unexpected convulsion during the creation of the two new wings, East and West Pakistan, the shape of free India remained highly unclear. Most significantly, the status of India's princely rulers was left unresolved at independence. Each kingdom had its own treaty with London, and control could not legally be handed over to the successor government—controlled by the Congress—without a signature.

Take Jodhpur as an example: Hanwant Singh was a volatile young man, and like most princely rulers he was not accustomed to being told what to do. Tall and bulky with a toothbrush moustache, he was called "Big Boy" by his father. He liked playing polo, shooting sand grouse and performing magic tricks. As heir to the dry, flinty kingdom of Jodhpur in the west of India, a princely state not much smaller than England, his life had been mapped out for him. When he went to boarding school, he took with him two cars, a stable of horses and a retinue of servants, including a tailor and a barber.[4]

In June 1947, life became more complicated. His father died, making him Maharaja of Jodhpur just as India was about to become free. On the personal side, the 23-year-old intended shortly to breach protocol by marrying a European, although not long before that he had taken a sixteen-year-old princess from Gujarat as his first bride. He dealt with the tension by going off on pig-sticking hunts, but the decisions facing him could not be postponed because he was in an unexpectedly important political position. Jodhpur bordered the emerging Muslim homeland of Pakistan, and its founder, Jinnah, had asked him to break with India and link his kingdom to the new nation. Unfortunately, the prince and most of his people were Hindu. Jinnah offered extraordinarily favourable terms: the maharaja could use Karachi as a free port, purchase whatever weapons he wanted, control the railway line to Sindh and receive free grain for famine relief. It sounded like a good deal. He agreed to sign up for Pakistan. Then, as he was about to touch his fountain pen to the paper, he learned that none of his fellow Rajput princes had yet thrown in their lot with the Pakistanis and he got cold feet. He told Jinnah he would go home and think about it.[5]

India's capital had moved earlier in the century from Calcutta to a processional new city on the edge of ancient Delhi. A few days after he met Jinnah, the maharaja was staying at New Delhi's finest hotel, the Imperial. A short south Indian man appeared there and told him he must come to Government House and meet the viceroy. This was unexpected. Unlike other members of the princely order, the Maharaja of Jodhpur disliked the British, and was glad they were leaving, even if his late father had been made a Knight Commander of the Most Exalted Order of the Star of India by the King Emperor George V. He claimed that as a boy he had at night crept out of his marble and sandstone palace (which had been built by his father over fifteen years, using 3,000 skeletal labourers) and put up anti-colonial wall posters. Hanwant Singh did as he was told, and accompanied the south Indian man to Government House.

Here the departing imperial power, in the form of the suave viceroy Mountbatten, told him it would be unwise to join Pakistan since his subjects could rise up in rebellion.[6] The maharaja was incensed. It was clear that what the viceroy was really saying was that independent India's new rulers—lawyers, agitators, socialists, Gandhians; the sort of people who had never shot a sand grouse—would foment revolution against His Highness. He wanted the imperialists to leave, but he certainly did not want their power or his patrimony to be taken over by the Indian National Congress. So would the new Indian government, then, give him what Pakistan had promised? Mountbatten looked to his adviser. No, said the short south Indian man—V. P. Menon, the senior political reforms commissioner—but they might offer a donation of grain. The big prince argued and blustered at Lord Mountbatten, and prevaricated and argued some more, and finally signed the instrument of accession.

At this point the viceroy left the room—he had other things to do—and the Maharaja of Jodhpur found himself alone with V. P. Menon. The encounter was too much. He had no entourage with him here, no cowering Rajput retainers to show him respect in the usual manner. All the young maharaja had was the painful knowledge that he had just given up control over the huge kingdom his family had ruled for many hundreds of years. Should he have gone with Pakistan? Might he have stood out for full independence, and approached the United Nations for protection, as some other rulers such as the Nizam of Hyderabad were thinking of doing? And why, anyway, was this snaggle-toothed southerner, this clerk, telling him what to do? Enraged, he pulled out a .22 calibre pistol, pointed it at his tormentor and shouted, "I refuse to take your dictation." He added for good measure that he was descended from the Sun, and would shoot down Menon like a dog if he betrayed the people of Jodhpur.[7]

V. P. Menon responded coolly and bureaucratically to the irate young Maharaja of Jodhpur, focusing on the matter at hand. His brief was to snare every princely kingdom for the new Indian union (few princely states fell inside Pakistan's borders).

"I told him," he wrote later, "that he was making a very serious mistake if he thought that by killing me, or threatening to kill me, he could get the accession abrogated."[8] The pistol disappeared. What Menon did not mention was that Jodhpur would soon be absorbed into the new state of Rajasthan, and that the days of the maharajas, rajas, nawabs and nizams were over, even if they were allowed to use regal red licence plates on their cars. Five years later, during the voting in India's first general election, Hanwant Singh died along with his Muslim third wife in a plane crash; he never did learn that he had just been elected as Member of Parliament (MP) for Jodhpur.[9]

Imagine for a moment you are the good-looking Jawaharlal Nehru, India's first prime minister. With your colleagues, you have to decide what shape the new system of administration is going to take. Gandhi and Jinnah are old, and shortly to die, one from an assassin's bullet, the other from lung disease. You are in your late fifties, a widower, and have spent in total nine years of your life in prison. How do you proceed?

Nehru had been given much time, like Nelson Mandela after him, to refine his political thinking. His jail during the Second World War was not a place of orange jumpsuits, black goggles and dead headphones: he and other members of the Congress Working Committee were installed in Ahmadnagar Fort, located in a dry region to the east of Bombay, and treated in something like gentlemanly fashion. He cultivated a small garden, and the group held impromptu seminars. He told his niece Chandralekha in a letter that he was "dabbling in Persian," and learning much from his fellow detainees. "Hindi, Urdu, Bengali, Gujarati, Marathi, Tamil, Telugu, Sindhi and Oriya—we practically cover every important language of India."[10] His family sent books to him, and he wrote *The Discovery of India*, an elegant combination of history and propaganda. It was an engaged, nationalist work which drew on the wide learning of his fellow detainees, including his room-mate, Maulana Azad, the Mecca-born scholar who, unusually for a Muslim, had become a Congress leader.

The book's premise was that India's present culture was linked to the Indus Valley civilization of four or five thousand years ago, a sophisticated sphere of planned cities, baths and sculptures. While Hinduism had been a common thread for millennia, he felt it would be "entirely misleading to refer to Indian culture as Hindu culture," since it contained Buddhist, Jain and Islamic influences too.[11] The emperor Ashoka had brought unity to the subcontinent more than 2,000 years ago, and it would be wrong, he said, to describe the repeated invasions by Muslim marauders over the last millennium as Muslim invasions, "just as it would be wrong to refer to the coming of the British to India as a Christian invasion . . . The Afghans might well be considered a border Indian group, hardly strangers to India, and the period of their political dominance should be called the Indo-Afghan period." Although the Mughals were outsiders from Central Asia, "they fitted into the Indian structure with remarkable speed and began the Indo-Mughal period."[12] Having travelled widely in India during the 1930s, Nehru knew the nation had "depth of soul" and realized that although its people varied hugely, "everywhere there was that tremendous impress of oneness, which had held all of us together for ages past, whatever political fate or misfortune had befallen us."[13] In this optimistic interpretation, India was a cheerfully composite and syncretic civilization, which would remain united.

London liked to think of Nehru as the last Englishman to rule India:

rather, he came from a wealthy, Anglicized, Hindu Brahmin family, originally from Kashmir, which had been influenced both by the West and by
the refined, mannered culture of the Muslim nobility. It was a world in
which literary references were expected to range from ancient Indian thinkers to contemporary European writers. His view of history came from this
intellectual collision: the culture of the nawabs met Cambridge University.
Nehru had a liberal, modern, perceptive, pluralistic view of India's past,
and his ambition was to make it come true for the future too. *The Discovery
of India* was a fine, slanted and sometimes romantic version of history.

Come freedom, how would he implement his nationalist dreams? Would
it be easier to borrow the mechanisms of the departed colonialists? You
could have an autocracy where one social group prevailed, or a dictatorship
where progress grew out of the barrel of a gun. Or—and this is where India
was unusual—you could have a public discussion about the ideal system of
government, and which outdated traditions should be given up.

First, it was necessary to secure the nation, the rashtra. When the British
empire closed down, it was near to collapse. The police were demoralized,
the army was breaking along religious lines and the administration was
cracking. The imperialists had left no effective peace-keeping force; nearly
bankrupt after depending on American financial support during the Second
World War, Britain's main concern was to get out.[14] In independent India
the situation was particularly unstable because, from a legal and practical
perspective, the government was inheriting less than half of the empire's
original land mass. The north-east and north-west became Pakistan, leaving
six complete provinces (Bombay, Madras, Orissa, Bihar, the United Provinces and the Central Provinces) which had been under British rule, and
the partitioned remnants of three others (Punjab, Bengal and Assam). The
princely rulers, whose states had covered more than a third of the empire,
were in theory free to do as they liked. Some had private armies, while the
larger kingdoms like Kashmir and Hyderabad—which had a government
income equal to that of Belgium—thought they might stand alone.

Congress had not come this far, had not endured the Morley–Minto
reforms (which allowed a limited number of Indians to elect legislators) and
the 1919 Jallianwala Bagh massacre (in which nearly 400 unarmed demonstrators were killed) and the Simon Commission (talks about talks) and the
Round Table conferences (further talks, in London) and the Government
of India Act of 1935 (which introduced some provincial self-government)
and the Quit India movement (total opposition to British rule during the
Second World War) and the Cripps Mission (a time-wasting exercise) and

the Bengal famine (in which several million people perished) and the Simlà conferences (further talks) and the tortuous negotiations with viceroys Wavell and Mountbatten and the baroque bigotry and chilly indifference of prime ministers Winston Churchill and Clement Attlee, let alone the beatings and marches and bandhs (general strikes) and dharnas (mass sit-ins) and the repeated terms of imprisonment, only to concede power to hereditary monarchs. According to the Gujarati lawyer and Congress power-broker Sardar Vallabhbhai Patel, the princes of India were parasites, "rotten fruit . . . incompetent, worthless human beings, deprived of the power of independent thinking and whose manners and morals are those of the depraved."[15] To break their substantial influence, though, would require subtlety.

This was where V. P. Menon proved the perfect flexible operator. Clever and thoughtful, he was the son of a schoolmaster from Kerala in the far south, and had worked as a railway stoker, coal miner and Bangalore tobacco company clerk before gaining a junior post in the civil service. He had an unusual home life: after his wife left him and returned to southern India, he had moved in with the Keralite friends who had arranged their marriage, and the couple helped to bring up his two sons. When the husband died, Menon married his widow, who was some years his senior.[16] In the years between the two world wars, he had worked his way up the civil service and become a respected senior bureaucrat.

Menon had recently drafted the text under which Congress and the Muslim League agreed the terms of independence. When Mountbatten asked him how to deal with the princes, he said they should be encouraged to join the new nation, giving up control of external affairs in return for the retention of autonomy and a chunk of local taxation—their "privy purses." He wrote craftily later: "The alternative to a peaceful and friendly settlement of the states' problem was to allow political agitation to develop in the states and to create, especially in the smaller ones, dire confusion and turmoil. Anyone conversant with the conditions in the country after partition must be aware of the inherent dangers of such a course."[17] Despite his own royal connections, Lord Mountbatten was a pragmatist who preferred Menon's plan to risking the possible Balkanization of India into a subcontinent of warring states, as had happened in China during the 1920s. So he personally persuaded the princes to sign up.

After independence, as the north imploded in the violence and chaos of partition, Menon worked under the iron guidance of Vallabhbhai Patel to integrate the remaining princely states. It was an epic task (there were estimated to be 554 kingdoms in all) which he performed with great speed and diligence. Patel was clear in his intentions, telling his staff, "Do not question the extent of the personal wealth claimed by [the princes], and never ever confront the ladies of the household. I want their states—not their wealth."[18] V. P. Menon's experience with the pistol-wielding Maharaja of Jodhpur was to be one of many bizarre encounters from Srinagar to Cape Comorin. His targets ranged from seriously obscure potentates to sophisticated royals who kept suites in the grander hotels of Paris or London; some taluqdars, or landowners, even approached him and asked to make treaties of accession despite having no princely status. The powerful and progressive Maharaja of Bikaner called on all hereditary rulers to be true patriots and embrace independent India, while an irate but inconsequential raja from near Mysore, who had only 16,000 subjects, refused to sign until the latest possible moment.

The complication was Kashmir, which should logically have joined Pakistan since it had a Muslim majority. The Hindu ruler thought otherwise, and India and Pakistan fought their first war within months of the end of empire. This led to the rough partition of its territory in a form that left everyone unhappy.

Each Indian kingdom was different, showing the sheer range of the subcontinent's social, ethnic and religious communities. Up in the ancient hill kingdom of Tripura in the north-east, the monarch was a child, and his mother signed away the state on his behalf. In Orissa, Menon found "excited aborigines" were fighting the local raja with bows and arrows in an effort to make him join India. A neighbouring Oriya prince was attempting to sell his kingdom's mineral rights in perpetuity before surrendering. In Rewa, a nervous V. P. Menon found himself gheraoed, or surrounded, by a fierce mob which refused to let him enter the palace. He suspected the ruler had himself arranged this reception, and asked him to put in writing that he refused to cooperate; the maharaja became nervous, and backed down.

Menon crisscrossed India by aeroplane, working out the best way to integrate the new nation. In Danta, a tiny state in Gujarat, a peculiar problem occurred: he could not contact the ruler. It seemed His Highness spent much of each day and night performing Hindu rituals, and between June and September in particular had not a moment to spare for official duties. In October 1948, he agreed his son could take the throne and sign the document of accession. In Cochin the royal family included several hundred princesses, and Menon made special provision for them because he thought they resembled "a rare collection of birds" that would be unlikely to survive if released into the wild. Where necessary, he made symbolic concessions, enabling rulers to retain their ancient princely dignity; in one case, he allowed a grant for the supply and maintenance of royal cars. "It is high statesmanship," wrote Mountbatten's press attaché admiringly, "that can cover a revolutionary act in the mantle of traditional form."[19]

Without the integration of the princely states, it would not have been possible for India to become a cohesive nation, or to invent itself as a modern democracy. In the crack-up of partition, the temptation might have been to reach for the gun and the edict. For many people, though, bloodshed would be the abiding memory.

The events of 1947 have an enduring capacity to shock. Bir Bahadur Singh is a retired shopkeeper, a handsome old man with an elaborate white beard. In the spring of that year, his village near Rawalpindi, in what is today Pakistan, came under siege. All the Sikh families in the area gathered together in a haveli, a large house with a courtyard. When they walked across the rooftops between the buildings, they risked being shot. There seemed to be no way out. In the distance they could see fires burning and, according to the rumours, a large gang of armed men was approaching the village, seeking revenge for horrific attacks committed against Muslims many hundreds of miles away in Bengal. Yet only days before that, everything had been normal: theirs was a lovely village, protected by hills which were dotted with trees and bushes, running down to fields of ripening green wheat and paddy and an orchard, and the houses themselves were well-built and well-ordered and the place was kept clean.

A local Muslim farmhand came to the trapped Sikhs and offered a solution. If they gave him a woman of his choosing, he would try to broker a settlement with the mob. It was discussed. What was the use of keeping the girl? Hadn't this one been having a secret relationship with the farmhand? Wasn't she a bad girl anyway? Why not give her up, if it meant saving all their lives? It was agreed: she would be swapped for freedom. But when the farmhand returned, Bir Bahadur Singh's father intervened and said no, this was a question of their dignity. A long cultural tradition of purity and sacrifice met raw fear. They would pay money, pay anything, but they would not give up a member of the community. He told them that even centuries before in the time of Mahmud of Ghazni, the first of the Muslim invaders of India, they had never abandoned their women to these raiders. "We brought those girls back," he said in Punjabi, casting his imagination across many hundreds of years, "and today you are asking us to give you this girl, absolutely not." They would preserve their honour, and face death.

What happened next has lived with Bir Bahadur Singh ever since. Tears came down his face and he turned his head away to one side as he described—sixty years on—how his father had prayed to the Sikh gurus. Seeing there was no way out, he would sacrifice the vulnerable before being killed himself, knowing the girls faced abduction, rape and forced conversion. Bir Bahadur Singh's father took his kirpan, his sword. A labourer confronted him and asked to be killed because he had swollen knees and would not be able to run. The labourer was beheaded. Another old man came and said to him: "Do you think I will allow Musalmans to cut this beard of mine and make me go to Lahore as a sheikh? For this reason kill me." So he too was killed. Now Bir Bahadur Singh's father approached his own daughter, Maan.

"My father said, 'Maan Beta, come here.' She was eighteen or nineteen years old, two years older than me. She sat down and my father raised his sword, but it didn't strike properly. My sister lifted her plait over her head, and my father angrily pulled her scarf back and brought down his sword. Her head rolled away. My uncles started beheading. All you could hear was the 'cut cut cut' sound. They just chanted god's name. Nobody ran away, nobody screamed."

Twenty-five women and girls were killed in this haveli, in this one village. Nearly all of the men died too, including Bir Bahadur Singh's father, but the son escaped. When he thinks back to those childhood days, he remembers the happier moments, like the times when he was little and sat with an old Muslim lady whom he called dadi, or grandmother. "Her name was Ma Hussaini, and I would go and sit on one side in her lap, and her granddaughter would sit on the other side. I used to pull her plait and push her away and she would catch hold of my jura, my hair [the Sikh topknot], and push me away. I would say she is my dadi and she would say she is my dadi." Relations between the communities were destroyed by the reciprocal massacres. Bir Bahadur Singh wondered, looking back over the decades, whether Hindus and Sikhs were themselves in part to blame, through their attitude to caste and religion. When they visited a Muslim household during his childhood, the family would refuse to eat, and if they were walking with a lunch box and happened to shake hands with a Muslim along the way, the food would become polluted and have to be thrown away. "If we had been willing to drink from the same cups," he said wistfully, "we would have remained united, we would not have had these differences, thousands of lives would not have been lost, and there would have been no partition."[20]

During the months after August 1947, similar scenes of retribution were played out across the north, and an estimated one million people were murdered. In Punjab, in particular, each community killed and was killed, raped and was raped, looted and was looted. Because India was perceived as the natural successor to the Indian empire and retained many of its institutions, Pakistan found itself in a desperate situation, financially insecure and lacking the key structures that were needed in a fledgling nation. In a terrible irony, it became the opposite of a place of safety. Jinnah's dream of a secular homeland for Muslims—"You may belong to any religion or caste or creed, that has nothing to do with the business of the state," he had told his people at its foundation—was replaced by a kind of chaos, as they struggled to establish a functioning country.[21] Many hoped the partition would be temporary, and Pakistan and India might reunite; you did not require a passport to travel between the two new nations in those days.[22] In the rush to gain freedom, nobody had worked out what division might entail. Nehru's niece, Nayantara Sahgal, unwittingly summed up the problem: "As children the idea of Pakistan was a joke—literally a joke. It was so outlandish and absurd to imagine that we would have such a thing happen in India."[23]

Everywhere, there was change, as traditions were uprooted. The character of Delhi altered forever as hundreds of thousands of Muslims fled to Pakistan, to be replaced by an even larger number of homeless Sikh and Hindu Punjabis. Yet despite the chaos, killing, kidnapping, food shortages and refugee camps, discussion was quickly under way in India about a constitutional settlement. Indeed, less than a week after the transfer of power from the British, politicians were busy in New Delhi debating such trivial matters as flag protocol in Hyderabad, and the president of the Constituent Assembly had to remind these leaders—never slow to express an opinion, or a number of opinions, since in India people tend to have more than one answer—of the matter at hand: "May I point out that we have met here today for the purpose of proceeding with the framing of the Constitution."[24]

Just over two years later, a document was agreed which has remained in place to this day, even during a brief hiatus in the 1970s when a state of emergency was declared. Free India was to be a secular, democratic republic, with strong reformist instincts. In the Muslim homeland, the framing of a constitution was postponed after Jinnah's death only a few months later and democratic politics were to be offset by decades of military rule; Pakistan's constitution has been suspended and reworked several times, and is still up for debate.

Earlier, both opponents of independence like Winston Churchill and supporters like Franklin D. Roosevelt had been sceptical of the idea that India would adopt a universal franchise. Could Asiatics rule themselves? Was democracy possible in such a fissiparous and undeveloped place? Remarkably, the new constitution was arrived at after vigorous discussion between rival interest groups: tribal people, communists, Muslim women and Hindu fundamentalists all had their say, and the final document, the longest constitution in the world, was overseen by Dr. Bhimrao Ambedkar, a formidable lawyer who had been born an "untouchable," a man who came from a community that was still expected to step aside when walking in the road rather than cross the path of someone from a higher caste.

Sovereignty was to be derived from the people, and justice, liberty, equality and fraternity were to be the aspiration of each citizen. Like the United States, modern India was founded on the idea that a few good men (and women, in this case) might come together and dream of a great nation, and enshrine that dream in law.

Stung by suggestions that the new dispensation would be a stitch-up for Congress, Nehru in particular was adamant that all shades of opinion should be heard. Dr. Ambedkar was recruited as law minister, although he had long been a political opponent. Nehru helped to shake up the very social rules that had brought him—the only son of a family of Kashmiri Pandits or Brahmins, who was sent abroad to be educated at the same boarding school as Churchill—to prominence. The constitution was to be about more than politics; it would be about society, on a grand scale.

The makers of the Indian Constitution met for the first time on 9 December 1946 (the very day on which a baby girl called Sonia Maino was born in Italy, handcuffed to history). In the Constituent Assembly in New Delhi bright new lights and electrically heated desks were in place, and leading figures in the soon to be victorious independence movement sat in tiered rows in semi-circles facing the dais. The assembly's members included historic names such as Nehru, Ambedkar, Patel, C. Rajagopalachari, Shyama Prasad Mookerji, Sarat Chandra Bose, J. B. Kripalani, Nehru's son-in law Feroze Gandhi, Jagjivan Ram, Maulana Azad and G. B. Pant. The chairman advised delegates to think carefully and to look to "the historic Constitutional

Convention held at Philadelphia by the American constitution-makers, for their country. Having thrown off their allegiance to the British King in Parliament, they met and drew up what has been regarded, and justly so, as the soundest, and most practical and workable republican constitution in existence."[25] The United States was an important example for Indians, a large and diverse nation which had thrown off the British colonial yoke and invented itself as a new country with a fresh identity.

Over the succeeding months, the Constituent Assembly framed the future shape of the Indian nation, for better or for worse. It would be a parliamentary democracy, rather than an executive presidency, and would use the first-past-the-post electoral system. Many leaders contributed to the discussions: Nehru drew the big picture, Patel did the heavy lifting in committee, Ambedkar thought on his feet. Although their ambitions were in the main liberal, diverse and progressive, nearly all of the delegates came from within the Congress family. Their intellectual influences combined Indian traditions and ideas with European and American principles of creative popular sovereignty. The process was full of questions. What is the ideal way to run a very large country? Should power be held at a local level, giving people the opportunity to make their own decisions about the best way to live? Or was it better to retain control at the centre, to help develop a common national purpose at a time of change and reconstruction? Who organizes elections? How do you select the judiciary? How do you respect the position of minorities without letting them dominate? Of course, there were digressions.

A delegate from Assam in the far north-east said the death penalty should be abolished since it gave glory to the recipient, while a Christian member from Travancore was concerned the assembly should not sit on a Sunday.

A representative from Orissa asked about the problem of nepotism: "We know today the Government of India contains people who are the wife's brother or sister-in-law's cousin . . . The evil tradition is there. It is a very bad tradition."[26] How would it be prevented, when everyday Indian life was still built around devotion to membership of the extended family (unlike the English, who went nuclear in the thirteenth century)?

A Muslim politician argued strongly that followers of minority religions should "consider themselves and one another as full and equal citizens of a secular state," because in her opinion the reservation of parliamentary seats for Muslims had encouraged cultural divisions.[27] But the reservation of seats for disadvantaged lower castes and undeveloped indigenous tribes was agreed.

Hansa Mehta, a Hindu lawmaker from Bombay who translated Shakespeare and Molière into Gujarati, believed the tradition across many communities of keeping women in seclusion was "an inhuman custom" which had to be abolished. "As far as the Hindu religion is concerned," she said, "it does not enjoin purdah. Islam does. But, I feel that Islam will be better rid of this evil. Any evil practised in the name of religion cannot be guaranteed by the Constitution and I hope that our Muslim friends will remember that."[28] The previous year, Mehta had been responsible for altering the text of Article 1 of the Universal Declaration of Human Rights from "All men are born free and equal . . ." to "All human beings are born free and equal in dignity and rights." Her objection was not a matter of feminist semantics; when Eleanor Roosevelt told Mehta that "the word 'men' used in this sense was generally accepted to include all human beings," she rightly pointed out this was not true in much of India, where a newborn girl child might be left unnamed or even left to die.[29]

A delegate from Mysore spoke in a language few listeners could comprehend: "My information is that he is speaking in Canarese [Kannada]," said a puzzled speaker. "This is the third occasion when a gentleman has spoken in a language which is not understood by the bulk of the members present here."[30] The member, T. Channiah, was making a valuable symbolic point: many Indians did not speak Hindustani, the widely used composite of Hindi and Urdu.[31] Another day he suggested—in English—that India's figurehead president should be chosen alternately from north and south, to avoid dominance by northerners.[32] India's presidents have been picked from all across the country, but only two out of fourteen prime ministers so far have come from the south, and neither was from the far south.

Although the Constituent Assembly contained political and social revolutionaries, there were also many traditional types who wanted a return to time-honoured values. They believed that religion, as practised in ancient times, offered a pure template for living. For many Hindus, it was essential the slaughter of cows be banned. Others wanted the creation of village republics, as Mohandas Gandhi had demanded. The *Gandhian Constitution for Free India*, drafted in 1946 by his disciple S. N. Agarwal, proposed the primary political unit would be the panchayat, or village council, which should control interest rates, the collection of land revenue and cooperative farming, with assistance from patwaris (keepers of land records, who had a reputation for taking bribes). Chowkidars, or village watchmen, would guard the polity, armed with sticks. Political parties would disappear or be abolished, and a strong central government would not be needed, only an

"All-India Panchayat" supervising customs, defence, the currency and economic development plans. India would be a radically decentralized rural society. Whether an army of Gandhian chowkidars would have been sufficient to check the invasion of Kashmir in October 1947 by Pathan fighters from Pakistan remains open to question.[33]

Ambedkar for one was determined that the village, which he regarded as "a den of ignorance"—not surprisingly, given the humiliations he had experienced as an untouchable—should never be empowered in this way. Drawing on other countries' constitutions and borrowing heavily from the surprisingly progressive terms of the Government of India Act of 1935, he fashioned what he called "a flexible federation." There would be a single integrated judiciary, which would be distinct from the executive. "Subject to the maintenance of the republican form of government," he said tellingly, "each state in the U.S.A. is free to make its own constitution, whereas the constitution of the Indian union and of the states is a single frame from which neither can get out and within which they must work."[34]

The list of new rights was substantial. The Indian citizen could not be turned away from a shop, hotel, public well, bathing ghat or water tank on the grounds of sex, race, caste, place of birth or religion. At the stroke of a pen, untouchability was abolished and its practice in any form was forbidden. Every citizen had the right to freedom of speech and expression, the right to assemble peaceably and form associations, and the right to move freely within the territory of India. No accused person could be compelled to be a witness against him- or herself. Minority groups with a distinct script or language (there were several hundred) were permitted to use them freely. No religious instruction was to be provided by state educational institutions. The sort of tribalism that beset many new nations after freedom from colonial rule was specifically refuted in this document. It did not escape the makers of the Constitution that other countries, such as Turkey, were seeking to promote unity by preventing minorities from using separate languages; or indeed that the former colonial power had an established religion and no written constitution. The range of options available to the creators of the Indian Constitution was enormous, and there was nothing inevitable about the framing of the final result. Much of the world was still colonized by the European powers: the Indians were the pioneers, with few political models to go by, seeking to achieve something luminous and unprecedented.

The solution to the clash between traditionalists and progressives was to turn contentious subjects into Directive Principles of State Policy—

meaning they were aspirations rather than laws. In this way, matters like the promotion of cottage industries or "prohibiting the slaughter of cows and calves" became directive principles of the Constitution. Crucially, and unwisely, a common religious or personal law for all citizens was not agreed. Instead, India retained the separate "civil codes" that had been created by the British after the mutiny or rebellion of 1857 to keep minority communities tame. This meant Muslims in particular were able to maintain antiquated laws on matters such as polygamy and inheritance. Changing this system ("The State shall endeavour to secure for the citizens a uniform civil code throughout the territory of India") became an aspiration that could be deferred indefinitely.[35] They got around the problem of "India" being originally a name given to the subcontinent by Persian outsiders by beginning the Constitution with the phrase: "India, that is Bharat, shall be a Union of States." After that, there were no further references to the subject except in the index: "BHARAT–*See* INDIA." It was a clever move: it had been presumed before 1947 that the new leaders would pick the less inclusive "Hindustan."

When Ambedkar presented the final draft of the document to the Constituent Assembly in November 1948, he was in a confident mood. The depression he had suffered from was lifting—it had been a life of many reverses—and he had recently got married again, to a reputable Saraswat Brahmin. "No constitution is perfect," he told his listeners, "[but] I feel that it is workable, it is flexible and it is strong enough to hold the country together both in peacetime and in wartime. Indeed, if I may say so, if things go wrong under the new constitution, the reason will not be that we had a bad constitution. What we will have to say is, that Man was vile. Sir, I move."[36]

Dr. Ambedkar was making an important point: a constitution is a mechanism, not a solution, and it has to be operated properly if it is to work well. What is notable from this distance is how eloquent, forward-looking and thoughtful these debates were.

India's Constitution, as Ambedkar said, was not perfect. Man and woman would sometimes be vile. But many of the good things that were to happen in India over the succeeding decades arose from it, and it offered a stability that proved to be lacking in most neighbouring countries. It was a clear, well-intentioned and cleverly thought-out document which balanced liberty and security, shared power and did not rely on the goodwill of any one leader. India was taking a gamble on democracy, on the precept that individuals would no longer rely on the whim of others to represent their interests. In 1966 the former Australian ambassador to India, Walter Crocker, wrote: "If India is not run by dictators, Rightist, or Leftist, or Militarist, she will be run by politicians, more and more drawn from, or conditioned by, the outcastes and the low castes. For this is the majority, and, thanks to the ballot-box, it will be the votes of the majority which will set up and pull down governments . . . In abolishing the British raj, and in propagating ideas of equality, so hastily and in the way they did, Nehru and the upper-class Indian nationalists of English education abolished themselves."[37]

Nehru's niece, Nayantara Sahgal, had just turned twenty when India became independent. Her mother, Vijayalakshmi Pandit, was shortly to become India's ambassador to the United States, and Nayantara lived for much of the time in her uncle the prime minister's house. She remembered the sheer excitement of those days, and the feeling that something new was being created. "We were infected by the sense of at last arriving on the scene to take charge of one's own affairs," she told me. "I had been in the U.S.A. during the Second World War, and the shops in India seemed very empty by comparison. All the English shops were winding up, and things like foreign cosmetics and English china were off the shelves by about 1950. The idea was that we didn't need foreign luxuries, and we would only be able to buy Elizabeth Arden if we went abroad. They wanted to make room for the new Indian products that were going to fill the shelves.

"It was extraordinary to be able to go around Delhi and visit people, and to meet the president in Rashtrapati Bhavan, which had been Viceroy's House. My family having been rebels, we hadn't visited these places in Delhi before. Many of the new leaders at that time were living a very austere sort of life. Some people were busy wanting to rename roads and to pull down statues like the one of King George V on Rajpath. My uncle didn't like that and always said it was an absurd thing to try to wipe out history. In Hyderabad after the police takeover, they wanted to name a street after him. He said no, on no account. I think the leaders were trying to reflect the idealism of what they were hoping to create. It wasn't an exclusive thing. The Constituent Assembly was composed of all opinions. Everybody had a say in it. We had a sense of trepidation and adventure. When my uncle came to power, he was out to make a new world: he was not about to fit into the imperatives of the old world."[38]

Like most victors, the founding mothers and fathers instinctively wrote history in their own image. Mohammad Ali Jinnah's earlier role in the nationalist movement (Nehru's father Motilal had said that Jinnah showed the way to Hindu–Muslim unity) was edited out, as were the missteps Congress had made in its dealings with the Muslim League. To justify the shape of free India, Jinnah was presented as a troublemaker who had subverted unity for his own purposes (in a later movie, he was played by Christopher Lee, who had previously been Dracula). With parts of the subcontinent reworked into a Muslim homeland, it became necessary to find a different basis for the new nation, in which religion could not be permitted to define identity: India would not be a Hindu homeland.

As well as other minorities such as Buddhists, Jains and Christians, 35 million Muslims remained in India and needed to be kept safe. Some were even now having their houses stolen under the guise of being homes belonging to migrants who had gone to Pakistan. Vallabhbhai Patel had no doubt that stability was more important than anything else: "the first requirement of any progressive country is internal and external security."[39]

In the months immediately following partition, some chief ministers forced Muslims to leave for Pakistan.[40] Although there were few religious riots in India in the 1950s, the Muslim community faced suspicion and discrimination, and found it hard to get jobs in public service or the police. In his regular letters to the chief ministers of all the states, Nehru stressed the need for a psychological integration of India's people. He believed passionately in the idea of non-alignment, that India could fashion a new global role and reputation for itself, outside the rules of the major power blocs. Outdated prejudices had to be abandoned, and the nation needed to see in itself a reflection of modernity. When he heard that a rabid monkey had not been killed in Lucknow because an official was fearful of offending devotees of the monkey deity Hanuman, he fired off a furious letter to the chief ministers: "I think it is little short of scandalous that such a question even should arise in the mind of a District Magistrate when a mad monkey is going about biting hundreds of people. We have to decide whether India is going to be a fit country for human beings to live in or for monkeys or for other animals to take possession of."[41]

Although he never made the point explicitly, I believe Nehru's attitude was conditioned by the trauma he experienced during partition as he toured riot-torn regions and refugee camps, sometimes intervening at personal risk to stop looting and mayhem. He was not averse to clouting miscreants and ordering crowds to be peaceful in a way that would be hard to picture in an unruly country today, in this era of suicide bombings and sequestered leaders. Mohammed Yunus, a Pathan politician from Peshawar in the north-west and the youngest of forty-two children, remembered going to Jamia Millia Islamia university with Nehru when they heard news of a riot. "We drove to the scene, and they were very surprised to see him. We could see there had just been great violence. Pandit Nehru climbed up on to a wall and addressed the crowd. He said, 'I want to be the prime minister of a country where Hindus, Muslims, Sikhs and Christians can live in harmony. Did we get our freedom so that you could kill each other?' He was very brave. The riot stopped."[42]

Nehru was also left miserable by the murder of his old guide and mentor, Mohandas Gandhi, by a Hindu extremist. Before independence, he had a naïve assumption that sectarian antagonism would end once the imperialists had departed, telling a visiting reporter, "When the British go, there will be no more communal trouble in India."[43] And now millions of citizens were dead or displaced. Should he have responded more cautiously after the Muslim League's dramatic gains in the provincial elections of 1945–46? If Congress had been more patient, might the horrors of partition have been avoided? During those terrible days, Nehru had the cruellest awakening imaginable to the dangers facing his own dream. Unless free India could be united around a modern, democratic ideal, unless he could hold on to the secular faith that he had tried to propagate, his life's work would be a failure. He disliked ardent followers of any religious tradition, whether they were Hindu babas, Muslim clerics or Christian missionaries, and he despised unscientific superstition.

In order to achieve social harmony in a battered land where most people followed and took comfort from religion, Indian children were taught now that an individual's primary allegiance should be to the nation rather than to any communal or caste identity. Jains, Jews, Christians, Sikhs, Buddhists, Parsis, Muslims and Hindus were all encouraged to believe in a common purpose. Before the first general election in 1952—at that time the largest example of organized voting ever, with an electorate of 174 million—the election commission did its best to educate the public about the virtues and implications of a universal franchise. The Constitution was drummed into the head of every pupil at school, and children are still given essays with titles like "Why Am I a Patriot?" Textbooks emphasize the importance of being a good citizen. The Class 7 civics textbook has chapters on "Directive Principles of State Policy" and "Citizenship." The junior citizen is taught that "After years of slavery under the British rule our people became very poor," and a good citizen "votes for those who, he believes, will run the government properly. He pays his taxes on time. He knows that the interests of the nation are much more important than his own."[44] Indian patriotism, while often strident and self-righteous, contains little jingoism compared to that of many other countries, for dissent is part of the national idea. Although the internal boundaries of India were soon to be redrawn along linguistic lines, increasing regional power, people were told to think of themselves as Indians first. When the French writer André Malraux asked the agnostic Nehru late in life what had been his most difficult task, he replied, "Creating a secular state in a religious country."

Historical elision was required too: it became necessary to say the Muslim invasions of earlier centuries had been part of a give and take, a contest for political space which had brought new food and music to India, and did not mark any real cleavage with the Hindu majority. It was suggested, pace *The Discovery of India*, that the country had a unique and admirable ability to absorb hostile external forces, and this should continue. So the formation of India's extraordinary diversity over many hundreds of years became politicized, and the past was required to be glimpsed through the prism of the present. Nehru's vision was warming and didactic, but it was not shared by all his colleagues.

Patel, now the deputy prime minister, was openly sectarian in private conversation, and doubtful Pakistan would survive: "The Muslims do not like to work hard. They want to wear fine clothes and sing ghazals. Who will do the hard work in Pakistan?" he asked.[45] As far as he was concerned, most Muslims were lower-caste Hindus whose ancestors had been converted centuries before, and for the first time in centuries the Hindus were in the driving seat. His department launched a campaign to drive Muslims out of the civil service if they were deemed sympathetic to Pakistan.[46] When Nehru wrote to him condemning some remarks he had made, Patel responded that while he opposed violence against Muslims, the basic cause was Pakistan's misbehaviour. He wielded the sword of Damocles, saying India's Muslims had "a responsibility to remove the doubts and misgivings entertained by a large section of the people about their loyalty."[47] But how were they to perform this difficult task? They might (or might not) have been Muslim League supporters, but this did not mean they endorsed the consequences of territorial partition, or were disloyal.

The rupture between the prime minister and his deputy, which to the credit of both men they did their best to resolve before Patel's death from heart failure in December 1950, was symptomatic of what was to become a running sore in India's public and intellectual life. Was a particular policy secular or communal? Had a politician made a communal remark, intentionally or otherwise? Bound into the idea of modern India was a belief that the state had a duty to remain neutral in matters of religion. In the aftermath of partition and its massacres, a commitment to secularism—a refusal to set India's religious communities at each other's throats—was seen by some as the true mark of the respectable politician. The historian Sanjay Subrahmanyam has observed that the word "secularism" has "a deep meaning and significance in India that many Europeans simply don't understand. Thus 'secularism' has become almost as Indian a word as 'preponed' or 'denting' (for removing a dent in a car)."[48]

In parallel to the rise of Congress in the early twentieth century, a new movement sprang up which sought to unify all Hindus under the banner of Hindutva, or Hinduness. This was a cultural rather than a religious definition: one of the movement's founders, Vinayak Savarkar—who had been sentenced to fifty years' imprisonment by the British for sedition—said you could be an atheist but still qualify as a Hindu.[49] Seeking inspiration, the early proponents of Hindutva were impressed by the racial ideas of the Nazis, which has led historians to connect them, with the advantage of telescopic hindsight, to the crimes of Hitler and the Holocaust. Their movement was in part a political response to the rise of pan-Islamism in India and beyond.[50] After the First World War, Mohandas Gandhi had given his backing to the Khilafat movement, which called for the restoration of the recently abolished Islamic Caliphate. This gesture was an opportunistic and finally unsuccessful attempt by Gandhi to gain mass Muslim support. (The demand for the Caliphate would later be taken up by al-Qaeda, which may explain Osama bin Laden's admiration for Gandhi, who he said brought down the British empire "by boycotting its products and wearing non-Western clothes.")[51] If Muslims were banding together, why should Hindus not do the same? As the pro-Hindu impetus grew, old wounds were prodded. If 70 percent of the population of India—this figure would rise to over 80 percent after partition—were Hindu, why were Hindus not more assertive? Surely they should go back to the wisdom of the rishis, and discover a purer way to live? What had made them so weak that they had suffered centuries of foreign enslavement? Why did they not band together and kick out the whites? Heroes from the distant past were invoked for their cunning and bravery in times of war.

The almost inadvertent end to the first surge of Hindutva came in 1948, when a follower of the movement killed Gandhi. Many of its supporters were imprisoned, and this strand of thinking was excluded from respectable political debate. The Nehruvian secular line, effectively a fudging of history, became the official view in an effort to maintain a unified society. This approach brought benefits, but also stirred a deep resentment among Hindu nationalists, which would bubble up in future years.

In 1996, I visited Gandhi's ashram in Ahmedabad. It was a sorry, decrepit place, some way from its founding principles. Even before his death Gandhi no longer provided the core ideas of independent India, and the ashram's neglect seemed unsurprising. In a nearby shop, I noticed a wall chart called "Top Officials of the World." It was a little out of date, and showed Margaret Thatcher wearing a glam-rock jacket, and Ronald Reagan covered in at least a week's worth of stubble, thanks to the haphazard printing process. After that, I began to collect Indian wall charts—some of which can still be found in provincial bookshops and stationery stores. The charts in many ways gave a better idea of the principles of the new nation. My favourite was "An Ideal Boy," which shows wonderfully evocative, stylized cartoons of an exemplary son of India.

The ideal boy is a chubby-thighed little fellow who gets up early, bathes daily, reads attentively at school and goes for a morning walk in a well-manicured garden, wearing shorts. He "brushes up the teeth," salutes his parents and "takes meals in time," his mother hovering shyly over his shoulder and popping a roti on to his plate. The ideal boy is paler than most Indians, and has a definitely Hindu look to him, but I doubt the chart was intended to be sectarian. Matching him on the "Bad Habits" wall chart are some less than ideal boys who play with electricity, tease a dog and purchase fly-blown snacks from a street vendor who, inadvertently I guess, bears a precise resemblance to India's first president, Dr. Rajendra Prasad. They also fly kites in a dangerous fashion, gamble (though with well-combed hair) and "take law in hands" by throwing a cricket ball through a shop window. On another wall chart, illustrating the law of karma, a naughty boy jettisons a banana skin and promptly slips on it.[52]

The pious sentiment, the optimism and strong moral ambition of "An Ideal Boy" arose directly from the nationalist project which began in India in 1950 when the Constitution came into force. Many injunctions which now seem amusing were aimed at people who had no experience of behaviour outside their immediate social context, and needed to be shown the way. They would be guided in the etiquette of railway stations, hospitals or bus stops, or telegraph and postal services. One chart shows "An Individual Family" (mother and father tend a tulsi plant, son and daughter draw water from a well) and "Combined Family" (father sits in a dhoti on a deck chair reading a newspaper, mother squats on the floor combing daughter's hair, sisters-in-law prepare vegetables quietly, boys do useful deeds). Other charts were aimed at the prevention of disease, in this land where many people were sick and hungry: recommendations included "sleeping on clean bed," "keep your nails short and clean," "always breathe through the nose," "destroy mosquitoes" and "always use latrine." The last instruction has not always been followed; I once saw a man at a Delhi market pissing against a painted sign which read, in English, "No Person Should Urinate Here."

The moralizing intentions of "An Ideal Boy" were in their way Nehruvian. Another popular picture shows Chacha Nehru—Uncle Nehru—reading a story to assorted children, who are chosen by their clothing and physiognomy to represent every variety of Indian. His ideas for the future nation were broad. He expected the state to intervene in people's lives in ways it had never done before in India. Like other postcolonial leaders, he was very ambitious. Nehru's aspirations ranged from enforcing lasting social change to reforming the holding of agricultural land, from developing an Indian space programme to building giant dams, from the creation of an economic planning commission to the promotion of a foreign policy built on queasy notions of Asian brotherhood. As prime minister, he had a rare ability to take the longer view of the country's destiny and global status, unconstrained by caste, religion or regional parochialism. This did not prevent him from getting things wrong, but his mistakes were made in the service of a larger idea, grounded in democratic participation.

He resisted any challenge to the Constitution. An attempt by President Rajendra Prasad in 1951 to take away power from the prime minister was blocked. Prasad said that he intended to rely on his own judgement when deciding whether to sign bills into law. His legal argument was specious, and Nehru at once referred it to the attorney-general and another respected lawyer. Their response was clear: the president's position was analogous to that of "a constitutional monarch in England" and any move to alter it would "upset the whole constitutional structure envisaged at the time when the Constitution was passed [and] make the President a kind of dictator." Prasad's move inadvertently strengthened the Constitution by clarifying the law and establishing the precedent that power rested with the prime minister and the cabinet.[53]

Nehru made a point of consulting Parliament, and refused to give peremptory orders. When his cabinet colleague Amrit Kaur requested him to intervene on a particular matter, he refused. "What you are asking me," he said to her, "is that I be a dictator. You have come to the wrong person."[54] Unlike other world leaders, he did not seek personal wealth. In his later years, he was supported and advised by his widowed daughter, Indira Gandhi, who became his official hostess. Living in a house formerly occupied by the British military commander-in-chief, Nehru attempted to pull the new rashtra together. Edifying measures were taken to emphasize the unity within the nation's diversity. He would start each day by seeing flocks of random visitors, some with petitions or grievances, others lobbying over policy, some just come to catch a glimpse of the new ruler. Refugees camped on his lawns and by his gate, and he did not send them away.

Nehru's premiership lasted nearly seventeen years, until his death in 1964. By the end, many things were unravelling. His devotion to insular socialist planning had not brought prosperity, and the country's share of world trade had halved. His government failed to introduce mass education or to enforce land reforms; the Portuguese colony of Goa was annexed at gunpoint; troops were used against the Nagas, a tribal people in the north-east who wanted to secede and had been fighting to establish a sovereign state. The Congress organization was dividing into factions and being challenged at the ballot box—in 1957 a communist administration was elected in the state of Kerala. Gone was the austere glamour of the freedom movement; the Congress uniform of white khadi, or homespun cloth, had become the vestment of a new ruling class. Nehru had colleagues who were mediocre, and in some cases corrupt. When powerful regional politicians like Pratap Singh Kairon in Punjab misused power or embezzled money, he tended to do little. When he did intercede, as in Kashmir—where the leader, Sheikh Abdullah, was imprisoned on dubious charges of conniving with Pakistan—Nehru still somehow managed to retain a personal link. At Nehru's cremation, a weeping Abdullah would stand by the pyre and throw flowers into the flames.

After Nehru's death, the democratic structures he had put in place came right: he had refused to groom or nominate a successor as prime minister, but it took Congress MPs only a week to choose a new leader, by consensus. He was Lal Bahadur Shastri, a small, impressive, scholarly man who had been born to a poor family in the United Provinces of Agra and Oudh, or what was known from 1950 as Uttar Pradesh.

Were the ideas of Jawaharlal Nehru and the founders too ambitious? Was India really a nation, or a collection of diverse peoples who had been thrown together under British rule, and granted independence? More than six decades later, there are 7 billion people living on the planet. Nearly 1.2 billion of them are Indian. So every sixth person walking on the earth is Indian, and a fair few more are ethnically or culturally Indian (though if you are Pakistani or Bangladeshi, you may not want to hear this). Is it right to ascribe unity and similarity to so many different people? Is it fashionable to do so? Is it possible to say that a nightworker in a call centre in Karnataka, an elderly Sikkimese princess, a displaced Adivasi, or tribal, from Madhya Pradesh, a deposed Rajput maharani, a Mizo craftsman on the Burmese border, a thrusting Punjabi garment exporter, a Malayali nurse, a magistrate from Kashmir, a Tamil Brahmin chef, a rock star from Meghalaya, a Gujarati stockbroker, a Musahar (a hereditary rat-eater) from Bihar, an eye surgeon from Thiruvananthapuram, a thriving Marwari businesswoman, a farmer from Karnataka, an Assamese tea picker, a lecherous Pahari politician, a Maoist revolutionary from Chhattisgarh, a languid Maharashtrian cricketer, an Ollywood (the Oriya-language version of Hollywood) actress and a Bengali painter-cum-civil servant have anything in common?

The prevailing intellectual convention, arising from the academic strait-jacket of poststructuralist theory, multicultural incomprehension and general postcolonial angst, is that it would be wrong to make deductions based on group identity or nationality. To say the French are arrogant, the Japanese inscrutable or the Germans Germanic is unacceptable, even if there is a discernible element of truth in each of these assertions. In the same way, deductions about different Indian communities tend to be made in private rather than in public, but few, even within the communities themselves, would deny their accuracy.

Take a popular email that has been doing the rounds:

BENGAL
1 Bengali = poet
2 Bengalis = film society
3 Bengalis = political party
4 Bengalis = two political parties

TAMIL BRAHMIN
1 Tam Brahm = priest at the Vardarajaperumal temple
2 Tam Brahms = maths tuition class

3 Tam Brahms = queue outside the U.S. consulate at 4 a.m.
4 Tam Brahms = Thyagaraja Music Festival in Santa Clara

MALAYALI
1 Mallu = coconut stall
2 Mallus = boat race
3 Mallus = Gulf job racket
4 Mallus = oil slick

GUJARATI
1 Gujju = share-broker in a Mumbai train
2 Gujjus = rummy game in a Mumbai train
3 Gujjus = Mumbai's noisiest restaurant
4 Gujjus = stock market scam

In each case, the depiction is close enough to reality for the stereotype to work: the artistic and disputatious Bengali, the clever, superior Tam Brahm, the Malayali from Kerala with its rivers and coconuts now transplanted to a job in the Gulf and the canny Gujju are all figures from Indian life, whether in the workplace or in a movie. These are only the stereotypes relating to particular states, rather than to more closely defined social, ethnic, religious or caste communities. There are further examples cited in the chain email, but to ensure this book is not burned on the streets of Patna or Lucknow, I will leave out the entries for Bihar and Uttar Pradesh.

One more:

3 Punjabis = assault on McAloo Tikkis at local McDonald's

Any member of a community may be distinct, but the wholesale effect of involuntary group identity is stronger in India than in most other countries. This is caused by two things: the fact that, until recently, marriage outside your community was difficult and unusual, and the absence of substantial immigration. There has been no large-scale migration to India for around 500 years, since the arrival of Zahiruddin Muhammad Babur's armies at about the time the first Europeans were peopling America. Protected geographically by the sea and by the Himalayas, Indian society managed to remain intact to an extraordinary degree during the colonial period. This caused, inevitably, a measure of integration or understanding between the existing communities. In the days of British rule there was little settlement except on a temporary basis, and social restrictions about eating, as well as the barrier of purdah (which had by now been borrowed by Hindus from Muslims, in the same way that caste had been borrowed by Muslims from Hindus), meant the opportunities for quotidian social interaction between Indians and Europeans were severely limited. Barriers of race, religion and culture, as well as their own national sense of identity and exclusivity, made the British less likely than earlier conquerors to be subsumed into India. Some wore local clothes and took a native mistress, but this did not amount to any sort of assimilation. At the start of the twentieth century, there were around 1,500 British executive officials in India, in addition to a much larger number of military officers and soldiers, and they existed in a separate world of dances, polo and the club, described in Kipling's short stories. After independence, apart from a small number of missionaries, tea planters and business people, the Europeans went home.

Traditions that are today identifiably Indian are rooted in a very distant past. Nearly a thousand years ago, the Muslim polymath Al-Biruni travelled through India and wrote a brilliantly perceptive account of the world and the systems of thought he encountered, *Kitab Tahqiq ma li-l-Hind*, commonly known as *The India*. Originally from Central Asia, Al-Biruni noticed the concentration on philosophy and mathematics, the emphasis on the purity of fire and water, the throwing away of earthen plates after use and the avoidance of touching between communities; he commented on the Hindus' religious flexibility, observing that "at the utmost, they fight with words, but they will never stake their soul or body or their property on religious controversy"; he recorded their "hideous fictions," like the notion that god could have a thousand eyes; he observed that Hindus "sip the stall [urine] of cows [during rituals], but they do not eat their meat," and that men wear earrings and "a girdle called yajnopavita [the sacred thread, worn by the higher castes], passing from the left shoulder to the right side of the waist . . . In their meetings they sit cross-legged. They spit out and blow their noses without any respect for the elder ones present."[55] When the emperor Babur wrote in his diary in the 1520s that Hindustan had "innumerable and endless workmen of every kind . . . a fixed caste for every sort of work," or that women "tie on a cloth, a half of which goes around the waist while the other is thrown over the head," he could have been writing about rural north India now.[56] The recipe for kulfi used by the wife of the emperor Jahangir, Noor Jehan, is the same as the recipe used today. The mricchakatika, or little clay cart, is a common child's toy (you pull a string to make the cart roll along, and it gives a tuk-tuk-tuk sound), but *Mricchaka-*

tika is also the title of a Sanskrit play dating back to 200 BCE, a play which Nehru was reading when he flew above the carnage of Punjab in 1947.

So the past becomes a part of the present, and ancient history is linked to everyday life in a way that is unmatched in any other world culture, in a form that is wholly unselfconscious. A seal found at the ancient city of Mohenjo-daro dating to around 2000 BCE shows a figure, seated in a yogic position, which seems to be a representation of the deity Shiva. To a Hindu today (who might sit in that very yoga position each morning) the pose, the trident, the bull and the phallus would be immediately familiar: a similar representation of Shiva might be found painted on a roadside rock or dangling from a truck's rearview mirror. Many Indians, conscious of their timelessness but often with no informed idea of their own history, are connected to their distant ancestral past every day. Modernity is converted to a purely Indian form.

The founding parents laid down the Constitution, but would the children follow it? A Delhi lawyer said to me while discussing the high ideals of Nehru and his fellows, "The problem with India is Indians." He meant that the rules were all there, but nobody obeyed them. Indians do not go by the book.

2

THERE WILL BE BLOOD

I N THE FALL of 1962 the dream of India as a secure, democratic nation which impressed the rest of the world with its peaceful values and ancient traditions took a savage knock. Nehru's docile policy of "Hindi-Chini bhai-bhai," Sino-Indian brotherhood, was trampled upon by tens of thousands of Chinese soldiers as they poured into north-east India and Ladakh in a violent attempt to resolve a Himalayan border dispute. Nehru, ageing and broken, went on All-India Radio to express his sorrow to the people of Assam, speaking as if they were lost forever because the hordes had breached the Se La, an impregnable mountain pass. Unexpectedly, his daughter Indira seized the headlines by deciding to fly to Assam and advance by helicopter to the front. The prime minister was aghast, worrying privately she might be kidnapped: "She is being very obstinate. Her visit is very dangerous, she should not go."[1]

Indira Gandhi, a striking woman with an angular face, already a widow in her mid-forties, took no notice of her father's fears and flew off in a plane stuffed with Red Cross supplies. She had been an admirer of Joan of Arc since childhood and made a rousing speech only thirty miles from the Chinese positions, ordered administrators back to work and commended the local tribals for their refusal to flee; then she flew to Delhi, picked up more supplies and went back again. The war was a humiliation for India even though the Chinese withdrew from Assam, but at least the press had a new heroine, a counterweight to the unpopular defence minister Krishna Menon, who was soon forced to resign. Mrs. Gandhi felt appreciated by the people of India. Krishna Menon referred to her as "that chit of a girl, Indira."[2]

More than any politician in modern Indian history, Indira Gandhi's behaviour was conditioned by her personal story. In the early 1930s, her mother, Kamala, had joined the protests against the British in their home city of Allahabad. Nehru, who was then in prison, was astounded to hear his shy wife had addressed public meetings, encouraged women to break purdah and even been hurt during a demonstration. One of Kamala's followers was Feroze Gandhi, a young chancer from a Parsi family who took it upon himself to become her attendant, helping out with household chores and political organization. He became part of the furniture at the family house, Anand Bhawan. Feroze grew close to the lonely Kamala, confiding that he admired her sixteen-year-old daughter and would like to marry her. Kamala discounted the proposal; Indira was still a schoolgirl at Shantiniketan in Bengal, a self-consciously Indian school started by the poet and philosopher Rabindranath Tagore, where lessons were taken beneath the trees. More importantly, she knew the heavyweights of the Nehru family, with their patrician aspirations, would never agree to such an unlikely match.

Kamala was a stubborn woman with intense feelings and a devotion to a mystical kind of religion. This led to the end of her sexual relationship with her husband in 1935; Nehru noted in his diary: "Apparently I am not to come in the way of God." The following year she became seriously ill, and was sent to Europe for treatment, accompanied by Indira. Around this time Nehru told their daughter he was handing over Anand Bhawan to his sister Vijayalakshmi and her husband: "The whole house will be at their disposal," he wrote. "If you want to put any of your personal effects apart, you may put them in my room." Indira was now homeless, aged eighteen, with her possessions in storage. Nehru added that she would have to shift for herself, and should remember her famous family had given her "a certain public position which you may have done nothing to deserve."[3] His own energy would be devoted to the freedom struggle. When Kamala died months later in a Swiss sanatorium, Indira was left alone, vulnerable and frail. She was probably suffering from tuberculosis, and now pursued a range of medical treatments in Switzerland and Britain.[4]

After his wife's death, Jawaharlal Nehru was taken up by a love affair with the buxom Congress politician Padmaja Naidu, and even more by his devotion to the cause of India's freedom: his passion was politics, and he was better at performing the self-regarding role of Chacha Nehru, loving all the children of India, than being a father to the teenage Indira. Later, he regretted the insensitivity with which he had treated his wife and daughter at this time. All of these events had the cumulative effect of leaving Indira feeling bruised, resentful and lost; she was both privileged and neglected, and felt her childhood had been "invaded" by politics. She went to Oxford University but dropped out, conscious of her lack of brilliance compared to other, better-educated Indian students. Her one solace, her anchor, was Feroze Gandhi, to whom she became secretly engaged in Paris. Quite what he was doing in Europe is unclear. He was supposed to be studying at the London School of Economics—his fees were paid initially by his aunt, who went by the name of Dr. Commissariat—and to make ends meet he had a job in a factory. He was busy, fleshy, outgoing and sensual, enjoyed Western classical music and had social abilities Indira lacked. They ate hot chestnuts on cold wartime nights on the London streets. Feroze made himself indispensable, as he had with Kamala. Indira kept the relationship secret from her father.

In 1941 she secured a passage on a ship sailing via South Africa to Bombay, with nightly blackouts for fear of the bombing. Back in India she stayed with friends and relations, filled with resentment but dutiful in her support for her busy, absent father. Although her grandmother pointed out that Feroze came from a different religious community and a different social class and had no money, she was determined to marry him: she wanted happiness, children, a quiet and private life. Her family, and it sometimes seemed the whole nation, were against the marriage. She found herself being interrogated by Mohandas Gandhi—who was a personal friend of her father as well as the guardian of the Congress conscience—about her desire for Feroze. When she told him that her feelings ran much deeper than physical attraction, the Mahatma suggested she might take a penitential vow of celibacy after marriage since "sex-pleasure" was no proper basis for a relationship. "I told him, 'You can ask a couple not to get married [but] to ask them to live a life of celibacy, makes no sense. It can result only in bitterness and unhappiness.'"[5] The couple married in 1942, with Nehru's pained, partial consent.

The strange thing about Feroze Gandhi is that having attained a position many men would have coveted—entering the family of the probable future prime minister of independent India—he remained resolutely his own person. He was a keen drinker and philanderer, and effectively unemployed, although he worked occasionally and with flair as an editor and journalist. His zest and unsuitability continued to attract Indira, although even before their second son, Sanjay, was born in 1946, he had got too close to Indira's first cousin, Chandralekha Pandit, and fallen in love with a woman from an aristocratic Muslim family.[6] It was an intense, damaged marriage, which continued unhappily, with occasional rapprochements.

All her life, Indira had been in the public eye—when she was arrested not long after her wedding, the policemen laid their turbans at her feet in apology—but Feroze found it impossible to adapt to being the nation's son-in-law.[7] He was elected as MP for Rae Bareli in Uttar Pradesh at the first general election, and was a vigorous lawmaker who worked to expose corruption and took special pleasure in targeting his incorruptible father-in-law's sleazier associates. As the prime minister's hostess, Indira had constant obligations, and Nehru was signally undiplomatic in failing to include his son-in-law in events at his house. As Indira's confidante Pupul Jayakar wrote: "Feroze was low in protocol and often found himself below the salt." Humiliated, he refused to attend official functions and shifted to his own house "where he cultivated roses and held his own 'durbars.'"[8] Jayakar believed their two sons, Rajiv and Sanjay, had a happier time with their father than with their mother. Feroze gave them his full attention and encouraged them to share his interest in carpentry and mechanics. The prime minister's residence was impressive and formal, a warren of working offices, although Indira made efforts to introduce childish pleasures like a garden of pets. Sanjay's favourite animal was a crocodile, but it was sent to a zoo after it nearly took off his mother's hand. The boys were brought up in large part by servants, including a stern Danish governess who insisted on cold showers and raw vegetables.[9]

The two children were very different in character. Rajiv was described by his mother as quiet and sensitive, a child who had trouble making friends. Sanjay was more outgoing, though at the age of six he had not yet learned to speak.[10] Lively, arrogant and sometimes amusing, he was feared when he was a boarder at the upper-class colonial-style Doon School. He bit a chunk out of the ear of a fellow student who is now an eminent national politician. When I asked a Doon School contemporary—the Maoist revolutionary Kobad Ghandy, who was to take a very different road—how he remembered Sanjay, he replied with a period putdown: "He was a lumpen element." It was not an unreasonable judgement: by his late teens, Sanjay was being accused of stealing and joyriding cars around Delhi.[11]

With her children away at boarding school, Indira Gandhi had more time to worry. She experienced feelings of anger and vengeance, and some days she felt tormented, thinking of giving up on Delhi and going away to live in London. Through all this she was surrounded by people who deferred to her as the prime minister's daughter and a possible source of patronage. She had a strong aesthetic sense, an eye for a hand-woven sari, and an eclectic interest in film, ballet, opera and passing intellectuals. Yet from early on, she had a peevishness and lack of proportion, particularly over those who crossed her, even in the mildest way. Having previously held minor positions, she was elected as president of the Congress party for a year in 1959, at the instigation of politicians who saw her as a potential route to the prime minister, and a possibly useful tool. She turned out to be more energetic, engaged and assertive than expected. Nehru's reaction was ambiguous. He had never rated his daughter's talents highly, but when she presided over a party meeting he said, "At first Indira Gandhi had been my friend and adviser, then she became my companion and now she is my leader."[12] Feroze was outraged, particularly when his wife persuaded a reluctant Nehru to topple an elected communist state government in Kerala and to invoke president's rule—the first time this had happened since independence—claiming the southerners were working with the Chinese.

In 1960, at the age of only forty-seven, Feroze Gandhi died from a heart attack. Despite their unhappiness as a couple, Indira felt isolated afterwards in a way she had never been before. Feroze was the one person who had stayed close to her at the worst point in her life, the years after the death of her mother. She resented many of the members of her father's family, and in particular her aunt, Vijayalakshmi Pandit, who was by now an influential politician in her own right, having served as president of the UN General Assembly and Indian ambassador to several countries. Her children were growing older, and would soon be going abroad. Sanjay, obsessed by speed, was apprenticed to Rolls-Royce in England, where his delinquent tendencies quickly alienated his employers. Asked to account for one of a series of mistakes, he told his supervisor: "You people mucked up my country for 300 years, so what's the big deal if I muck up Rolls-Royce?" When Sanjay finally quit his job, a Rolls-Royce executive said they were glad to see the back of him: "All he was interested in was booze and women."[13] Rajiv's approach was different. He lived a carefree life at Cambridge University, studying in a desultory fashion, growing a temporary beard, tinkering with car engines, learning to do the Twist, taking odd jobs as a fruit picker, ice-cream seller and baker at the Cambridge Co-Op, where he was assigned to the bread section with responsibility for stacking the hot loaves when they came out of the oven. Neither son came away with a qualification.

In the last months of Nehru's life, Indira Gandhi became his gatekeeper, supervising not only visitors but the government files that were brought to him. The modern Indian state had been made with his imprint, and now he was fading, leaving a hole at the heart of government. In the absence of precedent, it was not hard for his daughter to take a commanding position, issuing decisions about what the prime minister would and would not do. The process of transition between administrations was new for everyone. Sometimes Indira's only urge was to escape. "I feel I must settle outside India at least for a year or so and this involves earning a living and especially foreign currency," she wrote to her American friend Dorothy Norman weeks before her father's death. "The desire to be out of India and the malice, jealousies and envy, with which one is surrounded, are now overwhelming."[14] After he had passed away, she felt as if she was caught in a vacuum: the prime minister's house was being turned into a memorial museum and library, and she thought she was being made to leave in a hurry. Within ten days of his death, civil servants had migrated and workers were removing the office furniture. It gave her horrible echoes of losing her childhood home at Anand Bhawan, a hurt she had carried down the years. She was now an orphan as well as a widow, and her sons were away in England, pretending to study. The attention she had received for years as the only child of the most famous living Indian was evaporating, as power shifted. Indira Gandhi had long been a defensive and insecure person, and now she had good reason to feel unprotected.

The new prime minister, Lal Bahadur Shastri, told her he needed a Nehru in the cabinet to maintain continuity, and offered her a seat in the Rajya Sabha (the upper house of Parliament) and a position as minister for information and broadcasting. Indira Gandhi accepted, knowing this would give her a salary and a roof over her head.[15] Her elevation revealed new ambition. When she flew to Kashmir to visit troops during a stand-off with Pakistan, she was lauded in the newspapers as the only man in the cabinet. With a coterie of supporters forming around her, she made little effort to hide her contempt for some of the new prime minister's decisions.

In 1965 the Pakistani leader, the self-appointed Field Marshal Ayub Khan, sent tanks across the border and India fought an unwanted but successful war. During subsequent peace talks in Tashkent, Shastri died from a heart attack. At this moment of surprise, Indira Gandhi's entourage suggested she make a bid for power. The most obvious candidate for prime minister, the respected southern politician K. Kamaraj, declined to stand with the plaintive question: "No English, no Hindi. How?" Another likely leader, Morarji Desai, had too many opponents. For Mrs. Gandhi, the opportunity was irresistible: a woman who had long felt unappreciated was being offered an extraordinary chance. She had no experience of governing, but had watched her father at close quarters for years. Her late husband had been a theoretical socialist, even a soft Marxist, and Indira had observed his political ideas and developed her own alongside them. She knew everyone and could present herself to her father's colleagues as a unifying force. For the durable politicians of Congress, she looked like a suitable and malleable stopgap. Indira Gandhi would be a figurehead, drawing the nation together in the spirit of her late father while the party machine made the important decisions.

It was a fatal misjudgement by the party's high command. Mrs. Gandhi thrived in power, trouncing both her enemies and her backers, and dividing Congress. To the world, Nehru's daughter appeared to be a glamorous new leader. Fluent in English and French and looking unlike the elderly males who were running the world, she seemed an exemplar in international affairs. Her handling of the crisis that led to the creation of Bangladesh (the people of East Pakistan fought for independence from West Pakistan with help in the later stages from the Indian military) was assured. But her premiership was to leave two principal marks on India: socialism and conflict, as the state tried to make the people submit to its will. If things were not working out in the way the founders had hoped, it seemed easier to push their policies harder rather than to re-evaluate. If central planning had turned the economy stagnant, might it not be better to execute planning more carefully and vigorously, perhaps through nationalization of essential services? The country was suffering from drought, famine and a shortage of rice when she took over the job of prime minister, and she decided with encouragement from her advisers to become more radical.

Using her father's legacy and reputation, she tried to push through new policies centred around redistribution. She encouraged a nuclear programme, and later went to the trouble of amending the Constitution to turn India into a "Socialist Secular Democratic Republic." A key achievement was to develop a new agricultural strategy known as the Green Revolution, which had been started under Lal Bahadur Shastri in an effort to end the periodic mass famines that had disfigured India under British rule. By using high-yielding forms of rice and wheat, Indian agriculture was transformed, particularly in the northern states. Some farmers made sufficient profits to invest in technology and irrigation, and gained political clout with their new prosperity. The Green Revolution turned India into one of the world's largest agricultural producers.

The traits that made Indira Gandhi vulnerable, and afraid of internal political rivals, determined her style of leadership. She was a weak parliamentary performer, bad at thinking on her feet, and was nicknamed "goongi gudiya," or dumb doll. Not long after she became prime minister she was shouted down at a big party meeting in Jaipur. Her reaction was revealing. Lying in bed being massaged by a maid, she told a friend that her father's sister, Vijayalakshmi, had been responsible for destroying her confidence in childhood: "She called me ugly, stupid. This shattered something within me. Faced with hostility, however well prepared I am, I get tongue-tied and withdraw."[16] As a woman in a male political world, she was isolated from the start. Her reaction was to avoid Parliament when she could, and to depend on the advice of a close entourage. She liked to reach out directly to the public, accepting petitions wherever she travelled, trusting crowds more than she trusted individuals.

With Indira Gandhi, the personal was nearly always political. In her letters to Dorothy Norman—opening herself up to a friend who came from a different culture—she was often exasperated, depressed, vigilant, and facing difficulty from greedy, mean and petty people. Any attack on her or her administration was deemed a calumny. She drew strength from the masses who greeted her when she was campaigning, seeing the light in their eyes as a sign that she, despite everything, was on the true path and must not be deflected. A recurring trait throughout her premiership was the conviction that with so many things going wrong in India, only she could be trusted to put them right. Every order had to emanate from the prime minister's office. When she made a decision like accepting U.S. food aid, which seemed to go against her proclaimed principles, she balanced it with a more populist act, such as confiscating the former princes' privy purses, a symbolic move which generated paltry revenue. Her methods were autocratic. A senior bureaucrat recalled being summoned to her office in 1969: "She simply said, 'For political reasons, it has been decided to nationalize the banks. You have to prepare within twenty-four hours the bill, a note for the Cabinet and a speech to make to the nation on the radio tomorrow evening.'"[17] Mrs. Gandhi was not instinctively democratic, and lacked the necessary detachment of the good leader—the ability to distance herself from the whirl of events and take a dispassionate view.

During her time as prime minister, the way in which politics was conducted in India altered. She was respected, admired and even feared, but her lack of faith in institutions led her to move away from the emphasis on consensus and common endeavour of the 1950s. To implement policy, it became necessary to place increasing demands on the mechanisms of the state, and to limit the latitude of the individual. The political system no longer depended on the moral authority of Congress, although even as its status declined, the myths of the freedom movement were boosted, with criticism of the founding parents becoming unacceptable and public buildings being named after them. Party politics in New Delhi became more of a negotiation, whether with regional leaders or with other parties and political movements. This was where Indira Gandhi showed a particular, destructive talent. During her father's premiership and her own time as Congress party president, she had been able silently to assess the weaknesses of her potential opponents, and she now put this knowledge to use. More than ever, politics at a state level came to depend on "contractors" who could deliver packs of voters using money or muscle.[18] As the optimism of the past gave way to a more fragmented climate in the 1970s, with new political forces spinning off from the once monolithic Congress party, Indira Gandhi's response was to try to tighten the reins of power and micro-manage politics in a way her father had never attempted. This created lasting conflict, particularly in the states of Punjab, Assam and Kashmir.

In 1971 she won the general election with the slogan "Garibi Hatao"—"Abolish Poverty." It was a democratic victory, but behind the triumph lay a country that was failing. A mass movement led by the veteran socialist Jayaprakash Narayan promised strikes and "total revolution" against her administration. At first Mrs. Gandhi seemed paralysed by the agitation (Narayan's wife, Prabha, had been a close friend of her mother, Kamala). In 1975, she declared a state of emergency. Opposition groups were banned, newspapers shut down and more than 100,000 people arrested. It looked as if India might be moving towards a new form of government—dictatorship. "I want something done," she informed a senior colleague, Siddhartha Shankar Ray, shortly before the Emergency. "I feel that India is like a baby and just as one should sometimes take a child and shake it, I feel we have to shake India."[19] Most of her ministers were too surprised and in awe of her to raise any serious objection. Vijayalakshmi Pandit made it clear publicly that she thought Indira was betraying the Constitution and the legacy of Jawaharlal Nehru.

Indira Gandhi's chief adviser was her son Sanjay—prematurely bald, with extravagant sideburns and a pendulous lower lip. Previously, he was famous only for getting a licence to run a car factory which was unable to produce cars. After being given the opportunity to tour vehicle manufacturers in West Germany, Czechoslovakia and Italy, Sanjay expressed his own version of swadeshi, or self-reliance: he said he had nothing to learn from foreigners about car making. The Maruti project sucked in money for years from nationalized banks and private investors, with Indira Gandhi's connivance, and produced nothing but a few prototypes and some car parts. One visitor to Sanjay's amateur foundry described it as looking like "a dirty indoor barbecue."[20] During the Emergency, while his brother, Rajiv, stepped back from the action, worried about the dubious influence Sanjay was having on their mother, he was given the freedom to operate largely as he liked. Indira said later that nobody had shown her such selfless love as Sanjay.[21]

Sanjay Gandhi was a decisive operator, setting up a parallel operation alongside the mechanisms of government. He treated the Republic of India as if it were his personal fiefdom, with bribery becoming endemic. A friend of the family, the writer Khushwant Singh, remembered arriving at a meeting with him and watching a pair of supplicatory businessmen deliver two suitcases full of banknotes. "I found it hard not to like Sanjay," he admitted, "but I have to say he was a thug, and he was corrupt."[22] Mrs. Gandhi tolerated his conduct, although it appears she did not profit directly from the transactions. In the view of Sanjay's wife, Maneka, the benefits of the Emergency were later forgotten: "For a little while, things did work better and faster. Traders were ordered to put prices on their goods, and it's remained the same ever since—before that, you would have to haggle over a bottle of tomato sauce."[23]

One of his particular concerns was the rapid rise of India's population, which had almost doubled since independence. Notoriously, men were sterilized by a team led by one of Sanjay's friends, the jewellery designer Rukhsana Sultana. The population controllers paraded through the streets of Delhi, drumming up recruits. In numerous cases the operation was done without consent, although the usual reward was a tin of cooking oil, a transistor radio or Rs120.[24] "All our vasectomies," Sultana told the travel writer Bruce Chatwin, "were done in a lovely air-conditioned cellar. I and my workers had to sweat it out on the street."[25] Across India, several million men were sterilized. In Delhi, Lucknow and other cities, ancient buildings were knocked down as part of Sanjay's slum clearance project. Standing by Turkman Gate in Delhi's old city, he told a government official he wanted to be able to see the Jama Masjid, the main mosque. Over a period of six days the command was implemented and, according to the *Times of India*, 150,000 shacks were knocked down.[26] The police fired on a group of homeless protestors near Turkman Gate, killing several.

After less than two years, whether out of a belief she was still popular or a residual attachment to democratic principles, Indira Gandhi called an election.[27] This went against the wishes of her son Sanjay, who also objected when she ended press censorship and released political prisoners. Many government ministers, sequestered in their Lutyens bungalows in New Delhi, were truly surprised when Congress lost at the polls. Nehru's old colleague Morarji Desai, a rigid personality with a devotion to auto-urine therapy and cow protection, became prime minister in 1977. He tried to chart a new political course, cancelling the decrees of the Emergency and improving relations with the U.S. and China. Owing to the squabbling of the opposition parties in the governing coalition, Mrs. Gandhi was voted back into office in 1980, and her son looked set to return to power. Almost thirty years after India's first general election, the Congress party, though weakened, remained the eclectic and dominating force in electoral politics. As Karnataka's chief minister, Gundu Rao, said in self-abasement: "We are the actors of the Indira–Sanjay drama troupe."[28] Only five months after her election victory, the newly ascendant prime minister faced a heartrending shock. To the relief of the nation and the terrible grief of his doting mother, Sanjay Gandhi crashed while performing aerobatics over Delhi— illegally, one morning—in a Pitts S-2A light aeroplane.

It was now that the story of Indira Gandhi, played out increasingly in public, took on elements of tragedy and farce. Feeling more isolated than ever, and profoundly destabilized by the loss of her son, she turned to her remaining family. The household consisted of a clique of oddball advisers and hangers-on: Rajiv the pilot, who was now drafted into politics reluctantly; his shy Italian wife, Sonia, and their young children, Priyanka and Rahul; Sanjay's widow, Maneka, and baby Varun (she was only twenty-three when her husband died, and her son was 100 days old); and from time to time a handsome if highly dubious swami named Dhirendra Brahmachari, who ran a gun factory, did yoga performances on national television and knew how to perform some of the more obscure Tantric rituals. So it was that the daughter of the great religious sceptic Jawaharlal Nehru had shadowy rites performed to see off her enemies and counteract their evil intentions. When a friend told her she was devoting far too much attention to astrology and superstition, she answered, "It is because we did nothing and ignored what they said, that this happened to Sanjay. They had foretold the actual date."[29] Like many Indians, the prime minister believed her fate was preordained.

Indira Gandhi began to distrust her colleagues, and lost the political intuition that had oriented her strategies in the past. She fought with her daughter-in-law, Maneka, a strange, attractive woman who was apt to make outrageous allegations, and ordered her out of the house. Maneka refused to leave—instead she summoned her sister, ordered lunch and sat down to watch an Amitabh Bachchan movie on the VCR at high volume. Mrs. Gandhi burst into tears; Rajiv and his hulking cousin, Arun Nehru, told a security officer to remove the sisters from the house; the officer refused unless he was given the order in writing. Nearing midnight, Maneka, her sister and her baby, Varun, departed in front of the watching media. Mrs. Gandhi tried and failed to keep possession of little Varun, to whom she was devoted. Maneka published a letter accusing "Dear Mummy" of "literally torturing" her "in every conceivable way."[30]

Mrs. Gandhi's murder in 1984 was a kind of suicide, a fulfilment of the warnings she had hoped to keep at bay through manipulation and sorcery. The root cause was a conflict she and the late Sanjay had sparked in Punjab by attempting to influence a state election. To break a local coalition in Punjab, Sanjay had set up and sponsored an obscure Sikh preacher, Sant Jarnail Singh Bhindranwale, as an alternative political force. Bhindranwale was an extremist, a man with intense eyes who railed against any Sikh men who dared to cut their beards or touch alcohol.[31] In Canada, the U.S.A. and particularly in Britain, money was raised by Sikh activists for the cause of a separate homeland.

The scheming and plotting of mother and son ended with the break-down of civil order in Punjab when the Golden Temple in Amritsar, the most holy shrine of the Sikh faith, was taken over by Bhindranwale and his armed supporters. Indira Gandhi ordered Operation Blue Star, an assault which largely destroyed the Golden Temple. The director of the Intelligence Bureau had all Sikh personnel transferred out of her security detail, but she countermanded the order. In an atmosphere of doom, she visited a sadhu in Kashmir and spoke of death, and complained to friends that her personal security was organized in a haphazard way, while doing nothing to reform it. In a speech in Orissa, she said she had devoted her life to the service of her people, and did not care whether she lived or died. Just one day later, on the last day of October 1984, she was walking through her garden trailed by a servant, a male secretary, a security man and a constable, who was holding a large black umbrella to shield her from the sun. Waiting by a wicket gate were her two Sikh bodyguards, Beant Singh and Satwant Singh. As she raised her joined palms to them in the namaste greeting, Beant Singh pulled out his service revolver and pointed it at the prime minister. There was silence. Birds sang in the trees. Mrs. Gandhi looked at him, and said, "What are you doing?"[32]

Punjab is fertile. The land has tall thin trees and hayricks shaped like turbans. Buffaloes wander along the side of the railway line. I alighted at Chandigarh station where, as usual in India, there was a remarkable mix of people: a puzzled man with a pointed hat, some sort of holy woman standing on one foot, a modern girl in a tight sweatshirt, a large Sikh family with trunks and cases, the boys in orange shirts and topknots, and a Sikh guard in a royal blue outfit, holding a long spear. I drove through the sectors of the city to the house of Sarabjeet Singh. He was five years old when his father killed the prime minister.

"My father was an in-charge, he was good at his profession. He was very close to Mrs. Gandhi and even went on foreign tours with her. He had very much respect for her, and she called him by his own name, Beant Singh. My father had a stout build. He was not a follower of the dehras [religious bodies] or of a terrorist organization, nobody paid him or motivated him—he was not interested in Bhindranwale. It was just that he could not believe what had happened at the Golden Temple."[33]

After Beant Singh fired his revolver, he was taken to a guard house by the Indo-Tibetan border force and shot dead; the official story was that he was trying to escape. Sarabjeet remembers coming home from school and wondering why there were so many people at their house in Ashoka Police Lines. The security forces moved in with them for three weeks in the aftermath, before the family was transferred to Chandigarh.

The assassin's widow, Bimal Kaur Khalsa, became a martyr by proxy. She led a procession through Amritsar, was sent to jail on a charge of attempted murder and after her release was elected as an MP from Punjab. Sarabjeet had himself contested a parliamentary seat for a Sikh party in 2004. So like other families in India, their future role in politics was determined by the actions of those who had died before them.

Sarabjeet's sister, Amrit Kaur, took up the story: "It was a great moment for her. We were very young at that time. She sat right across from [Prime Minister] Rajiv Gandhi in Parliament and thought, this is our democracy. She raised her voice and said, 'Rajiv Gandhi, you have killed so many Sikhs and should be hanged.' What my father did was a great thing for the honour of Sikhs."[34] Sarabjeet said, "He sacrificed his life for Sikhism. Almost all our community were proud that he took a gun to Indira Gandhi. The common Sikh has a very high respect for us. They compare us to those who took revenge in the old times against the armies of the Mughal emperors."

He showed me things the family had been given: a big cardboard cutout painting of their father, silver-plated cups commending his action, an equestrian statue of the Maratha warrior Shivaji, an admiring plaque from the Sikh Foundation of Virginia.

Sarabjeet stood by the door as I was leaving. What, for him, were the central tenets of Sikhism? "To be honest, to give equal rights to ladies and children, to take pride in your religion but not to oppress others. The real Sikh is not casteist." As he said this, singing began outside the door, aggressive singing and stamping. Sarabjeet had recently got married and had a baby, and I guessed it was a choir of hijras, or eunuchs, come to celebrate the birth and demand money. Sarabjeet went out, spoke to them and came back in looking sheepish. The choir banged and rattled the door. He locked it. "They are just a backward class who come when they know a child has been born. Not hijras. This is what happens in Punjab."[35] The noise continued. He returned to the door, opened it a crack and the door was pushed open. Four women came in shouting, gesticulating and demanding money for singing the baby's celebration song. Sarabjeet was a big man with a long black beard and an orange turban. He paid up.

Mrs. Gandhi's daughter-in-law Sonia had just finished washing her hair when she heard what she thought were celebratory fire-crackers, but the bangs were followed by shouts and her children's nanny ran into the house screaming. Sonia went out to find her mother-in-law bleeding on the path. The driver of the prime ministerial ambulance was off on a tea break, and no one could find the key, so Sonia got into the back seat of an Ambassador car, wearing only a dressing-gown, and cradled her mother-in-law as they drove to hospital. Her greatest fear was that a killer might try to eliminate her children and the entire family, as had happened to the Bangladeshi leader, Sheikh Mujibur Rahman. It was a three-mile journey, and the traffic was thick. Within minutes, Indira Gandhi's saffron-coloured sari and Sonia's dressing-gown were drenched with blood. Mrs. Gandhi died that afternoon.

The events of the next few days showed, in microcosm, many of the things that had gone wrong with Indian politics in the twenty years since Nehru's death. During a flight back to Delhi from West Bengal, Rajiv Gandhi was encouraged to inherit his mother's job. A prudent suggestion by the finance minister, Pranab Mukherjee, that he might himself take the position on an interim basis was ignored. The Indian Constitution was consulted, and Rajiv's inflight entourage deduced that the president—who had been picked by Indira Gandhi for his sycophantic tendencies—could nominate whomever he chose. Before they even reached the hospital, the process was in train.[36] Nehru's grandson, a socially popular Indian Airlines pilot with no ministerial experience, would take power. In an ideal world, the premiership of the largest democracy on earth should not be an entry-level appointment.

At the hospital, no emergency preparations had been made, because nobody had thought to call and say the dying prime minister was coming. The atmosphere was chaotic. A young journalist, Vichitra Sharma, managed to get inside. "The hospital was on my beat as a reporter, and a doctor I knew took me up to the eighth floor, which had a VVIP [Very Very Important Person] space, saying, 'Blood donor, blood donor.' Once I got there, he told me I was on my own. I sat in a cubicle outside the operating theatre, behind a dark green curtain, watching the doctors go in and out through the swing doors. The body was puffing up and they were pumping blood and waiting for someone senior to tell them what to do." While surgeons attempted to conjure life into the corpse of Mrs. Gandhi, the ministers and courtiers of Delhi arrived in droves and milled about on the floor below. "In her years of power, she had taken away the manhood from every one of these men," said Sharma. "I remember a minister telling everyone how close he was to Madam, then hollering at his driver—'Go pick up my children from school!' They were just waiting for orders. It speaks volumes about her centralized style of leadership." Rajiv Gandhi arrived, composed but ashen-white. Sharma overheard a smartly dressed lady say, "I must go inside to show my face to Rajivji. He must know we took the trouble to come here at a time like this." Before long everyone had gone, pursuing a new source of patronage, leaving the corpse behind. Vichitra Sharma slipped into the operating theatre and saw the late Mrs. Gandhi "cold and lifeless. And no one was there to pay her the courtesy of guarding her body.

It was pathetic."[37] Her time as prime minister had left India in a vulnerable position.

Rajiv Gandhi's premiership began in 1984 with a founding slaughter. Within hours of his mother's assassination, news of the killing passed through the city, and by nightfall the shutters were down and the roads were empty. It did not take long for mobs, in some cases led by Congress activists, to target Sikh districts in Delhi and other cities—the men they were looking for were easily identifiable by their beards and turbans. On the same night Indira's old friend Pupul Jayakar received phone calls telling her Sikhs were being dragged out of their homes by their hair and thrown on bonfires. She raced to the prime minister's house. Rajiv was sitting with the home minister, Narasimha Rao. She poured out what she had been told. "Rajiv seemed helpless, bewildered. He turned to the home minister and asked, 'What shall we do?'" Narasimha Rao, famous for his silences, said nothing. Jayakar advised Rajiv, whom she had known since he was a child, to do what his mother would have done—go on television at once, "with all the prestige, power and strength of the Prime Minister of India" and say that although it was right to grieve, no one should take revenge and that butchery would not be permitted under any circumstances. Rajiv Gandhi hesitated and asked Jayakar to prepare a concept note. She did, and waited. The next morning he did not appear on television. Instead, the home minister appeared on the screen and read a statement. In her words, "The speech had neither the anguish of the son nor the massive authority of the Prime Minister."[38]

For days, mobs of rioters roamed the streets looting homes and setting people alight with kerosene. Only in Calcutta did the state government, run by a communist chief minister, Jyoti Basu, make sure no pogroms took place. More than 3,000 Sikhs died, and three days passed before Rajiv Gandhi decided to call out the army to stop the slaughter. When it was all over, he made a notorious comment—that when a mighty tree falls, the earth is bound to shake. His new government made only the most perfunctory attempt to investigate what had happened and to look at to what extent the killings were organized. It was to develop into a political tradition: after a small genocide, after a disaster, after a scandal, no leader would be held accountable.

Later in the year a general election was held, and a wave of public sympathy returned Congress to power with a large majority. There was a great sense of relief that the next leader from the Gandhi family would not be the late Sanjay. Everything rested on India's new Mr. Clean—unassuming, diffident Rajiv Gandhi, the man from the Co-Op bakery's bread section. His generation projected their aspirations on to him, hoping he would be the dynamic catalyst for a different India. Destiny had other plans for Rajiv: he would be remembered by history as Indira Gandhi's son, and Sonia Gandhi's husband.

Rajiv Gandhi had sensible, modernizing intentions, which was part of the problem. Early on, he hoped he could learn to be prime minister by reading textbooks on politics, just as he had learned to be a fine airline pilot by studying manuals. He wanted to do well, to bring India forward and make it run efficiently. As the first member of the family since Motilal Nehru to have had a regular job, he knew about schedules and workplace efficiency. All his achievements to date had been technical: he had assembled a radio, taught himself photography, flown different types of aeroplanes and experimented with recording sound. The aspiring technocrat was keen but out of his depth, impatient over the numerous obstacles he faced. Rajiv wanted to challenge the economic legacy of state socialism, but was not sure how to do it. There were some achievements: a peace deal with Assamese separatists, support for panchayats, or village democracies, some taming of the bureaucracy and a relaxation of duty on certain imported goods. Congress continued to manipulate vote banks. His government passed a law allowing discrimination against Muslim women during divorce in order to woo conservative elements, which infuriated many Hindus; this was balanced by a court decision regarding a disputed mosque—the Babri Masjid—which appeared to pander to Hindu traditionalists. After his death, this decision would have dangerous consequences. He responded to the setbacks and complications by relying on his popularity and dreaming up amorphous new initiatives, and working ever harder, eighteen or nineteen hours a day, tapping information into his treasured Toshiba T5200 laptop in the hope it might spit out some answers. Many of his initiatives were constructive, but they were never part of an overarching strategy.

To help him with his modernizing mission he brought personal friends with a similar agenda into his political circle. There was also a greedy clutch of less sophisticated hangers-on, some left over from Sanjay's day. The prime minister's office functioned in a haphazard and amateurish fashion, with the cabinet frequently being reshuffled. Rajiv Gandhi ignored corruption among his colleagues, and the payment of financial incentives became a growing part of Indian public life. The most serious scandal of his premiership related to the government's award of a contract for field guns to the Swedish arms company Bofors. He denied any money had been taken in bribes to facilitate the contract, only to be undermined by documentary evidence which showed he knew this to be untrue. Millions of dollars in commissions were paid into overseas accounts. Unlike his mother, Rajiv Gandhi did not start in office with a good working knowledge of international diplomacy, although he did develop a strong interest in areas such as the anti-apartheid movement. At a personal level, he was often better than Indira Gandhi at making a connection, but he lacked her strategic sense. He became involved in the politics of the neighbouring island of Sri Lanka, sending a huge peace-keeping force to implement a pro-Tamil agreement, only to find the Tamil Tigers refused to cooperate. When too many Indian soldiers returned home dead, the effort was abandoned. Sikh insurrection continued in Punjab, with the police being allowed to use savage methods against militants. By the end of the 1980s, as his wife, Sonia, wrote guilelessly, India contained "a dozen major terrorist outfits: for each of them he was the number one target."[39]

A general election was called in 1989, and Congress tumbled to defeat at the polls. A coalition government took power headed by V. P. Singh, a senior minister whom Rajiv Gandhi had sacked for investigating corruption too vigorously. During his brief period as prime minister, V. P. Singh brought in a major and exceedingly controversial affirmative action programme to help lower castes, reserving a quota of government jobs and university places for them. Rajiv began a period of introspection. He realized he had made mistakes and distanced himself from his courtiers. Some of his associates felt he would make a much better prime minister if he had a second chance in office.

In 1991 the minority coalition administration fell, and Rajiv Gandhi returned to the election trail. The new government had reduced his personal security. Near the end of the campaign, he arrived exhausted for a rally at a small town near Madras. Advancing through the throng in a plain kurta pyjama and red-and-white Lotto training shoes, he was surrounded and jostled by well-wishers and supporters. One of the crowd was a young woman called Dhanu, a Tamil Tiger terrorist set on avenging his government's military escapade in Sri Lanka. As she bent down to touch his feet, as if in homage, he stopped and bowed slightly over her. At that instant she pressed a toggle switch on her belt, exploding a bomb. Rajiv's old friend and media adviser Suman Dubey heard a low noise and watched the crowd dissolve "like a red flower unfolding in slow motion."[40]

When Sonia heard the news, she told her daughter Priyanka that she wished she had died too. She had an asthma attack and began to howl; her cries could be heard by the Congress activists who were gathering outside the house. In the days that followed, Mrs. Gandhi made it clear to visiting dignitaries, as well as to close friends and family, that she would never, ever enter politics.

3

THE CENTRIFUGE

T HE CONGRESS STORY is not the only story. If you are Lal Krishna
Advani, you might have bad memories of Indira Gandhi, not only
politically but personally, for what she did to you. When I asked him about
this, he said he was not bitter but was unable to forget she had taken away
two years of his freedom by putting him in prison. "I was protected by my
station: others had a worse experience." She returned to power, was killed,
her son came to power, was killed, and later her son's widow and son's son
would come to a different kind of power, orchestrating the government
from behind the scenes.

Advani did not like the idea, still propagated by the legions of Congress
sycophants, that one family had a destiny to rule a country. Resentment,
not surprisingly, was part of the undertow for him and his colleagues.
"When Manmohan Singh became prime minister he visited me and said he
had a list of five statues he wanted to be put up, and needed my agreement
as leader of the opposition. I looked at the list and said to him, they're all
from the same family! Can't you at least put up one of Narasimha Rao, who
made you the finance minister?"

At the time the Emergency was declared, Advani was president of the
Bharatiya Jana Sangh, an organization founded in 1951 to promote Hindu
culture, a non-socialist economy and a strong India. He was in Bangalore,

staying in a shared room in a hostel, when woken by news that prominent Congress and opposition MPs, including himself, had been arrested; so it was not a surprise when police officers arrived after breakfast and yoga. Together with his long-time colleague Atal Behari Vajpayee, he was taken into custody. They had time to tell reporters this was as significant a moment in national history as the mass arrests during the Quit India movement in 1942. His wife and children were not allowed to see him. The crackdown spread far. The private houses of several former princely rulers were requisitioned and damaged. Students, trades unionists, regional politicians, farming activists and personal enemies of Indira Gandhi were all scooped up, along with some of her late father's associates. J. B. Kripalani was an example: during the First World War he was a college professor who fought against colonial rule, in 1942 he was imprisoned by the British in Ahmadnagar Fort with Nehru, 1947 found him in the Constituent Assembly framing the future of India, and by 1975 he was protesting against the Emergency, although Indira Gandhi did not dare to detain him for long.[1]

In jail, Advani and his colleagues forged lasting bonds, as Nehru and his colleagues had before them. They were given books from the prison library, Vajpayee did the cooking and each evening they would take a two-mile circular walk inside the compound. The idyll did not last. They were released and rearrested, transferred north, shifted again and on arrival had their possessions pulled apart by a convict warder, searching for hidden papers. With other leading politicians, they were placed in a prison dormitory. Information from outside was patchy. They heard mass non-violent resistance was taking place, and more people were being rounded up. Then they were transferred back to south India. Sometimes the prisoners were able to pick up foreign radio stations like the BBC and Voice of America and learn of the opposition to "Madam Dictator." At times they would see direct evidence of what was happening. A young student caught distributing underground literature was brought to the jail covered in bruises, followed by another who was so terrified after being interrogated upside down for five days on a pulley that he was unable to talk. A 22-year-old Bharatiya Jana Sangh worker from Mangalore called Vishwanath was brought in with his back paralysed. Advani wrote pamphlets under the name "A Detenu" which were distributed illegally: *A Tale of Two Emergencies* compared the methods of Adolf Hitler and Indira Gandhi, and *Anatomy of Fascism* suggested her talk of discipline was a smokescreen for the concentration of state power in the hands of a single group. Meanwhile, scraps of news reached the prisoners, in one case via leaflets that were dropped from an aeroplane and fluttered into the compound. They announced a forthcoming appearance by Sanjay Gandhi. Advani noted in his prison diary: "One of them reads: 'If you miss this rally, you will be missing the unfolding of a new chapter in the history of the nation.' "[2]

Despite detention without trial and instances of torture, the Emergency was conducted with restraint compared to similar crackdowns in neighbouring countries. It always felt like a temporary solution. The strength of opposition and the instinctive Indian dislike of dictators, stemming from the tendency to believe in several possible solutions rather than a single answer, meant the prospect of an end was never out of sight. Unlike in Pakistan, the army in India had never had the political prestige needed to seize power. The most worrying moment came when a document was circulated at the end of 1975 proposing permanent constitutional change: power would pass to the president, the judiciary would be made subordinate to the executive and the fundamental rights detailed in the Indian Constitution would in effect be abolished.[3] The response to this proposal was so strong, with the Bar Council of India calling an emergency meeting to say it would lead to the destruction of democracy, that Mrs. Gandhi and her loyal ministers backed down.

"When I was picked up from the hostel," said Advani, "we were all surprised. It was a shocking thing for an MP to be arrested. Only a week or so before my arrest, an astrologer had said it was foretold in the stars that I would be facing two years in exile." Today in his eighties, Advani looked in remarkably good health. As a staunch follower of the Rashtriya Swayamsevak Sangh, or RSS—a pro-Hindutva organization which gave rise to the Bharatiya Jana Sangh, now called the Bharatiya Janata Party, or BJP—he was a believer in restraint and self-discipline. He followed a strict diet and never ate more than was necessary; I noticed each entry on his blog ended with the injunction: "If you enjoyed this post, make sure you subscribe to my RSS feed!"

L. K. Advani's view of the world was formed by his experience of partition. Unlike many of his generation in the RSS, he was not from a higher-caste Maharashtrian or north Indian background. His family were Amils from Karachi in Sindh in the far west, with links to the vaishya, or trader, community. In retrospect, he liked to stress the pious, syncretic culture in which he had been raised, with Muslims and Hindus attending the same shrines and fighting foreign invaders together in earlier centuries. He went to a Catholic school where there was one Muslim boy in his class. At his childhood home, the family "deity" was the Sikhs' holy book, the Guru Granth Saheb. He said he had joined the RSS because he was impressed by its patriotism.

In 1947, things fell apart—Karachi was now in Pakistan, and L. K. Advani had to depart. He was homeless, and would need to make his way in the world. "I came to Delhi. The contacts I had made in the RSS were the nearest thing I had to a family there. Previously I had been to Indore, Ahmedabad and Nagpur for training and had watched Hindi films, which I loved, but I couldn't speak the language too well. I knew some words of Hindi but could not read or write it. I was a pracharak, an old-timer who lived on the subsistence of the RSS." He spent his days touring the north, trying to establish roots for the organization. After the assassination of Mohandas Gandhi—whom Advani had admired for his ascetic qualities—he and numerous other RSS workers were arrested because the killer had tangential links to the organization. Like later political murders in India, it achieved the opposite of its objective: the killing made people turn against the perceived philosophy behind the assassin, and the Hindutva movement would for decades be tarred as violent and extremist. (Similarly, after Indira Gandhi was murdered, the campaign for a Sikh homeland was suppressed in a counter-insurgency campaign that left tens of thousands dead; and Indian sympathy for the Tamil Tigers—which had never been very strong in the first place—evaporated after Rajiv Gandhi was blown up by a suicide bomber; it took until 2009 for the Tamil Tigers to be annihilated, but this was inevitable from 1991.) The RSS continued, a conservative brotherhood organization which held regular camps where its members saluted each other and paraded in baggy khaki shorts. There was even such a thing as the "RSS honeymoon," when bride and groom, in an inoculation against Western decadence and purportedly un-Indian values, would set off on a holiday after their wedding accompanied by the groom's extended family.

How did Advani cope with the long decades of obscurity? Did he believe the Hindutva philosophy would ever gain mass political support? "No, no, no, I never thought we would form a government in New Delhi. For a long time it seemed we would not come to power, and would only remain a pressure group, with influence in one or two states. In a country as vast and pluralistic as India, an ideological party seemed unlikely to succeed at the centre. I wrote so at the time. It was the same for the communists." Did he lose hope or his temper? "I've read Dale Carnegie's *How to Win Friends and*

Influence People. I know there is no point in trying to force people to change their mind. You have to do it in other ways. It was in the 1970s, at the time of the Emergency, that I saw we might band together with other parties. I saw we might be able to succeed."[4]

For forty years, Hindu organizations rested on the fringes of the political mainstream. Advani and Vajpayee worked and plotted, hoped and waited, alert for the moment when Congress could be displaced as the natural party of government. In 1984, in the election that brought Rajiv Gandhi to power, the BJP returned only two MPs out of 542 in the Lok Sabha, the lower house of Parliament: a decade after that, the BJP was becoming the most important force in Indian politics. A perfect storm of events shot the Hindutva movement to the centre of national life. The Gandhi family seemed to have disappeared; middle-class shopkeepers and business people were ever more unimpressed by the stifling web of controls and regulations instituted by successive Congress governments, and by their willingness to manipulate communal politics for political gain. The BJP worked with this popular sense: Advani called the Congress interpretation of secularism an "allergy to Hinduism." A hugely successful television series of the Hindu epic the Ramayana produced a coincidental feeling of non-sectarian religious excitement. L. K. Advani took note of this and, despite being a displaced Sindhi from a very different religious tradition, harnessed the power of Lord Ram in northern India. Acting on the advice of Pramod Mahajan and Narendra Modi—two rising stars of the BJP, both born since independence—he set off on a rath yatra, or chariot trip, from the temple at Somanatha to the birthplace of Lord Ram in Ayodhya, where a mosque had been built on the orders of the first Mughal emperor, Babur. They would erect a Ram Mandir, a temple to Ram.

There was a difficulty here: Ram was a mythological figure, and there was no evidence he was born in Ayodhya, or indeed anywhere else. Because the mosque, like many religious buildings around the world, had probably been built on an earlier sacred site, it was deduced that it was the birthplace of Lord Ram. Advani himself wrote that once the rath yatra got started, it was less about "reclaiming a holy Hindu site from the onslaught of a bigoted foreign invader . . . It was about reasserting our cultural heritage as the defining source of India's national identity."[5]

This was the crux of what the BJP was trying to do. It wanted to redefine Indian identity by linking it to a mythologized Hindu past and at the same time turn itself into a busy, modern political movement. There were elements of Bollywood in L. K. Advani's long procession across north and central India. A naturally reserved man with a clipped white moustache now found himself the most famous politician in the country. As his chariot—really a decorated Toyota truck—drove from town to town, ceremonial arches were erected and enormous crowds turned out; in remote rural areas, the chariot would be stopped by apolitical villagers so that ceremonial pujas could be performed, honouring Lord Ram.

Advani was astonished by the depth of religiosity he encountered. From a political point of view, he had attained success. After years in the wilderness, wandering about with men in khaki shorts at hot RSS camps and avoiding large meals, he had found a deep, raw, colourful instinct through which he could channel his theoretical Hindu nationalism. Back in political circles in Delhi, the rath yatra was at first ignored and then—once the giant crowds turned out—spoken of as an embarrassing manifestation of mystical fervour. Who was this kacchawallah, this wearer of shorts, wooing the masses from a garlanded Toyota truck? The Congress-led minority government prevaricated over what to do. Could they allow a Ram Mandir to be built at the site of the mosque? The new prime minister, Narasimha Rao, a Brahmin from Andhra Pradesh who in his youth had been given a rough time by the Razakars, the Muslim guards of the last Nizam of Hyderabad, tacitly allowed the worship of Hindu deities inside the mosque. When more than 100,000 people gathered at Ayodhya in Uttar Pradesh, inspired by Advani's chariot ride, little was done to disperse them. The atmosphere at this time—and the surreal but not uncommon reasons for the veneration—was described by the journalist Jawed Naqvi, who noted the idol of Lord Ram "in his avatar as a toddler" placed on a platform inside the mosque, protected by a pujari, or priest, the whole overseen by security:

A tobacco-chewing policeman with a .303 rifle, stood idly under the southern dome. He claimed to know the entire history by heart of what many believe is the birthplace of Ram. I engaged him in his native Awadhi dialect. When was Ram born here? I probed. "Kahat hain ki nau laakh saal hoi gaye haye hain," he replied, mouth slanted upward to prevent the copious drool of masticated tobacco spilling over. (They say Ram was born nine hundred thousand years ago.) Where exactly was he born? I persisted. "Jahaan pujariji khadey huye hain, wahi ke jaano chaar paanch phoot yahan wahan." (He was born on the exact spot where the pujari is standing, give or take four or five feet.)[6]

This was Ayodhya a few months before sadhus carrying tridents and fre-
netic youths in saffron-coloured headbands climbed on top of the old
mosque and smashed the domes, some of the men plunging through the
rubble to their death, watched by an uneasy parade of BJP bigwigs, including L. K. Advani himself. With the mosque destroyed, Advani was careful
neither to embrace the violent desecration nor to repudiate it, but at the
general election four years later, the BJP displaced Congress as the largest
single party; the ruined Babri Masjid has remained under guard ever since,
the Ram Mandir unbuilt, the incendiary issue fading from public consciousness. More recently, Advani has said he never intended the old mosque to
be damaged in such a way, but it took no imagination to see what would
happen if you combined popular religious fervour with an angry determination to make good a perceived historical wrong. Against this, a member
of a family at the heart of the Ram Mandir movement told me: "We were
all watching it on television. The family were showing pure delight, the
elders knew exactly what was going to happen on that day, and disapproved
of Advani, whom they said was cowardly."[7] The implication here was that
hardliners had intended to destroy the mosque regardless of Advani's
instinctive caution.

For Nehruvians, the destruction of the Babri Masjid appeared to mark
the end of India as a secular state, with no mosque or Muslim now safe
from Hindu fundamentalists. The author Vikram Seth and his mother,
Leila Seth, who was the first woman to become the chief justice of an
Indian high court, published an advertisement in the Times of India saying
the demolition had "shamed the nation across the world" and "debased
Hindu culture."[8] Amartya Sen, the economist, deduced the destruction had
been caused by "the extreme gullibility of the uneducated." The Hindu
masses of the cow belt were unqualified: "While illiteracy may not be a
central feature of communal fascism or of sectarian nationalism in general,
its role in sustaining militant obscurantism can be very strong indeed."[9]

Several thousand people were killed in the riots that followed, most of
them Muslim, and in 1993 a series of bombs exploded across Bombay (now
Mumbai) in revenge, planted by a Dubai-based Indian Muslim crime and
terror mafia. The most damaging effect was local to Uttar Pradesh, the
largest state in India, where relations between Hindus and Muslims became
polarized. At aggressive rallies, loudspeakers blared the injunction: "Jab jab
Hindu jaga hai, desh se mullah bhaga hai"—"Every time the Hindus rose,
the mullahs fled the country." Aware of the degree of Congress duplicity
in what had happened, Muslim voters shifted to other political parties. In

the words of one man from nearby Kanpur: "There was now a view among the enabled class of Indian society that rabid feelings against Muslims were acceptable. It was regressive. As a child I was taught by the maulvi saheb [teacher or Islamic scholar] to be proud of being Muslim and proud of being Indian."[10]

In a broader context, the smashing of the Babri Masjid was less momentous than it appeared at the time. The act of destruction—widely filmed and photographed—did not prefigure the nationwide shattering of mosques or the emergence of a Hindu Taliban. The strictures of the Constitution and the broader Indian allegiance to secularism prevented this kind of focused religious assertion. Rather, the events of this year formed a pattern of atrocity since 1947, in which the usually harmonious relationships between hundreds of millions of people would at times turn loud and violent, spurred by politicians.

When Narasimha Rao took the premiership in the summer of 1991 after the murder of Rajiv Gandhi, the cupboard was bare. Many forms of economic stagnation had collided. The previous eighteen months had seen two prime ministers come and go, each one running a ragtag coalition of regional outfits, propped up in Parliament by a larger political party. Nobody owned the ensuing mess, with the result that the component parts or parties tried to take whatever they could, personally or regionally. Rao, near to retirement, was surrounded by ambitious colleagues within Congress like Sharad Pawar, Madhavrao Scindia, Rajesh Pilot (who had started out as a milkman, and changed his name after becoming an air force pilot) and Jitendra Prasada. He led a minority government, and there was every reason to think it would not last a full term.

It turned out to be one of the most important administrations since independence, headed by India's most elusive and inscrutable prime minister. Born in 1921, P. V. Narasimha Rao was a widower with eight children who had started as a legislator in Andhra Pradesh in the 1950s. In his spare time he liked to translate novels from Telugu to Hindi and from Marathi to Telugu; he was also thought to know Urdu, Oriya, Kannada, Tamil, Arabic and Latin.[11] The oddity was that he rarely spoke—I remember talking to an MP from the north-east who had just left a meeting with Narasimha Rao, unclear whether or not they had reached a deal because of the complete lack of verbal signals. Although he appeared to be a loyal servant of the Nehru–Gandhi family, it is apparent from his own novel *The Insider* that Rao had an ambiguous view of Congress politics, and an acute, cynical understanding of the arts of political manipulation and intrigue. He was careful to sideline Sonia, the widow of Rajiv Gandhi. Wherever possible, he kept every outcome open so that nobody knew in which direction his own thinking was heading. He was heavily superstitious and regularly guided by Chandraswami, a mystical adviser to the powerful and wealthy who was sometimes referred to in the press as "controversial godman Chandraswami."

When Rao took office, India faced grave economic problems. The first Gulf War and the high price of oil had created a balance-of-payments crisis. In response, structural changes were agreed which brought in foreign direct investment, enabled industry to become more competitive and allowed the market to function in areas that had previously been closed. He picked an economist, Manmohan Singh, and a lawyer, P. Chidambaram, and let them get on with taking down the enveloping mass of state-administered red tape known as the "permit raj" (or "rule by permit") which controlled much of the daily working of business. It was a revolutionary achievement. Although the economic reforms of his premiership would transform India, Narasimha Rao was not a neoliberal. Rather he wanted to raise government revenues through the generation of wealth by the private sector and hoped to have more money for the state to distribute. He continued the ruthless crushing of the Sikh insurgency in Punjab, improved relations with other Asian countries and devoted a substantial amount of his time to manoeuvring against his colleagues, sucking in money through corruption and paying it out to MPs to win crucial parliamentary votes.

His premiership came to an extraordinary climax in 1995 when he ordered the Central Bureau of Investigation to pursue more than a hundred politicians and officials who were alleged to have been paid bribes. The spur was some coded diaries which had been found in a raid on a businessman suspected of buying favours from politicians of several parties. They contained lists of payments to named individuals. The normal practice in such situations was for the people at the top to be spared punishment. For reasons that remain opaque (perhaps he was seeking to gain a reputation for probity, perhaps he intended to rout his enemies, perhaps he just wanted to invert Indian politics), Rao told the authorities to go after everybody— senior business people, friends of the Gandhi family, leading opposition MPs like L. K. Advani, even his own ministers. Several had to resign when legal cases were brought against them.

Things did not work out in the way Rao had perhaps intended: much of the material in the diaries was inadmissible as evidence, and he became

supremely unpopular within his own party. In the general election that followed, Congress lost ground, taking only 29 percent of the vote nationally.
In the crucial state of Uttar Pradesh it won a mere 8 percent of the vote,
against 33 percent for the BJP, with new rivals the Samajwadi Party and
the Bahujan Samaj Party taking 21 percent each.[12] No party won a nationwide majority, and a composite government was formed from smaller
parties. Rao was himself targeted by investigators, and his political career
was finished after five years as prime minister. Despite the political loss,
the economic changes brought in during his time in office were to be
transformative.

By the time the fiftieth anniversary of Indian independence struck in
1997, it looked as if the Congress party might be over. The once great movement of national liberation, which had sat astride the country's political
system for half a century, was in tatters. Narasimha Rao's machinations
had led to major politicians leaving, and his replacement as party leader,
Sitaram Kesri, was an elderly, incompetent Congress functionary. Voters
were bored by the corruption scandals, the obvious hypocrisy, the absence
of direction and the on-off support for the latest coalition government.
New parties were bubbling up across the country, and they seemed to have
a stronger understanding of the experiences facing millions of younger voters. V. P. Singh's affirmative action programme for backward classes was
producing important social change, but even the people who had opposed
it, such as the poor Brahmins of north India who felt they were now suffering discrimination, tended to avoid Congress.

The party was brought back from the edge by an unlikely person. Usually, when a political movement wins power, it is the result of a collective
shift, with a figurehead at the top. In this case, the impetus came from a
single, unlikely figure deciding to join a race that she had never wanted
to take part in—Sonia Gandhi, Rajiv's wife, who when she came to India
from Italy in 1968 had been nervous to enter a roomful of people alone.
She knew the party of her husband's family was fragmenting; she knew too
that this was probably the last chance to secure a possible political future
for her children; and there was even talk that she and her family might be
ordered to leave their large, government-supplied bungalow in New Delhi,
10 Janpath.

Half the people in the world who live in a democracy live in India, and an
Indian general election can be like nothing on earth. During the 1998 cam-

paign, when Sonia Gandhi joined politics, there were over 600 million registered voters, and ballot boxes had to be transported by donkey, mountain porter and fishing boat. Nearly 5,000 candidates ran for office, and some of these aspiring parliamentarians were bizarre. In Bihar, a candidate named Ravindra Kushwaha chose to file his nomination papers under the alias Santraj Singh because he was absconding from the police. In neighbouring Uttar Pradesh, the "bandit queen," Phoolan Devi, a gang leader turned politician, was standing despite having sixty-three court cases pending against her. Not far down the road, Dhruv Ram Chaudhary was up for election. He had two cases registered against him for murder, five for attempted murder and two for dacoity. Meanwhile a candidate in Maharashtra, the fifty-year-old Mr. Deshmukh, interrupted his campaign to kill two dogs and a buffalo and burn banknotes worth Rs10,000, for no apparent reason. In Meghalaya, voters could choose between Adolf Lu Hitler Marak, Hopingstone Lyngdoh and Frankenstein W. Momin.[13] (Such names usually came from parents in the north-east who liked their sound but did not realize the implications: others included Clutch, Billy Kid and Bombersingh. An academic in Shillong told me he had a student called Latrine Born, who had changed the name on her behalf to Laktrang—which means "something you really want" in Khasi.)[14]

The level of anarchic violence in the 1998 election was substantial. In the southern industrial city of Coimbatore, dozens of bombs were detonated, killing thirty-six people, but nobody claimed responsibility. Polling day in Bihar was savage. There was widespread booth capturing, which involved a gang of men arriving at a polling station, disabling the police guard, stuffing the ballot boxes with voting papers marked in favour of their own party and delivering the boxes to the local returning officer. Across the state, bombs were set off and rival groups shot each other with home-made guns. After the first day of voting, the *Hindustan Times* had this front page headline:

AT LEAST 40 KILLED IN BIHAR
POLL VIOLENCE—POLICE PATROL PARTY
BLOWN TO SMITHEREENS

After Rajiv's assassination, Sonia Gandhi had retreated from the world, seeing only her mother and sisters and a few close friends. Occasionally she would make public appearances or receive important foreign dignitaries, but most of her external contact was handled by intermediaries. In New Delhi, she became an object of fascination—the Sphinx, Jackie Kennedy,

Mona Lisa. Her house was turned into a shrine to her husband's memory, and she edited a moving and surprisingly revealing book about him, *Rajiv*, which contained a selection of his photographs. Initially derided as an uneducated outsider, an "Italian au pair," Sonia proved a canny political operator. Many who knew her well found it hard to believe what she was doing, having always thought of her as apolitical. In her book *Rajiv*, there is indeed little sense of her future strategic talent. Lines such as "Rajiv drove through most villages and towns in his jeep. Wherever people were waiting, we would stop. If we were delayed they would stand by patiently, to see him, to talk to him" appear naïve, and could have been written by the wife of almost any Third World leader who was sure to be received with rapture.[15] Over time, Sonia Gandhi would become an exceptionally commanding politician, exerting her unspoken will over the Congress party. Once again, the men in white khadi were afraid of "Madam."

I went to one of her first public rallies. Not far from Delhi's Red Fort, where the Mughal emperors once lived in state surrounded by half-naked eunuchs, lies Ram Lila Ground. People were streaming towards it, wearing Congress badges, Congress rosettes, sun shades and hair bands, chanting and jumping, shouting slogans, some barefoot in dhotis, some in shirts and ties. An auto-rickshaw passed, a pair of bell-shaped speakers attached to its roof, a man in the back blaring the injunction: "Aaj teen bajay sooniye Bharat ki ik lauti bahu, Sonia Gandhi"—"Today at 3 o'clock, listen to India's one and only daughter-in-law, Sonia Gandhi." Around 80,000 of us waited for five hours while a qawwal, singing as if from the heart, entertained the crowd. Up on the podium stood fabulously tall cutouts of Rajiv Gandhi, striding forward with his arm in the air, and beside him a giant Sonia, doing namaste.

When Mrs. Gandhi arrived, the crowd pushed forward against the bamboo barriers. Police shoved screaming people this way and that, and beat some of them with sticks. Dozens of Special Protection Group agents barked into walkie-talkies and cricked their necks as they listened to their earpieces. Head down, mouth set tightly, no time to waste, Sonia Gandhi scurried up to the front of the platform, wearing a man's watch like her late mother-in-law. Behind her came her daughter, Priyanka, and son, Rahul, both now in their mid-twenties, waving and smiling. Mrs. Gandhi began reading her speech in a woeful voice, in heavily accented Hindi, telling the story of her life and how she had sacrificed her husband for India. Beside me an old man with a long yellowing beard and a strong nose was sobbing, tears running down his pitted face. A middle-aged woman, huddled into her sari, dabbed at her eyes with a pink tissue, shaking her head. Sonia had arrived in India with a return ticket, "but Delhi was the place of my second birth and the ticket, like my past, was lost in the mists of time" (which ignored the fact that she and Rajiv almost quit the country for Italy during the Emergency). She concluded her speech with a line of unadulterated cinema. "Dar gaye," she rasped in her Italian accent, "ek aurat se dar gaye hain"—"The opposition are scared, scared of a woman."

Nothing in Sonia Gandhi's upbringing hinted at a political career. Born Antonia Maino, she grew up in the poor industrial suburb of Orbassano on the outskirts of Turin. Her father, Stephano, was a successful builder who had fought alongside the Wehrmacht against the Russians on the Eastern Front (he gave each of his daughters a Russian pet name, hence Sonia) and her mother, Paola, was a traditional housewife. Stephano remained an unrepentant fascist until his death, like many of his generation of Italian men, and kept a leather-bound edition of Mussolini's speeches in his front room.[16] The Mainos were a strict Roman Catholic family. The girls were not permitted to go out unchaperoned, and it must have been with trepidation that he allowed his attractive eighteen-year-old daughter to attend a language school in England.

Sonia stayed with a British family as a paying guest but felt homesick. One lunchtime at the Varsity restaurant in Cambridge, a mutual friend introduced her to Rajiv Gandhi. Sonia wrote later: "As our eyes met for the first time I could feel my heart pounding. We greeted each other and, as far as I was concerned, it was love at first sight."[17] The friend, Chris von Stieglitz, called it "pure, simple, personal magnetism. It never disappeared. Three months before his death I remember her sitting on his knee; they were still acting like teenage lovers."[18] After the marriage, which took place against the wishes of Sonia's father, they lived a carefree life in Delhi, away from politics, spending days with friends and going on picnics and excursions. Relations with Sanjay and Maneka were tense but detached. Sonia fulfilled the role of the faithful bahu, or daughter-in-law, buying impeccable clothes for Indira Gandhi and cooking her favourite dishes; in some respects, traditional family life in India and Italy was similar. Rajiv was a contented airline pilot, flying a Fokker Friendship and later a DC-3 on the domestic sector. Sonia Gandhi could never have anticipated how the untimely death of her brother-in-law followed by the murder of her mother-in-law would lead to her husband becoming prime minister, and how his assassination would in turn leave her with few alternatives but to become a politician herself.

During the 1998 election campaign, it was apparent that Sonia Gandhi was creating a popular reaction, but unclear whether this meant she could overcome the view that she was an outsider who had no business to be involved in Indian politics. Her opponents called her "Italy ki Maharani," the "queen of Italy," and Bal Thackeray, leader of the BJP's chauvinist ally the Shiv Sena, asked, "How is it that when we ask one white skin to quit India, you are welcoming another white skin? . . . Our ancestors, who fought for freedom, overthrew the British."[19] Her Catholic religious background offered another line of attack: Narendra Modi said she might be in league with the election commissioner, who came from a Christian family in Meghalaya in the north-east. "Has James Michael Lyngdoh come from Italy?" he wondered. "I don't have his janam patri [horoscope], I will have to ask Sonia Gandhi. Do they meet in church?"[20]

These jibes continued for several years, but it seemed from early on they had little genuine resonance with voters. I watched her visit the constituency of Medak in Andhra Pradesh, which had been Indira Gandhi's seat at the time of her death. Voters here were predominantly Telugu-speaking agricultural labourers, living in poor conditions. When she flew into Medak in an orange and white helicopter to speak to a cheering crowd of over 100,000 people, she represented some distant ideal, a deracinated image unconnected to the reality of cropping sugar-cane by hand for twelve hours a day. A local revolutionary outfit, the People's War Group, had ordered a boycott of her rally, but this was ignored. Some people came to see Sonia because they were paid by local village leaders, but most came voluntarily. One old man told me he had ridden four miles from Lingsanpally on his bicycle. "I have attended meetings of Indira Gandhi and Rajiv Gandhi, so let me see how Rajiv's wife looks." Unlike in Delhi, where outfits varied, all the women here wore saris and bangles and all the men had a dhoti and vest, except a handful of hard-faced local Congress leaders who wore slacks— and owned shoes.

As the crowd streamed towards the road, I spoke to Kondraopalli Pochamma, an agricultural labourer in her early forties with rings on her toes, poor teeth and a thin yellow sari. She earned about $20 a month, when she could find work. She had come to the political rally to see Sonia "and receive her message," she told me, speaking in Telugu. "But I couldn't follow a damn thing. Sonia's accent wasn't like Indira Gandhi's." All the same, she would vote for Congress. "Who else is there? Only the family has a soft corner and a wish to help the poor, especially women. I belong to a weaker [lower-caste] section. Our only hope is Sonia—we trust her, because she too has suffered." Nobody I spoke to there was concerned about her foreign origins. "She married into an Indian family and so we consider her as one among us," said Kondraopalli Pochamma firmly. "She is Indira Gandhi's daughter-in-law." In traditional Indian culture, the daughter-in-law is subsumed into the husband's family, so for a Medak voter she was not much more alien than a Bengali or a Kashmiri.

Sonia Gandhi's appeal rested in part on iconography. She had a transcendent ability to project herself as an Indian everywoman who shared the suffering of the huddled masses: she was the incarnation of a dynasty but also a tragic widow who tied back her hair and dressed in muted colours as a good widow should. Foreigners are notorious in India for looking foolish in a sari—six yards of cloth tucked into a petticoat and pleated over a blouse—but Sonia wore hers impeccably, and avoided Western clothes. Despite Bal Thackeray's jibes, most voters did not see her as a "white skin"; with her dark hair and light brown Italian complexion, she looked as if she might be from a similar ethnic background to the Nehrus, high-caste north Indians. Had she been of blond northern European or black African origin, she would never have been credible as an Indian leader. In a country where skin tone is noticed, this was part of her allure. It helped too that she was called Sonia—it was a name, like Natasha, which had become popular in the 1960s during India's love-in with Russia, and did not mark her as an outsider.

When the votes were counted in 1998, Congress and its allies had won 166 seats, an increase of twenty-eight from the previous election, and the BJP was short of a majority. The party had been rescued from oblivion. It still had some distance to go if it was to return to health and power, and it was at this point that Sonia Gandhi's skills as a leader began to appear. She made some blunders, learning as she went. Unlike her late husband, she kept her friends separate from her professional career and did not allow politicians to advance any further than the office at the back of her house. Her private, culturally diverse home life with her children was kept hidden from public view, and her close friends took a tacit vow of *omertà*. Priyanka got married and had two children, while Rahul went to college in the United States and Britain, and bucked family tradition by gaining qualifications. He developed the art of being discreet and unobtrusive, studying under an assumed name and avoiding any public profile. In his absence, the Indian press made up stories: his real name was reported to be Raol and his sister's was Bianca, and he had been arrested at Boston airport carrying wads of cash (in fact he had been spotted reading a flight manual a few days after 9/11—when questioned at Logan, he applied the precepts of secularism by refusing to say whether he was Hindu or Muslim, and when it became clear the problem was not going away, asked his questioners to call a contact at the FBI, who set matters straight).[21]

The mother and children were a strong unit, and unlike most politicians, Sonia Gandhi was not held back by family members with possible ambitions of their own. As she was an outsider, a European who had married into an Indian family, other politicians never knew quite how to handle the new Mrs. Gandhi. Where necessary, she could act detached and "Western." Her weapon of choice was repudiation. When three of her most senior colleagues suggested only someone born on Indian soil should head any future government, she resigned her post, saying her loyalty to her country (meaning India) was so great that she did not want to cause controversy. They went; she stayed. She built alliances with regional, caste-based and communist parties and avoided being identified with particular policies, except for nebulous ones like concern for the poor and secular values. Any Congress official who became too powerful was cut adrift, such as her husband's long-time secretary V. George. Mrs. Gandhi gave no one a second chance. In meetings she usually remained formal and aloof, using long silences to exert authority.

Despite this, Congress still had ambitious and qualified men who regarded themselves as potential prime ministers. Since Mrs. Gandhi had no experience of administration at any level, some wanted her to be kicked upstairs to a ceremonial post. She remained in a precarious and isolated position—people joked about her inability to speak Hindi well, and referred to her by her mother-in-law's nickname, "goongi gudiya," or "dumb doll." In 1999 she sat for one of the only interviews she has ever done, on Star TV. The unedited tape makes astonishing viewing. Mrs. Gandhi giggles nervously at the first question, stops herself and says, "I'm sorry, I just don't know how to face a camera." There are two more false starts; it is apparent she has had no media training. Blinking and swallowing, her upper lip perspiring, she finally gets into her stride, talking about bureaucracy, politics and her family tragedy. When the interviewer mentions that people mock her Italian accent, she says, "I don't blame them for making fun of it. I feel Indian. I don't feel one bit Italian."[22] By the end of the conversation, she looks ready to collapse.

Then, in an extraordinary series of coincidences, the internal opposition within the Congress party disappeared. In June 2000, Rajesh Pilot died when his car collided with a Rajasthan State Road Transport bus; in October 2000, Sitaram Kesri passed away following a heart attack; in January 2001, the 62-year-old Jitendra Prasada suffered a sudden and fatal brain haemorrhage;

in September 2001, Madhavrao Scindia was flying to Kanpur in an industrialist's Cessna C-90 for a state election rally when the plane abruptly fell out of the sky. After this, dissent stopped: the challengers were gone. Delhi's leading astrologers, who wield enormous influence in the political sphere because so many uncertainties are involved in a political life, warned that Sonia Gandhi was in her "shatruvinash yog," the astrological period when planetary forces are aligned in your favour and anyone who opposes you will be destroyed. Even more than the "raj yog"—the astrological period of "rule" that politicians seek, and try to hasten through pujas and the wearing of appropriate jewels—the shatruvinash yog is respected and feared. Whether Mrs. Gandhi gave any attention to these deductions, made by assorted astrologers in the employ of politicians' wives and mistresses, and retailed by the countless gossips of political Delhi, was uncertain, for she always kept her own counsel (though some of those close to her believed she had metamorphosed into a Hindu; after her mother-in-law's death, she ceased to take communion from the hand of the papal legate). In the 2004 election, against the predictions of the opinion pollsters, Congress came back to power.

During the campaign, the party avoided making a clear statement about who would be prime minister in the event of victory, but it was assumed Sonia Gandhi would take the post. When it became clear that Congress and its allies were going to form a government, the BJP stepped up its personal campaign against her. Sushma Swaraj, a homely seeming BJP politician, announced in histrionic tones that she would begin a fast and fight the forthcoming battle as a sanyasin: "If I see Sonia Gandhi take the oath as prime minister . . . I will shave my head, sleep on the floor and eat roasted grams [chickpeas]." At the same time, large crowds gathered outside Sonia Gandhi's house, demanding she accept. One man stood on the roof of a car noisily wielding a sword and a pistol, and threatened to shoot himself in the head if she declined.

When Mrs. Gandhi addressed her MPs in Parliament, she told them that after listening to her "inner voice" (a phrase borrowed from the Mahatma) she had decided to "humbly decline" the post. "Power in itself has never attracted me, nor has position been my goal," she said. It was a subtle response in a land where rejection of material ambition strikes a powerful religious chord. In case anyone missed the point, she was wearing a plain white ikat sari with a dark blue border, white being the Hindu colour of mourning. There was chaos and uproar. Might she still be persuaded? Mani Shankar Aiyar, a Congress loyalist, was first to the microphone. "Madam Prime Minister," he began, "we cannot betray the people of India." Another MP, Renuka Chowdhury, stood sobbing in front of the lawmakers saying that Sonia Gandhi "stood like a shiny [sic] armour" in defence of "the finest traditions of being Indian."[23] Her opponents were left irate by the manoeuvre she had pulled off. "She doesn't have a political idea," said L. K. Advani soon afterwards, "though she got smart advice. They have a dynastic culture in her party, where one family is supposed to be a royal family."[24] Her estranged sister-in-law, Maneka Gandhi, who was herself now an MP with the BJP, used stronger language, condemning both Sonia and the party's culture of sycophancy: "She was always adept at the management of people. The Congress party reacts strongly to mummies but you cannot always have mummy to take you through if you have no central ideology. It's theatre."[25]

Sonia Gandhi's decision was a historic act of renunciation and a shrewd political move. Her position was secure. The new prime minister, the respected Sikh technocrat Manmohan Singh, would serve at Madam's pleasure. This had been planned some years before. As far back as 1999, Mrs. Gandhi had told a close ally that she would give the job to Manmohan Singh if they took power. When asked why she did not announce this publicly, she answered astutely: "There would be a power struggle [in the Congress party] which Manmohan Singh wouldn't win."[26]

Although these political sequences might be blamed on the horoscope of Sonia Gandhi, it would be wise to consult the astrological charts of another body whose anniversary fell on the same day, the Constituent Assembly. When "Hon'ble Pt. Jawaharlal Nehru" signed his name in the register of the assembly on that day, the constitutional debates began and it was quickly agreed that India should become a democracy. The upper-class Indian nationalists had not quite abolished themselves—some aspiring mini-Nehrus can still be found in Parliament—but it did mean that less influential sections of Indian society would in time assert themselves through the ballot box. The vision of the founders took a while to come true, and in a dynamic and constantly changing form, as a multitude of political parties arose.

The smaller political movements in India today come in many shapes, but most have a link with a geographical region or a community. Some can be influential, such as the Telugu Desam Party (TDP) in Andhra Pradesh; its current leader, Chandrababu Naidu, is an energetic figure who has made pioneering attempts at "e-governance," publishing nearly all government documents, including draft budgets, on the Internet. Similarly the Biju Janata Dal (BJD) is strong enough to influence national politics and to define the parameters of political manoeuvring within Orissa; it is led by one of India's more unlikely statesmen, Naveen Patnaik, a figure on the Delhi and New York party scene who metamorphosed into an astute politician after the death of his father. Other parties are based on the combined power of a particular caste group. The Samajwadi Party (SP) is nominally socialist, but its main purpose is to speak for the OBCs (or Other Backward Classes, meaning they are socially disadvantaged, but in a stronger position than the Dalits, or former untouchables) of Uttar Pradesh; its leader, Mulayam Singh Yadav, is a former village wrestler with links to Bollywood who has also served as India's defence minister. His main rival is Mayawati, who heads another influential force in the state, the Bahujan Samaj Party (BSP), which is the voice of Dalits and others.

At the opposite end of India is the All India Anna Dravida Munnetra Kazhagam (AIADMK), a party from Tamil Nadu in the south run by the powerful J. Jayalalithaa (originally J. Jayalalitha—she added the extra "a" for astrological reasons), an actress who entered politics as the lover of the chief minister and movie legend M. G. Ramachandran; but the AIADMK should not be confused with another important Tamil party, the Dravida Munnetra Kazhagam (DMK), run by M. Karunanidhi and his son, M. K. Stalin (named after Joseph). Mamata Banerjee is a brisk, mercurial woman politician who runs the breakaway Trinamool Congress (AITC) in West Bengal and hopes to undo the Marxist lock on the political structures of her state. Smaller parties include the Indian Union Muslim League, the Sikkim Democratic Front and Shiv Sena, a flamboyant outfit from Maharashtra which attacks Mumbai cinemas when they show films featuring actors it does not like. The Janata Dal comes in various guises, which disagree with each other. The Shiromani Akali Dal, or SAD, is a collection of Sikh parties, while the Democratic Indira Congress (Karunakaran), or DIC(K), is a now defunct faction of the Congress party in Kerala. This is a shame, since "DIC(K)" is no longer found painted on walls and posters. There are two significant communist agglomerations in India, one based in the south and one in the east; the most important is the CPI(M), or Communist Party of India (Marxist), which has been running West Bengal for nearly four decades.

It took almost half a century for this process of democratic diffusion to happen: since 1996, the numerous smaller parties have held around half of the seats in the Lok Sabha, meaning neither Congress nor the BJP has been able to form a government without them. The centrifugal effect of popular democracy has been extraordinary, spinning out power towards people whose forebears had never had it. The idea that Mayawati, the daughter of a Dalit, could be one of the most influential politicians in the country could never have been imagined, much less have happened, in India's 4,000-year history. Those who in earlier times would have been classed as untouchables are gaining new status. As the nation changes, and long-suppressed communities find a voice, the paternalistic thinking of the independence era is losing its grip. A transformative revolution is taking place, and it is not always a pretty sight.

When the new nation was being built after independence, the Scheduled Castes and Scheduled Tribes were lumped together. They might more usefully have been treated in different ways, the depressed castes being integrated with the mainstream and the tribals allowed to live more traditionally. Instead, the Scheduled Caste label, which was in most ways a social disadvantage, could enable people to obtain certain benefits such as reserved jobs and college places, and seats in Parliament and on political bodies. Dalit comes from a Sanskrit word meaning "crushed" or "broken." Dr. Ambedkar started to use it to describe his community when making speeches in Marathi. Over time, it has been adopted as a generic term to describe oppressed and untouchable castes, or those outside the Hindu caste system—a term with a political ring to it when used by Ambedkar's inheritors.

As previously mute groups assert their power and identity in New Delhi, politics has become increasingly commercialized, with party leaders engaging in horse-trading to secure the maximum benefit for their own interest group. This has reshaped parliamentary politics, and was inevitable in some form—whatever decisions Indira, Sanjay and Rajiv Gandhi had taken during the 1960s, '70s and '80s, the monolithic Congress party would have fractured and given way to a multi-party system. The popular vote fractionalized between parties, and even when legislators were elected, there was a risk they might switch loyalty; everything depended on cunning and coalitions. Since the 1990s, the alliances between parties have become more complex and durable, but for the moment each prime minister has no choice but to seek unnatural allies. So when Manmohan Singh became prime minister in 2004, this man who was renowned for his personal probity was obliged briefly to sit alongside ministerial colleagues such as K. Venkatapathy of the DMK, who was charged with rioting armed with a deadly weapon, and Shibu Soren, an Adivasi, or tribal, political leader from the Jharkhand Mukti Morcha (JMM) who was later convicted (and acquitted on appeal) of murder.[27]

During the last twenty years, the only party that looked as if it might be capable of displacing Congress as a broad national force was the BJP. Advani's chariot ride to Ayodhya gave way to a more professional, middle-class public image as the BJP led a government for a full term, and voters were attracted by the idea that a fresh alternative was emerging. Business families switched allegiance, as did much of the massive, and massively wealthy, Indian diaspora, lured by a party organization that promised security and good governance. This was in part wishful thinking: for years business people had wanted a centre-right party in India that worked on merit rather than on redistributive rhetoric and family connections.

Following the scent of power, Congress politicians like K. C. Pant, a senior minister under Indira Gandhi whose father, G. B. Pant, had been a stalwart of the independence movement, began to defect to the BJP. He was followed by Najma Heptullah, the grand-niece of Maulana Azad, the most important Muslim in the Congress party at the time of independence. When she switched, Najma Heptullah attacked Sonia Gandhi: "The present Congress leadership has moved away from the ideology of Nehru, Azad, Patel and Gandhi."[28] This was an opportunist move, but it caught the popular sense at the turn of the new century that—despite its appropriation of a partially invented Hindu past—the BJP was the party of the future. Its leaders were going to be, if not clean, then a great deal cleaner than the prevaricators who had come before them. They would return to older, better and more traditional Indian values, and seek to kindle a Hindu national ethos based on social consciousness, the spirit of dedication, sterling qualities and good character. They would move away from the cult of the Congress party, with its exclusive version of India's independence movement.

In office from 1998 to 2004, the BJP-led government tested a nuclear bomb that had been primed by Narasimha Rao, led a steady privatization drive, fought a small war with Pakistan when Pakistani soldiers moved into Indian territory in Kargil in Kashmir, started road-building projects and boosted GDP significantly: they fought the 2004 election campaign on the slogan "India Shining," and did not expect to lose to Congress. The prime minister during this period was not L. K. Advani, who had made a notable misstep when accused of corruption in Narasimha Rao's coded diaries case. Knowing he was not guilty—even his many enemies saw him as a Spartan—Advani had rashly said he would not hold public office until his name was cleared. He had forgotten quite how slowly the wheels of justice grind in India, and the premiership passed to his colleague, Atal Behari Vajpayee, with whom he had been imprisoned during the Emergency. Vajpayee was a more popular choice, a gifted orator who wrote poetry in Hindi and was of a softer temper than Advani. When he became foreign minister in the Janata government at the end of the Emergency, Vajpayee had said he would consign Indira Gandhi to the dustbin of history. He represented an older, more conservative tradition of Indian or Hindu nationalism, and was a unifier, clever at handling his coalition partners. Nominally a bachelor, he had lived happily for many years with his college sweetheart, her husband and their daughters. As a less ideological and more ethereal figure than Advani, he offered an acceptable public face to the party. Yet the character of the modern BJP was best exemplified not by these two ageing warhorses, but by Pramod Mahajan and Narendra Modi, the two younger men who had flagged off the Toyota chariot in 1990.

Mahajan was a Maharashtrian Brahmin, a clever campaigner, a canny social manipulator and a financial wizard, adept at drawing in money from multifarious sources for the party and reputedly for himself too. Despite being an RSS man, he was known for having an extravagant life. He managed to position himself at the strategic heart of the party as the fixer, the dealer, the nexus without whom no essential political decision could be taken. In 2006—only months after Vajpayee had tapped him as the probable new leader of the party—Mahajan's brother walked into his sea-facing Mumbai apartment one morning and shot him with a pistol, before going to the nearest police station and saying what he had done. The nation was astonished by the fratricide of this prominent political leader, which appeared to be the result of a family and possibly a marital dispute. In the aftermath, Mahajan's son, Rahul, was seen on television gently comforting his mother and sister while his father passed away in hospital. In the presence of Vajpayee, Advani, the leaders of the RSS, the VHP (Vishwa Hindu Parishad) and Shiv Sena, Rahul Mahajan lit the funeral pyre while buglers played the Last Post and priests chanted Vedic prayers.[29]

Plans were made to draft the young man into a political career—but he turned out to be a less than ideal boy. A month later, the evening before going to immerse his father's ashes in the Brahmaputra, Rahul Mahajan settled into the Jacuzzi in his father's sprawling official residence, a short drive from the prime minister's house. With him in the bathroom were his father's secretary, Bibek Moitra, and several bottles of champagne. Later, they came out and had a small party accompanied by a bag of cocaine.

Mahajan vomited, staggered and asked his friends (some Nigerian and Kashmiri drug dealers) what was up with the coke—had they given him bad stuff? Then, in a scene that might have come from *Pulp Fiction,* it transpired the cocaine had been cut with heroin. The household servants had to be woken up and Mahajan and Moitra were taken to the nearby Apollo hospital, where Moitra died.

The debacle was reported initially as a case of food poisoning. Mahajan's uncle, another BJP politician, announced bizarrely that his nephew had taken no drugs: "The quantity of cocaine shown in the medical tests was within permissible limits, which can be found in any human being."[30] The Indian media covered this story as if it were a glamorous but sordid tale of drug use in high society, but it was a great deal more than that: the Hindu son of a leading figure of the Hindu party, hours before he was to perform one of the most important tasks of any Hindu man's life—scattering his father's ashes—was partying in a thoroughly un-Hindu way and engaging in the sort of behaviour that the moral police of Hindutva liked to decry as decadent and foreign.

Rahul Mahajan claimed to remember nothing about what had happened and was married off a month later to his childhood sweetheart, in an attempt to set him straight. He had a quick marital break-up before appearing on *Big Boss,* the Indian version of *Big Brother,* where he was seen flirting with Monica Bedi, a failed starlet and gangster's moll who had been arrested with Abu Salem, the convicted mastermind of the 1993 Mumbai bomb blasts. He went on to make the TV reality show *Rahul Dulhaniya Le Jayega*—"Rahul Will Take Home the Bride"—in which a gaggle of desperate-looking girls from all over India competed to marry him. The winner, a "Gladrags" model named Dimpy Ganguly, married Rahul Mahajan three days after the death of the uncle who had murdered his father.[31]

The other politician who had sent Advani's chariot on its journey was Narendra Modi. He was a different quantity, an ascetic Gujarati from a poor background who had started out with the RSS. His father ran a railway station canteen in Vadnagar. Dynamic and witty, Modi rose quickly through the BJP and became chief minister of Gujarat, an industrialized western state with strong connections to Mumbai. Business people admired his straightforward and efficient style, his effective management of the bureaucracy and his programmes for improved village health and electrification. In early 2002, a train of Hindu pilgrims was stopped at Godhra station reportedly by a Muslim mob and set on fire, killing fifty-nine people. In response, organized Hindu gangs took revenge on Muslims across central Gujarat; families were dragged out of their homes, cut to death and burned; mosques and Muslim dargahs, or shrines, were destroyed. Through all this, the police stood by in many places and did nothing, following orders from above. Around 2,000 people were murdered, and little effort was made to prosecute the killers or the organizers of the slaughter. Narendra Modi made no expression of regret, and focused on the victims of the attack on the train, implying that the Muslims deserved what had come to them. Vajpayee's government in New Delhi did not dismiss Modi as chief minister—in fact he later returned to power with a fresh electoral mandate.

For opponents of the BJP, this was incontrovertible evidence the party was showing its true, fascist colours. Advani responded that "the events in Gujarat in 2002 were an aberration in an otherwise consistent record of harmony."[32] All of this suited Modi, who became a nationally acknowledged figure, a self-constructed anti-hero.

Placed in the context of other riots and pogroms that have taken place in India since independence, the official response to what happened in 2002 in Gujarat was wholly familiar. People in authority had decided a mob should be given free rein to take revenge, and they allowed lower-level officials to facilitate the act; afterwards, when it was over, nobody would admit the horrible reality of what had happened. Almost nothing was done to help those who had suffered, and nobody in authority was punished. Similarly, in 1979 in Marichjhapi, an island in the Sunderbans in West Bengal, communist cadres had set upon lower-caste Bangladeshi settlers with the support of the police, burned and looted huts, raped women and murdered several hundred people, throwing their bodies into the river—Jyoti Basu, the veteran communist chief minister, did not express regret. In 1984 after the organized murder of Sikhs, the Congress party acted as if it had never taken place, and embraced and promoted some of those who were accused of the killings. Politicians behaved in this way because they could.

Might the BJP metamorphose into a party of the centre-right, a competent alternative to Congress, or was it still too busy trying to reinvent the dim past? I talked to some of its activists, seeking to get to the nub of what they believed. A conversation with the BJP president, Rajnath Singh, went nowhere: a former physics lecturer, he discoursed on integral humanism and humanity's integration, and I was none the wiser. I tried Ashok Chowgule, who had been emailing me for years, seeking to put across another point of view to a global audience. He was a vice-president of the hardline organization the VHP and an admirer of V. S. Naipaul. We met for lunch at the Cricket Club of India. Afterwards, I met a well-heeled Mumbai editor who said (speaking of Chowgule, not Naipaul), "His wife comes to parties, very well dressed, but he says *all these things*." This response—the reference to the clothes, as if a member of the VHP could not possibly have a spouse who wore designer outfits—was part of the unexpressed divide in Indian politics, the idea that the promoters of Hindutva were socially inferior to the Nehruvians. Certainly they could be rough: I had been in a roadside eatery in rural Maharashtra some weeks earlier when a load of buses stopped in the dusty yard outside. The lead bus had a banner across the windscreen: SHIV SAINIK CONVOY ON WAY HOME—MARATHA RESERVATIONS. The demonstrators had been to a rally at Mumbai's Shivaji Park in favour of reservation of jobs for Marathi speakers. The eatery had a "no buses" policy. So these sons of the soil beat up the guard in his down-at-heel uniform, pushed other members of staff and threatened to break up the place with their batons.

Chowgule had brought me some books by Kalidasa, the Sanskrit writer. He was proud that Sanskrit literary culture had spread around the world during earlier centuries, from Afghanistan to what was now Indonesia, and saw it as an undervalued Indian achievement. We sat overlooking the cricket pitch. He had been raised in Kolhapur and sent to England in the 1960s to study economics at Bristol University.

"It was a very dreary place, but I enjoyed my studies. After that I went to business school in Cleveland, Ohio, for two years but found U.S. society to be more shallow. I came back to join our family business—we do shipbuilding and owning, industrial-explosives manufacture, iron ore, some cement manufacture. As a child, there was no dispute we were from a Hindu tradition. To be pro-Hindu doesn't mean you are anti-anybody. One of my best friends at school was a Christian, and there were Muslims too. When I was a kid, you never saw anyone in a burqa, but now you see it all the time because of the international Wahabi movement. During my childhood in Kolhapur, Muslims would go to the mosque and to the Shivling [a phallic symbol of Shiva], and Hindus would go the other way, from the Shivling to the dargah. They were not dressed any differently from us. The Muharram procession was a big event, but now the mullahs have said it mustn't happen."[33] It was true there had been a change in relations since his childhood. By the 1970s, about half a million Indians, many of whom were Muslim, were working in the Middle East. They brought money and a new religious feeling to India, having developed a sense of commonality with other Muslims while living abroad. After the Iranian revolution in 1979, small groups of bearded, traditionally dressed young men began to propagate the idea of Islamic revival in Bombay, which in turn revived Hindu fears of Muslim fanaticism that had been largely dormant since the 1950s.[34]

"The big event in my political life was when Rajiv Gandhi turned out to be such a disappointment—instead of a modernizer, he was concerned with patronage, old economics and the Shah Bano case, which took rights away from Muslim women to appease the leaders in that community.[35] I went to an informal gathering of a Hindu organization on Nepean Sea Road in 1990: they spoke of resurgence, of bringing back our traditions and culture. I joined the VHP. Ram Rajya, the rule of Lord Ram, is just rule. The pub culture of England is not something we need. We have to talk about our ancient culture, our history, our sciences, and admit that the Aryans arose in India and the Vedas arose here. We were not some nomadic tribe. The Marxists who write about India are trying to eradicate all that history, to say our great past leaders were misguided patriots or mountain rats. These people are the reference point for Indians and foreigners who want to understand about India. It's the same with newspaper and magazine editors—they are all influenced by the same thinking. When I was young, we did not have the television, we used to read more widely and when the elders were talking we were listening. My children don't agree with all I say."

So it was not an unfamiliar experience: the parent, growing older and wondering why the young had different ideas. I asked Ashok Chowgule about what had happened in Gujarat, and he took the same line as Narendra Modi, focusing exclusively on the victims of the train attack. "After that, riots took place, and Hindus and Muslims all died. Violence is bad, but your objective should be to prevent the train being surrounded. If Congress wants to take up the issue of Gujarat, they should also take up what happened to the indigenous Hindus who were driven out of their houses in Kashmir." It was a circular argument. He continued: "Hindus do not have the chance to represent themselves. If there is a conference on Hindu nationalism, no Hindu nationalists will be invited. If a Hindu leader is killed it won't be reported, but if a Christian nun is raped it will be. It's part of the programme of trivializing our civilization."[36] We were back to the idea that the majority of Indians were victims, and "true" Hindus were misrepresented. It was incorrect to say the murder of a Hindu leader would not be reported: the Indian media were vigorous and indiscriminate in their willingness to report stories of political violence.

I felt this affable, successful industrialist had a sense of Hindu victimhood that was theoretical, rather than lived. His comments about the Marxist or post-Marxist tendency among historians were understandable, although slightly out of date. It seemed as if seeing his country in this way was for him a means of making people bond in a potential, abstract, mythic way. The Hindutva movement was too important a force to dismiss it only as ignorant bigotry, as most liberal commentators tried to, but every time I sought to move beyond this and understand it better, I came up against the irrational. In each of the last five general elections, the BJP and its allies have picked up around 100 million votes, and yet they have persisted with a view of the future that is rooted in a faraway past, arising from the historical imagination.

Take the BJP national election manifesto for 2009, which suggested ancient India grew volumes of rice which outshone even the bogus statistics used during Mao's Great Leap Forward:

According to foreigners visiting this country, Indians were regarded as the best agriculturists in the world . . . The Thanjaur (AD 900–1200) inscriptions and Ramnathapuram (AD 1325) inscriptions record 15 to 20 tons per hectare production of paddy. Now, even after the first green revolution, according to Government statistics, Ludhiana [in Punjab] in the late-20th century recorded a production of 5.5 tons of paddy per hectare. It is, therefore, imperative that India rediscovers an agricultural technology . . .

—and so it continued, borne back ceaselessly into the past.[37] Twenty tons per hectare! Australia today has the highest rice yields in the world at 10 tons per hectare, using intensive agriculture in lush conditions. This slice of the manifesto reminded me more than anything of a conversation with a literary type from Madhya Pradesh some years back, one of India's official writers. He told me, without a smile, that people in ancient times in India had aeroplanes. How did he know? Having studied the Vedas, it was clear to him they had sufficient knowledge to have made them. Why were there no remains of the Vedic aeroplanes? "They hid them in caves" was his answer.

I had another talk with the BJP, in the avatar of Murli Manohar Joshi, who had overseen the election manifesto. His janam patri, or horoscope, was reputed to say he would one day become prime minister of India, but this was looking increasingly unlikely. He was a Pahari from Kumaon in the far north, in the foothills of the Himalayas. Now in his mid-seventies, he had joined the RSS at the age of ten after watching its devotees parading in the park opposite his house. "I was impressed by the camaraderie and discipline." Joshi was dressed in a dhoti kurta and a flamboyant white, vermilion and gold stole. He wore four gold rings and a double-stringed pearl bracelet on his right wrist, and his room was done nicely with fresh carnations and lilies. Various deities were in attendance, in stone. We spoke on many subjects, but he only became animated about one thing—the cow.

"In Allahabad when I was younger, there was the Go Sevak Mandal, a movement towards cow protection. India was having a lot of food shortages. In the cultural life, the cow was considered to be as tolerant as mother earth. I looked at the role of the cow and its progeny. In Calcutta and Delhi, the cow was being slaughtered in an inhuman way. Most of these abattoirs were run by Muslims. Facts are facts. We had to challenge this because the export of beef is repugnant to the people of India. When I was a minister, I investigated it. The position of the cow has been most important since the beginning of our history. Cow's milk—it has been shown scientifically, the milk of the indigenous Indian cow—is nearest to mother's milk. It gives you immunity. So, the distillate of cow's urine has important medicinal effects. It makes your body able to absorb drugs, so you can have lower dosages. So Taxol, a drug for treating cancer made from yew-tree bark, can be taken in half-quantities if you have it mixed with distillate of cow's urine. There is no other society where the position of the cow is so important."

Why was the cow important? Some early source material suggests beef was eaten in India in ancient times, and that extreme reverence for the cow was a more recent social practice. Dalits and Indian Muslims, and presumably others too, had never stopped killing cows. I wondered if Murli Manohar Joshi was saying this because, as a Brahmin whose community had used cow's urine to purify themselves after contact with their inferiors, he wanted to return to a fading, archaic version of his own heritage, which increased his community's status. Did his theories about Taxol offer a link to the purported ways of his forefathers, just as the inscriptions about gargantuan rice yields "proved" the superiority of ancient agricultural technology?

He was still talking. "Every society must preserve its cultural values and traditions. India's love for the cow is one of these values, for the cow has done so much service to the society, for thousands of years. Some Indians who go abroad oppose and eat the cow, but this is because they are ignorant about their own value system. The cow is for us almost like a family member."

Other things paled after this part of the conversation. Did Murli Manohar Joshi still want to be prime minister? "I will wait for the design of the
divinity." Did he regret being present at the destruction of the mosque in
Ayodhya? "Congress did nothing to prevent that, and created a situation
where this thing developed. With their consent, religious men were washing the platform for the new temple in Ayodhya with water from the local
river. The action only should have happened through an Act of Parliament,
or by consensus." What were his ambitions for the nation? "India should
be strong. We are not congenitally anti-Muslim. I personally can't be anti-
Muslim because I listen to Sufi music during my morning yoga."[38]

Were Joshi and Chowgule detached from their own supporters or articu-
lating a deeply held view? I tried another tack, speaking to BJP workers
and enthusiasts in Lucknow, where Atal Behari Vajpayee, the acceptable
"mask" of Hindutva, was the Member of Parliament. More than any other
party, it seemed to have few women in public positions, and the women
who manifested were consciously conservative in appearance: a tame salwar kameez or sari, sturdy spectacles, a functional handbag, earrings and a
single-string necklace. The men who were helping to put the election campaign into effect at the BJP office here were mainly young or middle-aged,
and seemed genuinely enthusiastic. I talked to Manoj, a party worker from
north-eastern Uttar Pradesh who had ambitions to join the state legislative
assembly one day. He sat erect on a bench in a crisp white shirt and trousers
while a local activist, Arunav, translated his Bhojpuri into English.

"The Mussulman community doesn't accept that terrorism is cancerous,
that it has cancerous properties and if it is not shed it is going to ruin the
whole body." He felt strongly about this, and about other things too. "The
Mussulman community is a threat. Although they may be weaker economically, they have toughness of mind and nurse a grudge for partition. They
have a lack of education because Congress was content to keep them illiterate." It seemed as if he envied his own mental idea of Muslims for their
toughness. Manoj said he knew what they were up to, although he never
had any contact with them himself. "They work only as hair-cutters, or
they make goggles [spectacles] and don't know about the rest of the world.
We have to look at the root cause, which is their tendency to link each
and every act to the Quran. I want to say to them, 'Don't depend on this
book. Hindus have 33 crore [330 million] deities and it is a way of life, it is a
culture, and it is always evolving.' The nation must tighten. For 800 years,
invaders were coming and they took away a sizeable chunk of our country

[through the creation of Pakistan]. With the exception of emperor Akbar, they all broke down our religious centres, in Kashi [Benares], in Ayodhya, in Mathura." These were places in Uttar Pradesh with a religious resonance. "The Babri Masjid was a sign of our slavery. India may have achieved its independence in 1947, but the Hindu gods are still not free."[39]

It was quite a tirade, and I could not help feeling that Manoj, and other BJP types like him here, were similar to men I had talked to in Pakistan who imagined a purer nation. Their version of Hinduism was a direct match for politicized Islam. It was a similarly reductive way of viewing humans and the world, and it was as if their exclusivist, reductive, relentlessly male prejudice—which failed to acknowledge the loyalty most Muslims had to the Indian dream—was justified only by the threat of Islamist extremism.

I asked Manoj whether he was worried the leaders of the BJP were mainly old men. His hero was the 29-year-old Varun Gandhi, the son of Maneka and Sanjay who as a baby had been expelled from Indira Gandhi's house after his father's death. I had met Varun a few years before he joined politics, and he had struck me then as being an amalgam of his parents: lively, charismatic and somehow weird in his intensity, a young man who was likely to go somewhere, though possibly not to a good place.

At the age of twenty he had published a book of poems, *The Otherness of Self*:

> Of the end
> Seems to be
> Littoral noise
> Wash down the eucharist with water
> A euthanising silence
> strychnine
> Key to Eugenics
> Truth is the key to life and indignation.[40]

An aspiring MP for the BJP, and shortly to become a party secretary, Varun Gandhi had been jailed during the election campaign when he was secretly recorded saying he swore on the Gita that he would cut off the hand of anyone who raised a finger against Hindus.[41] After his release, he spoke about other subjects which he thought would hit a chord. Like Murli Manohar Joshi, he was keen on the cow: "If somebody attacks my mother, would I not stand in front of her to protect her? Cow-slaughter is not only a social crime it is also a criminal act," he told a rally.[42]

For someone like Manoj, he was exactly the sort of new leader the BJP needed.

"Varun Gandhi is a responsible youth. He has an emotional connect with the youth and he is the right torchbearer for Hindutva." Our interpreter, Arunav, interrupted. "Don't say 'Hindutva'—say patriotism." Manoj shrugged him off. "Varun Gandhi has been able to identify the threats that are posing a challenge to India. I met him at his rally yesterday. Maybe it is Sanjay Gandhi who will be put in the shade."[43]

4

FAMILY POLITICS

W HAT REALLY HAPPENS in an Indian general election? How does
it work? When the people of India got started in 1952, no one else
had tried anything quite so big. The new election commission had to make
2 million steel ballot boxes, and developed an idea begun in the 1920s of
having a symbol for each party—an elephant, an open hand—to make
things easier for illiterate voters, and decided to paint a streak of indelible
ink down the finger of those who had voted.[1] Before that, they had constructed a list of voters—but what of the electors in the former princely
states who did not want to give their names out of reverence for the ruler
and fear of democracy, or the women in Punjab who had no names to give
except daughter of _____ or wife of _____, or the people in Bengal who did
not want to say certain family names out loud to a stranger?

Somehow, it happened, and since then the elections have kept on coming,
fifteen so far since 1947. Amazingly, no one has yet managed to fix an Indian
general election. Certainly all sorts of bribery take place—one of Sonia
Gandhi's intimates told me you could buy journalists like prostitutes—but
the machinery or intimidation needed to capture an election at an all-India
level has not been found. There are too many voters, too many points of
view, too many conflicting allegiances. The practice of electoral violence
such as booth capturing has declined significantly since the 1990s. The

"model code of conduct" outlined by the election commission is enforced with increasing vigour, with rival parties being quick to complain of any breach: candidates break the law if they use an image of a deity on an election leaflet, their dummy ballot units (to show voters how to work the electronic voting machines) must be of a specified size and colour, political adverts cannot be printed "on back side of the bus ticket of Govt. owned buses," no more than five people are allowed to visit the returning officer at the same time and the display of party flags on moving vehicles is strictly regulated.[2]

After watching several Indian general elections, I had come to think they were self-regulating, like Gaia theory, designed for the public to fleece aspiring politicians as payback for the previous years when the transaction had gone in the opposite direction. For a small family business, urban elections could be like Diwali, the festival of lights: sweet sellers would produce special packages, caterers would charge double, loudspeaker rickshaws would be hired for ten hours and disappear after only two to a rival parade, printers would raise their prices, the sellers of flags, banners and bamboo poles would make profits, PR agencies would charge high fees to send out illiterate press releases, religious leaders would be paid to deliver the votes of the faithful (a car or truck was often the price) and the votes would not come in at the agreed level. A candidate in West Bengal said to me: "You can pay money for a certain district, but you are never sure if the neta [local leader] will deliver the votes. I would say that for election rallies, about two thirds of the money you pay to mobilize people gets wasted. They promise 10,000 farm workers will turn out, and you get 3,000." But he had lost his campaign; a more experienced candidate, always delegating the unsavoury work to a deniable third party, would butter the necessary parts of the constituency.

Money that had been stored up for years in cash would be paid out to officials and supporters. "When you see those IAS [Indian Administrative Service] officers' wives going shopping in the new mall," an oleaginous fixer told me, "there's usually someone like me in the car behind to pick up the bill." Semi-professional facilitators would pop up at election time, especially in constituencies which a member of a business family was contesting. In such situations, it was not hard for a fixer to say they needed to give a Montblanc pen here, a bottle of Blue Label there. A senior election facilitator from Mumbai told me a "big" candidate would have trouble spending less than $2–3m to win a constituency in the 2009 election (officially, each candidate was allowed to spend $55,000). One report calculated that if you had assets over Rs100m, your chances of winning an election to the Maharashtra state assembly were forty-eight times greater than if you had Rs1m ($23,000) or less. Just six of the state's 288 legislators were worth less than Rs500,000. The same report stated that celebrities were hired by campaigns in 2009 to give an endorsement, and newspapers moved back into profit by selling column inches brazenly to ride out the economic downturn: one candidate from Maharashtra had spent nearly $250,000 on local media alone during his successful campaign.[3]

This was one of the reasons why parties which were growing rapidly liked to pick "resourceful" candidates, who could spend their own fortunes trying to get elected. After an impressive showing in the 2007 Uttar Pradesh state elections, the leader of the Bahujan Samaj Party, Mayawati, wanted to extend her writ across north India to Haryana, Delhi and Uttarakhand. It was an ambitious plan, but she had never lacked ambition. Usually wearing gold and turned out in a pink or lemon salwar kameez, Mayawati was a squat woman born in 1956 and raised in a poor part of Delhi, one of nine children. When she was little, she travelled to her grandparents' home for a holiday, and the other passengers asked her parents where they were headed. They named the district. Acha, which village? They named the village. Ah, which part of the village, which mohalla? Chamar mohalla. And the passengers shrank away and stopped talking. Mayawati did not know why. Her mother explained that since they came from a caste of hereditary leather workers—Chamars—they were considered low and unclean. "From a very early age," she wrote in Hindi in her ghosted 3,300-page memoir, *A Travelogue of My Struggle-Ridden Life and of Bahujan Samaj,* "I learnt to hate the caste system with all my might."[4] Under her guidance, Dalits would claim their rights as Indian citizens.

Mayawati's response to the caste system has been extreme assertion, copying the methods of earlier rulers. After she took over the state of Uttar Pradesh in the 1990s, she built around 15,000 statues of her hero, Dr. Ambedkar, at the government's expense; for, without his ideas, she might never have gained the throne. To understand the extreme democracy of Uttar Pradesh, you ideally need a qualification in both statistics and chaos theory, and Mayawati knew how to play a game of numbers. The old elite hated her. "She should be given a broom," said one man, meaning she was a sweeper who should get back in her place. "How can she just take taxes from these poor people to build palaces and monuments?" asked a retired Rajput princess, whose ancestors had done much the same for generations. A rich lady in Delhi said, "Mayawati doesn't work, she just wakes up and dismisses some IAS officers. I've heard at midday she puts wax on, does manicure-pedicure, has massage and at six—like all the middle classes—she watches Hindi soaps." Stories circulated of her unexplained wealth, which included properties in some of the most expensive streets in Delhi. Despite having had no occupation but being a schoolteacher and a politician, Mayawati's declared assets when she ran for office in 2010 totalled 87 crores or more than $18.5m.[5]

Around half of the BSP's votes came from the Dalit community, and she wanted to widen the party's appeal and gain more MPs. If Congress and the BJP drew level at the 2009 general election, her hope was she could step in as kingmaker, and possibly become India's prime minister herself. She was picking her candidates from a variety of communities (for the seven Delhi seats, she had chosen three Muslims, two Brahmins, one Dalit and one Gujjar). The richer ones were probably running for office as an investment: if they gained power, they would have greater opportunities. And some were very rich indeed. Deepak Bhardwaj, who was standing for Parliament for west Delhi in 2009, was officially worth $134m—he described himself as "philanthropist, patriot, educationist, builder" and was to be seen driving around on a mini-tractor topped with a blue stuffed elephant, the party symbol. Haji Mohammed Mustaqeem was the candidate for Chandni Chowk in the heart of old Delhi. He was a meat exporter and a Muslim— the kind of person Murli Manohar Joshi of the BJP did not favour—and had declared personal assets of $4.5m.[6]

I went to see Haji Mustaqeem. His election office was in a run-down building extending over four floors, in a Muslim part of the old city of Delhi opposite Filmistan Cinema. The Bahujan Samaj operation was unlike that of other parties. In Lucknow, I had noticed the same thing: it was run by the firm edict of its leader, rather than in the usual haphazard way. Big posters of Mayawati, Ambedkar and the party's founder, Kanshi Ram, were on show by the entrance. The workers there were looking poor and edgy as they prepared to go campaigning, but they had a disciplined attitude which seemed to say, we might change things, our way.

Haji Mustaqeem had a canny face, with the sides of his head squashed in as if by forceps, and brown patches lay under his eyes. He was forty-seven years old. Guarded by BSP minders, he was sitting on a bed and looked as if he was not used to speaking to foreigners. "I have entered politics to help the poor and the downtrodden," he said in Urdu. One of his secretaries from the meat packing company was translating for me. "I am a good businessman. Congress and the BJP do nothing for these poor people." A minder who was visiting from Uttar Pradesh—UP—cut in: "He is very successful in business, he comes from a very reputed family and has no criminal record." I sensed that the party officials and Haji Mustaqeem did not make an easy fit. It seemed as if he was used to issuing commands, not taking them. He began again.

"The chief minister of UP, Miss Mayawati, said to me, 'You have earned a lot, now go out and serve your community.' My father was pro-Congress for fifty years, but in fifty years they have done nothing for Muslims in India. My father was a butcher before me. We don't have jobs in the defence services, in the bureaucracy, in the police. We are talking about people who have been neglected since years. The educational prospects are not good. The BJP is a communal party—so for me they are zero. My family used to be 100 percent Congress supporters. I have worked very hard, doing food export." This was true: under "education" on his election affidavit, Haji Mustaqeem had written only "Primary schooling from Rahima Madarsa." His was the sort of success story that was rarely mentioned in India or beyond: not being a software tycoon, he slipped under the net. Judging by his surroundings and appearance, he had little interest in displaying his wealth.

What sort of meat did he export? He looked surprised to be asked. "Lamb, goat and buffalo—fresh and frozen—to the Gulf, to Malaysia, to Egypt and South Africa. We are completely mechanized and automated, using equipment from Germany. We have one factory in Ghaziabad district in UP, one in Haryana and a government slaughter house on lease in Goa. We export 400 to 500 crores of meat per annum." That was about $100m a year, an impressive business. Was he bothered about some Hindus not wanting to vote for him? Earlier in the campaign there had been a story, quite possibly invented, about buffalo carcasses tipping off one of his lorries in front of a Hanuman mandir. The question did not interest him. He did not see the world in this way. The Haji was a businessman, not a politician. "My vote bank is in the walled city area. I have not approached any local leader to deliver my votes." Did he think the Bahujan Samaj Party could break into a constituency like this? "When we started, at the local election, our vote went up from zero to 16 percent—so we can win."[7]

As it turned out, Haji Mustaqeem did little campaigning, just tramped through the narrow lanes of the old city with an entourage who wore blue scarves, choosing days when he knew other butchers would be off work, counting on the votes of the Muslim sub-caste to which he belonged, the Qureshis. His essential purpose in this election was to put down a marker for himself and the party. He waved as he walked and rarely spoke or smiled. Haji Mustaqeem was the local man who had done exceptionally well. Elections were part of his journey.

Chandni Chowk was the number one constituency in India, the first on the electoral lists. In the 2009 general election, its size increased: delimitation gave it four times as many voters, with the proportion of Muslims reducing from one third to one fifth. In the 1990s the seat had been held by the BJP, but in 2004 it was won for Congress by Kapil Sibal, a Harvard Law School graduate who had joined politics after a successful career as a lawyer.[8] Now, with the redrawn boundaries, no one was quite sure where the result might be heading.

The main street of Chandni Chowk had once been a principal avenue of the Mughal empire, home to traders, poets, pilgrims and courtesans, and after the anti-British rebellion of 1857 the corpses of rebellious nawabs and rajas were displayed along the length of it. Now, it was a confusion of utensil shops, old havelis, flower sellers and street stalls trading currency notes. Every faith was catered for: a mosque, a Baptist church, a Sikh gurdwara, a Shiv temple and a Jain temple, beside a hospital for sick birds. A branch of McDonald's stood nearby, the steps thronged not with fans of the Maharaja Mac but with lean, squatting men in red turbans. Some had cotton buds stuck in the band of their turban, and each had a grubby towel draped over his shoulder. Others wielded sticks and wires, and were at work on their customers, crouching on their haunches, poking and twiddling, tutting and squinting: kaan saaf karne wallahs, the ear-cleaners of old Delhi. I asked one of them why he had chosen this spot to ply his trade. Drawing on a bidi, a leaf cigarette, he pointed out that McDonald's had chosen the location: these steps were where the ear-cleaners had assembled for generations, in sight of the Red Fort, and they had no intention of going elsewhere.

I went to visit another candidate, Dr. Sita Ram Sharma, whose office was nearby. He was seventy-seven, and his party, the Rashtrawadi Sena, was concerned with the salvation of traditional values. Although the election campaign in Chandni Chowk was a three-way race between the BJP, Congress and the BSP, in democratic style no fewer than forty-one candidates were contesting, for the excitement and to get their point of view across. Some were said to be standing as dummy candidates on behalf of larger parties, to enable more election agents to get into polling stations. One of the independent candidates seemed to be staking a third of his fortune: named Beer Singh, he had declared assets of $600, and was likely to lose his deposit of Rs10,000 ($220). Another candidate with an outside chance, a gentleman's tailor called Prem Narain, told a reporter he had no manifesto and when pressed as to why he was running answered sadly: "Hum bhi kuchh kar sakte hain"—"I too can do something."[9]

Dr. Sita Ram Sharma barked as I came up the steps to his office, "Open your shoes. Open them." I took them off and sat across from him on a mattress covered with a white sheet. A sign said: "PUNJABI SUITS AND SARIS." We were in a small enclave of Chandni Chowk run by Hindu cloth merchants. He started by complaining that Muslims were given money by the government to go on the Haj and permitted to have four wives under their separate civil code, but his real concern was about the values of the day.

"Our joint family, it was a sort of insurance against illness and old age, but it is disappearing because of Western culture," he said in English. Wasn't the joint family still strong in India, compared to most countries? "No, the social norms are relaxing. There are fads. The government sells liquor, and intoxication can make people murder and rape. Punjabi bhangra [a lively hybrid of music and dance] is now an influence in Delhi and people are dancing on the streets—which they shouldn't do. Modernization means Christian values. People used to honour the girls from other villages, and we would marry in neighbouring villages in the north-west of Delhi. We would say, 'Every girl is my sister, I won't look at her.' That is all gone." This was probably true. In Delhi, relationships between men and women were now possible in a way they would not have been when he was young in the 1940s. "It seems to be a conspiracy of some rich people to create an environment where boys and girls can engage in such activity. Some of these people import ideas from America and Britain. They are romantic in bus stands and parks, and they go to nightclubs. This is a hot country, and they should not be eating meat and drinking liquor. Men from this place are meant to eat nuts, fruit, berries and vegetables—and not chicken."

Dr. Sita Ram Sharma disliked social change, and his particular anger was reserved for the local press in Delhi. "I am a vegetarian, I don't take wine. They will not publish anything about my campaign because I do not bribe the journalists with liquor."[10] Part of the difficulty for him was that Hinduism offered no clear religious sanction against many of the things he was describing. A hair-stylist in Mumbai who prepared beauty queens for shows, Bharat Godambe, had summed up the conservative difficulty to me: "In India, you can do things that you can't do in our neighbouring countries. Here, it's an open culture. You can wear a two-piece swimsuit. Hindu culture doesn't say to people, 'You can't do it.'"[11]

The BJP candidate, Vijender Gupta, was a prominent councillor in the municipal corporation of Delhi. I felt as if I knew him already after seeing his Facebook fan page, with its elaborately mustachioed photo: "He is rendered with a pleasing personality, charming mannerisms, vibrant vitality and forceful and convincing oratory skills." We were going out on the road, and as I waited for his convoy to pick me up I received a phone call "on behalf of Mr. Gupta" to apologize that they were running fifteen minutes late. This was quite something in Indian politics, where leaders will happily keep people waiting for hours on end. (In one notorious instance in Bihar in 2008, a state politician kept flood victims waiting for thirty hours before arriving to inaugurate a relief camp. Until "minister saheb" got there, nobody could be assisted.)[12]

Vijender Gupta arrived in a large cream pick-up covered from bumper to bumper with a carapace of party stickers, with a loudspeaker on the roof. He was in white socks, box-fresh slip-on trainers, a tight pyjama outfit and a gold waistcoat; his wrists were wound with red strings from the temple. First we visited a newspaper office, where he complained he was being given insufficient coverage and waved his index finger at the editor, a grey-haired woman with a sceptical face. Next we headed for a rally being held in his honour by Gujjars. Their ancestors were cattle-herders in Wazirpur village, but now the village was part of Delhi and the Gujjars were classed as OBCs. They were looking for assistance, and ideally for classification as a Scheduled Tribe, which would bring them the benefit of job reservations. "After the Gujjars," said a worker as we bounced down the road towards Wazirpur, "we are going to meet some members of a particular community." This was BJP code for Muslims. I asked which community he meant. He looked at the other workers with a grin. "The Mohammedan community."

About 200 Gujjars were waiting under a large green tree in a courtyard. They had a long red turban to present to Vijender Gupta. All the senior male Gujjars had to feel or touch the turban to be sure it was of fine enough quality to be wrapped around the candidate's head. It was about 40°C. Flies were everywhere. Vijender Gupta made a vigorous speech, attacking Congress for not supporting the Gujjars. With a lot of cheering, we set off for Ajmeri Gate with a siren going on the roof of the vehicle and the driver announcing "make way" and "pull over" while shooting along the crowded lanes. Vijender Gupta settled on the front seat to have a sleep. "This is my bed. I spend nineteen hours a day here," he said to me.[13] "What is the name of Sanjay Gandhi's son?" asked one of his workers. Varun Gandhi had recently given his tirade about cutting off the hand of anyone who challenged Hindus, and they were trying to work up a press release.

When we reached Ajmeri Gate, crackers and fireworks were let off by a rowdy gang of BJP workers. The plan was to do a flag march through the almost exclusively Muslim section of the old city. Although it had been cleared with the authorities earlier, I did not realize it had been arranged, and felt anxious. We advanced in a convoy of vehicles through the tiny streets, travelling slower than a walking pace. Flag-waving, drumming and cold drinks had been arranged. People threw rose petals, waved advertising paddles and handed out sun visors in the BJP colours. The driver called out the Muslim greeting, "Salaam Aleikum," from his window, as if he were being clever. Most of the people we passed kept their heads down, avoiding contact, but some returned the greeting. A woman BJP activist joined us in the vehicle, and as we passed a clothing store she said in a hysterical voice, "What do you think they sell—ladies ki panty [ladies' panties] or burqa?" It was an unexpected remark. The other workers, all men, sniggered and looked embarrassed.

When we had been drive-marching in the descending evening light for about an hour through the busy, twisting maze of streets in the Muslim quarter, past a man hawking fish, past stalls which sold drill bits and stalls which sold metal cables, past food shops offering "broken chicken" and a bleating goat which was nearly the size of a cow, I realized the members of the convoy were more nervous than arrogant. It was not a triumphalist procession: rather, it was an obligatory pretence by the BJP that they were campaigning seriously in the Muslim area around Ajmeri Gate. They were in, for them, an alien world.

When we reached Asif Ali Road, I got down from Mr. Gupta's vehicle and took an auto-rickshaw out of the old city. Along the way I passed a scene, one of the Delhi scenes that flash like false images as you glimpse them for one or two seconds: a tipped-up handcart of rice sacks, a stopped bicycle rickshaw, a man lying in the road either unconscious, dead or dead drunk.

An absorbing aspect of the race in Chandni Chowk was the running battle between Vijender Gupta and Kapil Sibal, a high-profile cabinet minister who was frequently seen on national television as Congress spokesperson. Gupta, as the underdog, was seeking to gain parity by attacking him; that way, he could be assured of daily headlines in the thirty or so newspapers in the constituency. When Sibal was accused of being "a two-faced character" who exploited the parents of schoolchildren, he slapped Gupta with a defamation notice; Gupta responded that Sibal had "violated election norms" by using more than one loudspeaker on a car. As the legal writs flew, independent candidates jumped in to say these leaders should not be fighting. "Why are they tearing each other's clothes?" asked one. Gupta took the high moral ground, telling a newspaper: "I am not a TV boy. I am a street boy. Sibal is a high-profile lawyer. I am only pointing out the wrong things."[14]

Having mainly observed rural elections in the past, spread out over huge distances, I was surprised by how intensely the campaign was covered in the media. Each morning, Sibal would sit in his politician's white kurta pyjama beneath a canopy in the garden of his ministerial bungalow with two or three dozen journalists—section correspondents of national papers, reporters from Urdu or Hindi news sheets, film crews from city TV channels—who would ask him provocative questions while he tried to keep his cool in the blazing early-summer heat. Like many things in India, the press conference was a negotiation, a give and take: politicians, loiterers, helpers, minders, drivers, workers and reporters were all there, all wanting to be part of it. The media needed stories, ideally involving an endorsement—a Congress representative defecting to the BJP, an independent leader coming out for Congress.

With the press growing increasingly fond of stings and hidden cameras, every move had to be thought out. When a man with a foreshortened leg hobbled up to the gate of Sibal's bungalow with a Congress manifesto, seeking alms, no one dared to give him anything because it was presumed to be a set-up with a photographer in waiting. Each party campaign was required to file details of its expenditure every few days, which involved a member of the team filling in dozens of sheets of paper. If you showed you had hired 200 chairs for a meeting and there was evidence 500 chairs had been used, you might be investigated.

Mohan Kumar was an example of a small neta who was switching allegiance. He was a solid man with gold rings and a cotton trouser suit and stood nervously and a little pugnaciously in the garden of Sibal's ministerial bungalow. Kumar represented—or said he did—a few thousand voters in a poor area of the city. "We need the family of tigers," he said into a microphone, which was taken to be a reference to Sonia Gandhi. He was migrating, with his voters, from the Bahujan Samaj to Congress (at the previous assembly election he had gone the other way). When he spoke, his supporters raised slogans, "Bhai Mohan Kumar Zindabad!"—"Long live brother Mohan Kumar." As Kapil Sibal arrived, they cheered him with a similar slogan, but it was apparent their main aim was to build up their man while the television cameras were present. Sibal thanked Kumar—whom he described as a "coordinator"—for his support. Again, it was a negotiation: Sibal gained some more votes, Kumar was inflated within his own community by his fleeting proximity to the leading candidate, and his supporters, who were now rushing around in Congress caps and toggled scarves, got to eat. I asked one of them afterwards why he regarded Mohan Kumar as his leader. "He is a social worker. He gives out clothes every 1st Jan." It was apparent, watching the visitors, that one of the reasons they had come was for the food. They consumed the unremarkable snacks—samosas with tomato sauce, tiny cups of tea—with the attention of people who were not used to eating full meals.

Voting was held across India in five phases over successive weeks, to allow the election commission to shift 2.1 million police around the country to monitor 714 million potential voters. Once the national election started, more and more people sought involvement or just attention in the Chandni Chowk race. In the office of the Congress media campaign near Connaught Place, the staff had daily inquiries from random people: a non-existent Muslim magazine ringing up to sell advertising space, dubious public relations types wanting to become involved, a group of Christians wishing to meet and declare their support. Compared to the BJP and Bahujan Samaj campaigns, leave alone Dr. Sita Ram Sharma's attempt to convey his dislike of wine and romance, this was an efficient operation: text messages were relayed to organizers or precinct captains across the wards, and each day a press release in Hindi, Urdu and English was sent out, tailored for the appropriate audience, with fresh photographs of the candidate. A scholarly man with thin hair, glasses and a beard did the Urdu translation (although Hindi and Urdu are closely related languages, they use different scripts). His fingers skimmed over a Roman keyboard, stretching as if he were playing Rachmaninov, pressing three or four keys at a time to create the beautiful, flowing script on the screen. I heard one young office volunteer come out with a line which sounded as if it came from *The West Wing*: "I have a very meticulous system for ordering our coffee from Barista."

They were nearly tripped up when the leader of an international Sikh organization said he would publicly back the Congress. Chandni Chowk did not have many Sikh constituents, but this man had been recommended, and an endorsement was an endorsement. A photo opportunity was fixed. Then the office ran a quick background check, and things did not quite fit together. With just hours to go before the media snapped Mr. Sibal and Mr. Singh shaking hands in a common purpose, another story came tumbling out. Only weeks before, this eccentric, self-declared Sikh leader had done one of the most insulting things you can do in Indian public life: he had sent a garland of shoes to Sonia Gandhi in protest over the 1984 riots. He also turned out to be an admirer of the late Saddam Hussein, and even claimed he had visited him in his palace in Baghdad and given the Iraqi leader a wooden lion. "A great friend and a wonderful person. Five Mercedes cars came to receive me at the airport. I was treated like a king. I was given a special room and coffee in a golden cup."[15]

When the votes were counted nationwide in May—a remarkably quick process since it was electronic; no hanging chads here—Congress and its allies won a strong victory, gaining more seats in the Lok Sabha than in the previous election, enabling them to govern without support from left-wing parties. Sonia Gandhi and her son Rahul were in the ascendant. Manmohan Singh became the first prime minister since Jawaharlal Nehru to be re-elected after serving a full term in office. The BJP had run an ill-judged campaign, with Varun Gandhi talking of chopping off hands and not being repudiated, and L. K. Advani attacking Manmohan Singh as India's weakest prime minister when he was admired for encouraging stability and growth. The 81-year-old Advani even had himself photographed lifting weights at a gym in Ahmedabad in a feeble effort to capture the "youth vote." Mayawati made gains in Uttarakhand and Haryana but not the advances she had hoped for: although her total vote share went up by 1 percent, the success of Congress left her with no balance of power to hold. The communists and other leftist parties dropped back, still fighting over the grievances of the last century. Regional parties remained highly influential in some parts of India: the ruling BJD in Orissa, after dissolving an earlier strategic alliance with the BJP, boosted its vote by 7 percent.

In the Chandni Chowk constituency, the minor candidates evaporated (Dr. Sita Ram Sharma gained 609 votes) and Haji Mustaqeem scraped less than 4 percent. Three days before polling, a crowd had gathered outside his residence and shouted slogans in favour of Congress; rumours were spread at the tea stalls near the Jama Masjid that he in fact wanted people to vote for Kapil Sibal; Bahujan Samaj workers climbed on motorbikes and drove around the area, expressly denying this was true. The impetus had been running away from Haji Mustaqeem for weeks—his relations with his BSP minders had never looked good, and by the end he had lost interest in campaigning. For Vijender Gupta of the BJP, the election race had been in many ways a success: he took more than a quarter of a million votes, and was now a prominent figure in his party in Delhi. The victor by a large margin was Sibal for Congress, who secured a second term in Parliament by winning nearly half a million votes, and became education minister in the new government. A candidate in South Delhi suffered the indignity of arriving at a polling station and finding his name had been omitted from the voting list; he was so angry that he smashed up an electronic voting machine, and was promptly arrested by the police.[16]

Although Congress was back in power for a second five-year term, the complexities of national elections meant the underlying results were more nebulous and intriguing. Had Congress once again become India's natural party of government, and was the BJP in lasting eclipse? Straight after the election, my feeling after visiting about half a dozen very different constituencies was that the BJP's methods and message were seriously dated. The aggressive Hindutva rallying cry that had brought down the Babri Masjid in the early 1990s appealed only to their hardcore voters, and sounded old fashioned. India was more self-confident now, and a demand for better governance usually took priority over religious grievances. One man put it to me this way (he was a garment exporter who headed a small traders' association in Delhi): "Traders need communal harmony more than anybody else, because trade depends on cross-community work." What did he mean? "Look at my business. Who is doing the transporting? Sikhs. Our shopkeepers are all Hindu. Who does the weaving and embroidery for us? All Muslims." It was a very practical point of view. The BJP would need a fresh approach and new faces in order to return to power at the centre.

Against this, I had found it hard to detect a real wave of enthusiasm for Congress at ground level. Their victory was partly technical, in that their vote share (28.6 percent) was nearly the same as it had been a decade earlier when the BJP took office. The assumption made immediately after the 2009 election that the Congress party had been brought to power by the rural poor, grateful for the ministrations of the Gandhi family, turned out not to be accurate. Congress made its most significant electoral gains in urban areas: it won 34 out of 57 major urban seats. In addition, many of its voters were older people. So, statistically, there was no reason why the BJP or a mixture of other parties could not displace the current rulers.[17]

Everything—all of this—depended on the fluctuation of future events and personalities. The practice of democracy in India was deeply embedded, in a way that was rare in Asia. More than anything else, the campaigns had demonstrated in their complexity and illusion, in their duplicity and seeming chaos, that Indian elections were a self-balancing ecosystem.

The poll had run smoothly, yet there was something that niggled. It had first become apparent to me during the 2004 election campaign, and it niggled again now. The problem was the first-time MPs. With their spanking faces and sense of bland entitlement, these young men and women were treated with reverence by the Indian media, although their achievement was usually to have shared genes with an earlier leader (not far from the achievement of the pistol-toting Maharaja of Jodhpur, Hanwant Singh). I watched one of these new MPs on television as he drove through the dust of his inherited family constituency in an enormous Pajero, turning now and then to a waiting camera with a purposeful frown and saying things like, "I want to help these people, like my father did," or "We are going to make India number one." He looked like a giant baby who had been dressed up and put in a big buggy and sent off on an adventure.

The disjuncture between these fresh fruits and the hopes of the many millions of individuals they were supposedly representing was massive. In person they were perfectly affable and often idealistic, but as a phenomenon they were damaging. Was Indian national politics becoming hereditary, with power passing to a few hundred families, even as the elections themselves became more vibrant and open?

In the case of the new contenders, all you needed to know was the surname. It seemed India's strong women politicians were not reproducing themselves, for most of the new MPs were only sons, probably on account of the social convention in the 1970s that educated people should have small families. "Hum do, hamare do"—"We two and our two"—was the slogan. Rahul was the son of Rajiv Gandhi, Jitin was the son of Jitendra Prasada, Jyotiraditya was the son of Madhavrao Scindia, Sachin was the son of Rajesh Pilot and brother-in-law of Omar Abdullah who was the grandson of Sheikh Abdullah and son of Farooq Abdullah; Akhilesh was the son of the Samajwadi Party leader Mulayam Singh Yadav and Dushyant was the son of Vasundhara Raje, the BJP chief minister of Rajasthan and sister of Madhavrao Scindia. And so it continued.

I spoke to someone who was close to the new batch of Congress party MPs. What did they believe in? "It hasn't crystallized at all. These boys have all seen the world. They don't have an ideology." This was intended I think as a compliment, the idea being that India had suffered from, and to an extent still suffers from, ideological politics. Did the new hereditary MPs—for simplicity's sake we can call them HMPs—have plans? "They work really hard. Their constituents think they will just put in a call and get electricity for their village. They feel there is so much to do, they don't know where to begin." Why had they entered politics? "I can't promise they are not wanting to make money. I wouldn't say it's from idealism, except perhaps with Rahul. He's not sentimental, he has a clinical mind. The Congress party is a Mughal court, and no one can do anything unless the Gandhis say so. Sonia has tried to make it more democratic. The rest aren't interested because they want to keep their own position. Everyone likes to have the ear of someone who is influential, and nominate a few chosen ones." I tried to picture this in a British context and imagined, unhappily, how it would feel to have the nation's destiny in the hands of the children of Margaret Thatcher or Tony Blair.

Most political parties shared in this tradition of reincarnation, although the problem seemed to be worse in the Congress party. The trajectory of these scions was remarkably similar—they went from an Indian boarding school to college in Europe or the United States, followed by a stint in banking or commerce and a return to a safe family seat in their late twenties. They were generating an atmosphere that gave a dull echo of the feeling which greeted "Rajiv's Boys" in the 1980s, when bureaucrats and politicians were presumed to be dynamic simply because they were younger than those they were replacing. Press coverage of the HMPs would typically say how encouraging it was that "youngsters" were involving themselves in the future of the nation. The "young guns" or "young Turks" were projected as the future: "This is the era of Rahul Gandhi where to be young [he was almost forty, making him fifteen years older than India's median age of twenty-five] is to be politically correct . . . The disillusionment with politics as usual is at an all-time low. If there is a time when the young can make a difference, it is now. Their time has come."[18]

The problem though was not Rahul Gandhi: he was merely the latest incarnation of the lead dynasty, the most visible manifestation of a wider, much more serious fault. He had publicly expressed a measure of doubt about his inherited position, and rather than pursue the obvious course and become a minister, he was trying to restructure the calcified organization of the Congress party. His work before entering politics full-time—on his own terms, in his mid-thirties—had been in management, back-office operations and business consultancy. The further he proceeded with the process of reforming the party, the more he became aware how talent was strangled and individuals were prevented from rising on merit. He cultivated a mask of Buddhist detachment and purity in public, and most of his speeches were deliberately low-key. Even more than his mother, Rahul Gandhi avoided speaking on the record to the media.

"There are three-four ways of entering politics," he said frankly to a gathering of students in Madhya Pradesh. "First, if one has money and power. Second, through family connections. I am an example of that. Third, if one knows somebody in politics. And fourth, by working hard for the people."[19] Unlike many of the other young HMPs, he did not pretend otherwise. "Main apne pita, nani aur pardada ke bina us jagah par nahin pahunch sakta tha jahan main aaj hoon"—"Without my father, grandmother and great-grandfather, I could never have been in the place that I am now."[20]

For the middle and senior ranks of Congress party workers, the situation was highly frustrating. Like qualified employees of family businesses in India, they knew their achievements were much less important than the lack of a name. Younger people felt unable to progress, or to take a share of power, knowing their way would be blocked indefinitely. Often, the temptation was to switch to another party where paths might be more open. A senior state-level Congress activist described having to beg his boss to let him speak to Sonia Gandhi: "'Saab I want to meet Soniaji. Should I do so? Will you take me to meet her?' And when [he] does take me along, do you think I can say anything against him to Soniaji? Do you think I can even dare to open my mouth on how the party works at the grassroots level?"[21]

Even those who were well connected in politics found the party structure exasperating, and thought rival parties were lighter on their feet. Yusuf Ansari had run as a state legislator in Uttar Pradesh in 2007, and the tale of his unsuccessful campaign showed what a sorry condition the party had reached in its old heartland in the "cow belt." (In India's first general election, Congress took eighty-one out of the eighty-six seats in the state.)[22] The changes wrought on electoral politics by caste movements had left the organization disoriented. "It was summer," he said, "April, very hot. I was given Mahmudabad, a backward, rural constituency, and had to find workers, set up an office, organize the campaign. It was not long after the execution of Saddam Hussein, and the Shias were being blamed for this. I am Sunni, and about one quarter of the Muslims in the constituency are Shia. The imams and maulanas, my core vote, came to me and said they had decided to tell their people to go with the Samajwadi Party, because otherwise a Shia—the BSP candidate—might win. So my campaign was sunk by tensions produced in Iraq. The procedure in Congress is to delay, whereas the BSP had declared their candidates a year earlier. We had a week's notice. All my nominees had to be cleared at a district level by the Congress party, and you couldn't even get people on the phone. Our party is great on paper: there's a 'recruitment in-charge,' a 'natural disaster in-charge,' but none of it works. In the BSP and the Samajwadi Party, there is a grassroots structure operating twenty-four hours a day. The BSP have a president in each district who is always a Dalit, with a direct line to Mayawati. In Congress, even the most senior figures, the khadi-clad veterans, have secret or tacit arrangements with other parties, while keeping their positions. Mrs. Gandhi knows this—but people tell her, 'We can't do without X,' so they don't get rid of him."[23]

The rigid, archaic composition of Congress, where everything oriented around the often unspoken edicts of the first family, was not unconnected to its electoral success. At an election, the party was able to present the members of the Gandhi family—Sonia, Rahul and Priyanka, who had a talent for working a crowd—and let them speak nebulously of loyalty, secularism and their concern for the dispossessed. Despite his irritation with sycophants (even a minister had been spotted trying to carry his shoes), Rahul Gandhi was not above playing the game, coming out with this ill-judged line at a meeting in 2007: "I belong to the family which has never moved backwards, which has never gone back on its words. You know that when any member of my family had decided to do anything, he does it. Be it the freedom struggle, the division of Pakistan or taking India to the 21st century."[24] The words caused annoyance in Pakistan, Bangladesh and India, and demonstrated a natural or instinctive attachment to family tradition.

For political opponents, the yuvraj—the prince—was a soft target, but within Congress he was a source of possible future elevation. In issue after issue, the party mouthpiece, *Congress Sandesh*, fell over itself to praise the Nehru–Gandhi dynasty. A full-page image of "Indira Gandhi on her 91st birth anniversary" might be followed by a garlanded photo of the queen mother, Sonia Gandhi.

> Our pride is Mother India,
> Our guide is Mother Sonia.

In a land where so much was still based around reverence and the influence of family life, it did not seem implausible to appeal to family values for possible electoral gain, even if it contradicted the meritocratic values of the makers of India's Constitution. Praising dynastic leaders was, however, a declining strategy, one which held less appeal for younger people as they learned more about the world and gained experience of new corporate practice which depended on merit. With his background in consultancy, Rahul Gandhi was seeking to drive his party out of a rut. He travelled the countryside and spent the nights with Dalit families, interacting with the public and speaking better Hindi than his late father. Crucially, he boosted membership of the Youth Congress, democratized it and brought in outsiders to run internal elections. "People without financial muscle are now able to get good positions," a member of his team told me. "They must learn processes and protocols. The Youth Congress will become robust over time. Rahulji is very particular about that."[25]

It was a fine plan, and extremely ambitious. In 2009, a handful of parliamentary candidates arose through this internal democracy, and a few more were talent-spotted. So "Team Rahul," as the media liked to call his helpers, now consisted not only of the sons of his father's colleagues but a handful of interloping MPs like Meenakshi Natrajan, a Tamil biochem graduate from Madhya Pradesh whose family had no link to politics, and who had even been observed carrying her own tiffin box to work.

The reforms were a well-intentioned step, but it was hard to see them succeeding. Rahul Gandhi was up against a cascade of privilege and entitlement that reached to the heart of Indian politics at the centre and at state level. When other politicians sought to emulate his "Dalit sleepovers"— at the instigation of the Congress party machine—they missed the point. Shriprakash Jaiswal, the coal minister and MP for Kanpur, set off into the boondocks accompanied by music and movie equipment, his own food, a stock of mineral water and a brand new mattress with a set of sheets and pillows. He might be staying in a poor Dalit's house, but he did not wish to bed down on a straw mattress or a charpoy, a rope bed. After showing Richard Attenborough's *Gandhi,* a screen deification of the Mahatma, Shriprakash Jaiswal and his entourage left at 2 a.m., having completed the sleepover. "The purpose of the visit was to break caste barriers and understand life in Dalit villages," he said. "We were honest in our venture."[26]

The years Rahul Gandhi had spent living abroad anonymously had given him a closer understanding of the workings of different societies than most other privileged Indians. Many of his peers, not only in the Congress party, had only the most fleeting experience of life outside the bubble, away from admirers and servants. They perceived themselves as hereditary rulers, descended if not from the Sun then from a forebear who had worked to create modern India. Their usual justification, really a technical defence, was that they had been elected—ignoring the fact that almost no one else stood a chance of gaining the nomination. If Rahul Gandhi's plan were to succeed it would take fifty years, since many of these people were in their late twenties or thirties and the Indian political system was mistrustful of cabinet ministers aged under sixty—and many were older still. When the youthful British foreign minister David Miliband visited India and ingratiatingly addressed his elderly counterpart Pranab Mukherjee by his first name, New Delhi's bureaucrats made their displeasure clear.

The radical alternative was to compel sitting HMPs to step down, or at least face open reselection in a reformed party. This was Rahul's best and most likely bet, a re-run of the Kamaraj Plan of 1963 when senior Congress politicians had been obliged to put "party before post" and stand down. Having been shamed into retiring from office, these entrenched elements were expected to return to the grassroots and help revitalize the Congress party machine. This move had cleared the way for the rise of Rahul's grandmother, Indira Gandhi.

Nearly all aspiring politicians with a family connection did everything in their power to exploit it. When campaigning in 2009, Rahul's cousin, Varun Gandhi, said the Congress-led government was spineless and that "Wherever I go, I am told that if Sanjay Gandhi had been alive, the country would not have got reduced to such a mess."[27] Later in the year when the chief minister of Andhra Pradesh, Y. S. Rajasekhara Reddy, died in an accident, the local Congress party said 462 people had died of shock or committed suicide with grief. The purpose of this implausible piece of news was to force the national party to appoint his fabulously rich son, Jaganmohan Reddy, in his place. The move failed, and an investigation showed that families of people who had died in different ways were paid Rs5,000 [$105] by local Congress leaders for "funeral expenses," and persuaded to say they were victims of the mass grief.[28] Whichever way you turned, family politics were playing their part. In total, twelve of the seats in Uttar Pradesh in 2009 were won by women; but three were political widows, three were wives, one was a daughter, two were daughters-in-law, one was a movie star, one was the wife of a senior police officer and one, Annu Tandon, was the wife of a top executive at Reliance, India's largest and most powerful private company.

I had spent some time with Annu Tandon travelling around her potential constituency, Unnao, watching her speak to gatherings in village after village while buffaloes lay in ponds in the heat. It was clear that although she was sincere, she had needed to spend money through a family trust in Unnao to prepare her way for an election victory. Her idol was Indira Gandhi ("I used to copy her hairstyle and her clothes") and her electors were some of the poorest people in India. One woman, Mira Devi, told me that although she would vote for Annu Tandon ("She is a woman and may understand the problems of women"), she doubted any politician could change things: "We have no electricity, no good roads, no doctor for seven kilometres. It's very hard when children fall ill or a pregnant woman needs to go to the doctor."[29] This was the reality in the poorest parts of the nation, after more than sixty years of independence: although democracy functioned, its benefits were limited.

The media continued to report young faces admiringly in 2009, as a new generation coming in like a breath of fresh air. But how new were the faces? India's youngest MP, Hamdullah Sayeed from the Lakshadweep islands, was the son of a man who had once been India's youngest MP, and in 2008 the government had even gone to the trouble of amending the Constitution (Scheduled Tribes) (Union Territories) Order, 1951 to allow Sayeed junior to contest the seat, since he was not born in Lakshadweep.[30] The youngest minister, 29-year-old Agatha Sangma from Meghalaya, was the daughter of a former speaker of the house. According to *Savvy* magazine, "She stunned everyone sitting in the central hall by preferring to take the oath in Hindi"— the patronizing presumption being that because she came from the northeast, where people spoke in strange tongues and ate dogs and bees, Sangma would only be able to swear in in English. For the new minister herself, the experience was inspiring: "Soniaji and Rahulji both congratulated me after the swearing-in ceremony," she reported. "Rahul Gandhi is overwhelmed by my performance over the last one year."[31] So even within the family system, the hierarchy was closely defined: a young minister might inherit a seat, but the imprimatur would come from the first family.

As well as enjoying the comparative youthfulness of the new MPs, the Indian press admired their ability to work across political lines. They were "the bonhomie brigade" who played in each other's cricket matches and went to each other's parties. They formed parliamentary committees and refused to let party whips interfere. Supriya Sule, the daughter of Sharad Pawar, who had attempted to oust Sonia Gandhi because of her "foreign origins," worked happily with the children of her father's rivals. "It's all so lovely," she told a journalist who mentioned her willingness to bury the past. "Let's keep it lovely and not let past shadows darken it."[32] Was it any wonder the new MPs felt socially at ease together? With their prime education, overseas experiences and spare money they were socially much closer to each other than to their constituents. The younger government ministers complained that they had too little to do, since important decisions rested with the older generation of cabinet ministers.

The practice of nepotism in politics was so taken for granted that its effect on democracy in India had never been fully quantified. I was left wondering how deep the dependence on pedigree ran. Had it been this way for decades, or was it getting worse? What was the effect of a closed structure on bright, qualified people who might otherwise have entered public service? They knew they were more likely to get a break in business, or in a stable profession, than in this hereditary system. A stream of potential talent was diverted at source, away from politics. Would a self-made man like Rajesh Pilot have got anywhere if he had been born in 1975 rather than in 1945?

Some of the new HMPs and ministers would be good at their jobs, and others would be bad. The fact someone was born into a prominent family certainly did not mean they would be a poor lawmaker. If you were to exclude people on this basis, you would be knocking out Jawaharlal Nehru and William Pitt the Younger, as well as monarchs who had turned out to be great administrators and reformers, such as the Maharaja of Bikaner or the fourth King of Bhutan. And you would be excluding George W. Bush. The issue here was not heredity itself, but the tendency to draft in a child, widow or in-law of a well-known leader as a means of entrenching family power. The children of prominent politicians expected to be pressed to join politics even if they were unsuitable or content in another line of work. Not to be pressed and praised might suggest some sort of disloyalty on the part of the advisers by whom their family was surrounded. So when a young scion advanced, whether at state or national level, it was understood that talent would follow, rather in the way that love was expected to follow a well-planned arranged marriage.

How could you measure political nepotism? At the panchayat, district or state level, it would be difficult to see unless you were there. At the national level, members of the upper house, the Rajya Sabha, might be picked for ulterior reasons since they were chosen in part by nomination (state assemblies voted on who their Rajya Sabha MPs would be, which meant in practice it was a horse trade between parties). So I decided to direct attention only to the directly elected lower house of Parliament, the Lok Sabha, which has 545 members. My intention was to find out how each of these 545 MPs came into politics. With some, the answer was obvious and could be found out within moments; with others, published sources offered an answer; and with a high proportion of MPs, it was impossible to learn anything of substance. The Internet, which I had presumed would have the answers hidden away in one of its corners, was of marginal use. Surprisingly, around one third of India's MPs were almost invisible online, except for their page on the Parliament website, which detailed matters such as their name, party, constituency, state and postal address.

I was stumped. I had a certain amount of data, but it gave an incomplete picture. It was not enough to take prominent names and make larger deductions from them. Equally, much of the information did not seem to exist. Only someone who worked at a local level, perhaps as a political journalist, would be likely to know how each MP in their area entered politics. So I took the plunge and began to ask friends and contacts in different states across India if they would help to fill in the gaps. Some remarkable biographies reached me this way. For example, the member for Nagarkurnool, Manda Jagannath, had started out as a labourer on the Nagarjuna Sagar Dam, become a doctor and slapped a bank manager for refusing to give loans to tribal people; Shatrughan "Shotgun" Sinha of the BJP was described as "an actor, politician, publicity hound and crusader"; Ram Sundar Das, a Dalit MP from Bihar, had started in politics more than seventy years ago; Inder Singh Namdhari, a Sikh from Jharkhand, had switched between four different parties: "A deft player in statecraft," the journalist Rasheed Kidwai wrote to me, "his favourite Hindi song is, 'Mere pairon me ghungroo bandha de to phir meri chaal dekh le . . .'—'Strap on the anklets and watch me move.'"

It was too good to stop now. Once I had about 200 names, I asked Megha Chauhan, an efficient reporter on a Delhi paper who had worked with me in the past, to double-check the information and find out the trajectory of some of the nation's more obscure MPs. The only rule was that the MP or their office should not be taken as a reliable source. We made a separate spreadsheet for each state, and a picture began to develop.

It was at this point, when we were approaching 400 names, that I realized I was moving into deeper waters. We had a growing file of information about the Lok Sabha MPs: name, sex, date of birth, age, party name, constituency, state, whether or not the seat was reserved for a member of a Scheduled Caste or Tribe, political background, biographical notes and the source of the data we had obtained. But how would I catalogue it? What methodology would I use to analyse it? How did you classify the son of a political leader who was also a well-known cricketer and had been inducted into politics, or a successful lawyer who had been a student politician, or a prosperous industrialist who was a member of a dynastic family? What would be the best way to make larger deductions from the material? It was at this point that I thought I should take advantage of India's reputation as a hothouse for nerds, geeks, techies and assorted data fiends.

Arun Kaul's CV looked promising. He was twenty-two, lived in Noida, had a BA and an MA, spoke German (I never asked him why) and had been "Jt. Secretary Cleanliness" at his school. He was hot with statistical software packages. The moment I knew I had found the right person was when I asked him to describe what sort of people lived in Noida, and he replied: "I think if one were to plot the ages of the inhabitants of Noida on a graph, it would be a bimodal curve, which would peak at about eighteen to twenty years, then fall, become a plateau and rise up again around the sixty to sixty-five years age bracket." I asked him to take the information we had assembled on the family politics project, process it and see what conclusions emerged. Arun asked whether I needed code lists, cross tabs, cutoffs and logit regression, and I said I thought so. When he started to use the phrase "beta coefficients," I surrendered.

With Megha's help, I completed the charts for each state (our last piece of information was the estimated birth date of a rural MP whose parents had not recorded it) and passed them over to Arun, who turned the political background of each MP into numerical code and converted the data to SPSS, a statistical package used by social scientists. We decided that when an MP had several routes to a political career, the most important would be entered, with the alternatives left as an observation but not included in the analysis. This usually meant that if a "family" element existed, it dominated. So, for example, if someone had an active background in student politics and a mother who was a chief minister, we felt it safe to assume that the mother was more important to their success than the student union membership.

Now we could ask the question: how hereditary is Indian politics? How did the 545 MPs in the fifteenth Lok Sabha enter politics?

No significant family background	255
Family	156
Student politics	47
Business	35

RSS	18
Inducted	16
Trade union	10
Royal Family	7
Maoist commander	1

Initially, it appeared that heredity was not the most important aspect in Indian politics, in that "Family" was not at the top of the list of routes to Parliament. In total, 28.6 percent of MPs had a hereditary connection. "No significant family background" covered nearly half of all MPs, which meant they had found their way to Parliament by a similar mixture of idealistic and weaselly routes as lawmakers in any representative democracy. "Business" covered everybody from chief executives who were joining public service to members of a land or mining mafia who needed political clout. "Inducted" usually meant the MP was a famous actor, but it could mean someone who had done well abroad and was returning home, or even in one case a commando in Rajiv Gandhi's security cordon who had been parachuted into politics. "Royal Family" meant an old princely family which had retained its influence—another form of family politics, but not what we were looking at in this study. The Maoist commander came in a category all of his own (I had considered listing him under "Business"). Rasheed Kidwai gave me his potted biography: "Baitha Kameshwar cleared his matriculation examination in 1975, and then decided against college and headed for the jungles to join the People's War Group instead. He has rewards on his head from three state governments and has been labelled as a 'dreaded Maoist commander.' He won the election while in custody at Rohtas district jail without campaigning in person. He faces forty-six criminal cases ranging from murder and extortion to carrying out explosive acts." Lately, the Communist Party of India (Maoist) had disclaimed Kameshwar as a rogue operative.[33]

Second question: which political party was the most hereditary? (Or, what percentage of a party's MPs had reached the Lok Sabha through a family link—excluding parties with fewer than five MPs?)

RLD	100.0	5 out of 5
NCP	77.8	7 out of 9
BJD	42.9	6 out of 14
INC	37.5	78 out of 208
BSP	33.3	7 out of 21
DMK	33.3	6 out of 18

SP	27.3	6 out of 22
CPI(M)	25.0	4 out of 16
JD(U)	20.0	4 out of 20
BJP	19.0	22 out of 116
AITC	15.8	3 out of 19
Shiv Sena	9.1	1 out of 11
AIADMK	0	0 out of 9
TDP	0	0 out of 6

The RLD ranked first, with all its MPs being hereditary. The runner-up was the NCP, a splinter from the Congress party, with seven hereditary MPs (including Agatha Sangma). The BJD at 42.9 percent came third. The results for these parties were statistically insignificant, since they had so few Lok Sabha seats. At the opposite end of the scale, two parties did not have a single MP from a hereditary background, but the TDP had only six MPs, while the AIADMK had nine; its leader, Jayalalithaa, expected strict loyalty and promoted cronies, but had not taken the family route. The Shiv Sena on 9.1 percent had eleven MPs, but was itself run by one (increasingly fractious) family, the Thackerays. In the middle of the table came Mayawati's BSP: a full third of her MPs were hereditary, although in every case they were not Dalits, but had been brought in from one of the communities she was seeking to woo for the party, such as Muslims or Brahmins.

The most important result concerned the two largest parties in India, the BJP and INC, or Indian National Congress. Since they had 324 MPs between them, the sample survey was large enough to be genuinely revealing. Only 19 percent of the BJP's people were HMPs, which helped to explain the party's appeal to the Hindu middle classes across swathes of middle India: they knew that more than four fifths of the party's MPs had ascended by other means, rather than descending from on high, which made them seem more representative and regular. An additional 11.2 percent of BJP MPs came to politics through a background in the RSS, which for true believers in Hindutva was a family in itself. When the corpulent Nitin Gadkari became president of the BJP in 2009, he described himself as a "simple worker" who had reached the top by his own effort. "This can happen only in the BJP," he said. "The BJP is not like other political parties where dynasty rules. My father was not the prime minister of the country."[34]

What, then, of Congress? Thirty-seven and one-half percent of its MPs had reached the Lok Sabha through a family connection. This was almost twice as many as its principal rival, but it was not a fatal statistic. The Congress leadership could still argue that more than 60 percent of its MPs had arrived on some alternative merit—through student politics, business or simply personal ability and ambition.

The third question: was this a regional issue? Were some states more hereditary than others? Here, the results were diverse. Family politics was at its strongest in Punjab, Delhi and Haryana.[35] After that, there was a significant drop. Apart from Andhra Pradesh, all the southern states had 75 percent or more of their MPs from a non-hereditary background. Generally the newer states, such as Uttarakhand, Chhattisgarh and Jharkhand, which were only formed in 2000, were less nepotistic, presumably because family politics did not have enough time to become entrenched. In the same vein, MPs who came from seats reserved for Scheduled Castes or Tribes were statistically less likely to be from a family with a political background, although not by much.

The answer to my fourth question was inevitable, given the way in which Indian politics works. Were women MPs more likely to have reached their position through a family link? Yes: 69.5 percent of women MPs fell into the family politics column. The exceptions were powerful self-made women leaders like Mayawati, Jayalalithaa and Mamata Banerjee, whose extraordinary success was not often replicated in the middle ranks of political parties.

When the information about all the MPs was coming in, I had been struck by how many of the older ones had risen from a grassroots background— people such as 78-year-old Danapal Venugopal, a respected and modest man who had started out in a block-level panchayat in Tamil Nadu and served five consecutive terms in Parliament. The tradition of seats being passed within families seemed more recent. To an extent, this was inevitable: it was not until the 1960s that there would have been significant numbers of MPs dying or coming up for retirement. So any MP aged seventy or over (our benchmark date for age-related calculations was 1 January 2010) who had started out in national politics at a relatively young age was unlikely to have had a parent in Parliament. So my fifth question was: is politics in India becoming more hereditary?

Arun sent me an unusually excited email while he was looking at this question: "Your hunch was spot on: as age decreases (i.e. as one moves from older to younger MPs), it may be noted that incidence of 'family politics' increases! Just ran the analysis—such a nice, perfect little linear trend. Researcher's delight!"

I asked him to produce a simple graph of the perfect linear trend. This

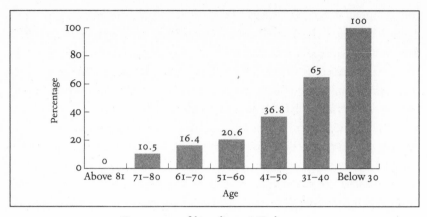

Percentage of hereditary MPs by age

was a shocking result. Every MP in the Lok Sabha under the age of thirty had in effect inherited a seat, and more than two thirds of the sixty-six MPs aged forty or under were HMPs. In addition, this new wave of Indian law-makers would have a decade's advantage in politics over their peers, since the average MP who had benefited from family politics was almost ten years younger than those who had arrived with "no significant family background." In the Congress party, the situation was yet more extreme: every Congress MP under the age of thirty-five was an HMP. If the trend continued, it was possible that most members of the Indian Parliament would be there by heredity alone, and the nation would be back to where it had started before the freedom struggle, with rule by a hereditary monarch and assorted Indian princelings.

Already, the tendency to turn politics into a family business was being emulated across northern India at state level, with legislators nominating children and spouses. There was no reason to believe it was not also spreading to the districts. Nepotism was written into the working of democracy, as it was in other areas of Indian life, ranging from medicine and the legal profession to the media and the film industry. An advert for an investment website encapsulated this attitude, which was that even if you were self-made you would do your best to dispense patronage if you made it to the top: beside a photograph of an ambitious young man was the line: "I don't have an influential uncle. But I will be one someday." The Bollywood movie *Luck by Chance*—about young actors who try to make it on merit rather than on family connections—itself starred Farhan Akhtar and Konkona Sen Sharma, the children of famous parents.

Looking at Arun's analysis more closely, the difference between older and younger MPs was marked. For those over fifty, the proportion with a father or relative in politics was not unreasonable, at 17.9 percent. But when you looked at those aged fifty or under, this increased by more than two and a half times to nearly half, or 47.2 percent. I checked some of the people involved, and the news was not reassuring. Of the thirty-eight youngest MPs, thirty-three had arrived with the help of mummy-daddy. Of the remaining five, one was Meenakshi Natrajan, the biochem graduate who had been hand-picked by Rahul Gandhi, three appeared to be self-made politicians who had made it up the ranks of the BJP, BSP and CPI(M) respectively, and the fifth was a Lucknow University mafioso who had been taken on board by Mayawati: he was a "history-sheeter"—meaning numerous criminal charge-sheets had been laid against him—who had been involved in shootouts and charged four times under the Gangsters Act.[36]

I asked Arun for another chart. Looking only at the Congress MPs, how hereditary were they, by age? Here, the curve was more dramatic and it concealed an even more worrying phenomenon, which was that the tentacles of extended families were now winding themselves ever more tightly around India's body politic. While compiling the main list of MPs, I had noticed that a few seemed to be more than simply the sons or daughters of a politician—rather, their links spread in several directions at once, making them not just hereditary but "hyperhereditary." So Preneet Kaur, for example, was the daughter of a senior bureaucrat and daughter-in-law of a former maharaja, and her husband, mother-in-law and two brothers-in-law were either former ministers or senior politicians. In other cases, the links

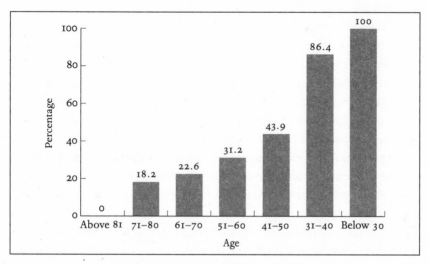

Percentage of hereditary Congress MPs by age

were more nebulous and might connect to close family members at a lower level, for instance in a state assembly.

I asked Arun to look at the MPs who had multiple family links. He responded, "The problem is the sample size, it is twenty-seven. As a rule, one does not consider stats run on sample sizes less than thirty to have any statistical meaning." I promised to bear this in mind and not to look at the data in percentage terms. The twenty-seven hyperhereditary MPs were concentrated in certain states: Uttar Pradesh, Andhra Pradesh, Haryana and Punjab in particular. Again, their age distinguished them. The average age of an MP with no significant family background was fifty-eight; for a hereditary MP it was forty-eight and for a hyperhereditary MP it was forty-six. They were identifiable, unsurprisingly, by their party. The BJP had only three hyperhereditaries—and two were Maneka and Varun Gandhi. The Congress party had seventy-eight hereditary MPs, of whom nineteen were hyperhereditary. In some cases they had combined their political take-over with a successful business, like Dr. Gaddam Vivekanand, a prominent and wealthy asbestos manufacturer from Andhra Pradesh whose father and brother were politicians.[37]

One other aspect concerned me: the possible effect of the 108th Constitution Amendment, passed by the upper house of the Indian Parliament in 2010 to reserve 33 percent of seats in national and state-elected bodies for women. This had been a much disputed bill, with supporters saying it would give women essential national representation, and opponents saying it would disadvantage other groups—Muslims in particular—who did not have reserved seats. The driving force behind the change in the law was Sonia Gandhi, who announced: "It was my husband Rajiv Gandhi's vision and promise."[38] But in the light of "family politics," would this change in the law—which might have been genuinely influential had it taken place a few decades earlier—do anything other than entrench the power of existing political families, when wives and daughters were nominated for the reserved seats? The exact implementation and details of this change were not yet clear, but it seemed inevitable that at India's next general election the number of hereditary women MPs in the Lok Sabha would rise. Going by present trends, more than 100 extra hereditary women MPs might be elected. This was a conservative estimate: if prominent MPs like Sonia Gandhi were to run in unreserved seats, and male MPs who were obliged to step down were to hand over their seats to their wives or daughters, the number of hereditary women MPs in the next Lok Sabha could cross 150.

Congress presently had 208 MPs, of whom 23 were women. This was the same as average, 11 percent. So far so low; now comes the difference: 19 out of the 23 Congress women MPs were hereditary (and of these, 4 were hyperhereditary). This left only 4 Congress women MPs who appeared to have reached Parliament on their own merit: Meenakshi Natrajan, Annu Tandon, and two other stalwarts. Who were they? Dr. Girija Vyas, the president of the National Commission for Women, and Chandresh Kumari Katoch, who turned out to be hereditary by another measure, being the daughter of none other than our old friend Hanwant Singh, the Maharaja of Jodhpur.[39]

The Indian republic was founded on the truth that power should not be handed over by the colonial rulers to the princes. India's next general election was likely to return not a Lok Sabha, a house of the people, but a Vansh Sabha, a house of dynasty. Nehru, Patel, V. P. Menon and others went to enormous lengths to make sure heredity was knocked aside as a criterion for rule, and to ensure the 554 princely states were absorbed into a modern and democratic nation. The Indian Constitution was based on the principle that sovereignty was derived from the people.[40]

PART II

LAKSHMI · WEALTH

5

THE VISIONS OF
JOHN MAYNARD KEYNES

JOHN MAYNARD KEYNES was full of surprises. Not long before the
First World War, he found himself working at the India Office, without
enough to do. He had recently graduated in mathematics from Cambridge,
and the new job involved a six-hour working day with an hour's break for
luncheon, though it was sometimes necessary to work from eleven to one
on a Saturday, which was offset by two months of holiday, bank holidays
and time off for Derby Day. It was a giant department of state in London—
the network of offices filled 100,000 cubic metres—overseeing the government of India by remote control. In one of the oddest methods of colonial
administration ever conceived (the system would be reformed in 1919)
India was at this time run by an executive council based in England. When
he attended a committee of the council for the first time in 1907, Keynes
noted: "The thing is simply government by dotardry; at least half of those
present showed manifest signs of senile decay, and the rest didn't speak."[1]

In other respects, the India Office tried to run along modern lines. Speaking tubes had been installed between offices, and the telephone could be
used to communicate with other government departments. One resident
clerk was known to travel the corridors of the building on roller skates,
until ordered to cease. The department was so big that it even housed its
own printers in a basement backing on to the prime minister's house in

Downing Street, ready to send off despatches to the subcontinent. "Boy copyists" had been replaced by "female manipulators," who operated type-writers in a secure office at the top of the building to ensure their safety, with work coming in and going out through a small hatch in the door.[2] This whole mechanism, along with civil and military salaries and pensions, was paid for by the Indian taxpayer: Indians had, without being asked, out-sourced the running of their government to Britain.

After examining military accounts for several months, Keynes moved to the Department of Revenue, Statistics and Commerce, and passed each day in a large room overlooking St. James's Park, inspecting files and circulat-ing them back and forth. He was worried by the quality of the statistics he received, and told the head of his department it was absurd they were pre-pared without technical knowledge. He suggested the India Office appoint a statistician. This was one of the difficulties with running a government from on high: it was detached from lived experience, and bred resentment. The politician Harold Cox, who had taught mathematics at Aligarh Muslim University, was once advised by a judge in India: "Cox, when you are a bit older, you will not quote Indian statistics with that assurance. The Govern-ment are very keen on amassing statistics—they collect them, add them, raise them to the nth power, take the cube root and prepare wonderful diagrams. But what you must never forget is that every one of those figures comes in the first instance from the *chowty dar* [chowkidar], who just puts down what he damn pleases."[3] Keynes, charged with preparing a report on "The Moral and Material Progress of India" for Parliament, distracted himself by studying stock market fluctuations. "A special feature of this year's edition," he wrote to an occasional male lover, "is to be an illustrated appendix on Sodomy."[4]

Like numerous imperial officials through history, Keynes had no strong interest in the country he was helping to control. It was easier to hold the prevailing view that it was best governed from a distance; although he was acquainted with some Indian students, he never himself went further east than Luxor. At this point, only 6 percent of entrants to the civil service in India were Indian, since many practical obstacles stopped them from join-ing. A proposal by the Indian National Congress that the entrance examina-tion be held not only in London but in Bombay, Calcutta and Madras was rejected; one British official inadvertently undermined the idea of racial superiority when he wrote that "half the service would be Bengali" if it were opened to this sort of competition, since Indian students were "infi-nitely quicker" at exams than Europeans.[5] Keynes found the India Office a frustrating place to work, although he enjoyed having enough spare time to go to wild Bloomsbury parties, the ballet, the theatre, art galleries and suffragette meetings. With an agile and capacious brain and a range of interests, he spent his spare office hours working on an academic study of probability. Soon he was so bored and so convinced the people around him were his intellectual inferiors, that at the age of twenty-five he resigned from the India Office and returned to Cambridge to relax, coach students and give lectures in economics.

Keynes is known today as the figure who revolutionized perceptions of the link between the economy and the role of government, principally through his influential 1936 book *The General Theory of Employment, Interest and Money*. He was the panjandrum of economics, married to the cheeky Russian ballerina Lydia Lopokova (he appears to have been genuinely bisexual), who offered world leaders solutions to complex problems. His achievements were not only academic: Keynes attended the Versailles negotiations, was the lead British representative at Bretton Woods in 1944 and is considered the father of the World Bank and the International Monetary Fund. In the 1970s in an era of high inflation, failing socialist experiments and the rise of monetarism, his reputation went into eclipse as he was blamed for sins he had not committed. After the world financial crisis of 2008, he fell back into fashion. His argument that during a slump the government had a duty to spend money in order to kick-start the economy (he referred to it as "magneto trouble") was widely accepted. In fact, the earlier equation of Keynesian thinking with uncontrolled government borrowing was wrong: he regarded deficit spending (using money the government did not have, in advance of future tax receipts) more as a technical fix. He viewed risk as central to the free market, and foresaw a safer and better regulated form of capitalism.

Ensconced in Cambridge eating anchovies on toast and drinking coffee, Keynes maintained an intellectual interest in India's economy. Although the existence of an interconnected global banking and monetary system is now assumed, economists were at the time groping towards an understanding of how such a thing might work. Large quantities of silver had been discovered in the United States, and in the 1870s Germany and other countries had abandoned bimetallism (by which their currency could be converted at fixed rates to gold or silver) and adopted a gold standard. This meant currencies like the rupee which were on a silver standard dropped, and debts the Indian government incurred in Britain, which was on a gold standard, became increasingly expensive to service. To boost confidence in the rupee, the India Office ordered gold sovereigns to be distributed from Bombay, but Indian bullion dealers had the bright idea of melting them down and selling the gold at a higher price than the face value. Panicked, the authorities shipped a large part of India's gold reserves to London, and as a temporary measure went on the "gold-exchange standard," meaning the rupee was now supported by assets held in a stable foreign currency—sterling.[6]

India's monetary problems had for some time been a matter of public and political concern. In Oscar Wilde's 1895 play *The Importance of Being Earnest*, Miss Prism tells her charge: "Cecily, you will read your Political Economy in my absence. The chapter on the Fall of the Rupee you may omit. It is somewhat too sensational. Even these metallic problems have their melodramatic side."[7] In 1912 news broke that Samuel Montagu & Co., a firm of London brokers, was secretly purchasing silver on behalf of the Indian government for its reserves. This was a sensible move designed to avoid speculation, and the silver was bought below the market rate, yet the press preferred the idea of possible impropriety: senior Jewish politicians might be enriching themselves by passing business to bullion dealers, to whom they had family connections. Were India's monetary arrangements a disgrace or a danger?

It was a typically English story, concentrating on the minutiae of a possible scandal while missing the larger point that the arrangements of the world's currencies were changing. (Nearly a century later, the British media would focus more attention on MPs claiming £1m in dubious expenses than on the government's creation of a debt nearing £1tn.) Irritated by the level of ignorance and the India Office's inability to state its case properly, Keynes decided to write a book in explanation, *The Monetary Affairs of India*. He began it in December 1912 and had proofs in his hand less than four months later when he left for a much anticipated holiday in Egypt, his first trip to the east. He was to stay with his old friend Robin Furness, a magistrate in Alexandria, who had promised him "all the attractions which made Gomorrah such a popular resort in the good old days," including his houseboys.[8]

The book on India's monetary affairs, with the final title *Indian Currency and Finance*, was published in 1913 and sold fewer than 1,000 copies in the year following publication. Keynes came to several important conclusions, specifically that the ancient link between money and metal was no longer necessary. His contention was that far from being dangerous, as monetary fundamentalists suggested, India's interim use of the gold-exchange standard should be made permanent. It was part of the evolution of global finance and would benefit business through a greater elasticity of money. In the long run, rather than pegging national currencies to the price of gold, the world should think about using a global reserve currency.[9]

Looking at India, he tracked the development of its paper currency. Although silver coins had been circulating in the subcontinent for more than 2,000 years, rupee notes of various denominations (promissory notes payable to the bearer on demand by the government of India) were presently issued by as many as seven different centres: Calcutta, Cawnpore, Lahore, Madras, Bombay, Karachi and Rangoon in Burma. Until recently, these notes had been accepted only in their area of issue.[10] In addition, several princely states had their own currencies, and the rulers of Goa issued rupee notes printed in the name of "India Portuguesa"— Portuguese India.[11] Keynes suggested immediate reform: paper notes should be circulated more widely in the subcontinent, the direct link to gold should be permanently curtailed and an Indian reserve bank established. The peg to sterling would secure the value of the rupee. He subsequently joined an official royal commission and managed to promote these proposals, although the Reserve Bank of India would not be created until 1935.

As well as developing his ideas about currency in the book, young Keynes elaborated a theory of money, value and hoarding, which would later become the concept of liquidity preference outlined in his *General Theory*. His supposition undermined the previously accepted thinking of Adam Smith that money saved was used either by the saver as capital or by another person to whom it was lent through the banking system. Keynes suggested that liquidity preference determined the rate of interest, since at times of uncertainty people hoarded money—not spending it, but not putting it to economic use either. In *Indian Currency and Finance*, he wrote breezily of the "needless accumulation of the precious metals" by Indians, "an uncivilized and wasteful habit" which damaged the Indian economy by absorbing redundant bullion from the West.[12] At the least sign of danger, people in India hoarded gold or cash. "I know, for example, a very conservative Brahmin family, small landowners in Eastern Bengal, where this is the case. Once a week the head of the family will retire privately to a corner of the roof of the house, take out the little hoard of notes with ritual care, count and check them, dust each with a feather brush, and lay them out in the sun to air and to recover from any trace of damp."[13]

It is apparent that Keynes was writing here about the family of a Bengali Brahmin student, Bimla Sarkar, with whom he was having sex. Keynes had arranged for him to be admitted to one of the Cambridge colleges, although Sarkar had already been blackballed for falling under "dangerous influences" at the university. Over several years Keynes gave him substantial amounts of money, which appear to have been prompted by an uneasy mixture of goodwill and desperation.[14] "He is a strange and charming creature," wrote Keynes to another lover, the painter Duncan Grant. "I don't know how our relationship is going to end. I have had all to-day the most violent sexual feelings towards him . . . yet I don't feel at all certain what feelings there are in his odd Indian head."[15] When Sarkar ran up debts with a muscular clergyman at his college and his family were unable to pay his fees (he had come to England without telling them), Keynes threatened to bring the monetary affair to an end and have him deported. The relationship was predicated on imbalance and incomprehension, and was indicative of the attitude of the British ruling class at the time. Keynes had been born to a world of privilege at a particularly stable moment in British history; he wore a top hat to the royal commission on Indian finance, risked his career with illegal sexual escapades and spent weekends at country houses with cabinet ministers and Virginia Woolf. Consumed by Edwardian optimism and a sense of entitlement, he could not understand how people from other backgrounds might flounder or respond in different ways. Sarkar, with his chaotic finances and unformed interest in Marlowe and Shakespeare, was an enticement and an irritant.

In some kind of subtext, Keynes played out his desire and exasperation in his little-known first book, seeking to put a price on a country he had envisioned only through statistics. What he could not see, for instance, was that the Indian emphasis on what he called hoarding was a logical response to circumstance: there was no formal national banking system, and no certainty the prevailing power would still be in place for the next generation. While England had not been invaded since 1066, north India had faced repeated invasions and disturbance since around the same time. There was no reliable mechanism to invest money, and borrowing only happened within the extended family or from particular caste communities, at exorbitant rates. Gold and jewellery were the ideal movable asset, as Queen Victoria had realized when she plucked the world's largest diamond, the Koh-i-Noor, from the ruler of Punjab and implanted it in her imperial crown. In India's joint family system, gold was one of the most effective forms of retaining and displaying wealth. New money did not usually go into banks or real estate (whose house would it be when you had paid the cash—your father's, your brothers', your own?) but into gold necklaces, bangles, rings, buttons, waistbands and headpieces to be displayed on rich men and women. Gold in India was, and is, a hedge against uncertainty. It could be hoarded, guarded and dusted, like the unfortunate Bimla Sarkar's father's rooftop notes. In his way Keynes, however distantly, realized through his inadvertent connection to India that the assumptions of the classical economists about human behaviour were insufficiently flexible. India had a preference for liquidity.

A year after this saga unravelled, Europe went to war. Many of Keynes's generation died; five of the students at his college were killed before the end of 1914. After the Versailles treaty, he wrote a furious denunciation of the level of reparations Germany would be obliged to pay, believing it would cripple the German economy and breed resentment. Unfortunately, he was right: hyperinflation and the rise of Hitler came next. *The General Theory of Employment, Interest and Money* was written out of the depression that followed the Wall Street Crash of 1929. Towards the close of the Second World War, Keynes's earlier proposals for a new monetary system came to fruition in the snows of Bretton Woods. With Britain almost bankrupt and the United States ascendant, Keynes's proposal of an international currency unit was adjusted so that the U.S. dollar became the new global reserve currency. It was not until 2009, in a very different world economy, that his idea was revived by Zhou Xiaochuan, the governor of China's central bank, who suggested the dollar should be dislodged in favour of a new IMF-backed currency. (China disliked having to hold its massive foreign exchange reserves in U.S. dollars.) Creating a fresh global monetary system needed "extraordinary political vision and courage," said Zhou, and he acknowledged his debt to John Maynard Keynes.[16]

After Bretton Woods, Keynes prepared a document for Britain's war cabinet saying that the UK had debts of £3bn which were principally the result of cash expenditure in Africa, the Middle East and India. Unless spending in these colonies was brought "under drastic control at an early date . . . our ability to pursue an independent financial policy in the early post-war years will be fatally impaired."[17] Keynes was in poor health now, having passed from the Edwardian era to two world wars. He was nursed by his wife, Lydia, on a diet of sour oranges, coffee and raw cabbage.[18] His note to the war cabinet was not taken up, and by the time of Indian independence, two years later, he was dead.

When the British East India Company had started out in 1600, it had £35,602 in bullion and goods, stuffed into just four ships which were setting out for the unknown limits of the Indian Ocean.[19] Now, at the close of business nearly 350 years later, Britain was indebted in sterling to India to the tune of £1.3bn, through circumstances nobody had anticipated. In 1939 the debt had been running in the opposite direction, as the Indian government paid for the machinery of empire controlled in London. When war broke out, Britain found itself having to pay troops and convey them across Asia, as well as to build airfields, railways and military installations, ratcheting up debts to the administration in New Delhi in the process.[20] When supplies of small arms or clothing were sent from India to Singapore, or Indian troops were sent to fight in Egypt, London incurred a liability to the Indian government. By the end of the war, this debt had developed a life of its own, and the money was a substantial potential asset for the newly independent nation.

In 1947, London and New Delhi discussed what to do about these sterling balances. When the prime minister, Clement Attlee, suggested they might be forgiven, Sardar Vallabhbhai Patel quickly put him right: repayment of the debt to India was "Britain's sacred obligation."[21] The difficulty was that the British empire had total gold and dollar reserves of £500m, and Britain's external liabilities were nearly eleven times that amount.[22] So even if India wanted all its money, the money was not there to get. With remarkable goodwill in the circumstances (the British delegation was led by Jeremy Raisman, who had been India's wartime finance minister and was well regarded on both sides) agreement was reached. Amounts would be released gradually by Britain to fund Indian imports, and money was put aside to buy out British assets in India and pay pension annuities to retired civil servants. The debt would also be shrunk through the devaluation of sterling. The British government agreed to pay India a tapering sum each year, culminating in a theoretical final transfer of £72 in the 2007–8 tax year.[23] Although it was not the full shilling, this gave India a useful advantage in the years immediately following independence and partition, an asset which would need to be carefully husbanded. By 1958, when Jawaharlal Nehru's government implemented its second Five Year Plan to create an industrial economy, the money had all been used up. Without this surplus, the gap had from now on to be filled by deficit financing and foreign aid.[24]

In the words of the governor of the Reserve Bank of India, C. D. Deshmukh, the new government had run through the sterling balances "as if there was no tomorrow."[25]

Why did the Indian economy go wrong in the decades after independence? Whose idea was it? Arriving at Cambridge in 1907, Nehru imbibed the liberal atmosphere in the lull before the First World War. He studied natural sciences, and attended lectures given by Keynes, Bertrand Russell and other figures of the day. He read H. G. Wells and G. B. Shaw, and considered Fabian socialist theories, as well as self-consciously modern ideas about human psychology and sexuality. He travelled in different parts of Europe and observed the rise of Irish republicanism. Much of his energy was devoted to behaving like any other well-off student: reading, thinking, meeting people from different countries, visiting the pantomime at Drury Lane, going for walks, going to parties, behaving in a mildly dissolute way, drinking champagne and getting into debt repeatedly, to the anger of his father Motilal. He was restless, and it was not until the 1920s back in India that Jawaharlal Nehru found real direction, realizing the battle for his country's freedom would occupy his life. It was not a unique trajectory: after the First World War, both Chou Enlai and Ho Chi Minh studied in Europe and honed a more extreme form of revolutionary thinking.

Nehru's economic ideas, such as they were, chimed with the progressive thinking of the time, particularly after the economic slump of the 1930s. Although he was not a communist, a visit to Soviet Russia in 1927 had left him impressed. He did not believe in Mohandas Gandhi's idea of village industry and a spinning wheel in every hut; he wanted new, fast, scientific progress. In retrospect, it is extraordinary how optimistic he was about the prospects for immediate advance in *The Discovery of India,* as if putting words on paper would make them possible. He described the discussions of the National Planning Committee, set up by Congress in 1938. Its aim was:

> to ensure an adequate standard of living for the masses, in other words, to get rid of the appalling poverty of the people. The irreducible minimum, in terms of money, had been estimated by economists at figures varying from Rs15 to Rs25 per capita per month . . . We calculated that a really progressive standard of living would necessitate the increase of the national wealth by 500 or 600 percent. That was, however, too big a jump for us, and we aimed at a 200 to 300 percent increase within ten years.[26]

These were big numbers, and a long way from what transpired. It was a case, again, of ambitious people formulating plans for other people that were not based on the reality of how humans work. Nehru's thinking was outsourced in part to Subhas Chandra Bose, who as Congress president at this time helped to push through proposals for planning and industrialization against opposition from Gandhi.[27]

Underlying Nehru's philosophy was a widely accepted belief that the economy could be made to grow by applying remote, organized, rational precepts. There was an assumption, based on the experiences of other countries, that India would need subsidies and state assistance during the early stages of industrialization. Even after the reverses of the late 1950s, Nehru did not change his economic ideas in any substantial way. He was an example of the dictum laid down by Keynes at the end of the *General Theory*:

> Practical men, who believe themselves to be quite exempt from any intellectual influences, are usually the slaves of some defunct economist . . . for in the field of economic and political philosophy there are not many who are influenced by new theories after they are twenty-five or thirty years of age, so that the ideas which civil servants and politicians and even agitators apply to current events are not likely to be the newest.[28]

His economic thinking was a hardened version of the social democratic outlook of Clement Attlee's postwar Labour government, a Keynsian idea of a mixed economy taken to extremes that Keynes would have found fiscally impossible. Even as the American economy boomed in the postwar years, Nehru's relationship with the United States would be scratchy. India's wartime links to the Allied economy, which had been important to military success in the Middle East and Burma, were largely severed.

The fashion for socialism and central planning had an intellectual logic which attracted many of India's brightest minds in the middle of the twentieth century. The theory was that since the nation was rich in land, resources and people but lacking in capital, it would not be possible to invest in the roads, power and steel needed for industrial development unless the government put up the money. It would be dangerous to risk being exploited or swallowed up by predatory foreign companies, in some new form of imperialism. The Indian economy during the last half-century of colonial rule had been in a stagnant condition, with annual per capita GDP flatlining at 0.1 percent.[29]

Nehru was impressed by a fresh orthodoxy which appeared to be endorsed by some of the world's finest economic planners. The concept developed into the quasi-science of development economics, which was highly suspicious of the role of the market. Native entrepreneurs in newly decolonized countries were not thought likely to provide a serious engine for growth. Nehru was by no means the first world leader to have trouble with the financials—his British contemporary Alec Douglas Home had to use matchsticks to understand economic problems—and his idealistic outlook was linked to the rejection of the benefits of a financially secure background. It also came from the potent Gandhian ethic of abandoning possessions, which was contrary to the Indian tradition of saving (not forgetting Sarojini Naidu's quip about the Mahatma: "If only that old man knew how much it costs us to keep him in poverty").[30] As a young radical, Nehru told his father to throw himself into India's freedom movement and give away his capital, but his father responded in a letter in 1921: "You cannot have it both ways—insist on my having no money and yet expect me to pay you money."[31] It was this approach, wanting to spend money but not to make it, that was to cause the new nation many problems.

Nehru, though, was not alone. With the exception of the Tamil politician C. Rajagopalachari, the first Indian governor general of India, who vigorously opposed what he called the "permit/licence raj," and the late Sardar Patel, who thought the idea of central planning unproven and unrealistic, his views followed the consensus. He did not want a communist system, nor did he wish to replicate the social injustices of nineteenth-century industrial capitalism. Few people by this time were taking Gandhi's idea of village republics seriously; indeed, Dr. Ambedkar thought this economic philosophy "with its call of back to nature, means back to nakedness, back to squalor, back to poverty and back to ignorance for the vast mass of the people."[32] Pushed from the left during his premiership, Nehru may even have felt he was taking a middle path.

If a single document catches this heady, ambitious vision of how the subcontinent could be made a better place, it is *A Plan of Economic Development for India,* published in Bombay in 1944. Its authors were not firebrands or revolutionaries: rather, they were staid and successful businessmen like J. R. D. Tata, Sir Shri Ram, G. D. Birla and Sir Purshotamdas Thakurdas, as well as the respected economist John Matthai, who became finance minister after independence. Although most were mill owners or industrialists who had made outstanding amounts of money by the usual capitalist methods, they thought the new India would need to be constructed along different lines. From a distance, their plan seems breathtaking in its idealism and detachment, the work of people who were philanthropic but unrealistic. Its origins were more prosaic. India's business leaders realized that when a Congress-led government took power, some form of disciplinary economic planning was inevitable. The "Bombay Plan" was in part a tactical move to outflank the hard left. "The inevitability of a change in the direction of a socialist economy must now be recognized," Matthai wrote in an internal minute to his fellow "planners," when much of the country was destabilized by the Quit India movement, "and leaders of industry would well be advised to take this into account and be prepared to make such adjustments as may meet all reasonable demands before the socialist movement assumes the form of a full-fledged revolution." His hope was that industrialists could take up and endorse the "sound and feasible" elements of socialist thinking.[33]

The Bombay Plan was a short pamphlet, clearly written. The authors aimed to double per capita income over fifteen years, increase agricultural output and raise industrial output by five times. It was an ambitious idea, but not impossible given the underdeveloped state of Indian industry. Like Nehru, they hoped not to have to rely on foreign countries for plant and machinery. Moving on to social ambitions, the proposal started to become outlandish. Since people in Germany and Denmark used around thirty yards of cotton each year, Indians must do the same. Then there was new scientific research showing that everybody needed 3,000 cubic feet of fresh air per hour. This worked out at around 100 square feet of floor space per person, meaning the size of the average house would need to expand to 500 square feet. As residents of Bombay had around 28 square feet each (today the average figure is around 31 square feet—and bear in mind that some houses on Malabar Hill are very large indeed), this would involve extensive residential rebuilding.[34] Their apparent dream grew. The quantum of personnel required for "large scale economic planning" could be gleaned from the Soviet Union: the Russians in 1939 had needed 582,000 "managers of state and collective farms" and 450,000 "heads of administration." The process could only go forward with public agreement and goodwill. "In the execution of a comprehensive plan of economic development, it is essential that we should be able to count on the willing cooperation of the people. This will be possible only if the masses are able to read and write and are in a position to understand for themselves the broad implications of the developments embodied in the plan."

How was India to pay for all this? Through a favourable balance of trade, money created by issuing government bonds, sterling securities held in the UK, "the hoarded wealth of the country, mainly gold" (they had been reading their Keynes), and foreign borrowing. Once "a national government comes into power in whom people have full faith," the hoards of gold would quickly come out from their hiding places.[35] *A Plan of Economic Development for India* reads like a spoof, but it was the reality.

The early years of central planning might best be seen through the person of Prasanta Chandra Mahalanobis, the epitome of organization. Privately austere, he never carried cash and had assistants to do such things for him, although his private and office money and assorted grants were all mixed up together.[36] He was a product of the Bengal renaissance, the social and religious reform movement, a man for whom intellectual activity was a virtue in itself. Tall, crafty, thin-lipped and difficult to work with, Mahalanobis impressed Nehru with his knowledge of mathematics and his bursting self-confidence. He was a skilled statistician, an expert in large-scale sample surveys and the inventor of the "Mahalanobis Distance"—a measure used in statistics to assess group divergence and detect outliers. A friend and promoter of the poet Rabindranath Tagore, he had taken a first in physics at Cambridge (from Keynes's college) a couple of years after Nehru. Notably, he was the founder of the Indian Statistical Institute in Calcutta, a body with a high and continuing international reputation. The prime minister liked the idea of putting the economy in the hands of this clever technician, a Bengali Brahmin who dabbled in poetry and impenetrable philosophy and dreamed of a noble future for India.

Mahalanobis came to economics only in his forties, and had spent the 1920s pursuing subjects such as the pseudo-science of eugenics (he wished to discover the racial origins of Bengalis). He had written a paper, "Analysis of Race-Mixture in Bengal," in which he recounted how by using "anthropological measurements such as stature, head-length, head-breadth, nasal length, etc. of 300 Anglo-Indians in Calcutta," he had discovered that Anglo-Indians were taller than Bengalis and had variable head-lengths. He invented a mathematical formula of "caste-distance" to determine the eugenic gap between Anglo-Indians and specific caste groups by contemplating variables, measurements and pooled variance. His conclusion was that Europeans had bred with Bengalis rather than with people from other regions, and that the resultant half-breeds were "singularly free from contact with the Chotanagpur tribes, but appear to have intermixed to some extent with the Lepchas of Darjeeling."[37] There was more. In 1949, by which time such ideas were falling out of fashion, he took part in an anthropometric survey of several thousand Indians, busily measuring their brows, noses, elbows and shinbones.

Extending himself from skull measurement and statistics to the ideal future for the nation, he invented a theory of economic development—the "Mahalanobis Model," inevitably. It had much in common with a mathematical model used in the Soviet Union, although Mahalanobis arrived at his conclusions independently.[38] Standing over an early computer at his institute and examining punch cards, he worked out the details. His notion was that since the economy was composed of various sectors, and they all fed into each other, it should be possible to devise a mathematical table to regulate the flow between the sectors. It was an input-output model, drawing on the prevailing economic theory that one industry's output could be considered another industry's input and they could be correlated in a matrix (economists still argue that an input-output model can function in wartime). So when the table expanded, rows and columns could be added to show an array of different businesses, all happily feeding in and out of one another. Investment would be directed towards heavy industries, engineering, petrochemicals, fertilizers and refineries, rather than towards agriculture, rural employment, healthcare or education. A mine would produce coal to make steel for railways to transport coal from mines—and the process would all be orchestrated centrally. The glitch was that for this model to work, some harsh theoretical conditions had to be met: factories must work at full capacity, entrepreneurship must be brought under government auspices, prices must be fixed and the economy should be closed, with international trade restricted.

In November 1954, Mahalanobis made a speech in Calcutta in which he outlined the skeleton of India's Second Five Year Plan. The occasion was attended by Nehru and other dignitaries, to emphasize how important it was to the nation's future. Finding that indigenous economists were doubtful about the practicalities of his expansive dream—John Matthai had resigned as finance minister in 1950 because his power was being given away to the new planning commission—Mahalanobis travelled the globe, meeting supporters in Europe and North America.[39] He hoped well-wishers from abroad would chivy the likes of Matthai: these "trained and experienced economists can help us a great deal in speaking their own language to Indian economists (which we are unable to do); and in carrying conviction to administrators and political leaders."[40] There might as well have been group discount rates for foreign economists, such did they flock to India.

Most of them endorsed what was going on, finding it new and exciting. Milton Friedman was a dry exception: he went to India in 1955 and judged the Mahalanobis Model excessively mathematical. Friedman suggested the mixture of village handicraft units and monumental heavy industry was a potential disaster: "This policy threatens an inefficient use of capital by combining it with too little labour at one extreme and an inefficient use of labour by combining it with too little capital at the other extreme." It encouraged inefficiency and discouraged entrepreneurs. Foreign exchange controls brought "delay, uncertainty, and arbitrariness into domestic business activities."[41] Although most of India's economy remained in the private sector, it was bound by a theology of red tape.

It is worth quoting some lines of what Mahalanobis said in his speech in Calcutta in 1954, for although his thinking did not match what was coming out of China at this time in its folly, the inhumanity of his approach and its disengagement from normal commercial experience were extraordinary. He began with a haze of numerical examples, designed to stress the uniquely scientific quality of the new project: "Different models of economic growth are being constructed and studied on the basis of different sets of relations (sometimes expressed in a mathematical form) between relevant varieties." India, in its infinite variety, would become an input-output matrix: the Mahalanobis Model. Materials would be allocated to different industries from the centre: "When an approximate allocation of investments is ready, the anticipated consumer expenditure is known, and the requirements of final flows of consumer goods have been settled, it would be necessary to work out the total output of the different industries (inclusive of all intermediate products and consistent with the bill of final goods) . . . Work is already in progress in 12 sectors (that is, a 12 x 12 table); and arrangements are being made to prepare a 90 x 90 table." What a thought, 90 x 90—or 8,100 table cells, in a time before computer spreadsheets! In Mahalanobis's dream of the future, India would industrialize rapidly and full employment should be assured within ten years. To get there, he announced that both large and small industries across the nation would now be obliged to "increase productivity by all other means such as working 2 or 3 shifts," and the resultant surplus of goods would be purchased by the state "on a large scale to build up inventories which would be used to meet the increase in demand later on."[42]

It was fantasy, an imaginative piece of Bengali creativity and an implausible economic vision. An exceptionally damaging consequence of all this thinking and action was that as new nation after new nation tried to make itself afresh following the European retreat from empire, postcolonial leaders and their economic advisers turned to India and to Mahalanobis. They went not to Chicago for guidance, but to Calcutta. As one such thinker, Hans Singer, said: "P. C. Mahalanobis became the prophet (or guru) of the development economists" in the postwar decades.[43] Later in life Mahalanobis even proposed the creation of what he called a Labour Reserve Service, an idea that fortunately never turned into reality, in which a giant pool of surplus workers on half-pay (half-pay, for labourers on a few rupees a day) would be shifted around the country from project to project on the whim of government officers, like something out of pharaonic Egypt. He had it all worked out: "The Labour Reserve Service (LR) would then act as a buffer against unemployment and would serve as a (perhaps socially more useful and psychologically more preferable) form of or substitute for unemployment insurance limited, however, in the first instance, to persons who are already factory workers."[44]

What did it mean for Indian business people, in practical terms, to have their day-to-day commercial decisions controlled by the theoretical strictures of successive Five Year Plans? Some of the larger conglomerates, such as those owned by the Tata and Birla families, were left to get on as they liked. The enthusiasm of the owners of capital for the aspects of socialism contained in the Bombay Plan soon dissipated. From 1966 to 1969, India had a "plan holiday," largely because of a lack of finance, but it did nothing to unravel the stifling structure Nehru and Mahalanobis had created.

In the years immediately following independence, the new system had appeared to be working. Import substitution (making goods locally rather than importing them from abroad) and unmatched public investment had generated economic growth. During Nehru's premiership, per capita GDP rose on average by just over 2 percent a year, which was a noticeable improvement on the preceding half-century. By the 1960s, serious structural problems were becoming apparent. The new Third Five Year Plan was dependent on foreign assistance in order to make it possible.[45] The worst period came during the 1970s, when India's annual per capita GDP grew at 0.76 percent.[46] Under Indira Gandhi, the country was in the illogical position of getting American food aid while denouncing American capitalist hegemony, and looking over its shoulder at countries like Japan and South Korea admiringly even while disapproving of their methods. A developing cult of the larger national cause made it somehow unpatriotic to question the economic system that had been created by the victors of the freedom movement—even if it was not really working. Indira Gandhi started to use economic policy as a form of political patronage, pacifying farmers who had grown richer under the Green Revolution with subsidized power and fertilizers one minute, and championing the poor the next with populist moves like taking money from the former maharajas or proposing to nationalize the wheat trade.

Shortly before the outbreak of the First World War, a lawyer named T. V. Sundaram Iyengar had started southern India's first motor bus service, using the dense network of roads in the Tamil region. It was an innovative idea; he offered a promise of wayside meals in an effort to recruit passengers, knowing that many people would be frightened of using such a novel form of transportation. Over the years, he had diversified into road building, car parts manufacture and rubber retreading. The south of India had fewer merchant capitalists than the north. Prominent trading communities like the Chettiars had largely stayed away from industry (unlike the Marwaris, a prosperous mercantile community originally from Rajasthan) and done business abroad, giving a rare opportunity to people like T. V. Sundaram Iyengar.

The TVS group that was named for him had grown and grown, and today it has an annual turnover of about $1bn. His grandson, Gopal Srinivasan, remembered how in order to make anything happen during the Mahalanobis era, the company had no choice but to woo government bureaucrats.

"Nineteen fifty-six to 1984, when Rajiv Gandhi came in and started to make some changes, was a black period in our history. We were ruled by the DGTD, the Director General of Technology Development. If you wanted to import a $10 machine, he would make the decision. Before 1956—after the Brits went into decline in the 1930s—Indians were used to doing business largely as we liked. You had the textile businesses in Ahmedabad and Coimbatore, and my family were involved in truck and car distribution. By 1960 we had obtained the licence to make Dunlop wheels, Lucas electricals, Girling brakes—but we had nothing to distribute!"

So each effort that TVS made in the international market in the 1950s and 1960s was hamstrung by the planning regulators.

"We needed to import steel and copper, and had to make the payments to an English company. So that meant we had to: one, get an import licence; two, ask the Reserve Bank of India to release the foreign exchange; three, get the payment released; four, get permission to manufacture.

"For foreign collaboration, like we had between TVS and Lucas, we had to prove it was justified: how much it would cost, how long it would last, whether expatriates were needed, then how much they would be paid, how many days' travelling would be required. Each stage—each permission—took us six months to a year. We had to set up a large office in Delhi in order to apply to the ministries. Twice every month my father had to fly from Madras to Delhi."

This was a journey of more than 1,000 miles, in a four-prop Viscount aeroplane, from India's southern reaches to the nation's capital. Because their brand was based on reliability and trust, Srinivasan said TVS had refused to pay bribes to the bureaucrats. Some of the important ministers and civil servants originated from south India, which made the process of winning their support easier.

"You needed to develop a social relationship. In the 1950s and '60s, I would say there was still some sense of purpose connecting business and government—that we were all in it together, building the new India—but by 1969 it had become bureaucratic to the point where . . . it was really a lost era."

In the first years after independence, the Indian economy had managed a reasonable growth rate, since it was starting from such a low base. By the late 1960s, the initial surge had ceased. During the premiership of Indira Gandhi, Srinivasan's father decided to make a cheap moped; he called it his "mechanical horse" and envisaged the people of India being able to go from town to village without having to walk, or drag their goods up and down the dusty roads on undignified handcarts. The rigid official obstacles that he faced demanded an imaginative response. "My father wanted to make a two-wheeler for the common man, the TVS 50 moped. He was told that since it would be a luxury item, no foreign exchange could be used and he was not allowed to import a prototype, or any machinery, or any parts at all. Say he needed a bearing, or a carburettor, he couldn't get it. And he would have to export 25 percent of production. My father would have to generate an overseas market for this moped. It took him four years to start up. We sold around 10,000 mopeds a month."

The numerous blocks on commercial activity meant that a large number of talented Indians went abroad for opportunities, especially to the United States. The nation was left with a pool of good, frustrated engineers and scientists. Those who remained in India had no choice but to negotiate the official hurdles; that was business. By the 1960s, the government had another reason not to dismantle the permit raj—it depended on revenues from the tariff system.

"The controlling was so entrenched that before you travelled abroad for work, you had to secure letters of invitation. You had to specify the number of days, and what you were going to be doing, to get foreign exchange. If you were the head of the company, you were allowed a 'once per trip' entertainment allowance. On return, you had to show your receipts. Your personal belongings would be examined with a fine-tooth comb. It created a lack of dignity as a nation. Here in Madras, there was a place by the port called Burma Bazaar where you could buy things from the pavement that had been smuggled from the ships—deodorant, chocolate, pens, underwear, soap, talcum powder, liquor."[47] Across India, this sense of restriction during those closed years created a constant and unquenchable demand for everyday consumer goods. So when the businessmen of Madras entertained their contacts in the 1960s, they had to rely on India's street capitalists, and send their servants down to the docks to buy bottles of French wine and Black Label whisky.

Sitting in his office in the sullen southern heat of Tamil Nadu, Srinivasan had the restless demeanour of a born (or bred) entrepreneur. He had spent time in the U.S., studying at the University of Michigan. Anticipating change, he had moved in and out of numerous fields during his career in India, first with TVS and then on his own—car seats, moulded plastics, vehicle locks, computer peripherals, engineering design services and now private equity, scouting India for new business propositions. On the day we met, I had a conversation with another industrialist, B. Santhanam, who headed the French glass manufacturer Saint-Gobain in India. He believed lower levels of government investment in industry and services in southern India had been to their long-term advantage.

"We have a calmer mentality here," said Santhanam. "Government has taken care of infrastructure, but not of industry: that has always been entrepreneur-driven. We have no great resources such as mining, we don't have defence investment like in the north, we are not trying to defend a border. Historically this area had no large kingdoms, and for centuries it was lightly ruled. We have always had a great emphasis on education. The College of Engineering in Madras was established 200 years ago—the first outside Europe. So most of our business success comes from the ambition of our people." He viewed the permit raj as "a pure dark age," and was young enough to have little personal knowledge of its strictures.

"The late 1980s were not bad for us, in our industry. I feel that at a micro-level, things were OK but the macroeconomics were all wrong and we were living on borrowed time. In 1996—as MD-designate of Saint-Gobain

Glass—it took me six weeks and no bribes to get approval from the commerce ministry to set up our operation. And over the last decade, we have invested $400m in India." I mentioned my conversation with Srinivasan and the difficulties TVS had experienced in the old days, trying to get permission to import a bearing. "We employ 800 people," B. Santhanam said. "Only two of them work on imports."[48]

What is the matrix—or, what did it mean to be inside the input-output matrix?

In order to make the most important industries work in a planned economy, it was necessary to have somebody make the heavy stuff, the capital equipment: cranes, mineral crushers, blast furnaces, deep-hole boring machines, excavators, railway materials, crank shafts, draglines, forged rolls, pig casters, slag cups, wagon tipplers and apron feeders. The Heavy Engineering Corporation, or HEC, was created in 1958 and situated in a poor, mineral-rich part of east India near Ranchi. (It is still there today, and in 2006–7 went into profit, prompting the government to describe it in 2010 as a "navratna," one of the nine gems of the state, and to propose listing it on the stock exchange.)[49] One difficulty was that its main output was intended for the benefit of India's steel industry, which planned to grow capacity by one million tons each year. But as things turned out, steel production grew at only around half that rate. New steel plants were not built, and when they were built they were sometimes sourced not from HEC, but from the Soviet Union.

Between 1973 and 1978, the corporation received no major orders. A prudent early suggestion that HEC should start out gradually, and construct infrastructure in phases as demand increased, was dismissed. Because of the absence of steel plants, HEC's line on the matrix choked up and things ground to a halt. Against this, state companies which matched the intentions of the economic planners were sometimes successful. For example, Bharat Heavy Electricals, which supplied power sector infrastructure, went into profit in the early 1970s. It had good leadership, and the market for heavy electrical equipment in India was broadly in line with the planners' anticipation.

Until the mid-1960s, the Heavy Engineering Corporation had substantial teething problems because of the capital and technological barriers involved in setting up such a gigantic public undertaking. The corporation had three units: a heavy machine-building plant, a heavy machine tool plant and a foundry forge. The tool plant might have been useful for companies such as TVS—which needed to find its bearings—but had trouble getting off the ground. It never came close to operating at full capacity, which had been deemed essential under the Five Year Plan for the input-output matrix to work effectively.

Here are some figures for capacity utilization in the heavy machine tool plant, in percentage terms, which show how the matrix did not work:

1968–9	3
1969–70	11
1970–71	11
1971–2	8
1972–3	9
1973–4	12

These are not misprints: 3 percent of capacity, 11 percent of capacity. Only during Mrs. Gandhi's Emergency did production rise above 25 percent of capacity, before dropping back to 6 percent in 1977–8. In the foundry and heavy machine-building plant, things were little better. The largest forging press in Asia operated at the feeblest levels. The heavy machine-building plant averaged a capacity utilization of 21 percent during the period 1965–80.[50]

So year after year, the gargantuan enterprise lay idling and bleeding public money. Over time, politicians realized the system was not functioning in the way they had intended. At first, it seemed easier to blame external forces for the economic stagnation—a poor harvest, another war with Pakistan or the failure of aid donors to live up to their promises. In June 1980, this question was asked in the Lok Sabha: "Will the Minister of Industry be pleased to state: (a) Has the HEC, Ranchi, the capacity to fabricate a one million ton [steel] plant per annum? (b) If so, whether this capacity has been utilized so far, and (c) If not, for how long the capacity has remained underutilized?" The minister may have been in a hurry (he went on to become a movie producer) because he responded as follows: "(a) Yes, sir, (b) No, sir, (c) From the beginning up to this time."[51]

It is apparent that senior managers at HEC were unhappy about the way it was working (or not working) but were locked into the grid in such a way that it was hard to make anything change. The management was not frightened to raise objections, as they would have been in the Soviet Union or China; rather, they had no means to break out of the system. Lacking skilled employees, they were initially obliged to hire local farmhands as workers. One director said later they had been dragged down by "the mass recruitment resorted to in the early years, unrelated to the production needs. Large bodies of idle men led to slackness and unhealthy practices."[52] During the 1970s, HEC employed around 20,000 people and nearly 200 "foreign experts," who were visiting from the Soviet bloc. Although HEC was set up as a "model employer," much time was taken up with industrial disputes. It was nearly impossible to sack anyone. Rival trade unions—each one tending to represent a different caste or tribal group—would fight each other at the plants, and the management would have to call in the police. Strikes, slow working and mammoth demonstrations were frequent, usually calling for incentive payments, overtime payments or changed working hours.[53] In some cases "tight delivery commitments" forced the corporation to subcontract work to private companies, or to import orders from abroad. Young engineers, who had joined HEC with first-class degrees and gold medals from their institutes in a blaze of optimism in the 1960s, began to flee in the early 1970s to other firms in India or abroad. As Ravi Ramamurti, now a professor at Northeastern University, wrote in 1987: "The irony of the situation is that while HEC was losing the people it most needed, it was forced to hire those it did not need, and to retain those it could afford to let go."[54]

Worried that the Heavy Engineering Corporation was not running according to plan, politicians tried to help. One of their methods was to parachute in new chief executives on a regular basis: a man who ran a sewing machine company, the head of the state coal company, a major general, a manager from the railways, even a left-wing politician who had lost his seat in Parliament (and who stayed for less than a year before leaving to contest another election). During a critical period from 1964 to 1974, HEC had eight different chief executives. One left because he thought his deputy had closer links to the relevant government minister than he did, another quit because there were riots in the sprawling township, which contained more than two dozen schools and a hospital, adjoining the plants in Ranchi.

In 1968, a committee of MPs visited HEC and wrote a report. They found a large number of Soviet advisers running it, trailed by interpreters. Almost all sections of the plant were used below capacity, and attendance and time-keeping were poor. "It is with the help of Russian Experts and considerable work of foreign trained engineers some of whom are heading the shops and departments and the Junior USSR trained supervisors, that the company have been able to produce whatever they have so far."[55]

During the Emergency, HEC ran a little more efficiently and the chief executive fired 170 workers and officers, the first to lose their jobs in the history of the company. When the Janata government (an assortment of opposition parties, including the forerunner of the BJP) came to power in 1977, the workers were reinstated. So year after year, HEC made the Top 10—meaning it featured in a survey of the "Top 10 Loss Making Public Sector Undertakings" in India.[56] The sheer scale of the giant meant no government would dare to kill it.

The Heavy Engineering Corporation is one of the more extreme examples of how big dreams in India went wrong. A lot of what it could make was not wanted or needed. At the opposite end of the scale, or on the other axis of the matrix, was a commodity that many industries needed, often in larger quantities than was available: coal. Here, the problems became more creative, for whatever happened, the nation could not do without coal.

Indian coal is usually of poor quality and contains a lot of ash. At the time of independence, it was mined mainly in open pits in Bihar and West Bengal, and in 1956 a state body was set up to develop an indigenous coal industry. After a decade, the Ministry of Steel, Mines and Metals noticed it was not getting very far. The public sector had produced merely 37 percent of its target for coal under the Five Year Plan, while the private sector had hit 93 percent.[57] The production targets had been set centrally using forecasting techniques, when the demand for coal from every sector of the economy had been aggregated, using an input-output model.

The Ministry of Steel, Mines and Metals produced a report in 1967 which stated that each nationalized mine should "prepare cost data reflecting the actual expenditure and showing separately the direct costs which vary with production"—implying nobody had thought of doing this before. "There may be scope for improvement in regard to such matters as planning, administrative and organizational set-up, staffing, procurement of equipment, control of stores, financial and budgetary control management, employees' relationship and marketing."[58] Or, everything. Each industry in the input-output model claimed it was suffering from the inefficiencies of another. Coal blamed rail for not supplying wagons, rail blamed steel for not producing materials and steel blamed coal for not providing a regular power supply. The conditions in the mines were dangerous, with accidents caused by cave-ins, gas explosions and flooding; many miners suffered from pneumoconiosis, or black lung disease.

After her 1971 "Garibi Hatao" election victory, Indira Gandhi decided the best way forward for the floundering coal and steel industries might be to nationalize them completely. Her chosen men were Mohan Kumaramangalam and a senior bureaucrat, K. S. R. Chari, "Secretary, Coal." Kumaramangalam was a recognizable type, and following his untimely death in a plane crash Mrs. Gandhi wrote: "He came from a wealthy, very conservative Brahmin family of Madras. While in Cambridge he fell for the 'idealism' of the Communist party . . . I took him into the Cabinet to clean up the mess that was our steel production. He did a marvellous job, but it was only just begun."[59]

When the nationalized Coal India Limited, or CIL, was formed in 1975, it was apparent as production stagnated that the company was failing for the most basic reasons: a shortage of explosives, problems with transportation, non-receipt of shovels and drills, thriving corruption. Its figures for "output per man shift" were way below those of other countries. Equipment would be bought at grossly inflated prices from a single supplier, without a tender. An MP asked in Parliament how it was that a large, highly mechanized conveyor belt had disappeared from the Churcha colliery, which operated for twenty hours a day: "If that belt can be stolen then anything under the sun can be stolen."[60] CIL's losses for 1978–9 came to $258m: this money, frittered away by just one state-run company in a single year, could have sponsored all the social welfare schemes (family and child welfare, women's welfare and welfare of the handicapped) and all the nutritional support schemes covered in India's entire Fifth Five Year Plan.[61]

By the 1980s, the company had almost 700,000 employees. One year, it reported a $12m profit when it had on closer inspection made a $65m loss.[62] In 1988, the co-creator of Coal India Limited, K. S. R. Chari, did an about-turn. He admitted that despite boosting production, the nationalized coal industry needed urgent and radical change. The coal had to keep on coming, because the nation required power. In a report he detailed the incompetence of the management, the fiddling of statistics, the manipulation of coal prices and interference by bureaucrats. Chari added that CIL's management, while far from blameless, was "a virtual prisoner in the hands of buccaneers, charlatans and mafias enjoying political clout." Law and order problems in the coalfields of what is now Jharkhand were so serious that "there can be no solution to them without political will."[63] India's coal industry combined the rigidity of a communist system with the latitude of a democracy—a fatal combination. In its very inflexibility at this time, the matrix was profoundly un-Indian.

During Rajiv Gandhi's premiership, an official board was formed to suggest "preventive, ameliorative, remedial and other measures" for the "timely detection" and potential recovery of sick industries.[64] A subsidiary of CIL was referred to the board when it reported a negative net worth of $55m and accumulated losses of $412m.[65] The total declared losses of Coal India Limited at the time of Rajiv Gandhi's assassination were around $1.4bn. In addition, it had overdue arrears to the government exceeding $1.2bn.[66] CIL remains the world's largest coal-mining company, and has been at times a source of corruption, with politicians from smaller political parties being given the coal ministry as a trade-off for backing the government.[67]

What would John Maynard Keynes have made of all this? We can be certain that such crazed deficit spending would have dismayed him no less than a global boom built on credit default swaps, with banks lending out the same money time after time and feeling safe because they had insured it with other banks. Keynes was not a Keynesian, at least not in the sense the word was used during the 1970s, as a term of abuse by economists frustrated with his nominal followers and the paralysed creations of P. C. Mahalanobis. At the core of Keynes's bisexual, liquid mind was an acceptance of risk and a belief that any rigid system would be likely to fail, whether in economic, political or personal philosophy.

6

A DISMAL PROSPECT

W HEN THE TREATY OF PARIS was signed in 1783, breaking British
power in the new United States and bringing the American Revolutionary War to a close, it took a little time for this information to reach
India. At Cuddalore, a humid port on the south-eastern coast, a desultory
battle continued between the French and British fleets until a messenger
arrived with news that the shooting could end. For centuries, Cuddalore
has been a place of interaction, a lush city, home to a wealth of Vaishnavite
temples and what may be the oldest mosque in southern India.

When C. K. Ranganathan was a child in Cuddalore in the 1970s, his prospects were poor. As a young chemistry graduate, he did not know what to
do with himself. Rejecting "the Hindu mythology about the family"—by
which he meant the idea that senior males should be deferred to, regardless
of their ability or character—Ranganathan refused to work in a subordinate
position to his elder brothers in the family business. The phrase "family
business" implies something substantial, but this was a part-time operation
started by his father, a mathematics teacher, to bring new goods to those
who could not afford them. His father had made sachets of shampoo and
sold them to people who could not manage to buy a whole bottle, along
with tiny packets of Epsom salts and talcum powder. When he started out,
he sealed the shampoo in lengths of rubber hose for his customers.

So here was the young Ranganathan in the early 1980s, burdened with what he remembered as "a terrific inferiority complex," because unlike his elder brothers he was educated in Tamil and knew barely a word of English. He lived in a single room in Cuddalore which tripled as his bedroom, office and kitchen, and also rented a unit for $6 per month in a nearby town, to which he bicycled each day. His hope was that he might raise chickens, but for chickens you needed space, and he had only $300 in savings. So he decided to compete with his brothers selling sachets of shampoo. Using his knowledge of chemistry, he mixed the components in the rickety unit to make sodium lauryl sulphate, the frothable basis of most shampoo, heated it to 70°C, cooled it to room temperature, adjusted the pH, added perfume, colour and viscosity, if required, and squirted the mixture into a PVC sleeving screen-printed with the logo of his new company, Chik, named for his now deceased father, Chinni Krishnan. (A south Indian's first name usually indicates the home village, the second the father's name and the third their own, although this can vary and polysyllabic names like Sivaramakrishna, which include different gods, are often abbreviated; the Tamil actor and singer Mayavaram Krishnamurthy Thyagaraja Bhagavathar was known as plain M.K.T.) Then Ranganathan climbed aboard a pedal-operated polythene seal welder, not unlike a giant exercise bicycle, which he had bought for a magnificent $70, and divided the sleeving into "pillow packs" of shampoo.

He trudged the streets, trying over the course of each long day to persuade shopkeepers and other retailers to take his new product. It was humiliating: they called him a "copycat"—a loanword that has passed from English to Tamil and other Indian languages (as in "copycat, copycat, copycat killed a rat!" an insult used gleefully by schoolchildren). His family were irate at what he was doing. Ranganathan saw he would have to do something different: he would need to move and innovate, constantly. He was persistent, and like many Indians he was instinctively versatile, adapting to each change in circumstance. His philosophy was that you must differentiate your product, or your product would perish. He did not learn this at business school—he learned it on the street. If a move failed, he moved on.

"At first," he said, "I thought that since ladies have long tresses, I will make a bigger sachet for them: 10 ml." Tresses—an old-fashioned word, probably important in the world of shampoo, perhaps left over from the British days like "stepney" for a spare car tyre. "It didn't sell. I tried using fuchsia, an expensive imported fragrance. I was losing money." Then Ranganathan realized the problem: when people asked for a sachet of shampoo in a Cuddalore shop, they usually used the brand name of his brothers' company, Velvette. But when they said, "Velvette," shopkeepers would produce whichever brand of copycat shampoo offered the highest margin.

Lacking the financial resources to undercut his rivals, Ranganathan understood he would need to do something original. In the early 1980s no banks would lend money to small businesses, and the best rate offered by the local Marwaris was 4.5 percent monthly interest. That rate assumed you had assets to set against a loan. So he tried to make people take notice by offering a free sachet of Chik if they returned five empty sachets of any shampoo, and combined this with a flyposting campaign. It worked, until the local shopkeepers offered schoolchildren "some small chocolate" if they picked up empty sachets from the riverbanks where women washed their hair. So now he declared it could only be empty sachets of Chik. Sales rose. "Every retailer started taking orders," he said.

Ranganathan had not been much of a success at school, but as the months passed by he found he had a genuine talent for business. He employed three casual workers, who buried the empty, redeemed shampoo sachets each day in gunny bags, and later sold the waste for reprocessing. His business spread across the southern state of Tamil Nadu: prominent film actors agreed to promote the brand and Chik sponsored the screening of movies featuring the regional superstar Rajnikanth.

By 1986, C. K. Ranganathan was manufacturing more than 20 million sachets of shampoo each year. Today, his company has an annual turnover of $140m and employs 1,000 people, making toiletries, cosmetics, cleaning products and food. He has a reputation in India as an innovator; he was the first person to put pickles in a sachet, something that had previously been thought impossible because they would leak. His products are promoted on regional radio and at big urban bus terminals, with free sachets of jasmine shampoo catching the wide-eyed visitors who are starting to move between the village and the city. His target is less the existing market than new customers: lower-middle-class families who might spend a few rupees here and there on items their parents would never have thought to buy. He has more than 20 percent of the Indian shampoo market and is known as the man behind the sachet revolution, bringing small quantities to people who cannot afford to buy more. When I mentioned the sachets of Chik to a radical journalist in Delhi, he had never heard of them; but his wife had: "Our maid uses them."

It would be simple to depict Ranganathan as the predatory capitalist who has turned villagers into consumers (his company now calls itself

CavinKare, with a possible echo of Calvin Klein), but the sachet revolution is a major feat of democratization. People who have previously been too poor to buy the products they see on billboards and movie screens can now sample the experience, and aspire to the pleasure of having shiny hair and softer skin, and washing with something other than rough country soap; at current prices, $1 buys you about a hundred of the smaller sachets of shampoo. Most CavinKare products are useful and cheap, although some such as Fairever, a cream designed to make you whiter, are unlikely to be of much benefit to anyone's health. It plays on the Indian obsession with skin tone, where every variation of colour is mentioned and compared, and matrimonial adverts specify shades ranging from very fair to fair to wheatish to not fair. CavinKare's Fairever, with its Kashmiri saffron and creamy milk, plays on a particular prejudice: Kashmiris are known for being fair while south Indians are usually darker; on the Fairever television advert, available on YouTube, a bride who is noticeably paler than her parents visits the house of her intended: regular applications of the cream must have worked.

Sitting in his office, bursting with energy and still struggling with his English, C. K. Ranganathan retained the intuitive, open-minded approach that got him going in business. It pleased him that his initial success came from breaking convention. His family were from a farming community, but their switch to selling was not especially unusual in Tamil Nadu, where strict caste barriers had been breaking down since the 1920s. Retail distribution, however, remained in the hands of the old merchant community, and the merchants set the rules for small manufacturers: forty-five days' credit, take it or leave it. Ranganathan tore up tradition by recruiting a new class of distributors. He described to me how he went about it: "First I got a man who hired out bicycles to help me, then I found some retired civil servants and small landlords who wanted to go into business. I called them to a big hotel, so they would think I was rich. They gave me a payment in cash and I gave them sachets of shampoo." He sprayed the boxes with perfume of rose and jasmine, to give the impression they contained something special. "Soon I had a distributor in every town in Tamil Nadu—perhaps 150 of them. I helped them to make a success. It was, you might say, the blind leading the blind. Even today, I don't extend credit."

The rise of Chik shampoo took place during the later days of the permit raj, so India's gradual economic liberalization in the early 1990s was a possible threat to Ranganathan. For example, during the 1980s, a company would be charged a numbing 120 percent excise duty if the annual turnover of the factory exceeded about $10,000. He dealt with this problem by paying others a good return if they opened small factory units to manufacture his products.

"After 1993 the law changed, and it was not important whether you had a big or a small factory. All the foreign cosmetic brands were coming to India. Our advantage had disappeared. It was a leadership challenge for me. I thought, we are here to stay. I hiked salaries by 50 percent, hired people from IIMA [the Indian Institute of Management in Ahmedabad, which has a high reputation] and designed new products. We advertised. Before shampoo, Indians used to take a bar of soap or shikakai, a traditional herb, to wash their hair. So we launched Nyle, a herbal shampoo range containing traditional ingredients like shikakai. It made us stand out against the new big brands. After three or four years, we came back with synthetics—and hair dye, fairness cream, lotions, deodorant. All the banks came knocking on my door, wanting to extend capital. They came to my own office. I could never have imagined that! Now, I can put a proposal to four banks and go with the one which offers the best rate. We have good machinery, we have automation, and importing quality materials is much easier than it used to be. We are starting to export to Singapore, Malaysia and the Gulf."[1]

Ranganathan was so excited to be talking about his early days in business that he let our meeting overrun, and through a glass door I could see members of the CavinKare board assembling for a conclave. In appearance, they were mainly south Indian men of middle age in drab slacks with pens lined up in the top pockets of their checked cotton shirts, looking modest and solemn. If India is the land of talented nerds, south India may be the source, the fountain.

They were known for their tendency to innovate and for their dedication to a project once it had started. Arunachalam Muruganantham, a college dropout from Coimbatore, a little further south, always had ambitions to do something different with his life. He was in his mid-thirties, the son of a handloom weaver, and frustrated by working as an assistant in a welding shop. One day he came home and had the sort of encounter that would be embarrassing in any culture but was particularly awkward in a conservative Tamil family. His wife was holding something. What was it? She refused to let him see. He insisted she show him. It was torn strips of old cloth that she was using as an improvised menstrual pad. Why did she not buy sanitary towels, he asked, shocked. Because, his wife told him, if all the women in our household bought sanitary towels, our milk budget would have to be cut by half. He had touched on a serious problem, which was that poorer women in India still relied on strips of cloth when they had their period. So Muruganantham set to work.

For four years, he dedicated himself to the invention of a low-cost sanitary towel. He bought new ones and pulled them apart. He experimented with the absorbency of pine wood pulp padding and cotton gauze. He made samples and distributed them for free, and collected the used pads to see how well they had worked. He researched methods for sterilizing the materials, the causes of cervical cancer and the risks from dioxin exposure. He built simple machinery to manufacture the pads, which used little electricity, and perfected the production. His family were humiliated by his obsession. His sisters avoided him; his mother even moved out of the family home. By 2008, Muruganantham had sold more than a hundred sanitary-towel manufacturing machines around the country, focusing on rural areas where women could buy and operate the equipment themselves, and start their own cooperative business. Each machine produced around 16,000 pads a month, and he was planning a new design.[2] Plans were now being made to roll out this low-cost project across the country.

Ten years before Sonia Maino went to the Lennox Cook School in Cambridge to do an English language course and met her future husband, Rajiv Gandhi, Manmohan Singh arrived in the town to study economics at the university. He was a diligent and teetotal Sikh student, somewhat withdrawn and polite, and he seemed to be interested in nothing but his academic work. Maybe this was because he had seen too much to want to have fun. His mother died when he was a baby, and he was brought up by his grandparents in a poor farming village in what is now Pakistan. His father, finding it hard to scratch a living from the land, had moved to Peshawar and became a munshi, or bookkeeper, for a businessman who imported dried fruits from Afghanistan. Aged eleven, Manmohan Singh went to live with his father and his new wife. During partition, he walked to school in Peshawar past dead bodies sprawled in the road. His grandfather, who had helped to raise him as a child, was murdered in the communal violence and the family home was burned down. At the age of fourteen, he escaped over the border to the new India with his father.

After spending some time in Haldwani in the Himalayan foothills, the family migrated to Amritsar. Manmohan Singh had three half-brothers and six half-sisters, and made it clear to his father that he hoped to study rather than to work with him in his retail business. At this desperate and dislocated time, he succeeded in winning a university place in Chandigarh and later gained a scholarship to study abroad. Singh said his interest in economics had stemmed from a puzzling question he read in a book when he was a child: why was India, a potentially rich country, full of poor people? After winning the Adam Smith Prize at Cambridge, which Keynes had won in 1909 for an essay on index numbers, he departed to do a D.Phil. at Oxford. Manmohan Singh was now accompanied by his wife, Gursharan Kaur, and their young daughter.[3] His chosen subject was the collapse of India's export market and its prospects for recovery.

In the second half of the nineteenth century, sometimes known as the First Age of Globalization, the Indian economy grew by 1–1.5 percent per annum, aided by the export of commodities like tea, jute and cotton.[4] It was during the period of recession following the First World War, when the population grew rapidly while per capita income dropped, that India gained a reputation as a desperately poor country. Nationalist campaigners like Nehru, appalled by the suffering they saw around them, took up an explanation first suggested by Dadabhai Naoroji, a Congress patriarch and mentor of Jinnah who had served as a Liberal Party MP in the UK Parliament, about why India was suffering from extreme poverty. Naoroji said it faced "the continually increasing, exhausting and weakening drain" of its resources by the colonial power. He was joining up different things here: debt servicing on infrastructure projects like canals and railways, money that was being made by European firms and spending on forced imperial services like the India Office. By 1947, London was in debt to New Delhi through the sterling balances, but in a newly independent nation this was less important than the sense that money would no longer be draining away to a foreign country. The benefits of the infrastructure supplied by the British could not be separated from the memory of their cultural presumption and racial contempt.

The new national leaders believed a policy of "laissez-faire and free trade" had been the root of the problem. They disliked the way that for nearly a century India had been importing large quantities of foreign manufactured goods rather than making them indigenously, and Nehru himself thought international trade was a "whirlpool of economic imperialism."[5] It was also an antagonistic response to the intrinsic Indian tendency towards capitalist activity. As the business strategist C. K. Prahalad said, on a typical street "virtually every individual is engaged in a business of some kind—whether it is selling single cloves of garlic, squeezing sugar cane juice for pennies a glass, or hauling TVs."[6] So India—a country with a tradition of trading dating back over thousands of years, an established financial network and a population of notoriously hardworking citizens—backed away from buying and selling in the world economy, preferring to try to become self-sufficient. Trade, the ancient and natural link between nations, was replaced with imposed, state-sponsored cultural interchange; Bharatanatyam dancers were sent to Uzbekistan, and Russian circuses arrived in Delhi. The economist Meghnad Desai suggested the "drain theory" expanded and developed into "a general theory of nationalist economic critique . . . The most blatant case of this thinking was in the case of Bangladesh, whose leaders argued when it was East Pakistan that it was being kept in poverty because of a drain to West Pakistan. Since independence, one has failed to locate this surplus."[7]

Writing a year before Nehru's death, Manmohan Singh began tentatively to suggest the policy on trade should be changed. His postgraduate thesis, which became a book, *India's Export Trends and the Prospects for Self-Sustained Growth*, was the first complete analysis of the causes of this problem. He argued that policymakers were acting as if "the stagnation of India's export earnings was an inescapable phenomenon," and that unless it changed, the country could not sustain itself "in the sense that the economy ought to be able to balance its foreign exchange budget without resorting to external aid."[8] What he meant, essentially, was that unless Indians gained money by selling things abroad, they would have no foreign currency with which to buy essential imports from other countries. Unless export earnings rose substantially by 1970, the predictions for self-sustained growth in the Third Five Year Plan would fail, and India would have to depend on begging from the Soviets or the Americans.

Much of his book was a meticulous, case-by-case study of the trade in jute, tea, textiles, oilseeds, minerals, tobacco and coffee. His worry was that these commodities were insufficient for growth, and that India should start manufacturing for export and sell things like iron, steel, chemicals and drugs. In the short term, it should boost bilateral trade with countries in the Soviet bloc. He was aware that the rapid disappearance of the sterling balances had left the nation in an impossible position, with a looming balance-of-payments problem. "The foreign exchange reserves of the country having been nearly exhausted the Indian economy now faces a dismal prospect: even a minor dip in export earnings or a shortfall in the expected amount of foreign aid can induce a magnified cut in industrial production and employment."[9] He had little sympathy for "responsible economists" who were claiming "that import substitution, whatever it meant, would by itself be able to solve India's balance of payments difficulties."[10] Singh was referring here to the popular idea that by making imitation goods across every sector, the difficulty would be cured. (It was this philosophy that meant TVS could not import bearings.) He suggested that export controls and import licences needed to be urgently reviewed—and looking at the list of regulations in his footnotes, it is not hard to see why: typewriter ribbons, pearl barley, biscuits, paper-lined hessian bags, cashews and hurricane lanterns had all had their import status specified by the civil servants of the permit raj, some of whom were making money out of these controls.

India's Export Trends, like most books, was widely ignored and has never been reprinted. Manmohan Singh went on to academic posts in Chandigarh and Delhi, combining teaching economics with assignments in the civil service, and in his fifties became governor of the Reserve Bank of India and later deputy chairman of the Planning Commission. He had a reputation for being reticent, modest and incorruptible. A stint in Geneva at the end of the 1980s confirmed his feeling that conditions in India needed to change urgently. His more dynamic contemporaries in academia saw him as a time-server, a perfect bureaucrat. One of them said: "He was a solid applied economist. None of us rated him very highly as an economist, I can tell you that—though he's a very nice man."[11] This was the brilliance of Manmohan Singh: he was never going to do the breathtaking research, or create a differential equation for pricing derivatives, or concoct a "Singh Model" of inputs and outputs. Rather, he took a simple idea and ran with it when he got the chance.

A series of disconnected events catapulted Manmohan Singh into history, enabling him to turn a calamity into an opportunity. At the end of 1989 the Berlin Wall came down, followed by the wobbling and ultimate collapse of the Soviet Union, which had long been one of India's main trading partners. In August 1990, Saddam Hussein invaded Kuwait and hundreds of thousands of Indian workers were displaced across the Gulf, leading to the loss of their remittances home. More significantly, the price of oil spiked and the cost of India's petroleum imports tripled, creating the prospect of a fatal balance-of- payments crisis. In 1991 Rajiv Gandhi was assassinated, and in the aftermath a Congress minority government was elected with Narasimha Rao as prime minister. India was close to bankruptcy.[12]

Since the economic disasters of the 1970s, much of the political class in India had wanted reform, although in public they had to utter the prevailing platitudes. In some cases the impetus for change came from their

fathers of our republic. We shall pay any price, bear any burden, make any sacrifice to realize those dreams. India is on the move again." Responding to the speech, the constitutional lawyer Nani Palkhivala said the budget marked "a new chapter in India's economic history. It was our ideological socialism which had been responsible for India remaining the twentieth poorest nation on earth . . . We must get rid of the illusion that we are still fighting the East India Company." Somnath Chatterjee of the CPI(M), or Communist Party of India (Marxist), was having none of it: the Congress government would "go down in history as the one which has mortgaged our country to the imperialist financial marauders for some tainted lucre"— Indians were now slaves to "those agencies whose imperialist and capitalist design so far as the Third World countries are concerned is very well known . . . Pandit Jawaharlal Nehru has been given an indecent burial."[19]

To be a technocrat is to wear an invisibility cloak. Despite his apolitical background (not being an elected Lok Sabha MP, he had to make do with the Rajya Sabha), Manmohan Singh was to emerge as a canny political operator. In 1998 he would negotiate an unlikely electoral alliance for Congress with the notoriously abrasive Kanshi Ram of the BSP.[20] His unassuming manner and ability to defuse tension, and above all his reputation for being "clean," enabled him to do things no other leader could have done. Together with Chidambaram in the commerce ministry, he reworked fiscal, economic and trade policy. When Congress MPs and even the prime minister, Rao, expressed doubt, he cleverly harnessed the legacy of the late, apotheosized Rajiv Gandhi, saying that reform was Rajivji's wish. It was true that economic reforms had been included in the election manifesto in 1991, but very doubtful Rajiv Gandhi would have implemented them on this scale.

At first government revenues fell, but the reforms delivered growth, a 5–7 percent annual GDP rate, growing to 7–9 percent during the following decade. As the market deregulated, carefully positioned businesses managed to make huge sums of money, with much of it evading the tax system. Government borrowing remained high, and inflation rose to unexpected levels. Singh's calculation was that although in the short term the benefits of growth were dangerously uneven, without them India would have no chance of raising the overall standard of living and be left in the position it had been in before, of redistributing poverty rather than redistributing wealth. Further reforms were needed but seemed politically impossible: the removal of unproductive subsidies in the power and agricultural sectors, a widening of the tax base, a culling of further unnecessary business regulation, a simplification of foreign direct investment and a change in the law on industrial disputes, which prevented large companies from making anyone redundant without government authorization.

Manmohan Singh's hopes in *India's Export Trends* for a boom in the export of goods and services took time. India's share of world exports grew, though slowly by comparison with China. New markets for textiles, jewellery, manufactured products, computer software and pharmaceuticals opened up, but it was not until his return to office in 2004, this time as prime minister, that trade really took off. Through the 1950s and 1960s, India's export earnings had hovered between $1bn and $2bn a year; by the time of the economic reforms of 1991 they stood at $18bn; a decade later they had reached $45bn, and a decade after that they were heading for $200bn.[21] In a Pew global-attitudes survey in 2009, 96 percent of Indians responded positively to the question: "What do you think about the growing trade and business ties between your country and other countries?"—the highest figure for any nation surveyed.[22] India could sell to the world, even if the progress was gradual.

When Manmohan Singh became prime minister at Sonia Gandhi's behest in 2004, his government's lack of a majority limited his opportunity to make further reforms. The communist parties on whom he depended for votes would not back further liberalization, while L. K. Advani of the BJP said he was in power but not in authority, a puppet of the Gandhi family. This was to misunderstand the quality of his relationship with Sonia Gandhi. She might not know an endogenous growth model from a fiscal

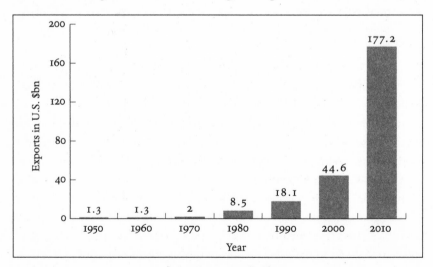

India's export trends, $bn

deficit, but she had strong intuition and accurate political instincts, keeping command of electoral manoeuvring while he got on with being prime minister, with Chidambaram as his reliable finance minister and Montek Singh Ahluwalia, a Sikh economist who had previously worked at the World Bank, running the Planning Commission.

It was a careful, understated two-step, with Mrs. Gandhi always calling on the prime minister rather than the other way round, a reverse of the symbolic arrangement by which Congress leaders were required to pay obeisance at her residence, 10 Janpath. His style did not change when he took the premiership—to the consternation of officials, he continued to go home for lunch with his wife each day—but he moved rapidly to encourage growth and push forward infrastructure and rural development projects.

Spotting the global economic crisis some way off, Manmohan Singh raised spending in advance of a dip in an attempt to boost the economy during 2008–9. Working with the Reserve Bank of India, he made sure the Indian banking system was not exposed compared to that of other countries where banks were less strictly capitalized and regulated—a residual benefit of the controlled economy. His thinking on the stimulus was explicitly Keynesian, spending in advance to avoid greater calamity. Sanjaya Baru, his media adviser, recalled a flight to Mumbai with the prime minister in 2006, when he presented him with a draft speech. Singh glanced through it and wrote an extra paragraph: "If the rich had spent their new wealth on their own enjoyments, the world would long ago have found such a regime intolerable. But like bees they saved and accumulated, not less to the advantage of the whole community . . . the capitalist classes were allowed to call the best part of the cake theirs and were theoretically free to consume it, on the tacit underlying condition that they consumed very little of it in practice. The duty of 'saving' became nine-tenths of virtue and the growth of the cake the object of true religion." This was a quote from Keynes's *The Economic Consequences of the Peace,* perfectly remembered.[23]

Manmohan Singh preferred saving to consumption, and in the years after his 1991 reforms, India's private savings had indeed grown along East Asian rather than American lines, with money stored for the future. At the close of 2009, the Reserve Bank of India bought 200 metric tonnes of gold from the IMF to diversify its assets. One financial analyst described this as "the biggest single central bank purchase that we know about for at least 30 years."[24] Like the Chinese, the Indians did not want to rely only on U.S. dollars or U.S. Treasury bonds at a time of economic flux. It was a dramatic turnaround from the anxious days of 1991, when gold bars had been sent from Bombay to Switzerland in a desperate move to raise $600m. India's foreign exchange reserves were now approaching $300bn.

Politics in India tends to be seen only in close focus. An outsider watching a television debate, with its cheerful shouting, cross-talking, references to "the creamy layer" (privileged people from minority communities who benefit from affirmative action) and frequent acronyms, might be left unaware what subject is under discussion. Indian politicians love intrigue and detail, and like to turn debates about policy into philosophical discussions, but they tend to avoid drawing back from the close focus to look at the wider picture. This is a problem around the world, but in India it can be acute. Like Nehru, Manmohan Singh had the ability to take a long view, and in 2005 he pursued a contentious nuclear deal with the United States, realizing it offered India an extraordinary and possibly unique opportunity. With Sonia Gandhi's backing, he risked bringing down his government.

During the Cold War, U.S.–India relations had been tense, with the CIA running agents inside ministries in New Delhi to counter extensive Soviet infiltration, and Indian politicians busily attacking American hegemony.[25] In 2000, Bill Clinton became the first U.S. president in more than twenty years to visit India. Except for a few minor politicians who engaged in a public fast at the Constitution Club, drinking only water and fruit juice while Uncle Sam was on Indian soil, the visit was a surprising popular and political success, with Clinton taking the chance to join in with a group of iridescent dancing women in Rajasthan.

Five years later, President George W. Bush offered to accept India as a nuclear weapons state and to share technology, all without India signing the Nuclear Non-Proliferation Treaty. This move was a rare example of a neoconservative dream becoming a reality. The U.S. ambassador, Robert Blackwill, had arrived in New Delhi shortly before 9/11 with little prior knowledge of the country and deduced that, as a large, diverse and vibrant functioning democracy, India would be the perfect ally for the United States in the twenty-first century, especially since Pakistan was no longer stable. He convinced Bush there should be a strategic shift, and that by building up India against China, Asia would not in the future be dominated by any single power. Both the U.S. Congress and Indian political leaders had understandable doubts about the proposal.

In a parliamentary debate in 2008 that was disrupted by MPs waving wads of cash which they claimed had been given to them to abstain from voting on a confidence motion, Manmohan Singh explained his belief that India needed energy security, and slapped down the opposition BJP for their cynical refusal to back the deal, despite having done much to engineer a rapprochement with America when they were in government. Standing before Parliament, with his calm voice, trained white beard and pale blue turban, Singh told the MPs: "The nuclear agreement that we wish to negotiate will end India's nuclear isolation, nuclear apartheid and enable us to take advantage of international trade in nuclear materials, technologies and equipment . . . Every day that I have been Prime Minister of India I have tried to remember that the first ten years of my life were spent in a village with no drinking water supply, no electricity, no hospital, no roads and nothing that we today associate with modern living. I had to walk miles to school, I had to study in the dim light of a kerosene oil lamp . . . my conscience is clear that on every day that I have occupied this high office, I have tried to fulfil the dream of that young boy from that distant village."[26]

Through all these reforms, it was not hard to find people who condemned Manmohan Singh and his works. He was, one commentator said, "the harbinger of the neoliberal economic policies of liberalization-privatization-globalization" that made India "the junior military ally of the U.S. and Israel" and "demolished the image of India as the peace-loving, sovereign supporter of the people of the Third World, and made it the target of Islamic fundamentalists."[27] The benefits of the system Singh developed were questioned, especially after the global credit crisis of 2008, as if the meltdown was evidence that capitalism was a flawed operating system. If things had gone so wrong, how could economic liberalization be good for India? Surely it would be better to return to a command economy? In the words of the leader of the Communist Party of India (Marxist), Prakash Karat: "We, communists, have had no illusions about the nature of globalized finance capital and imperialist globalization. We have doggedly fought the neoliberal policies being imposed in India . . . We should continue the fight against the military collaboration agreement with the United States."[28]

Was the global financial crisis caused by capitalism? In the U.S., a poor person would be offered a loan to buy a house. Sometimes the loan would come to more than the cost of the property. If the value of the house rose and the person paid the mortgage, all might be well. Some of these mortgages—debts—were rolled up into bonds. By 2005, $507bn of high-risk, subprime loans had been repackaged as mortgage bonds.[29] Spinning around inside the global financial system were securities worth more than $500bn which were in fact questionable loans, loans made to part-time maids in Indiana and air-conditioning-unit maintenance men in Florida. The bonds were sliced up, depending on how likely the mortgages were to be repaid, and the weaker tranche repackaged and given a new credit rating and sold on to investors. Once U.S. property prices flattened, the house of cards fell and the effects cascaded around the world. The crisis had many causes—greed and incompetence, the collusion of credit rating agencies, America's failure to control the high-risk lending of its banks, financial instruments few people even in the institutions themselves understood—but at root it was an enormous pyramid scheme, not capitalism exactly. The problem was human nature: if people are encouraged to cheat, they will. India, with its more strictly regulated banks and its deep tradition of saving, was to an extent protected from the worst effects of the global credit crunch. *

Socialism, or the principle of equality, did not come naturally to the subcontinent. In a society with a system of gradation in the form of caste which extended across communities and to every aspect of life, it would have been impossible for any ruler to expect uniformity, even if the ruler had been a great deal more coercive than Jawaharlal Nehru or Indira Gandhi. Nor did Indians have any hesitation or embarrassment about wanting money, even if they were abstemious and interested only in saving. There was no suggestion it was easier for a camel to pass through the eye of a needle than for a rich man to enter the kingdom of heaven; materialism and religion were united. For Hindus, the worship of the goddess of wealth and prosperity, Lakshmi, was assumed, and in some cases emulated by other religions. At the festival of Diwali, you seek the blessings of Lakshmi, and at any Hindu temple it is usual to see gods and banknotes intermixed.

When I visited India for the first time, in 1986 as a teenage student, hoping to see the world, I brought with me a selection of electronic goods to sell. I had been told this would be a good way to fund the trip, so I left China through Hong Kong and stocked up on calculators, digital watches, digital games and even a few bottles of branded whisky—the sort of things that were difficult to obtain in India at that time. Bringing them into the country turned out to be straightforward, since the customs officers at the sparse airport were all off duty that night, and on the streets of Delhi these rare goods were snapped up with no trouble, with taxi and rickshaw drivers being the conduit to the Punjabi dealers in such low-level foreign desirables. In those grey, Soviet-style days, everyone wanted shiny goods from overseas and enjoyed the idea of something new which said: "Made in Hong Kong" or "Made in Taiwan."

Apart from the government stores selling handicrafts and finely made hand-woven cotton items, little was available to buy except on the semi-legal street stalls. Bookshops offered cheaply priced Russian novels translated into English, which seemed to have quite a following. I was able, by braving the touts in underground shops on the fringes of Connaught Place (looking back, it seems strange that I risked being robbed for a few thousand extra rupees), to secure a dollar exchange rate about 20 percent higher than the official rate, since the rupee was not a freely convertible currency.

I had travelled previously in Poland, where the communist system left the shops even emptier, but the surprise in India was that nobody appeared cowed by the system. Rather, they worked around it, using ingenuity to manipulate regulations. The restrictions of the state seemed if anything to make people more entrepreneurial and self-reliant, so that the permit raj was like a stagnant obstacle rather than a threat. The tendency in India was to call the choked bureaucracy a legacy of the colonial period, but British form-filling was less pervasive and the state's direct interference in business was lighter before independence. This seemed more of an indigenous development, something that had evolved in the way that further sites of devotion spring up around an existing shrine. The economist Kaushik Basu suggested in 1992 that the market economy in India worked in the wrong way, since:

> its freedom is in the wrong domains. In some parts of India you can buy university degrees; in most parts of India you can bribe to get a driving licence and you can buy your way out if caught for a traffic offence. In these domains our problem is that of excessive marketization: there is a price at which everything can be had.[30]

Many of the regulations—for example, the law requiring a bureaucrat's permission to sack people if you had more than fifty employees—would have been positive in intent, but in their implementation they became a source of corrupt money and did more to protect poverty than to protect the poor.[31] The restrictions on choice were in some ways attractive, with the ban on Coke and Pepsi creating odd local fizzy drinks like Campa Cola, Limca and Thums Up, with its missing "b." The system looked stuck; in the pre-reform era, politicians took pleasure in making it impossible for foreign corporations to do business in India. A senior Western ambassador in New Delhi told me he was informed by an official from the Ministry of External

Affairs in the course of a difficult negotiation during the 1980s: "All foreigners are basically spies."[32]

Indians did things their way, and outsiders had to adjust. Even in more recent times, when a minister kept nearly a hundred international delegates waiting for more than three hours, including assorted high commissioners and ambassadors, he saw no need to apologize: "Slowly, they will also get used to living like this in India."[33] A vigorous opponent of this national tendency was P. Chidambaram, who in 2009 outraged the officials in the home ministry by introducing fingerprint scans to ensure everyone reached their office by 9 a.m. and only left at 5:30 p.m. Bureaucrats at "the joint secretary level and above" had mistakenly assumed these new regulations would not apply to them.[34]

In the era before liberalization, India was known around the world for its poverty and its mysticism. Comprehending the country was a specialist interest, rather than a necessity, as it is today. It could be a playground for foreign visitors, a place where backpackers might pretend to be hippies or sadhus for months at a time and survive on a few dollars a day in Pushkar or Goa, and still feel superior to the general dereliction. The unspoken assumption behind the Western view of India at this time—all disease, dirt and deities, stemming from Mohandas Gandhi's exaltation of village poverty and the romantic attitude taken by anti-colonial writers like E. M. Forster—was that it would always be like this: India was exotic, eternal, to be admired and patronized, but incapable of helping itself. It needed the pump-priming charity of outsiders and was certainly not a competitor, not a country that might take off and revitalize itself. Had Bob Geldof been less busy organizing Live Aid, he would perhaps have gone there to plead for an urgent increase in foreign aid.

Yet at the very time that Westerners were travelling to India in search of suffering and spirituality, and writing replica accounts of it, a more interesting shift was taking place. Indians, and in particular those who came from extended business families, were migrating to North America and Western Europe in search of modern opportunities. They moved into a range of businesses: import-export, shopkeeping, automobile parts, fuel dealerships, steel, catering, jewellery, construction, computers, hotels, motels and potels. (A potel is a motel run by someone from the Gujarati community of Patels; Indians now control around half of all U.S. lodging properties, and the officers of the Asian American Hotel Owners Association are Hemant D. "Henry" Patel, Tarun S. Patel, Chandrakant I. "C.K." Patel, Ashwin

"Ash" Patel, Alkesh R. "Al" Patel and Fred Schwartz.)[35] Across the cities of America and Europe, neatly dressed professionals from the subcontinent can be spotted playing their part in a global success story, shifting formally and securely back and forth between cultures. With its annual output of dedicated software, medicine and engineering graduates, India was seen as the natural home for any business process that could be outsourced. Yet through all this, poverty and affluence have grown side by side, and many foreigners still find it nearly impossible to work out how to do business in India.

I visited Andhra Pradesh in 2002. On the day I reached the capital, Hyderabad, known optimistically by local software enthusiasts as Cyberabad, twenty men and women dressed in the olive-green jungle uniform of the banned People's War Group attacked the railway station at Chalana, about a hundred miles to the north. After herding the railway employees and their families into a hut, they disconnected all telephone lines, blew up the station buildings and the signals box and exploded an improvised mine under a stationary locomotive, causing several of its carriages to run down a hill into an advancing goods train. Then, in a scenario worthy of Monty Python, they lectured the assembled railway workers for an hour on the evils of the capitalist system and wrote revolutionary slogans in the stationmaster's register before melting away into the forest.

Chandrababu Naidu of the TDP was chief minister of Andhra Pradesh at the time, doing his best to draw foreign investment and build infrastructure. Bill Clinton and Tony Blair had both recently been to see him, and one of his aides told me about a remote monitoring project he had established for the restoration of a temple complex at Tirumala: each evening, an engineer on the site had to make a video of the work and email clips to the chief minister in Hyderabad, and as a result the project was completed at a fraction of the expected time and cost. Naidu seemed the very model of a CEO chief minister. I asked him how he coped with the People's War Group, who had tried to kill him on several occasions. "The days of revolution are over," he said. "Now people want employment, they want their land to be developed and to have proper electricity and water supplies."

He had sent a paramilitary police unit, the Greyhounds, in pursuit of the Maoists, but believed a purely military victory over them was unrealistic. "How can you win a war against terrorism?" he asked rhetorically. "They only need three or four people to put a mine in the road and explode it, and the problem is there." The People's War Group targeted infrastructure like railway tracks and representatives of the state.

Revolutionary violence had intermittently raised its head in independent India. In 1967 an improvised army of tea plantation workers and landless peasants revolted against their landlords at Naxalbari in West Bengal. The rebellion was the start of a protracted phase of violent unrest, and the Naxalite or Maoist movement became a significant threat. China was then at the height of the Cultural Revolution, and Beijing applauded it as "the front paw of the revolutionary armed struggle," which would "start a prairie fire and set the vast expanses of India ablaze." Insurgency became popular among poor people in some rural areas, urged on by intellectuals and a generation of Indian university students, who in turn were encouraged both by the romance of Chairman Mao and the évènements in Paris and elsewhere. A Maoist political party was formed, which soon splintered into factions, one of which was the People's War Group. The revolutionaries turned against the "class enemies" of Nehruvian India; even poor Mahatma Gandhi was charged with "devoted service to imperialism, feudalism and the comprador bourgeoisie."

In Andhra Pradesh in the early 1970s the People's War Group gained control of 15,000 square kilometres of land, aided by social hatreds and resentments dating back to the days of the Nizam of Hyderabad, who had ruled before independence. The reclusive Nizam was an exceedingly rich Muslim (he used a diamond the size of a gull's egg as a paperweight) but most of his subjects were Hindus who lived in extreme poverty. His feudal political approach formed the backdrop to the present unrest in Andhra. In the 1970s the Maoists had forcibly redistributed large amounts of land, with some popular support. In areas such as Warangal they ran what was effectively a parallel government, holding "people's courts" and collecting "taxes" from businesses and forest contractors. In the 1980s their popularity faded, but now appeared to be growing again. They were the only armed movement in India that was not perceived as secessionist; they did not look different, or follow a minority religion. Although the Maoists were widely condemned, they had tapped into an anger felt by many against the Indian state, and the sense that the fruits of economic liberalization were bypassing swathes of central and eastern India.

In 2004 the People's War Group merged with other Naxalite outfits to form the Communist Party of India (Maoist), causing distress to comrades in the Communist Party of India (Marxist), who thought it sneaky to take out their "rx" and replace it with an "o." The Maoists continued to target the Marxists, viewing them as traitors to the left because they took part in government. Their leader was Ganapathy, alias Ramana, alias Srinivas, alias Dayanand, alias Chandrashekhar, alias Mallamma, alias Rajamma, alias Balreddy, alias Radhakishen, alias Shekhar—his name changed according to where he was. Aficionados knew him as plain "G.S.," because he was general secretary of the Central Committee of the Communist Party of India (Maoist). All these names sounded more glamorous than the one his parents gave him: Muppala Laxman Rao.

One of the few outsiders to have met Muppala Laxman Rao was K. Srinivas Reddy, a journalist from Hyderabad, who was summoned for a jungle interview in 1998. He told me how he was taken on a long and remote trek, escorted by relays of shadowy armed guards, in search of Ganapathy. Reaching a clearing in the forest, he saw a large mounted machine-gun pointing down at him from a tree. A military parade began, and the leader of the Maoists greeted the reporter with a clenched fist and a shout of "Lal salaam!"—"Red salute!" "I thought that I had better do the same back to him," said Reddy, "which felt kind of strange. Ganapathy is a straightforward, open sort of guy, with grey hair and spectacles. He's medium height, lean build, medium complexion—not too fair, not too black. He speaks frankly about politics and tactics and his hero, Che Guevara, and often refers to Mao and the Long March—and to Sun Tzu's 2,500-year-old *Art of War*, which is like his handbook. He spends a lot of time on political education. Of course, he's been underground for decades now, so he's out of touch with what's going on in the rest of the world."

Why had he devoted his life to overthrowing the state? "He was attracted by what was going on in Bengal, by the Naxalite movement. Perhaps he saw certain failures of democracy, the exploitation of landlords, and was motivated to do something."[36]

More than a decade passed before Ganapathy gave a second interview. This time, aided by the Internet, he had a more up-to-date grasp of events elsewhere in the world. His main aim was to continue fighting, only by stealth, never in the open, never at the ballot box: "The real terrorists and biggest threats to the country's security are none other than Manmohan Singh [and] other ruling class leaders and feudal forces who terrorise the people on a daily basis," he told the journalist Rahul Pandita. This was the consequence of "pressure exerted by the comprador bureaucratic bourgeoisie and the imperialists, particularly U.S. imperialists, who want to plunder the resources of our country without any hindrance." He was not a fan of President Barack Obama: "The hands of this new killer-in-chief of the pack of imperialist wolves are already stained with the blood of hundreds of women and children . . . bail-outs for the tiny corporate elite and attacks on democratic and human rights of U.S. citizens continue without any change." Although he disapproved of al-Qaeda's "social outlook," Ganapathy thought Islamist extremists were motivated by the "bullying, exploitation and suppression" of imperialist wolves. Nor was he complimentary about his comrades who questioned the party, and was plain bitchy about one leader who had turned his back on Maoism: "Papi Reddy surrendered due to his loss of political conviction and his petty-bourgeois false prestige and ego."[37]

Rahul Pandita had done something unusual: he had studied the movement at ground level for more than a decade, growing ever more interested in the way it functioned, travelling through the remoter jungles of central India for weeks on end and spending time with the tribal people. He was himself a Kashmiri Hindu who had been driven out of his home at the age of fourteen by Muslim separatists, at the start of the insurgency in 1990. "When I met Ganapathy, he asked me where I was from. I told him Kashmir, and he said they were pro the secessionist movement but saw fundamentalists as 'obscurantist.' I talked about my own exile. He was surprised. He thought the Indian government had expelled us. They have a lot of romantic ideas about secessionist movements. I've met other top Maoist commanders and they will speak about Amitabh Bachchan, Stalingrad, Sachin Tendulkar, local cultural traditions—it's as if you're having a couple of sundowners at the club with an Oxford professor—but when they talk about politics their whole face and demeanour changes. Their eyes become opiated. When a policeman was beheaded in Jharkhand, one said to me, quoting Mao: 'Revolution is not a dinner party. You're talking about one beheading. In the French Revolution, they had to invent the guillotine to cut off heads.'"[38]

Later I asked Pandita about his own exile, another war. He wrote to me in an email: "I left Kashmir on April 4, 1990, along with my family, leaving everything behind. We could not take anything with us except my parents' educational degrees and some of my mother's jewellery. Life was very tough initially and we had to sleep on newspaper sheets for days altogether. Life had become very difficult in Kashmir. One of my father's friends was waylaid by terrorists, shot in his knees and then they sprayed pee on him, and after torture, he was shot dead. A woman, a nurse, was kidnapped, gang-raped for days and then cut alive on a mechanical wood-cutting machine. On the roads, people from the majority community would jeer at us, saying, 'Go away, this is Pakistan.' We had become the Tutsis of Kashmir." Another exile, another war.

The dense jungles of India where the Naxalites function are also home to various aboriginal Scheduled Tribes. In many cases, Adivasi or tribal life was a response to a particular geography: communities such as those in the foothills of the Himalayas simply could not survive if required to live more conventionally. Part of the complication was that the term "tribal" covered everybody from Angmo, a businesswoman who ran a successful trekking agency up in Leh, to Agatha Sangma, the young hereditary MP from Meghalaya. Scheduled Tribes ranged from the Asur people of Jharkhand and West Bengal, a small tribe who worship spirits and smelt iron, to the Kattunayakan from Kerala and Tamil Nadu who collect forest produce like wild pigs and honey, and the Gonds of central India, a tribe several million strong with a recorded history going back more than a thousand years. Since 1947, with a policy run from New Delhi and the state capitals, the covenant between the remote regions and the government has broken down. When large mines, dams and factories were built, the rehabilitation or resettlement was usually nominal. Tribal peoples were often given colonial treatment, as if they were somehow separate from the rest of India, despite usually being the Indians who were Indian before the rest arrived.

This problem was at its worst in the north-east, in the pocket of states bordering Burma, China, Tibet and Bhutan, which were linked to the rest of India only by a narrow corridor or "chicken's neck" between Bangladesh and Nepal. The Constitution made a distinction between the tribal peoples of this region and those in other parts of India, but since independence this had rarely been observed. There was little sign of any policy except containment of separatist activity by the military when it occurred, and reliance on a handful of local ruling politicians. The north-east had several hundred tribal groups, and although a Karbi from Assam and an Ao from Nagaland might have little in common, they were perceived by the public as being the same: "Chinkies." The region was sparsely populated, and with only twenty-five MPs it was difficult to exert political influence in New Delhi.[39] Nearly all its funding came from the centre, and much of this money ended up in the pockets of bureaucrats and separatist extortionists. Little effort had been made to develop a more creative policy of administration, which recognized the links between remote regions and sources of power outside India: in 1965, the tracks of the Bengal–Assam railway that linked the Assamese city of Guwahati to Dhaka (now the capital of Bangladesh) were torn up.[40] A Khasi from Meghalaya told me he believed that all insurgency in his state would stop if the Indian army returned the land they had appropriated for their various operations and military bases.[41]

Millions of people whose ancestors were from Nepal found they were perceived as outsiders in India. Munish Tamang was a lecturer at Delhi University who wished to be perceived as a loyal citizen, but found it hard when many other Indians made assumptions based on his physical appearance. "Most of us came to India in the nineteenth century, to help with the tea cultivation," he said. "My parents were part of the Indian National Congress and contributed to the freedom struggle. When my daughter's friends saw me for the first time, they asked her: 'Is your dad a Chinese or a Japanese?' There was a Gorkha signatory to the Constitution of India. It was only in 1992 that Nepali became an official language in India. If you look at Bollywood films, we are shown only as guards, watchmen or 'road Romeos' who look at girls. Or we're presented as fighters—brave, loyal Calibans." Tamang's organization, the Bharatiya Gorkha Parisangh, campaigned for a Gorkha state within India. "We want a Gorkha state as a mark of our identity, just as the Nagas can say they are from Nagaland. Back in 1907, the Hill Men's Association was demanding that Darjeeling should not be part of Bengal, but should have a separate Gorkha administration. So we want to be more integrated: it's separation for integration."[42]

No resolution was apparent in the clash between modernization and the needs of India's many minorities. The government's wish to integrate or assimilate Scheduled Tribes was in many cases impractical, and the country had neither the spare land nor the social temperament to set up reservations for protected forest-dwelling tribes. Many Adivasis themselves liked to journey back and forth between modern and traditional life, yet tribal living was sometimes impossible under present conditions; moving from place to place or hunting and gathering from the forest had in practice been criminalized in parts of India. Rahul Pandita told me he had been to villages where the last time a government block development officer had visited was in 1967.

"You go to the huts and there is nothing. They have a lot of malnutrition. The Adivasis take the liquid of the mahua flower, which turns into alcohol. You can see women and children drunk. People from the outside look down on them for this, but the reason they drink is because they need the calories. They get mistreated by forest officers, who take their goats and their chickens and try to take their wives too. In the old days the Adivasis could get a monkey or snake from the forest and drink water from a river. Now they find—because of all the mining and industrial processing—that the water is contaminated with fluoride and arsenic. The Maoists have set up schools in some places which have a mix of education and propaganda. They even show BBC science programmes. If you ask the Adivasis who they support, they say, 'The police come here and beat us. The Maoists come and demand food, and then go on their way.' You could call them sympathizers."[43]

I went to Warangal and other destabilized parts of the Andhra region to meet the Maoists. The first was Gaddar (his name meant "revolution"—he was born Gummadi Vittal Rao), a bank clerk turned balladeer who could draw hundreds of thousands of people to his concerts. He was a legend among leftists, the founder of an organization that had spread revolution via cultural performances in the 1970s. Gaddar sang some of his songs to me, heartily, in Telugu, but was interested mainly in repeating slogans. At one point he even broke off our conversation to do a telephone interview with a foreign radio station:

"If you slap me once, I'll slap you four times."

"If I sow a seed, it has to break the earth in order to grow."

"Coca-Cola is killing us every day."

In 1997, Gaddar took six bullets to the chest, in what he believes was a contract assassination attempt by off-duty policemen, but survived. Without prompting, he removed his shirt to show me the gruesome scars.

The second revolutionary was Madhu, a squat and stunted man with a look of terror on his face, who looked as if he had been physically destroyed by a life of poor nourishment in the jungle. We met in a decrepit room, with lookouts all around, where flocks of mosquitoes bit us. Madhu had fever and the scars of old wounds on his legs. He told me he had joined the Maoists after being beaten by his landlord for not working properly. Again, he spoke mainly in slogans. When I asked him why he followed Maoism when it had been abandoned long ago in its country of origin, he said that I was following revisionist propaganda and added: "Revolution is a duty. We are not following Mao. We are following Maoism-Marxism-Leninism. Officially, we are following the mass line given to the Chinese Communist Party plenary in 1969 by Lin Biao, who said revolutionary groups in oppressed nations should not take part in elections or trades unions, but should follow the armed struggle."

This was quite a claim: Lin Biao was a paranoid wreck of a man, a military commander who had been promoted as Mao's loyal servant and possible successor, and had been so mentally disturbed by the inversions in China that he had to be injected with tranquillizers before appearing in public. Lin Biao was discredited even among old-fashioned communists. This was a central aspect of the problem with India's Maoists: they relied on dead mantras. The initiator of the Naxalite movement back in the 1960s, Charu Majumdar, had believed above all in bloodshed as a route to purity, the theory that if you annihilated the correct landlords and moneylenders (though in these backward areas, the landlords were themselves often not far from poverty) ancient social ills would disappear.

The third revolutionary was a more unlikely figure, though more representative than either of the others. Suneetha Kukka was a "surrendered" militant, meaning she had given herself up in exchange for the bounty that was on her own head—Rs20,000, or about $430—and agreed to abandon Maoism. Slim in her best pink sari, she said she was only twelve when she ran away from home to join the militants. A gang of revolutionaries had come to her village and made vigorous speeches against injustice, social evils and the oppression of women. For Suneetha, whose parents were landless labourers who had worked for a lifetime in return for less than a dollar a day, it seemed like a reasonable message. She had never been to school, and was one of eight children; the prospect of a career as a coolie was less appealing than joining a war. Suneetha had been attracted by the singing of the People's War Group. The more Maoists I met, the more I heard about how they had been motivated and inspired by the local literature, poetry and songs of "resistance."

"I loved the revolutionary songs. My favourite ones were 'Land to the Tiller,' 'Red Flag,' 'Oh, Brave Lady' and 'Down with the Boorjuva.'" Suneetha was speaking in a rural Telugu dialect, and I asked the interpreter what "boorjuva" meant: it was an appropriation of "bourgeois." She continued: "After I had been living in the forest for about one year and had done my basic ideological education, I was given a revolver. Since they thought I had a military temperament, I was told to join a Special Action Team. Then I was given a Sten gun. I was the only woman in the team. Our job was to target local politicians and MPs."

At the age of sixteen, Suneetha became second-in-command of a unit of seven trained killers. Their principal weapon was the home-made land mine, or IED, a devastating device they had learned about from the Tamil Tigers, the rebel group which assassinated Rajiv Gandhi. Sympathetic local coalminers sold them blasting gelatin, which they used to make bombs.

"We would take a bucket and put in about five kilograms of gelatin," she explained, demonstrating with her hands like a children's television pre-senter, "and fill it with metal nuts, bolts and nails, and put a polythene cover over the top to make sure nothing got wet. At night, we would bury the device in the road and run wires to a hideout, and connect a camera flash-gun to the wires. We would set up a three-point alignment, usually by tying a strip of cloth to the branch of a tree." What was a three-point alignment? "We needed an exact alignment between the landmine, the strip of cloth and the hideout—like the sights on a gun—or there was a risk we would detonate at the wrong moment. Then we sat and waited, maybe for days, until our target drove past."

Suneetha told me all this in a matter-of-fact way. She was nineteen now but did not look much older than the schoolgirls with ribbons and satchels I had passed on the way to the police camp in Warangal where we met. She left the revolution because she was ill and being molested by a fellow mili-tant, and felt the Maoists were not achieving very much. Using her uncle as an intermediary, she let a local policeman know of her intention. He brought her before Warangal's feared superintendent of police, 33-year-old Nalin Prabhat, who accepted her surrender.

In a damaged, brutalized place where the forces of the state had retreated and lawmakers were afraid to visit their own constituencies, the police held great prestige and power. On the way to see Suneetha I had passed Hanamkonda police station, which had been blown up using directional mines hidden in gunny bags. A lone wall was all that remained, attached to the blackened metal frame of the building and shaded by a lacerated tree. In revenge the police had rounded up suspected local militants. Early one morning, four of them were taken to hills on the edge of the town and shot dead in what police referred to euphemistically as an "encounter." Later that day, the police chief told a press conference they were "cowardly and dastardly criminals."

Nalin Prabhat was trim and friendly, with high, Himalayan cheekbones and cropped hair, sitting to attention behind his desk, in khaki shirt-sleeves. He was a fan of the thriller writer Jack Higgins, and seemed to revel in his position. Prabhat had been promoted fast, and now he held the power of life and death in his hands. For several years he had faced assassination, after being officially labelled "a threat to the party" by the local Maoists. "There's no use in worrying about it. These days most of them are riff-raffs, uneducated people. One of their leaders said recently that our chief min-ister, Mr. Naidu, was using a 'low-intensity conflict strategy' given to him by the World Bank. That's how much they know. They think it's romantic to be a revolutionary. For the women, it means they no longer get treated like a sexual commodity. If you go into a village with a gun, even the rich landlords have to kiss your feet.

"I know we're winning. Five years ago there were 3,500 active terrorists here and now there are just over 2,000. We have a generous surrender programme, and the ones who don't want to surrender will be surgically excised, like unhealthy tissue. I sleep easily at night. I sleep easily because I don't doubt that any of the people we have killed are guilty. I say prayers every morning. The human rightists don't realize we are dealing with beasts. I have a colleague, a signals man, who was recently blown up in his vehicle by an IED. His wife was with him, and they left two children, aged five and six. Does anyone ask about their human rights, about the human rights of those children?"

Nalin Prabhat was exuding a cold anger, the anger of a man under extreme, constant pressure.

"I tell you, the Maoists should give up. What good is it in today's world to continue?

> The old order changeth, yielding place to new,
> And God fulfils Himself in many ways,
> Lest one good custom should corrupt the world.

"It's from Tennyson's *Morte d'Arthur*. I quote it to the terrorists when they surrender."[44]

I left Andhra in 2002 feeling the Maoist insurgency was in decline. It would not disappear—as Chandrababu Naidu said, you only needed to bury a mine in a road once in a while to keep it going—but I felt the combination of vicious policing, the surrender programme and a redundant ideology would diminish the movement. Instead, the opposite happened: the CPI (Maoist), in its various incarnations, opened a "red corridor" through Dandakaranya, a forested expanse stretching up from Andhra Pradesh through parts of Maharashtra, Chhattisgarh, Jharkhand and Orissa. In 2006 revolutionaries in Nepal overthrew the monarchy, emboldening their Indian neighbours. By 2010, Maoist guerrillas controlled about 40,000 square kilometres of territory in India. It was a flimsy control—they were always on the move—but it prevented the infrastructure of the state from functioning, which in turn promoted the conditions in which rebellion flourished. Some officials privately praised the Maoists for their skill in setting up schools and water management projects. The deaths of both militants and security forces usually remained below 1,000 each year, but large numbers of police and paramilitaries were tied up trying to cope with the Maoist problem.

There was an identifiable link between places with extensive rural poverty, rich mineral reserves, a high tribal population and exploitative feudal landlords and a Maoist presence. Government programmes such as a scheme to give guaranteed employment on projects in rural areas had failed to reach outlying areas, with false lists of workers being compiled and money stolen. The Indian government recognized the circularity of the situation, saying in an official report: "Naxalites operate in the vacuum created by functional inadequacies of field level governance structures, espouse local demands, and take advantage of prevalent disaffection and feelings of perceived neglect and injustice among the underprivileged and remote segments of population."[45] An MP in Orissa, who had no sympathy for the Maoists, remarked on their organizational abilities. A timber merchant near Gopalpur-on-Sea by the Bay of Bengal had raped a girl. "The next day he was tried by the 'people's court' of the Maoists. The girl had the choice—death or reparation. They confiscated all his assets, expelled him from the district and took a ten lakh fine [$22,000]. The Maoists gave justice there, and they have a family for life."

A deeply destructive government response to the insurgency was the creation of a police-backed militia, the Salwa Judum, in Chhattisgarh in 2005, with funding from the state government and local industries involved in the extraction of iron ore. The members of the militia were recruited in many cases from other Scheduled Tribes, who had grievances against their neighbours. In one district, the Salwa Judum used the strategy of expelling people from villages in "red" areas and putting them in camps as a supposedly temporary measure. When this had been done, anyone left in the red area could be labelled a Maoist and treated brutally. It was a cruel and hopeless solution, which had the paradoxical effect of generating support for the Maoists.

Speaking to a constable in the COBRA contingent of the CRPF, or Central Reserve Police Force, I was surprised by the strictness of the rules of engagement that he had to follow. At the end of 2009 he had been based in Lalgarh, a poor part of West Bengal where villagers were caught between the violence of the revolutionaries and the violence of those who had come to hunt them down. The CRPF constable said, speaking in Hindi: "It's dense in the jungle, you can't see anything in there. We are dropped from a helicopter in groups of four. You shin down a long rope with your pack—water, salty biscuits, toffees, two grenades, an AK-47 with 200 rounds, a 9 mm pistol and a long knife like a sword. We have a radio and a sat-nav each. They tell us on the radio where to go, which people we can trust. You won't believe how the terrorists fight. When we search and see a weapon, we assume they are Naxalites. They are willing to give their lives. If ten Naxalites are in a village, they will give country-made guns to the others and all fight. If one of their people gets shot, they tie a rope and drag him back to the jungle. When we are patrolling, the villagers act as if we are the terrorists—they don't even speak to us. They are dark, like Biharis. The terrorists have looted the police stations. I have seen so many police stations where there is not a single rifle left in Lalgarh district." I had known this CRPF constable for years, and he had no reason to lie: I asked him what happened when they caught Maoists or took prisoners who had survived a gun battle. "If we catch someone we have to hand them over to the local police, and they will be taken to jail. We aren't allowed to do encounter killings. Do I feel sorry for these people? I don't feel bad for them—I feel like killing them on sight, but we don't do that because we don't have the order."[46]

The strategy of the Maoist leaders had changed little over the decades, although they had become more efficient. Muppala Laxman Rao, otherwise known as Comrade Ganapathy, was still content to be judge and executioner. If anyone broke the strikes or curfews of the Maoists, they risked death. Kaushik Dutta worked as a contractor for the state electricity board in West Bengal. If he delivered an electricity bill, he was paid Rs2; if he took a meter reading, he was paid Rs2.5. One day in April 2010, Kaushik went with a colleague to a neighbouring village and took some meter readings. He had to support his sickly, elderly parents as well as his wife, Rupali, and their daughter, and knew the Maoists had called a bandh, or general strike, but assumed it did not apply to meter reading. On the way home, the two men were intercepted by Maoists. Their bodies, when they were found, bore marks of beating, stabbing and shooting. The superintendent of the local electricity office said later: "The two were nice, decent, honest and hardworking. I could never have imagined that they would be killed by Maoists."[47] Kaushik Dutta and those like him, many of whom were Adivasis, knew they were easy targets and that the state government could and would do little to protect them.

The portrayal of the Maoist conflict as an *Avatar* type of story—good people with bows and arrows facing down bad people with machinery, one atrocity paralleling or excusing another—was a romantic and spurious version of a complex reality. In some cases, Maoists faced policemen armed with sticks and whistles. It was a fatal philosophy, not simply because of its brutality, not simply because of the chilling absurdity of Charu Majumdar's theories about the cleansing effect of bloodshed, but because it was the wrong tool for the conflict. The security apparatus of the Indian state was too powerful to be faced down, and would never be pulverized in the way it could be in smaller, neighbouring places like Nepal. As long as the CPI (Maoist) continued without a fresh approach, the weakest people in the red corridor would suffer, caught between an indifferent state and a dated political idea. It would be the poor who died, whether they were the police or the Maoist foot soldiers.

Whenever the Maoists ambushed a police patrol or blew up a minister's car, the Indian media would refer to them as if they were an abstract and intractable phenomenon, like a hurricane or an earthquake. Some people assumed they must be funded by China because of their name, though the leadership in Beijing had long ago moved on from their ideology. They liked to remain anonymous, rarely gave interviews and preferred to present themselves as the voice of India's dispossessed, the authentic leaders of the revolution. In practice they were a bunch of ageing men from upper-caste backgrounds, most of them from landed families in Andhra Pradesh and West Bengal. Ganapathy had grown up on family landholdings near Karimnagar in northern Andhra Pradesh, and after gaining degrees in both science and education he had worked as a teacher before leaving his wife and young son to become a Naxalite. He was from the Velama caste, who were traditionally the feudal lords in the Telangana region. They were known for their dislike of productive work. Other castes had a saying about the Velamas, which translates roughly as: "Even if burning coals fall on a Velama's thighs, he will expect the bonded labourer to lift them from his body instead of saving himself."

Ganapathy had turned sixty. The killing continued. In April 2010, in the largest Maoist attack yet, eighty-two police jawans, or constables, were murdered in an ambush in Chhattisgarh because they were "class enemies"; every one of them, Hindu, Sikh and Muslim, came from a poor family, most from the villages of Uttar Pradesh.[48] More than forty years after the campaign of strategic slaughter had begun, the Maoist superstructure was composed of the same old types. When the Hyderabad journalist Srinivas Reddy read out the names of the senior leadership to me, I asked him whether any Adivasis had yet come on board. He looked down the list: "Forward caste, landed, Brahmin, wealthy family, middle class, lower rung, landed gentry, Brahmin, middle class, landed . . . not yet. There is one tribal woman in prison who might be a leader." Only in the middle and lower rungs of the CPI (Maoist) did you find "the people." What did the leadership want? Another senior member, Mallojula Koteshwar Rao, a Brahmin with a B.Sc. in mathematics who enjoyed calling up newspapers and television channels, had spoken: "Our first role model was Paris [he was referring to the commune of 1871]. That disintegrated. Then Russia collapsed. That's when China emerged. But after Mao, that too got defeated. Now, nowhere in the world is the power truly in the hands of the people . . . So there is no role model."

That was his answer: there was no role model. Every society, every government, was bad; only the Maoists could improve things. "To create a new democratic state," said Mallojula Koteshwar Rao, "one has to destroy the old one."[49]

In the late 1960s and early 1970s, during the Bangladesh crisis, the later part of the Vietnam war and the eruption of Maoism, a generation of students was attracted by the idea of reinventing the world. In India they were responding, although they would not have seen it in this way at the time, to an economy stripped bare by ideology. In a society with innumerable problems, in which the opportunities to pursue a rewarding career were limited, they reacted, ironically, by turning further to the left. Most well-off Naxalites returned home after spending a few months in the jungle, turned off by the bad food and the bloody reality of killing moneylenders, and in some cases they were sent abroad by their parents, usually to the United States, at the instigation of police officials who did not wish to prosecute the children of the rich.

The origin of this political feeling lay in earlier times, in a more practical but still idealistic attempt at social and land reform in the immediate aftermath of independence. The parliamentary constituency of Vadakara in Kerala passes along a palm-filled coast and is home to a mix of communities: Christians, Muslims and Hindus. Haphazard roads run past paddy fields and fertile forests, and up through rubber and coffee plantations. All along the way, there are rivers, and even glimpses of the sea. Kerala has the highest literacy rate in the world, hovering close to 100 percent, which is in part the result of educational campaigns carried out by communist volunteers. For many years, K. P. Unnikrishnan was MP for Vadakara. In his thinking and outlook when he was a teenager, Unni was typical of a generation of educated Indians. The age of imperialism was over, and he believed something modern and politically exciting was happening that was going to cure old ills—socialism.

"In June 1957 I was invited to Moscow by the Communist Youth Movement," Unni remembered. "I was only nineteen. We took a train to Delhi and a special flight to Kabul, and on to Moscow. I was impressed by Moscow. There were maybe 30,000 or even 50,000 of us, young people from Iceland, Tahiti, South America, the United States. It was difficult in those days to travel outside of India. In Moscow, we had a cultural programme, theatre, science and technology, lectures about flights into space. Khrushchev inaugurated it. The idea was to influence young people, and it was a big gain for Moscow to get us at that impressionable age. It was the pinnacle of Soviet glory, and I was quite impressed by what I saw.

"I had been to Presidency College in Madras and my father was a lawyer in Calicut, although my mother had given away her jewellery to the freedom movement. I was in the Socialist Party, which was critical of the communists both in India and abroad. A lot of people were on the left, but the communists were unpopular here because they were calling Nehru 'a running dog of Anglo-American imperialism' and that sort of thing.

"After Moscow, some of us were invited to continue on to China, though the Americans were not allowed to go. We did a ten-day rail journey to Beijing, going past Lake Baikal. China seemed much more familiar than Russia. About twelve Indians were in our group, and I was the youngest. We met all the leaders. Mao looked quite impressive, but he didn't say much. We met Deng Xiaoping, and he took us to his house. I had four conversations with Chou Enlai. He would ask us to drink a toast—GAN BEI!—in rice wine and we were given fantastic food. I remember thinking he was a great host. He asked me what I thought of his country. I answered, 'It's a bit drab because everyone is wearing a blue tunic.' He laughed and said, 'But did you see anyone naked? In some countries—in your country—people go naked.' I had to agree. He was speaking through an interpreter, though I think he understood French and English."

While food and wine were being served to impressionable foreign students, Mao was preparing to launch the Great Leap Forward, in which nearly every Chinese family would be herded into a commune—by 1961, approximately 30 million people would have died in China in an engineered famine.

"Some American students were with us too who had resisted the State Department's ban on coming to China. Chou Enlai was very interested by them: 'They are the future. If you want world peace, there is no alternative to world peace, but the Americans want to have war.' He criticized Britain and France. Then we went on tours of Xian, Shanghai, Canton. I was impressed by the idea of getting rid of poverty, and that everyone had clothes. I made a second trip to China in 1959. The student officials didn't talk: they just gave us two pamphlets attacking Nehru. It was said Mao had written them. The atmosphere was completely different, because Nehru had welcomed the Dalai Lama to India. By the time the war came with China in 1962, I had joined the Congress party and Indira Gandhi had put me in charge of the youth section to organize anti-China rallies and seminars."

Unni went on to have a long career as an MP, first as a Congress loyalist and later with the IC(S), or Indian Congress (Socialist) party, a breakaway faction formed when Mrs. Gandhi fell from grace after the Emergency. He continued to be elected from the same constituency, Vadakara. By the time of the first Gulf War he was a senior minister in New Delhi with responsibility for transport and shipping. By now in his fifties, he had to go to Iraq to see Saddam Hussein. One hundred fifty thousand migrant workers, many of them originally from Kerala, were stuck in Kuwait. Unni was brought to a palace on the edge of Baghdad by helicopter. "Saddam Hussein was in military uniform. The future of all these stranded people depended on what he said to me. He talked about friendship, about India, about how strong his claim was over Kuwait. I told him our problem plainly: we had our people stuck between Kuwait and Jordan. We couldn't send ships to collect them because the Americans had mined the harbours. Well—he said they could leave. He acted like quite a reasonable person."[50] A massive airlift was arranged out of Amman.

Half a century after K. P. Unnikrishnan's extraordinary teenaged journey to China and Russia, intellectual fashions had changed, but pragmatic communism remained an important component in Indian life, most notably in Kerala and West Bengal. His children were not members of any socialist party. One of his daughters was a Bollywood lawyer, and I observed that the other, who worked in finance in London, wore a red T-shirt featuring a crossed hammer and sickle and the slogan: "The Party's Over."

In 2009, Kobad Ghandy was arrested in Delhi, where he was said to have gone to seek medical treatment for prostate cancer. He was a throwback to earlier times, a man from a Westernized, prosperous Parsi background who had gone underground to stir up armed revolution. The police had been after him for years as the head of "party publications" for the Maoists. Born in the year of independence, he had been sent to the Doon School at the same time as Jawaharlal Nehru's grandsons, and studied chartered accountancy in London. His family had lived in a sprawling apartment in Worli Sea Face, an expensive part of the city then still called Bombay, and his father was a senior executive with Glaxo who also had an ice cream business called Kentucky's, making the first ice cream in town to contain chunks of real strawberry.

Kobad Ghandy and his wife, Anuradha, a former college lecturer who used to drive a TVS moped and according to one contemporary was "a petite bundle of energy, bright eyes sparkling behind square glasses . . . who introduced us to that feminist bible, Germaine Greer's *The Female Eunuch*," were unusual in that they stayed the course, devoting themselves exclusively to the Maoist cause and living on the run for decades, using numerous different aliases and identity documents.[51] Much of the time, the demands of the revolution kept them apart; when united, Kobad would cook for her. Anuradha died from cerebral malaria a little over a year before her husband was arrested.

I went to see him in Tihar jail, on the edge of Delhi. Since he was in judicial custody and had not been convicted, I was only permitted to make a social call rather than do an interview; my guide to the prison was S. A. R. Geelani, who visited the inmates regularly. Geelani was a Kashmiri academic who had himself spent two years in Tihar, charged with involvement in the attack on the Indian Parliament in December 2001, before being acquitted. He had nearly died in an assassination attempt in 2004—everyone had theories about who did it, but no one knew for sure—and since the shootout he had been under the obligatory protection of the Central Industrial Security Force.

We set off from Delhi University, Geelani a composed figure in a long, dark-green kurta driving his vehicle, a policeman with an automatic weapon beside him in the front, myself in the back seat and a more junior policeman riding in the boot. Along the way we stopped at a traffic intersection, and a man with a ponytail and a big grin ran out to us carrying two bags. He approached and handed over the bags: cooked, packed food. At the jail, Geelani told the junior policeman to carry the bags of packed food to the entrance; it seemed that he regarded his paramilitary escort with resigned exasperation.

Before we entered the jail, the food had to be checked. A policeman and a policewoman, both huge-bellied, sat behind a table inspecting. Only plain vegetarian food was allowed, and only rotis, no rice. There was no definite reason for this, but it was written in the prison regulations. Geelani put the polystyrene cartons of food on the table, one at a time, opening each lid. The policewoman stirred interminably with a plastic spatula, the sort you might use for stirring sugar into coffee or tea. All went well until she found a mushroom, and extracted it.

"Mushroom nahin. Mushroom allowed nahin hai."

"Mushrooms kyu nahin allowed hain?" said Geelani.

Were mushrooms allowed? A more senior policewoman came out, debated, disappeared, returned; mushrooms were allowed.

In the reception, we were photographed ("London friend," said Geelani, explaining why I was visiting the prisoner) and given the kind of pass you get when you go to an office, a piece of paper slipped into a small, clip-on transparent wallet. Beside our photographs were our names and next to Geelani's name the words "HIGH RISK." Perhaps this was because he had previously been a high-security prisoner, and was considered a returning danger. We waited, looked inside the shop, which sold items made by prisoners, including TJ Chips—Tihar jail potato chips—and went through security scanners.

Now we walked some way to the restricted part of the compound. Geelani said he came to visit here once a week. Having been inside, facing execution at one stage and enduring repeated attacks by other prisoners, he knew it was a lifeline for the inmates; he made no distinction between those he thought guilty or not guilty. In the next staging room, the prison guards repeated the rigmarole with the food, which was smelling quite oily by now. They prodded and stirred the curries, mainly because they were bored and had nothing else to do. Finally we were in the anteroom to the high security unit, which held India's most dangerous and politically sensitive prisoners, many of them Sikhs and Kashmiris. After another security check, we were allowed to go in, a parade of about a dozen; the wives, the mothers, the fathers.

It was like visiting a bank. The prisoners were behind bleary windows and we had to speak through a malfunctioning sound system. After thirty minutes, the system would be turned off. Kobad Ghandy had a sad, engaging face; behind him through the window I could see two men dressed like hip-hoppers, a pair of young Kashmiris who according to Geelani had been framed years before. Ghandy spoke to me about the "lumpen" behaviour of his Doon School contemporary Sanjay Gandhi, his own time in London and how he did well in his chartered accountancy exams but became increasingly involved in politics. At a rally in north London attended by rival outfits he had been caught in a skirmish, and he and others had been sent to prison, he believed for racial reasons, although they were not responsible for the trouble. His moment of full awakening, when he reached some sort of idealistic plateau from which he had never come down, was at this time. He had returned to Bombay in the early 1970s and devoted himself to dismantling what he saw as India's feudal, colonial state. Kobad Ghandy was earnest and likeable; he reminded me of the armchair communists who lived in greater style in Delhi and Kolkata.

He was having some problems with his legal case and had to speak to Geelani. Only one person could fit at the window, so I went to the neighbouring counter and who should be behind it but Mohammad Afzal, the most feared man in India.

He was smiling from ear to ear. Afzal had a bushy black beard, round glasses and a white skullcap.

"Hello, sir," he said in English, "what do you know about me?"

"You're Afzal," I said. What did I know about him? That he had been convicted of organizing the attack on Parliament in 2001 which brought India and Pakistan close to war; that he had been sentenced to death; that at present his case was pending—and that many people in India wished to see him hanged.

I asked whether he talked to Kobad Ghandy much in prison. He said he did, and was fascinated to have learned about the problems facing the people in the jungle, which he thought were similar to those facing his fellow Kashmiris. Afzal was Indian enough to be obsessed by books; we discussed French novelists, and he said he had recently finished Samuel Huntington's *The Clash of Civilizations* and agreed with much of its thesis. Through all of this, Afzal kept smiling. He seemed to have some sort of joyfulness, and it was hard to know if this was religious fervour or some other instinct. Like many Kashmiri militants, he had been gruesomely tortured, and it seemed almost as if he had arrived in some new mental place where he had known everything and nothing could get worse. During the last few minutes of the visit, I switched back to Kobad Ghandy's window. When I mentioned that Afzal thought they shared many political insights, he looked sceptical and said he had been surprised by how little interest most inmates had in politics.

I had one last question for Ghandy about Maoism, the same question I had asked Madhu in the forest in Andhra Pradesh years before—how could he follow Mao after everything that had happened in China, with its political system that had killed tens of millions of people? His answer was that there may have been mistakes but the philosophy was right, and I thought at that moment how overrated conviction was as a way of facing the world. When taken to an extreme, idealism is little more than a form of prejudice.

Before we left, Geelani had to hand over the food. In a corner of the area by a grille, each roti was checked before being passed through, each dish was stirred once more. However unappetizing the food looked, it was better than what was inside. Through the bars I could see Kobad Ghandy, hunched forward, waiting to return to his cell. Afzal was still up by the window, and he beckoned me over in his manic, smiling way. He did a mime, imitating the guards who were searching the food. I asked what he missed most. "Roast chicken," he mouthed at the dead glass. "I miss roast chicken."[52] Then the guards ordered everybody out.

7

FALCON 900

IN THE LAST CENTURY, the world's personal wealth was held in American, European, Arab and occasionally East Asian hands. Something
changed—by 2008, four of the eight richest people alive were Indian.
Alongside them in the *Forbes* Top 10 were a German, a Russian, a Swede,
two Americans (Bill Gates and Warren Buffett) and the Mexican tycoon
Carlos Slim Hélu, whose father was a Maronite Christian from Lebanon
who had, in the son's words, "escaped the yoke of the Ottoman empire" at
the age of fourteen by moving to Mexico.[1]

Sunil Bharti Mittal's net worth was estimated at $8bn. Unlike many
other successful Indian business people, who had developed existing operations or used their talents to flourish in a foreign market, he was wholly self-
made and had created his fortune on Indian soil. Now he was expanding.
When I met him in 2010, Mittal's company, Bharti Airtel, had just taken over
the telecom operator Zain in fifteen African countries. Like other aggressive entrepreneurs, Mittal saw undeveloped territories as the future; the
purchase of Zain for $10.7bn was the largest ever cross-border deal in an
emerging market.[2] His intention was to grow in Africa as rapidly as he had
in India. It was not unlike the rough capitalism in the U.S. in the nineteenth
century, when men like Cornelius Vanderbilt and John D. Rockefeller made
sudden, inconceivable fortunes. While Russian oligarchs had bought up

state assets at knockdown prices, Indian entrepreneurs were able to take advantage of sudden advances in technology, or to corner a particular market when the economy expanded in the wake of globalization. Sunil Mittal had placed himself in exactly the right position to take advantage of a moment in his nation's history when a great fortune could be made.

At the Bharti Airtel offices in Mayfair, the brass Zain Services plaque was still in place beside the front door. Mittal was on a flying visit to Europe, zipping between countries and spending just over a day in England. Except for a receptionist or secretary and a tank of fat goldfish, the office was empty: the new dispensation had yet to put its people in place. While I waited for Sunil Mittal, a member of the old regime arrived. This man was tall, white, stooping, grey-haired, distinguished, and he peered at me over the top of his half-moon spectacles as he sat down at a desk. He tapped listlessly at a computer keyboard. The secretary walked over to him, and they had a little exchange.

"I didn't have time to do your refund for the hotel bill. I've been doing things for Bharti," she said. Ignored, she went on: "I'll do my best to do it this afternoon."

He stared straight ahead and said in an acidulous upper-class English accent, in which the emotion conveyed the opposite implication to the words: "You're very kind."

Next, an executive of the Bharti empire knocked on a glass-panelled door. She was stuck on the wrong side of it. The secretary rushed to open it and wedged the door ajar. "How am I meant to get in if you are not here?" asked the Bharti executive. "Mrs. Mittal will be here in ten minutes. Have you met Mrs. Mittal before? You might want to go down and meet her." She was tense, serious. The keycode for the door was produced.

Sunil Mittal appeared out of the elevator. He had come from a meeting in another part of London. In his early fifties, he wore a suit with a blue shirt and tie, and red strings from the temple were wound around his right wrist. He had no entourage with him. Bypassing both the old and new guard, we went to a meeting room. His manner was direct, unpretentious. I asked him how he had started out. When asked this question, many people in India will give a disquisition on the achievements of their forebears. Mittal did not do this. Instead, he said how much he had hated studying at college.

"I preferred rifle shooting, playing cricket and table-tennis, flying gliders. My father said I had to graduate, and then I could quit. With a friend—or a colleague—from college, I started making bicycle parts. I had a tiny amount of family capital, about $1,500."

Sunil Mittal was born in Ludhiana in Punjab, a city known for manufacturing knitwear, hosiery and motor parts. He graduated in 1976, at the time of the Emergency. His home life was unusual, in that he was not part of a joint household.

"We were more like a Western nuclear family. My parents were both Punjabis, but my mother was from a Kshatriya family and my father was a Bania." Punjabi Banias were mostly shrewd traders, shopkeepers and small industrialists. So the bride was considered a bad match, who would bring no dowry. "My father was a student politician and my mother was in the audience when he was giving a speech. They had a love marriage. My father's family were not happy and they almost disowned him. I never knew my uncles or my cousins. My father would have been cashed in at a higher level. In his time, it was important you came from the right family background." His father, Sat Paul Mittal, later became a Congress MP in the Rajya Sabha and a prominent parliamentarian who campaigned internationally on matters such as apartheid, population growth and social development. "When he did well as a politician, some of his family came to meet him again."

Although Sunil Mittal's father was in politics rather than in business, many of the people in the family's social group were involved in trading or manufacturing. Ludhiana was one of the busiest commercial centres in Punjab, a place where it was usual to be trying to set up one thing or another. At the fledgling bicycle parts factory in his early twenties, Mittal "dreamed of owning a large-sized business entity," and knew it was not the ideal industry for him. "I saw it as a means to an end, and knew it would not be enough. We manufactured special high-tensile-strength crankshafts for export to Germany. I did a few other things in my twenties—trading in copper, zinc, zip fasteners. I wanted to be important in my sphere. Even though I was not even a speck in the copper market, I wanted to be in a position to decide the market price one day." He dreamed in numbers and in big ideas.

"I have always been a capitalist in my mind, but misery and poverty were at our doors—you could hardly not see them—and my father was a politician during a socialist time. So we were socially connected. I was uncomfortable with the control or permit raj, being told what you can and can't do. When I was starting out, all the prospects were with a handful of business families. People would say to me: 'Take an agency for gas or cars. Do some work for Birla or Tata. Your father's a politician, you'll have a comfortable living.' I didn't want to do that, I wanted more, and I thought that if you look to the U.S. or to Europe, in each decade there is a business idea that breaks the mould."

I began to import portable generators from Suzuki in Japan—the sort that in another country might be used for a picnic or a party or an ice cream stand. In India I thought we would need them in homes when the mains electricity failed, which happened all the time in those days. It was hard work and pain from 1976 to 1982, but it was the first time I tasted success. You could put that on my tombstone. I was able to buy a good car and an apartment. I had revenues of $100,000 a year, which at that time was really a lot of money. In 1983, generators were banned. It was decided by the government they should be manufactured in India, because of the import substitution policy. Birla and Shriram [two large, established and politically well-connected business houses] got letters of intent [from the bureaucracy in New Delhi] and the ban on imports was immediate, even though they hadn't started to manufacture any generators."

Sunil Mittal laughed, as if he still could not believe it, and hunched forward in his chair. His hair was closely cropped, black flecked with grey. "So I picked up my bag and went to Japan. God has guided my life. I looked at the street markets, seeing what was there. Some of the time I took an interpreter with me, other times I got by using English. I considered importing VCRs. I went to Korea, went to Taiwan. I looked at Teflon-coated products, at sports shoes, even at plastic tents. In Taipei at a trade fair, I saw push-button phones. I went to visit the factory of a man named Richard Wu and signed an MOU with him immediately to import the parts and assemble them in India. Only rotary phones existed at that time, and I knew these would be popular. We called the company 'Mitbrau,' which sounded German—foreign products sold better—but it stood for Mittal Brothers as I was working with my brothers by then. We sold about 10,000 phones a year, with a 300 or 400 percent margin. I realized I loved telecom. We started to make answering machines, did a tie-up with Siemens and imported cordless phones and fax machines from Korea. Then the mobile phone market opened up, and we bid as the outsiders. We had to go through courts, litigation, challenges—I'm compressing a lot of things here—but we ended up winning the Delhi licence and launched Bharti Airtel in 1995. The rest is history."

Three years before the telecom sector opened up, Sunil Mittal had asked a consulting company to do a report on the market potential for mobile phones. Getting a landline connection in India was a long, tedious and corrupt process, and it was apparent the new technology might enable people to bypass the obstructions. "They said we could sell 50,000 phones over the next ten years. I thought the number was closer to half a million, so I threw away that report. I can't truthfully say I saw the full market potential in 1995. By 2000 or 2001, we knew the future was going to be huge. I was convinced India would have more phones than it had vehicles. Today there are 20 million cell phones in Delhi. We have 135 million subscribers in India."

The invention and spread of mobile telephony had a significant impact on Indian society. The mobile phone spread faster than in countries with a more efficient landline system. It had become an Indian object—a status symbol and a commonplace tool. The phrase or word "missedcall" had passed into Hindi and other languages. When foreign publications illustrated stories about contemporary India with inevitable photographs of a sadhu or a sari-clad woman clutching a mobile phone—as if this were the most outlandish juxtaposition, an Easterner holding a Western product—they were missing just how mainstream and indigenous the technology had become. Bharti Airtel's own revolution had been ignited further east, when its founder visited Taiwan in the early 1980s and was captivated by the idea of a push-button phone.

When his commercial idea exploded, Mittal made a decision which went against accepted business thinking. He was under threat from other Indian companies that were moving into the telecom market, like Reliance, which had more capital to spare. So rather than finding new employees, Mittal did something unexpected—he "reverse outsourced," giving his work to foreign companies like IBM, Ericsson and Nokia, who opened up larger operations of their own in India. So instead of an Indian company "taking" jobs from richer nations, he was creating business for them. The strategy worked: even while Bharti Airtel was hiring fewer people, it became India's largest telecom provider a little over a decade after its foundation.

"I looked at the size and infrastructure of telecom companies around the world," he said. "I looked at Verizon, British Telecom, France Telecom, AT&T—and I thought there's no way I could build that infrastructure in twenty-four months. It's not going to happen. So I let other companies do the IT and call centres while we focused on markets, customers and innovations." Bharti Airtel no longer obtained and maintained their own equipment. Their network operations were run by Ericsson, the management of their transmission towers was outsourced and most of their IT staff moved to IBM, with protected salaries and the right to return within two years.

"None of them came back!" Even the computer on Mittal's own desk at his head office was maintained by IBM. "When I decided on this strategy, one of the big European companies called me to say I was making a fatal mistake, and that I was taking away the heart of our business. I told them telecom companies are not technology companies. We're not the ones who understand how wireless technology works. If something goes wrong with a switch and the network goes down—nobody in our office can fix it. I've sat all night watching engineers trying to get the Airtel system running. The heart of our business is not technology, it's the customers. I prefer speed to perfection."

Although Mittal was still a small player at the time, he had three meetings with Sam Palmisano, the chairman and CEO of IBM, who realized his own company needed to evolve fast if it were not to have its business eaten up by the nimble new IT companies in India. With the exponential growth of Bharti Airtel's subscriber base, IBM had every reason not to exploit the contract by ratcheting up costs.[3] "Sam told me he would personally keep a watch on this project. I told him, if this fails, IBM will fail, and the world's telecom companies will open to you if it succeeds. He kept his promise. Soon I was talking at IBM conferences, celebrating our partnership on stage. Once that happened, I knew we were in a good place and it would hold together."

As more and more people in India acquired mobile phones and handheld devices, Mittal thought he might be moving towards easier times. He was wrong. "We get regulatory curveballs all the time—new rules, a minister denying spectrum, issuing licences. It's still war." He was now seeking to move beyond telecom, in various directions. "The number of dollars I have doesn't interest me. I love the journey. What excites me is the new." What was new now? "Our work in Africa. The possibilities for retail in India. There's huge waste in fruit and veg, and we don't have a cold supply chain. A lot of stores are run by family, but the sons and daughters want to work in modern shops." He was starting gradually, and had opened about 100 stores in partnership with Wal-Mart. They were branded—innocuously—"Easy Day." Although his point about the waste in the system in India was true, many family-run shops like dry-goods stores and chemists were highly efficient and versatile. Changing this embedded system, which was linked to ideas of family and caste, was not likely to be easy.

Did he think the economic revolution over the last two decades in India was too narrow? Had it helped only a handful of clever, lucky business people? "Well—each year 20 million more people are having a second meal every day. I don't like the vulgar display of wealth. I think the government should run social programmes and we should pay our taxes and not resent it. The fuel for change comes from the development of the economy. Bharti Airtel employs around 50,000 people today, but we provide indirect employment to around 1.5 million. The Bharti Foundation will soon be sending 100,000 children to school, and the schools we have set up are in very poor catchment areas." It was, in effect, an affirmative action programme. "Most of our children and most of the teachers come from Scheduled Castes or Tribes or from the OBC category. We provide the children with a uniform, one meal a day and free books, and we take care of the fees." Was this a way of promoting his brand? "No. It's a way to unlock India's potential. A lot of these families wouldn't know about our business. You can change a whole family if the children get educated. We want to open many more schools like this, at primary and secondary level."[4]

Although he did not express it in this way, I felt Sunil Mittal was saying that when you have made a certain amount of money—say $1bn, for the sake of argument—then trying to change the world through philanthropy becomes an attractive way to spend the cash, more interesting than buying another aeroplane, house or company. In his case, the Bharti Foundation was overseen by someone he trusted and who shared his social vision— his older brother, Rakesh Mittal, himself a successful businessman. The annual cost of the schools was 28 crores, a little over $6m. The possibilities for his foundation to effect social change in India—with its comparatively low employment and infrastructure costs—were exceptional. Sunil Mittal had said recently in a television interview that he was inspired by the stories of American tycoons like Rockefeller and Andrew Carnegie. "I sit on the Carnegie Endowment board in Washington, and it is incredible how they left most of their wealth for public causes. I think that has to happen here. So if you ask me what is Bharti Foundation's vision, it's to be one day known like a Carnegie Endowment or a Ford Foundation or a Rockefeller Foundation. We have started well. Hopefully we will end well."[5]

In the past, rich people in India were princely rulers or members of extended business families who had made a fortune in textiles or manufacturing. Industrialists would hoard capital, and there was a limited expectation of seeking to outbid your neighbours in gross ostentation. Since liberalization, an unbound social class had grown with extraordinary speed. Sunil Mittal's objection to the vulgar display of wealth was not widely shared. For members of this new global community—the Indian super-rich—geography had become flexible. They could carry their world wherever they chose and station themselves in whichever city they needed to be in at the time. Their passports, and those of their family members, might not always be Indian, but culturally their attachment to their homeland remained strong. One businessman told me he was able to compress time, and that a ten-day journey to his work sites in Mozambique could be reduced to four days by using his own plane. Invitations to house-warming parties were likely to specify any of a number of cities between Los Angeles and Hong Kong. In Mumbai, the industrialist Mukesh Ambani had built the world's most expensive private residence, a 27-storey confection involving three floors of gardens, swimming pools, a cool room (which in the ultimate Himalayan dream blew flurries of fake snow), three helipads, a six-storey car parking garage and several "entourage rooms"—for who travels without an entourage?[6]

The steelmaker Lakshmi Mittal (no relation to Sunil) was presently the only Indian richer than Ambani. He held the principal celebrations for his daughter's wedding in Paris, and even hired the palace at Versailles, which nobody had managed to do before. In 2006, Mittal Steel's hostile bid for Europe's largest steelmaker, Arcelor, had been met with dismay. The head of Arcelor, Guy Dollé, said sorrowfully that the predatory company was "full of Indians" and his own Luxembourg-based operation had no need for "monnaie de singe"—meaning money without value, which in direct translation became the insulting "monkey change."[7] Lakshmi Mittal won the battle, Dollé was ousted and Arcelor Mittal was now the world's largest steel company.

I had first noticed the spread of Indian wealth about ten years ago, when I had to judge a prize in London for "Asian Women of Achievement." In North America, "Asian" usually means east Asian, but in Europe it is often taken to mean south Asian, or more specifically north Indian or Pakistani. At the awards dinner, new money was on display—in the clothes, in the jewellery, in the willingness to pay for tables for the night. It was small-scale compared to what was going on in Mumbai and Delhi, but it marked a cultural shift. Social competition was high. Punjabis, Sindhis and Marwaris were there in numbers, some from triumphant business families. They observed each other's necklaces, handbags and rings, chewed over fashion designers like Manish Arora and discussed tax shelters, cricket results and private jets. The Dassault Falcon 900 seemed to be a particularly popular model of plane, because it could do the Delhi–London hop without the ignominy of having to refuel in Dubai or Baku. Many of the women and men at parties like this one had legal, medical or financial careers, and some pursued unusual lines of work: one man told me he supplied notes to the foreign exchange bureaux of the West End, another that his business was import-export, "mainly shoes and helicopter parts." Shoes, as in, shoes? Yes, and clothes. And helicopter parts.

It was a change from earlier decades, when south Asians were associated with poverty. Indian, Pakistani or more specifically Punjabi culture was a strong culture, a brash force that could thrive under globalization and not be worried greatly by what was going on around it. We might have been in almost any country, for the guests carried their own ethos with them. It transferred easily to Britain, where the economy was open but assimilation was difficult. This was a product of the British attitude towards immigration, a hangover from colonial times. The expectation after the Second World War was that new arrivals would come to the mother country from the poorer parts of the disbanding empire: Africa, the West Indies and rural India or Pakistan. Unlike other nations which accepted or sought rich immigrants, Britain preferred the poor, to whom charity could be extended through the state. The two largest south Asian communities in Britain came from Sylhet and Mirpur, two impoverished parts of rural Bangladesh and Pakistani Kashmir. Between them, people of Bangladeshi and Pakistani origin made up nearly 2 percent of the UK's population and had some of the worst indicators for housing, health, education and employment. Other people of south Asian origin, some of whom were Muslims and Hindus who had been expelled from east African countries like Kenya and Uganda in the 1960s and 1970s, had achieved greater economic success. They had flourished away from India during the early and middle years of the twentieth century, and had now moved on around the world. England was for them more like a staging-post or an amenity.

The British did not know quite how to take them. Politicians from all parties, some of them dressed in Indian clothing, made a point of attending the Asian Women of Achievement awards ceremony each year. Unlike the Conservatives, Tony Blair's Labour Party had been quick at obtaining money and support from subcontinental grandees. Prominent among them was Swraj Paul, who made steel strips, gave large sums to the party and had published a book lavishing praise on Labour politicians like Gordon Brown, Robin Cook and Tony Blair: "Gordon is both tough-minded and sensitive . . . Gordon is a man of vision [with] a constant desire to do what is right for the country."[8] Paul also showed a talent for winning the admiration of British journalists: a profile in the *Independent* suggested, preposterously, that he "could have accepted the post of India's ambassador to Washington when it was offered, and might then have had the chance to succeed Indira Gandhi as prime minister."[9]

Tony Blair and Gordon Brown rewarded Swraj Paul by making him a lord, a privy counsellor, an ambassador for overseas business, a stalwart of the Foreign Secretary Robin Cook's fatuous and short-lived "Cool Britannia" panel and chairman of the India–UK Round Table.[10] Paul was a curious choice of envoy to India, since he was well known for funding Indira Gandhi during her wilderness years after the Emergency, and the government at the time of his appointment was led by the BJP, which loathed the Gandhi family. When Indira Gandhi lost power in 1977, Swraj Paul had telephoned her and said, "Indiraji, as long as I have something to eat, you will eat first."[11] Perhaps the Labour Party thought this was not important; they certainly never explained why someone who was non-domiciled in the UK for tax purposes (avoiding paying tax because he intended to return to India, his country of origin) should represent Britain abroad. The India–UK Round Table achieved little, at substantial cost to the taxpayer, but gave Swraj Paul exceptional access in New Delhi. In 2007 he promised to bankroll the Labour Party at the next general election, and distributed 6,000 free copies of Gordon Brown's dud book *Courage* to schools to celebrate his becoming prime minister; in 2009 he was found to have claimed £38,000 in expenses from the House of Lords authorities by pretending his main home was a tiny one-bedroom flat attached to a three-star hotel he owned in Oxfordshire. The money was repaid. Lord Paul of Marylebone's net worth was estimated at $750m.[12]

So Britain continued on its way, drawing in a little cash from the non-domiciled, paying out some more to the economically inactive, continuing with a perception of the world that depended on the imprecations of earlier times. When London needed a monstrous sculpture to commemorate the 2012 Olympic Games, it was designed by Anish Kapoor (ex-Doon School) and paid for by Lakshmi Mittal; the Indian media called it "a permanent Indian presence in London," the mayor Boris Johnson called it "a piece of modern British art" and Kapoor, presumably conceiving the overstretched tower as a metaphor for Britain, described it as "an eccentric structure that looks as if it's going to fall over."[13]

At high-functioning south Asian parties in London, prestige was graded in commercial terms, to the disapproval of the few Indian representatives of old money, those who played the game that was popular in the 1950s and 1960s of copying the manners of English gentlefolk. Their approach was out of date; few were interested in people who acted like people who were themselves becoming irrelevant, a social group which relied on the mantra of proud inaction, "Keep Calm and Carry On." When Lakshmi Mittal entered the room there was an understanding he was the guest of honour, since he was the richest person in Britain—of any ethnicity. I remember waiting by the front door to leave one party and finding myself beside Lakshmi Mittal. He had an intelligent and reserved face. His wife, Usha, a squat woman with movable assets on her neck, ears and fingers, was surrounded by admiring women wearing shimmering metallic outfits. It was something close to the worship of pure wealth, the worship of Lakshmi. One old man was saying over and over again to nobody in particular: "Lakshmi, Usha, so nice," with a glow on his face like the glow of reflected gold.

Indians were turning global, in Europe, in the Americas, in east and west Asia. In Australia, the fertilizer tycoon Pankaj Oswal outraged his neighbours by building the country's biggest house in the genteel suburb of Peppermint Grove; his wife, Radhika, banned builders working on the site from eating meat pies and ham sandwiches, saying, "Meat eating is creating bad karma."[14] The unshackling of talent extended far beyond the flamboyant new rich. An idea of Indian exceptionalism had developed, a conviction that the country could achieve something unique at this point in its history.

In India, the middle class had a chance to shape its own destiny in a way that had never been possible before. You could move to your own house using a home loan and live outside the joint family; you could buy a car that was not an Ambassador or a Fiat; it was possible to travel abroad and see how people in other countries lived; you could watch your politicians accept bribes or dance with prostitutes on television in media sting operations while surfing your way to *Desperate Housewives* or *Rahul Dulhaniya Le Jayega*. Alongside this, business people who had been successful on their own merit overseas were projected as national heroes, like Arun Sarin, the CEO of Vodafone, or Indra Nooyi, a graduate of IIM Calcutta who became the head of PepsiCo and one of the most powerful businesswomen in the world.

Abhishek Bachchan—in an inversion of the rebellious roles once taken by his father, the Bollywood star Amitabh Bachchan—could be seen in the popular 2007 movie *Guru* extolling the joys of capitalism. In one dramatic scene he gives a speech to a government inquiry that would have been impossible on the Indian silver screen even a decade earlier. He talks of walking in the steps of Mahatma Gandhi and declares the need for a second freedom. The first freedom was from foreign rule; the new, second freedom was . . . freedom to run a successful business without government restriction and make lots of money. *Guru* was based on the story of Dhirubhai Ambani (like Gandhi, a Gujarati from the Modh Bania caste), who founded the brilliantly innovative chemicals, textiles, energy and retail conglomerate Reliance Industries. He was adept at gaining favours from politicians of different parties and at playing the permit raj: he would export spices at a loss and use the resultant replenishment licences to bring in rayon; when rayon started to be manufactured in India, he exported rayon and imported nylon, selling it on again with a 300 percent profit margin. An investor who bought Rs100 worth of shares in Reliance in 1977 would have found that twenty-five years later they were worth Rs16,500.[15] His sons, Mukesh and Anil, had been engaged in a protracted family and business dispute, but had used economic liberalization to make Reliance grow.

A new dispensation was beginning, focused on Asia, the effects of which were not yet fully understood. Much current thinking about India and China is the product of old knowledge and expectation. Three out of every five people alive today are Asian. It would be easy to assume American hegemony in the late twentieth century, or European hegemony in the late nineteenth century, means occidental supremacy must continue. The assumption that the rest of humanity will acclimatize to Western precepts, as happened in various forms over recent centuries, no longer holds true. Rather than examine the reality of the present, which is that all certainties are being turned upside down and everything is fluid, there is a tendency to look at superficial signs like the Asian love of brands (Cartier, Bulgari, *Hello!*) and deduce that, with some adjustments to existing business models, Western power will remain intact. This is an outdated and fantastic view. The Beijing government's quiet and swift diplomacy has proved lethally effective in making economic gains, and particularly in securing raw materials like iron ore and natural gas from African countries. China's authoritarian capitalism, while very different from India's self-critical, democratic and sometimes unbalanced entrepreneurship, is part of a realignment of existing global patterns of political, economic and ideological power. Multipolarity is coming.

Although slower than China's transformation following the death of Mao, India's rapid success has induced a sense of baffled wonder elsewhere in the world. What on earth is happening? Why are Indian businesses suddenly doing so well and buying up foreign companies? Is India rich or poor now? Does devotion to the extended family offer a template to other countries, where family structures have broken down, and is the Indian business

family the supreme embodiment of this structure? Why does Indian identity remain so powerful even while globalization is altering the country profoundly? How does it feel to be part of a freshly minted meritocracy, where
genuine social mobility is possible in parts of the country for the first time
in history? Is India today—diverse, democratic, dissenting—potentially a
unique strategic ally for the West, and a possible antidote to the rise of
stricter global powers like China and Russia? With so many things shifting
internationally, and the spread of Indian entrepreneurs and software engineers across the world, India's reputation was being redefined.

Financial analysts were suggesting that if present rates of growth continued, India's economic position would be further transformed. Guessing
precisely where the country was heading was a popular pastime, since no
one could be certain of the answer. One of the more influential projections,
which shocked foreign business people into acknowledging the possibility
of a radically reshaped global economy, was a 2003 Goldman Sachs report,
Dreaming with BRICs: The Path to 2050. It suggested that by the year 2050, Brazil, Russia, India and China (BRIC) might collectively overtake the economies of the G6 (the United States, UK, Japan, Germany, France and Italy)
in GDP terms. By 2032, India could overtake Japan, and, by 2041, China
could overtake the U.S. India was projected as the only BRIC economy that
would still have high growth rates by 2050, since it had a younger population. China, because of the demographics created by its one-child policy,
was set to decline from a paramount position in around 2023.[16] There were
many arguments against this dream of the future—like climate change, the
shrinking of the Himalayas, political instability or inertia, river pollution,
severe water shortages in parts of north India, mineral depletion and the
running conflict with Pakistan—but it seemed inevitable that before the
middle of the twenty-first century the global balance of economic power
would have shifted and India would lie somewhere near the centre.

The largest economies in a multipolar world would not be the richest
in per capita income terms, because their populations were too big, and
this would make strategic business decisions much more difficult. If you
were selling to a market where perhaps a third, or two thirds, of people
would never be likely to buy your product, how should you arrange brand-
ing, advertising and distribution? Marketers jumped at the chance to project
speculative new interpretations of the Indian customer to hungry foreign
firms. One Indian report estimated the country presently had about 100 million people in urban areas who belonged to the top three socio-economic
classes, and that they consisted of "partition's generation," which had a

"high regard for functionality"; a "transition generation," which believed in "credit/debit living"; and a "no-strings generation," which had "unchecked optimism" and apparently thought "bad is the new good."[17] Could you sell to such people? Or should you keep your prices low in order to try to capture a new type of consumer and win their loyalty? If a billion Indians were now drinking 100 grams more tea each year as their incomes rose, where would it come from—Africa, perhaps? Imagine if you could sell fifteen razor blades a year to 400 million men, or a small car to 60 million families; or might it be better to identify your customers from among the super-rich? When Chanel launched itself in New Delhi in 2005, the company held a fashion show and an exhibition of its iconic jewellery at the Imperial Hotel. The clothes certainly sold fast. Then, it being India, there were inquiries from the wealthy onlookers whether it might be possible to buy the antique jewels and the entire exhibition too.[18]

A follow-up report to *Dreaming with BRICs* by Goldman Sachs in 2007 advised that India's position had been understated. It now thought an increased growth rate of 8 percent represented "a structural increase rather than simply a cyclical upturn" and might continue until 2020. India was racing along, with some of the fastest-growing urban areas in the world. This report made the valuable point that if these projections were correct, India would only be returning to its historic position as a major economic power: before the late eighteenth century, its share of world GDP had always been higher than 20 percent. "By the 1970s, after two centuries of relative economic stagnation, that share had fallen to 3 percent—the lowest in its recorded history."[19] The global credit crisis, which started a year after the Goldman Sachs report was written, did not significantly alter these optimistic projections since the Indian economy was comparatively unexposed, and more than half of its GDP depended upon consumer spending.

India's creaking road and rail infrastructure restricted its ability to make the necessary leap forward. Certainly some new building projects were speedy, including several offshoots of the Golden Quadrilateral Highway project started by Atal Behari Vajpayee when he was prime minister, linking Delhi, Mumbai, Kolkata and Chennai. Parts of Delhi were being transformed: the metro was a revelation, with cheap fares, sleek Japanese-style trains, air-conditioned coaches and a simple, well-designed layout. A journey which might take an hour by a clogged and pitted road could be completed in

eight smooth minutes. A large sign warned that travelling on the roof of
a train would attract a fine of Rs50, although I doubted it would be possible to get on top of a train without being electrocuted. New Delhi, a city
conceived and executed by the British as their power waned, was now part
of a criss-crossed and ever expanding national capital. I went to see one of
the roads in the sky that was being built over the city, following an ancient
drainage ditch dating to the time of the Mughal emperor Babur.

This new elevated road would be 2.5 miles long and three lanes wide on
each side, and would ease the traffic that was presently crawling helplessly
through this part of the city. It was being built for the government by a
private company. They were working out of a casting yard, with the road
being constructed like a giant Lego model, piece by piece. Cement, sand,
water and chips of crushed stone from a mine near Gurgaon were mixed
together and poured into an immense cage of steel bars to create a slice of
the road. "The whole beauty of this," said Dilip Mathur of the construction company as we watched, "is that each segment is matched." Every
giant slice, a D-shape, was made either straight or curved according to a
computer model of the complete road, and matched to the one it would
sit next to in midair. Not many workers were required, just great precision.
All around us were notices saying: "Think Safety" or "Use the Appropriate
Tools." The casting yard worked twenty-four hours a day under floodlight
(P. C. Mahalanobis would have been pleased), and when a dozen segments
had been cast, they were taken to their resting place not far from the banks
of the Yamuna and joined together with long wires to make a prestressed
span of road, a solid unit 34 metres long. Each span was lifted into place
using a launcher—it was an enormous device, the sort of thing you might
see in a dockyard—enabling the stretch of road to rest securely on rubber
bearings between two piers. Every third span of road was joined using an
expansion bolt, to cope with changes in temperature.

I drove with Dilip Mathur to look at the work. Delhi was going about
its business. A section of the elevated snake was sitting in the sky. "Here,"
he said, pointing upwards, "we had to raise it an extra four metres because
of an old tomb." A family of aggressive pigs was rootling in the drainage
ditch. The future route of the road was clear; you just followed the dirty
water. This was to the advantage of the builders, as they did not have to
destroy buildings to sink piers. We drove further. "Others would take three
or four years to make this road," said Dilip, "and we will do it, start to finish, in fifteen months." It was being constructed in twelve different places

at once; when I first arrived at the casting yard, I had imagined it would be constructed in one go, from A to B, rather than organically.

At a junction we climbed up a long spiral ladder and walked along the elevated road. Each section had been covered with a coat of bitumen. Workers were putting the barriers in place along the edge. How much were they paid? "Rs10,000 a month [around $230], plus overtime. If you don't ensure lodging, fooding and pay, you don't keep the good ones." Dilip explained things that seemed obvious to him, and obvious to me once they had been explained. The outer curves or edges of the aerial road were super-elevated. Why? "Otherwise the centrifugal effect would pull the vehicle off the road and make it skid. The surface is engineered—raised—by 4 percent on average." So it was like Scalextric, on a real-life scale; if you did not raise the curve, the cars flew off. We looked out across the city, in various directions. It seemed an epic thing, building a road. "We have a small priest who comes," said Dilip, "he brings coconuts, flowers, incense." When did he come? "When we finish 1,000 segments, when we put a pile cap [the base of a pier], when we start the casting yard or the launcher, or if it's a festival. That's for the luck of the project. Sometimes we do a bhandara, when we give common food to everyone from the top officers to the workers. It's lunch for all. We might do a puja to remove ghosts from along the course of the road, especially if we're working in a far-flung area. We also do a puja for tools and tackles. Seventy percent of people in India will do a puja every day after taking a bath; they will worship god for a few minutes. We do the same for the course of the road. There is a god, Vishwakarma, who invented the cartwheel in ancient times, and he is the god of machinery."[20]

With the subcontinent now seen as a gargantuan potential market, global brands were seeking to reach new consumers, recruiting Indian staff and trying to buy up companies in India. The predatory activity worked the other way too, with Sunil Mittal buying Zain, and Europeans feeling astonished when Tetley, Jaguar Land Rover, Corus (containing the remnants of British Steel) and a chunk of Piaggio Aero were snapped up by Tata. A colossal Indian property developer, K. P. Singh's DLF, bought the luxury hotel group Aman, and the Chinese firm Nanjing Auto bought MG Rover, Britain's last mass production carmaker. When Tata made a move to buy the hospitality firm Orient-Express, which was listed on the New York Stock Exchange, the CEO of Orient-Express responded that any association with the Indian company might reduce the value of the brand. Tata was livid, calling this a "prehistoric" response and saying Orient-Express should realize Indian companies would "take their rightful place in the international arena . . . Enterprises and individuals must recognize and adapt to these fundamental economic changes. We believe that those with a fossilized frame of mind risk being marginalized."[21]

Cadbury was an example of a once British company that was creating a new Indian market. They had been in the country since a year after independence, selling at low volumes in a land with no tradition of eating chocolate. When you found a Cadbury's chocolate bar in India in the past, the heat had usually damaged it.[22] Now they wanted to target the new consumer by developing or inventing traditions, using products like Cadbury's Celebrations, aimed at people who usually bought mithai—Indian sweets—on special occasions. A TV and cinema advert showed an aspirational couple passing on an unwanted gift, which was passed on by a similar couple until eventually it found its way back to the first couple. The suggested solution was instead to give a Cadbury's gift box, which had a starting price of Rs100, or a little over $2. At the opposite end of the scale they sold individual Cadbury's éclairs, and small fruit and nut chocolate bars. The adverts focused on occasions when Indians celebrated by "sweetening the mouth"—such as a birth, a religious festival, an election or passing an exam—and aimed to persuade people to substitute Cadbury's chocolates for the local halwai's sticky traditional confections made of sugar, milk, ghee and nuts, topped with silver or gold leaf. According to Cadbury's head of marketing: "The products are also more hygienic in comparison to most mithais and are a convenient food." Other adverts showed human heads exploding in a chocolaty mess, and raunchy college girls using éclairs to entice money out of a boy. In the words of a company statement, detailing new publicity: "One of the most significant sequences in the commercial shows a pizza delivery boy working overtime on the eve of Diwali. He gets surprised with a Cadbury's Celebrations being gifted by the customer he delivered pizza to. The gesture warms his heart and makes him feel appreciated."[23] Everything about the positioning of this famous British chocolate brand (started in the nineteenth century by philanthropic Quakers who wanted to steer people away from alcohol and towards coffee, tea and chocolate) was put into a distinctive Indian cultural context—even if the lucky delivery boy was handling American fast food.

By 2009, Cadbury's sales in India were growing by 30 percent a year, and they had ambitions for further growth, although annual revenue was still only around $300m. They were in the process of persuading south Indian coconut farmers to plant cocoa alongside coconut palms, with the intention of giving India 3 percent of world cocoa production by 2020 (presently, it was minuscule). In lower-middle-class street markets like the one by the metro station in Vishnu Garden in the west of Delhi, Cadbury was catching new customers. As many as fifty-five outlets in this little market sold their chocolates, and the luckier ones were given display cabinets or fridges in which to keep them. Each time the salesman on this beat, Rajesh Sharma, visited a shop he would check that the Cadbury products were out on display. One of his strategies was to persuade mithai sellers to stock chocolate alongside Indian sweets during a festival. If they agreed, Rajesh Sharma was able to give them an extra 2 percent profit margin. The combination of TV adverts and clever marketing made Cadbury attractive, but it also had an unexpected result—it encouraged the interest of another kind of purchaser, the giant U.S. food group, Kraft.

In 2010, Kraft bought Cadbury for $18.5bn. A Cadbury's factory in England was closed, with production being shifted to Poland. Since Cadbury sold 70 percent of India's chocolates and Kraft had almost no presence in this vital emerging market, the United States was able to leapfrog over Britain to reach Asia. On a flying tour of Indian cities, an executive vice-president of Kraft International, Sanjay Khosla, said, "the energy is just phenomenal in this country" and that "the Cadbury acquisition was aimed primarily at getting a footprint in markets like India." Khosla was himself an IIT Delhi graduate who had made his career in different parts of the world before moving to the United States.[24]

Although many of the newer companies in India sought to separate themselves from an old image of graft and backhanders, in some cases by having firm and transparent rules on corporate ethics, the tentacles of bribery still snaked from the bureaucracy. The problem of corruption was closely linked to poverty and social imbalance. Often the poorest members of society, those with no protection, suffered disproportionately, paying out money to the police to be allowed to live in an illegal shack, or to someone with a keycard in order to use a locked water pump, or to a local thug for the chance to beg at a road junction. At the other end of the economic hierarchy, there were frequent cases of embezzlement: a civil servant in

Chhattisgarh discovered with over $20m of unaccounted assets; or the for-mer chief minister of Jharkhand, Madhu Koda, arrested with his associ-ates because more than $500m appeared to have been diverted from public funds; or Shibu Soren, who accepted money to support Narasimha Rao in a crucial trust vote in Parliament and took it straight to the Punjab National Bank, where he opened an account and deposited the cash. Both Koda and Soren were Adivasis from poor backgrounds—Koda had been a labourer in a mine, and one of his associates had sold milk and sewing machines from door to door—who were caught because their laundering was amateurish; more sophisticated operators, including some at the very top of politics, used "bagmen," people who looked after their worldly goods in return for a cut, and who sometimes kept the money.[25]

One of the strongest weapons against corruption was transparency—or a fear of being caught. Taking bribes was now becoming annoyingly diffi-cult for senior bureaucrats and politicians, such was the fear of spy cameras. The 2005 Right to Information Act, combined with the new media's love of spying and bugging, appeared to be undermining certain types of graft. An investigation into arms sales by the website Tehelka in 2001 sparked this shift, catching and shaming people for the sort of behaviour that had always been rumoured but never so graphically demonstrated. The sting revealed that numerous politicians, military officers and bureaucrats were taking money on defence deals. The undercover footage was as shocking for its content as for the nonchalance and foul language with which the guardians of the nation's defences sold their services for cash. Tehelka was then in its heyday, and two of its reporters, Mathew Samuel and Aniruddha Bahal, posed as representatives of a fictitious London-based arms manufacturer, West End International.

They claimed to be selling "4th generation thermal imaging equipment" and military hardware. Bangaru Laxman, a token Dalit who was president of the BJP, was filmed taking Rs100,000 in cash as an initial sweetener and saying, "you can give dollars" next time. The Samata party's treasurer, R. K. Jain, boasted he had made a fortune for his party and for himself in similar scams. Bangaru Laxman, the defence minister George Fernandes (who in his days as a firebrand had thrown out Coca-Cola from India) and his col-league Jaya Jaitly resigned, with Laxman claiming there was a conspiracy against him because of his lower-caste background, and Jaitly asserting that "dubious blackmailers" were trying to destroy the country.[26]

The recorded dialogue between the journalists and their targets yielded material worthy of Joseph Heller's *Catch-22*, as reworked by a subcontinental absurdist playwright. Aniruddha Bahal described how his fellow sleuth, Mathew Samuel, was a painfully inept conspirator. Asked by an army general who his firm's bankers were, he answered: "Thomas Cook"; asked where he stayed in England, he said: "Manchester United." His military knowledge was no better than his geography (Samuel was a Malayali who had never travelled outside India). When the potential purchasers of the latest thermal imaging cameras asked him what their range was, he replied: "Unlimited." Noticing a baffled expression, he corrected himself: "No, no . . . after a long distance the vision gets blurred."[27] Everyone, from the director of ordnance and supply to the deputy secretary of the ministry of defence, took money. Using a broken mix of Hindi and English, senior army officers, middlemen and politicians chatted away to the fictitious arms dealers over drinks in New Delhi's five-star hotels:

LT. COL. SHARMA: We don't involve ministry in our world. We do it directly.

BRIG. SEHGAL: This bhenchod [sisterfucker], they've done a very smart thing. He has kept everything with him.

LT. COL. SHARMA: Fuck it . . . We issue the tender, call the bloody parties, do the PNC [Price Negotiation Committee], give the supply order. Screw you.

TEHELKA: We will get the tie-up done. With whoever you want, we will get a tie-knot . . .

BRIG. SEHGAL: Bhenchod, see I have a counter offer and all these fuckers know about it. Either I give money bhenchod to all of them. Include all. This maderchod [motherfucker] is the way here . . . All these politicians are chutiyas [cunts]. They are all different behind your backs . . .

BRIG. IQBAL SINGH: Cultivating MGO [Master General of Ordnance] is my problem . . . I will find out somebody from his country-cousin side, whether he is game or not otherwise.

TEHELKA: Yeah, okay . . .

MAJ. GEN. AHLUWALIA: Now understand, if you are talking about a deal which is 20 crore [$4.5m] here, 60 crore there, make a profit of

5 crore, saala [brother-in-law, though implying worse], if you come to my house to meet me on Diwali, you can't talk without bringing Blue Label . . . Isn't it?

TEHELKA: True fact, sir.

MAJ. GEN. AHLUWALIA: So, if, when you are talking big, you got to also project big . . . Every other fucker knows bloody Putin. Everybody knows George Fernandes, everybody knows bloody Putin, everybody knows bloody Saddam . . . There are 25 buggers who are carrying a letter from exports. This is big. The carrot at the other end is one bloody deal. This Kaun Banega Crorepati [*Who Wants to be a Millionaire?*—or technically, who wants Rs10m] . . . People are happy . . .

ADDITIONAL SECRETARY L. M. MEHTA: What is the product range?

TEHELKA: Which one . . . Sir, we have a tank navigation system . . .

ADDITIONAL SECRETARY L. M. MEHTA: *Achha.*

TEHELKA: And that is smart ammunition, and some very typical type of bombs . . .

ADDITIONAL SECRETARY L. M. MEHTA: I see.

TEHELKA: So, a lot of products, we are supplying NATO countries also.

(Pause)

ADDITIONAL SECRETARY L. M. MEHTA: So you must remain on their payroll.

TEHELKA: Yeah . . .

MAJ. S. J. SINGH: I am, basically, you can call me a fixer . . . There was a deal of Krasnopol [a laser-guided artillery projectile]. That was 50 crore deal . . . It was not being cleared and . . .

TEHELKA: Due to what?

MAJ. S. J. SINGH: Firstly, out of six tests, it was only one test which was successful. Five test failures. Then the bureaucracy was not at all in favour of it . . . but, ultimately, we were able to push it through . . . and now it is a repeat order.

TEHELKA: This is called smart ammunition something?

MAJ. S. J. SINGH: Yeah.

TEHELKA: Same thing.

MAJ. S. J. SINGH: Krasnopol is the name of the bomb.[28]

The image of the Indian military communicated here was not reassuring; the following year, India and Pakistan came close to going to war, with India mobilizing half a million troops on the frontier. The most outrageous thing about this exposé was not the corruption, nor even the idea that a weapon might be bought after repeated test failures, but the state's response to the dishonesty. The prosecution of those involved was half-hearted, and much more effort was devoted to persecuting Tehelka, which was nearly destroyed by repeated investigations and court cases (it has since revived as a weekly magazine for the socially concerned). The BJP was in power at the time, but even when Congress came back into office they showed no interest in quashing the various cases. Many of the people caught in the sting operation simply pretended that all the videos had been faked. This became something of a tradition in India whenever a prominent figure was caught on camera: the 86-year-old governor of Andhra Pradesh, N. D. Tiwari, said he was innocent of any scandal after he was photographed in bed with several unhappy young women: "They are using the electronic technology to combine photographs."[29]

Corruption and poverty were part of the same story in India. If the economic reforms were to mean something, they had to reach those who had never been privileged before, those who had previously lacked an opportunity to alter their position in society. If money only passed to the rich and corrupt, no sincere progress would have been made. Did the ambition of raising government revenues through the generation of wealth by the private sector succeed in undermining poverty? The figures were complicated, with the argument swinging back and forth depending on who was telling the story.

The first thing you had to decide was what poverty meant. Tashi Norbu, the old man who saw Nehru's plane land in Ladakh in 1948, would qualify as poor. He lived almost by subsistence in one of the most remote parts of India. His family farm had four hours' supply of mountain water each day, by village agreement, designed to give them two harvests of barley a year before the snow fell and winter set in, with temperatures dropping to minus 30°C. Life depended on the efficient labour of every family member (which explained the higher status of women in the Himalayas; they were needed for survival). Yet Tashi Norbu had enough to eat, and although his existence was tough, it was culturally rich and did not seem like poverty. Similarly, when I visited the slum of Chetan Basti in Delhi during the 2009 election and spent time in some of the houses, it was noticeable how clean and airy they were, despite lacking running water. The risk of looking at poverty in this subjective way was to romanticize it; these places did not seem poor to me, while the houses or huts in Chandni Chowk and the blazing villages of Uttar Pradesh did.

Analysis of poverty began in a serious way in India in the 1950s under the guidance of (who else but) P. C. Mahalanobis. He set up one of the world's first household expenditure surveys. The thinking behind it was that people did not usually report their income accurately, and since payment at this time in India often came in the form of crops, it would be difficult to obtain useable data. So instead Mahalanobis used a method that recorded household consumption over a thirty-day period. By the 1970s a government task force had decided what level of income was necessary to secure a basic calorie intake. The all-India poverty line was the weighted sum of rural and urban poverty lines. After 1973–74 it could be updated using a price deflator to account for inflation, rather than recalculated each time. Every five years, the Indian government now did a "thick" or detailed consumer expenditure survey in order to estimate national levels of poverty. Exact comparison became possible over several decades.[30]

What did these official estimates reveal? Starting in 1973–4, they showed that 56.4 percent of rural Indians and 49.0 percent of urban Indians lived in poverty, a national total of 54.9 percent. A decade later the national figure had fallen to 44.5 percent and by 1993–94 it had dropped to 36.0 percent. By 2010 (projecting forward from 2004–05 assuming an annual decline of 0.8 percent) the figure stood at 22.9 percent.[31] The preliminary implication here was that extreme poverty had been falling steadily since the sampling system began, but did not decrease any faster after the economic reforms. In absolute terms, the number of poor people in India had not changed significantly between the 1970s and 1990s, because of the rise in population. When Manmohan Singh came to power in 2004, there were still 300 million Indians living in dire poverty.[32]

A country's estimate of its own poverty levels may not be the best source—the U.S. federal government has long been accused of setting its poverty line too low (and announced a change to the system in 2010). The World Bank uses global reference lines set at $1.25 and $2.00 per day at purchasing power parity, meaning they are weighted for the cost of staple goods in a given country. In 2008, Shaohua Chen and Martin Ravallion of the World Bank published a revealing research paper titled *The Developing World Is Poorer Than We Thought, But No Less Successful in the Fight against Poverty*, explaining an overhaul of methods of estimating poverty and deducing that although it was pervasive in developing countries, it was declining fast. The most noticeable change was in China, which since Mao's death had managed a world-altering programme of poverty alleviation. Another World Bank publication estimated that, by 2015, only 84 million Chinese would be living on less than $1.25 per day.[33]

How did India look when judged by these international standards? It looked even worse. The government's all-India line, when matched to the World Bank's method of calculation, turned out to be set at only $1.03 per day.[34] The international poverty line was higher, at $1.25 or $2.00 per day, which allowed some latitude in deciding the relative extent of poverty. These shocking figures showed that at the time of Indira Gandhi's assassination in 1984, 17 out of every 20 people in India lived on the equivalent of less than $2.00 per day, and more than half lived on less than $1.25 per day.[35] The levels of poverty have been dropping steadily since then, although it was only in 2005 that the effects of earlier economic reforms started to make the numbers drop rapidly. If things continued at their present rate, India should reach a position in around 2025 where less than 10 percent of the population is caught in extreme poverty, when defined as an income of less than $1.25 per day.[36]

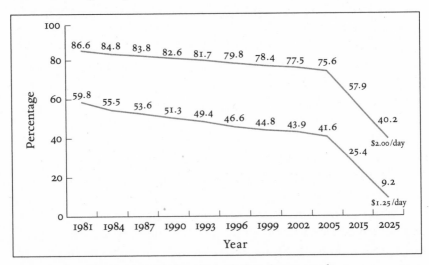

Percentage of Indians living below the poverty line

Another calculation was the "squared poverty gap" (the poverty gap index weighted by itself), which measured the severity of the problem by taking greater account of the very poor. It suggested the intensity of poverty in India had declined in recent decades. Under this analysis, Rajiv Gandhi's time as prime minister emerged as a time of significant improvement. In 1981 the squared poverty gap stood at 8.5, in 1990 at 5.6 and in 2005 at 3.7.[37] Certainly photographs or film footage taken of India during the 1950s or 1960s—or at the time of British rule, when famine was often rife—indicate a way of living that was substantially worse than anything seen today. Even in the poorest parts of India, where children die of disease, foul water and malnourishment, I have never come across the depths of human suffering that were visible on the streets of Calcutta when I first visited in the 1980s: an old man lying dying in the dust by Howrah station, and human figures who gave a sudden meaning to the previously empty phrase "skin and bone," for that was all they had left.

Whatever political view you take of India's economic liberalization, two things are clear: large numbers of people have been lifted out of extreme poverty, and around one quarter of the population have so far gained very little. People still die from poverty, finding that eating rats or ground mango kernels does not save them from starvation, migrant workers continue to break stones by hand and live in pipes or under plastic sheeting, and parents continue to sell their children into servitude.

This was the central political and moral quandary of how the nation would develop. Would India go the same way as some Latin American countries, where the benefits of economic growth were restricted to a few? This was the standard criticism but looked unlikely: the new Indian middle class was visibly dynamic. Yet a wide gap remained. The growth of the economy would not eradicate poverty, but it could not happen without it. Judging by their unchanged position over previous centuries, the villagers of Uttar Pradesh would be no better off if Lakshmi Mittal had not held a lavish family wedding at Versailles.

Kaushik Basu, chief economic adviser to the finance ministry, proposed in 2010 that the government implement its promise of "inclusive growth" by measuring progress through the rise in per capita income of the poorest 20 percent; unless their income rose at the same level as the rest of society, the government would be failing.[38] Basu proposed various solutions, such as issuing food and fertilizer coupons rather than relying on subsidized products in the open market, which had previously had the effect of creating a shadow economy; government "ration shops" were a fount of corruption, with grain adulterated with grit and some of the stock sold illegally. If Basu's method were to succeed and be effectively targeted, it would depend in part upon a scheme that was currently under way to give every Indian a unique biometric identity card, with online verification. The plan, perhaps the most ambitious IT project in history, was being organized by Nandan Nilekani, one of the founders of the Bangalore-based technology company Infosys. In the meantime, poverty declined while injustice remained—although some escaped their fate.

When Rajeev Samant was at the Cathedral School in Bombay in the 1980s, he formed an Ayatollah Khomeini cult. This was not because he was a Shia fundamentalist or indeed a Muslim (although Salman Rushdie was a former Cathedralite) but because he thought it might entertain the other children and annoy the teachers. He also ran a gambling syndicate, betting on cricket matches, Wimbledon and the U.S. Open, but managed to fix the odds so he and his friend Cyrus always won. As a student at Stanford he was, in his words, "basically a party guy." He went on to work in the finance department at Oracle in California before deciding to return to India. Samant was coming home, wanting to do something different in the new economy.

His father had a small-scale plastics manufacturing business and had started a commercial diving company. One day they drove together a few hours out of Bombay to look at a patch of land the family owned near Nashik. It was a dry area on the northern end of the Deccan Plateau, not far from the source of the Godavari river, and close to an important pilgrimage site where Lord Ram was reputed to have bathed. His father was inclined to sell the land, but Samant had an idea: he could grow mangoes on it. He would need permission to pump water from a nearby lake. He employed Dattu Mahadu Vanse, a local labourer, to clear the earth.

Over time, Dattu would lift himself from poverty in a way that would not have been possible in earlier times, and life for him and his extended family would be transformed by India's economic changes. With Samant, he cut down grass six feet tall and dug up the scrub, avoiding the cobras and leopards. The plan to grow mangoes worked, but there was no commercial market for them. Samant tried growing tomatoes, roses, peanuts. The problem was the same. The land was fertile, but it was nearly impossible to make a business succeed. One day he noticed farmers eating grapes. Nashik's grapes and raisins were popular. Might it be possible to make wine?

Dattu Mahadu Vanse was a stocky man in jeans, trainers, a shirt and a necklace. He remembered what happened next: "Rajeev sir went back to America for three months. He returned with some vine cuttings and said, 'It's a wine grape.' I said, 'What is a wine?' He said it was a product made from grape juice. I had to grow the saplings and to water them." After growing some grapes successfully, Samant persuaded Kerry Damskey, a Californian winemaker, to come to India and show them how to go about making wine commercially. The climate was deemed to be similar to Brazil's, between tropical and temperate, although Nashik suffered from a monsoon—which was unheard of in any of the world's wine regions. During the growing season, the climate was not unlike that in Sonoma County in California or the Barossa Valley in Australia. No bank would lend Samant money for this untested project, and he had to borrow from family and friends before a commercial bank eventually agreed to make a loan. In 1999 they produced their first bottles of Sula Sauvignon Blanc, and a decade later Sula Vineyards was selling 3 million bottles a year and starting to export around the world.

Their principal ambition was to grow a local market for wine (annual per capita consumption in India was less than a tablespoon, against more than 50 litres in Sonia Gandhi's country of birth) by attracting the new middle and upper classes. Until the late 1960s there had been prohibition in Maharashtra, and drinking alcohol was still seen by many as an improper activity, particularly among women. Samant was astute at marketing the product not as alcohol, but as a way of life. The Sula website said: "Mr. Samant is an avid sportsman and enjoys running, yoga, diving, windsurfing and playing tennis in his playtime. Sula Vineyards is also a leader in sustainable winemaking, and has created direct and indirect employment opportunities for thousands of rural youths." His first coup was when he convinced Mumbai's best-known hotel, the Taj, to stock his wines. "I got to see the man at the Taj because we were both old Cathedralites. He said he could get French wine at the same price. I said that's true, but it's bad wine. He tasted our Sauvignon Blanc and put it on their list."[39] Samant also persuaded the state authorities to see wine as an area of potential economic growth and not to put an excise duty on it as they did on spirits like rum. There were now more than twenty functioning wineries in Maharashtra.

Before the winery opened, Dattu had almost no way to make a living. He came from a tribal group called Mahadev Kolis, known in Maharashtra for following their own customs and for suffering discrimination and poverty. Producing no surplus crops on their scraps of land, they had nothing to sell but their labour. Members of the Mahadev Koli community, who tend to be short and dark, would often fall into debt to farmers, and find that in practice they had become bonded labourers. Dattu had no education at all. He went to a school once, but there was no teacher and he came home again. At the age of twelve he became a fisherman, sitting in an inflated tyre tube and paddling around a sun-splashed lake with a hook and a net. This sounds almost glamorous, like something from *Huckleberry Finn*, but it was bleak work. I asked Dattu how much he had earned. "That depends if I caught any fish. I sometimes made Rs100 per week. Sometimes Rs200." Even on a good week, that was a lot less than $1.25 per day, and on a bad week it was about $0.30 per day.

We were sitting in a café above the Sula winery. Rajeev Samant ran the place along Californian lines, with the vineyards open to visitors, a tasting room and two restaurants: Kareem's and Little Italy. The quality of the wine had improved over the years, as the vines matured. Nearly all of the visitors were Indian. Dattu spoke in Marathi, with his words interpreted by one of his younger colleagues, Santosh.

"My mother and father grew millet and chickpeas, enough for themselves. They were very poor because we are from a backward community. My first job was cutting the wild and thorny trees. Rajeev sir needed reliable people. I grew tomatoes and roses. When they were going to build the winery, I did other things like digging an eight-foot pit for a consultant engineer, and when the construction started I was a supervisor. I cleaned out the big tanks when they came from the manufacturer in Nashik. Mr. Kerry taught me how to clean a stainless-steel tank. It's very, very difficult to make good wine. You have to be careful. I learned how to operate the press when we were doing the crush. I learned about racking [separating the wine from the lees or sediment]. Mr. Kerry had to explain all of this by sign language. If Rajeev sir was there, he would translate. I learned about the chilling plant, about adding bentonite to remove protein and how to avoid getting crystals in the wine. I understood how the automatic bottling plant would operate. I came to learn all the different parts of the winemaking process, although we did not speak the same language."

A French wine grower had been with me when I toured the winery and been frankly astonished. As this man, Laurent, said: "In the south of France we cannot afford to employ the human beings. Otherwise, it is exactly the same. I can see the same love, the same passion to make the wine." In the vineyards, they used the Israeli technology of drip irrigation.

I asked Dattu what his favourite wine was. "Shove you"—Sauvignon. "The first time I tasted liquor was at a post-harvest party when I had some champagne. I found it sour, and I felt a bit sleepy." Did other members of his community like wine? "My father prefers a local rum made of molasses. The Mahadev Kolis are Adivasis and they normally prefer Chenin Blanc, which is not too expensive, and Madeira because it is sweet." Santosh said, "Indians like fruity wines. Zinfandel is quite popular. You can see it being loaded there." Out of the window, beside a stand of motorbikes which belonged to the workers, we could see an army truck being filled with cases of wine. On the way to Nashik I had seen the democratization of wine drinking—a roadside dhaba serving batata vada, potato fritters, with white wine.

Dattu's talent and hard work had led to him getting a key position in the winery, even as graduates with degrees in subjects like microbiology were brought in by Rajeev Samant to take other posts.

"I am the cellar master. I look after all the cellar operations and have six people with me as a helping hand. We execute any instructions that come from the laboratory. I can't write up the forms because I am still illiterate. I have a secretary who writes my report—he is my cousin-brother—detailing all transfers and additions. I know that information in my head, but other people need to have it written down, so they can read it. I know how many bottles are in each place, what date a process took place. We have to check oxygen levels, the torque on the caps, bacteria levels, cork moisture, the taste, the blending."

This was not the first time I had heard of a clever person who was illiterate having exceptional powers of memory. The act of not writing down forced you to store knowledge in a different way; perhaps writing was a way of removing knowledge from your mind. "My salary is Rs20,000 [$450] per month. I have bought land and invested in life insurance. I grow grapes on my land and sell them to the winery. A lot of relatives come to me and ask to get their children into the business. I try to do my best for them, if they are capable. I don't want to spoil my name. They have opportunities. I have five daughters and one son. The younger three are getting education. My son goes to an English-medium school and I want him to go to college. I'm not sure what he should study, as I have nobody in my community to guide me. Nobody has ever gone beyond the tenth grade. As he gets older I might seek advice from the Mahadev Kolis who live in the city."[40]

Dattu was the world's only Adivasi cellar master.

8

A QUARRY NEAR MYSORE

INDIA IS NEVER SHORT of horror stories. A bride was burned to death in Jodhpur on the orders of her mother-in-law because her family had not delivered a dowry. In Imphal, an unarmed young man was shot by police commandos, execution-style, only paces from the state assembly. A widely syndicated newspaper photograph showed a mentally ill girl tied to a post on a grimy city street while her mother went to work each day. A journalist reported from Patna that children had replaced oxen on the farmland of Raghubansh Prasad Singh, the rural development minister: in an accompanying photo, little boys dragged a heavy plough across a sodden field. The father of a boy was quoted: "Yahan par tractor nahi chal sakta hai, aur bail nahi jot sakta hai. Issliye bacha log hi jotega"—"A tractor or oxen cannot be used in this field and so that's why children have to plough the land." The minister laughed it off when confronted by a reporter: "They are just doing some small work in the field and it is just being blown out of proportion."[1] In Rajasthan, girls were injected with a cattle hormone to bring on puberty prematurely, so they could be sold to brothels in the United Arab Emirates.[2] Dozens of handicapped children in Gulbarga were temporarily buried up to their necks in a garbage dump during a solar eclipse in the hope their disabilities might miraculously disappear. Several families in a village in eastern Uttar Pradesh were massacred because they came from the wrong caste.

Foreign correspondents, or Indian writers seeking a docile foreign audience, can make a living by reporting ceaseless tales of woe. Deracinated and placed in an alien context, they become India's only story. Such accounts seem, in their enormity, to emerge from a distant or eternal past, and to offer evidence of the impossibility of progress. For outsiders who have not visited India, they reinforce long-standing prejudices and underline the subcontinent's brutal, shocking and alien nature. For Westerners, poverty can be a source of entertainment: if the BBC wants a television show about child-trafficking in India, they send Lindsay Lohan from *Mean Girls* to West Bengal. Lohan helped the process along on Twitter: "Over 40 children saved so far . . . Doing THIS is a life worth living!!! Focusing on celebrities and lies is so disconcerting, when we can be changing the world one child at a time . . . hope everyone can see that . . . never too late to start helping others, however u can."[3]

This is presumed to be the only explicable way to deal with India; a celebrity, or a second-generation South Asian with passing knowledge of the subcontinent, visits with a view to saving something—the tiger, the destitute, the elephant, him- or herself. India is made frightening. Take this representative opening paragraph, from a first-time traveller writing in the *New York Post*:

> Let's face it. India is really intimidating. The heartbreaking poverty, the heat, the crazy traffic, the begging. It's an unpredictable place, in fact, there are few things you can count on when visiting—except, perhaps, a week-long bout of Delhi Belly. Of course, for every reason to stay home, there's at least one to go. The food—you haven't lived until you've eaten the real-deal curry slathered in homemade lime pickle; the history, from maharajahs to the British Raj; the swoony neon colors. (Legendary fashionista Diana Vreeland once noted that "Pink is the navy blue of India.")[4]

Here, the heartbreaking poverty, begging and putative stomach trouble are linked to the swoony colours and slathered food, so that India becomes above all a surfeit, a place where a visitor's sensory experiences are sure to be intense.

For several decades after independence, the stock Indian response to reports of extreme human suffering was to pretend it had not happened, or had been misunderstood, or was being exaggerated for political reasons by a combination of anti-national forces and the menacing foreign hand. As sections of the country have become prosperous, patriots have started to admit or acknowledge the horror of many Indian lives. Although the Oscar-winning movie *Slumdog Millionaire* received a tepid reception in India for being implausible and miscast (apart from Azharuddin Ismail and Rubina Ali, most of the supposed children of the slums spoke in upper-class accents), few of its detractors tried to pretend life in Mumbai's heart was anything other than degraded. Vikas Swarup, the author of the book on which *Slumdog Millionaire* was based, was a senior Indian diplomat; in earlier decades, an overlap between shocking social commentary and diplomacy would have been impossible.

In 2003 I met a magazine editor in Cochin, or Kochi, who gave me an article he had published in his magazine, *The Week*, some years earlier. More than any Indian horror story I had read, it lodged in my mind. The report, titled "Life in Chains," was simple. A man, a Dalit who worked in a quarry in nearby Karnataka, took a loan from his boss and found himself under the yoke of an implausible debt. To make sure he and his family members kept working, the man was taken by the boss's goons to a welder in Mysore, who fitted him with a pair of fetters linked by a bulky metal chain. The bolts were welded over, to ensure they could never be undone. The cost of the fetters and the welding was added to the man's burden of debt. There he remained for years, cracking stones, until a group of farming activists chanced upon him during an election campaign and secured his release. The report compared the liberated quarry worker's tentative steps to those of a little child learning to walk, while the man himself, Venkatesh, said he felt unbearably light: "It is a strange feeling. It is like coming out of water."[5]

It was a very Indian story, and one that had emerged from a prevailing social order. More extreme human rights abuses happen in neighbouring countries, but the absolute indifference shown to Venkatesh was an unexceptional Indian response to another human being's suffering. Many people, including the local police, would have known the quarry contained chained labourers, but nobody had bothered to do anything about it. It was the same indifference that allowed modern India to ignore the plight of Adivasis and let "Maoists" become their spokespeople, and in turn allowed the Maoist leadership to slaughter police jawans because they were "class enemies." Compassion (in the original sense of "suffering with," which implies a commonality) is not a Hindu concept, except where it involves ritual donation in pursuit of a religious obligation. Loyalty is shown to the family or to your particular community, rather than to people in general. The idea that all are equal in the sight of God is Islamic, while "Do as you would be done by" is a Christian concept. In this case, Venkatesh was not seen as a fellow human to whom care might be extended; he was nobody, nothing. His incarceration, or slavery, happened in a country with democratic rights and genuine constitutional safeguards, less than a hundred miles from one of the nation's most prosperous cities.

I was left wondering about the real story behind the story, and finally went in search of Venkatesh. How did this tragedy happen? What did Venkatesh himself think about it? By luck, the journalist who had written the original report in *The Week* was able to accompany me. He had published the story under a pseudonym, because he was doing another job at the time; his real name was Bhanu.

We set off in the morning half-light from Bangalore, or Bengaluru, passing large construction projects and roadside hoardings where white models advertised lingerie. Around nine o'clock, we stopped for a breakfast of vada and coconut chutney at a hotel, New Maddur Tiffanys (Maddur Tiffanys faced us on the opposite side of the road). Here, a hotel meant a restaurant, set up when people were starting to travel for the first time. "Before 1900 or 1920," Bhanu said, "nobody in the Mysore area would have eaten food cooked outside the home. They were worried the wrong caste might be doing the cooking. In Mysore and Bangalore, you can still see places called Brahmin Hotel." The atmosphere here was different from Delhi, where I had come from—more restrained, less fashionable, more respectful. As we drove along the road, I noticed Hindu Military Hotel—"military" meant they served chicken and mutton. These restaurants would have been opened for the meat-eating north Indian soldiers who were posted among the vegetarians of the south, surely feeling less than at ease in a faraway culture.

The day grew much hotter as we drove through the lush, sensuous, green landscape of paddy and coconut groves, spotted with many temples, towards the village where Venkatesh was believed to be living. We were near to Srirangapatna, which the British called Seringapatam, and I was queasily conscious of our proximity to a colonial horror story. In 1780 the Muslim ruler of the predominantly Hindu kingdom of Mysore, Tipu Sultan, inflicted an important and bloody victory over the British, checking their expansion in the south. In response, an East India Company army besieged Seringapatam, only to be greeted with rockets packed in iron tubes, a major advance in artillery, which was recorded by artists of the period. When Seringapatam was finally stormed, the British troops slaughtered Tipu Sultan and several thousand Mysore people. So the beauty of the land was drenched in cruelty, in the horror of past wars and in the indifference that had led to Venkatesh's slavery.

We reached the village of Ganjam fairly easily. The road was good because it was home to an important temple, and prosperous families needed to be able to visit. We stopped by the temple entrance, where some people were sitting in a neat line on the ground beside a stall, begging in a formal, ritualized way. Bhanu explained to them that we were looking for a freed quarry worker named Venkatesh. A man looked up at him and said simply: "I am Venkatesh." It seemed impossible, or an impossible coincidence, and it was only later in the day that it came to seem less extraordinary: in India a man with such a fate was likely to end up begging outside a temple. Venkatesh had dark-brown skin, black, oiled hair and the physique of a boy, but at sixty-five he still looked strong. Gathering up his mat, he asked us to come to his house and speak there.

When we reached the building, it was clear we were not going inside: it would be too small to accommodate Venkatesh, Bhanu and myself.

I sat on a stone step in the sun and Venkatesh squatted opposite me, chewing betel. He was wearing a dhoti and a dirty shirt. The government had given him and other quarry workers a row of bad houses when the story of their incarceration came out. Other things, such as a water supply, had been promised but had never materialized. By now it was maybe 40°C, and one of the women who had been begging at the temple crouched behind me holding a large black umbrella. Then plastic chairs were brought and we visitors sat on them while the woman holding the umbrella sat on the step, shielding us from the sun.

"Swathantra bandaaga naanu innu chikka huduga," said Venkatesh. "Nehru, Gandhi avarella budhivantharu. Naavu yavagloo Congressige vote hakodu."

"Independence came when I was a little boy. Nehru and Gandhi were very intelligent people. We have always voted for the Congress. It was about casting your vote. We don't have the brains of those leaders: that's why we crush stones. Indira Gandhi, Raja [Rajiv] Gandhi—didn't they take bullet wounds and die? I've learned more about this since my release. For us it was a struggle for food, for sustenance." He was one of four children, and had been crushing stones since he could remember. His father, Annamayya, had been a migrant worker from an arid region on the border between Karnataka and Andhra Pradesh, the state to the north. When the big Krishnaraja Sagara dam was built on the Cauvery river, he had helped to make it. "When we were children there was a Congress leader, a Muslim, who owned a rice mill and let us have split [rejected] rice at Rs5 a kilo. Now you wouldn't get it for less than Rs10. We lived with the rest of the Scheduled Castes and Muslims at one end of a village near Srirangapatna. We have a caste name, Voddollu, which we use among ourselves, but here they call us 'Bovi'—stone crushers. It's not our own name: Bovi is a Kannada word."

Venkatesh and Bhanu then began one of the detailed conversations that happen in India when people from different places are establishing social information about each other. Until now, they had both been speaking in Kannada, the local language, but as it became clear that Venkatesh's family had migrated originally from further north, they switched to Telugu, which Bhanu happened to speak because his parents came from Andhra Pradesh.

It was not unusual for an educated person to be able to shift fluently between languages in India, the land of conversation. You had the local language of the street, English and Hindi for general interaction, and your mother tongue as well, usually meaning the language spoken by your father's family. The ancient Dravidian languages of the south (Telugu, Kannada, Tamil and Malayalam, which are grammatically different from Indo-European languages like Sanskrit, Hindi and English) have phonetic similarity. They are made with the tongue at the front of the mouth and sound to an alien ear like water gurgling in a stream. If you learn the languages from childhood, it is possible to speak them all, minus occasional words of vocabulary. In the case of Bhanu, who spoke perfect English, he could also manage Hindi, Kannada, Telugu, Tamil and Kodava, a dialect spoken by people from Coorg, a lovely hilly area of southern Karnataka where coffee is grown and the elephants eat jackfruit. He had picked up the "extra" languages during his childhood in Bangalore.

"I made a mistake when I wrote the report about his release last time," said Bhanu. "He is from a Scheduled Caste, but he is not an untouchable."

So the story became more complex: this was not, it seemed, about caste oppression. I wondered where Venkatesh was positioned in the caste hierarchy. He was adamant that as a Bovi, or what his community called a Voddollu, he was distinct from Dalits.

Still speaking in Telugu, he told Bhanu: "We are different. We would not enter an untouchable's house, or intermingle with them. They are lower than us. We are stone crushers. We are invited to interdine with OBCs, but we wouldn't interdine with untouchables."

"Interdine." It was a word from Gandhi's time, a word that made sense only in a rural Indian context, where the old caste restrictions were so ingrained.

"I started working full-time when I was twelve years old, carrying soil away from a canal. My father had me married at eighteen. I worked in different stone quarries, usually breaking granite." I noticed that Venkatesh had nicks and scars all over his feet and legs, presumably from the flying chips. "My job was to use a sixteen-pound hammer to make stones about this size"—he described a loaf of bread with his hands—"which could be put in a crusher to get jelly stones for reinforced concrete.

"It would have been in around 1995 that I went to the 'prison' quarry, because I had heard you could get food there. I didn't know the reputation of the owner, Puttaswamy Gowda. He was good at first. I didn't suspect anything. I asked for an advance of money, and he gave me a loan and said there was no need to repay it. He could be strict. If the stones were the wrong size, he would beat us horribly. He would tie us to a tree and beat us and leave us there for the night. Then, because he paid less than other quarry owners, I decided to leave. That was when the chaining started. My sons Krishna and Siddaraju ran away and were brought back by his men to the quarry, and he chained them.

"There were seven people, all from my family or community, who between us had borrowed maybe Rs850 [$19]. The owner said we had borrowed more, and that we now owed Rs20,000 [$450]. We were taken by car, one at a time, to a factory where they made metal wardrobes. They wrapped a cloth around my ankles, put on the cuffs, bolted them and welded the bolt. It took about three hours. It wasn't painful. Nobody said a word. The thing about wearing chained fetters is that you can't put on underwear or trousers. You can only wear a lungi, and you must take tiny steps. I was in chains for twenty-one months. There must have been a hundred people working in the quarry, and nobody did a thing. Cow-herders and shepherds were outside: they all saw us, but they couldn't challenge the quarry owner. He was too powerful."

I had not thought of this—that if your ankles were chained, you could not put on underwear or trousers. I asked whether he had thought of trying to send out a message to the police. For the first time, Venkatesh and the women around him laughed.

"The police? The police and the tehsildar [local government official] were in the pay of Puttaswamy Gowda. I never believed I would be freed. I thought I would be there for the rest of my life. When the farming activists came to free me, I was terrified. I only got the courage to speak when I was in the police station. It was my karma. What has to happen, will happen: it was god's doing." Venkatesh looked pensive. "I will never know why he decided to tie me up. It's as if you came here today to visit me, and I just chained you." Even the possibility of this frightened me.

By now the sun was overhead and we walked to the other end of the row of houses, where a coconut palm could give a little shade. On the way, we asked some of Venkatesh's neighbours what they thought about his experience. One woman was unsympathetic: "People kept on running away from the quarry and not doing their work. The owner had no choice but to chain them." The legal case against Puttaswamy Gowda had not yet come to court, although Venkatesh had been promised protection by the district commissioner if he would agree to testify. Instead, he told me he had gone back to the quarry in the hope of being paid off. He was given Rs3,000 by Puttaswamy Gowda: that was his price.

"I have anger against the owner, but what is the point of having anger? He is a rich man, and I have to beg. He can bribe boys who have just grown moustaches and they will testify against me. I can do nothing."[6]

Now the conversation was over, Venkatesh and his wife, Venkatalakshmamma, showed us a photo of their daughter-in-law, who had died of TB, leaving two young children who had been playing near us while we talked. Venkatalakshmamma said she herself was tubercular. There was more tragedy in the background: their son Krishna had been murdered two years ago during an argument, and his killers had been released. It seemed their neighbours had been involved. His brother Siddaraju was working far from home, and returned whenever he could. As we left, I asked Bhanu whether I might give Venkatesh and his family some money.

"I wouldn't offer more than Rs500, or it could cause a quarrel. I will say it is for their grandchildren."

When I gave Venkatesh the banknote, he bowed down in front of me, cringing. It had been a miserable experience talking to him, most of all because I knew this was the better time of his life. Bhanu and I walked to the temple on the banks of the Cauvery which was dedicated to Lord Shiva's consort, Parvati, known here as Nimishamba. Stalls sold coconuts and jasmine garlands and bunches of bananas for the pilgrims to take in as offerings. Plenty of people were visiting, in huge family groups. They bathed in the river wearing trunks or salwar kameez. Inside the Nimishamba temple we proceeded barefoot in a slow line, passing the hereditary priests with their naked chests and oiled hair. They made a point of treating pilgrims brusquely, snatching money and offerings and pushing us towards a grille behind which a statue of the goddess could be seen. Further back, coconuts were being broken for her. Snaking again in line, we were wafted with a flickering flame by a priest, smeared between the eyes with red paste and handed a piece of wrapped newspaper containing prasad and flower petals.

Then we were out on the stone steps, looking over the Cauvery. It was wide and beautiful although, away from the ritual cleanliness near the temple, the banks were strewn with rubbish. As we drove away, Venkatesh and Venkatalakshmamma were back in their position by the entrance to the temple, begging.

Our day was not over. News travels fast in India even without the Internet or a mobile phone, and our visit to Venkatesh's house had reached the ears of the campaigner who had secured his release from the quarry. Bhanu thought it would be rude not to visit him, so we arranged to meet by the Sri Bhavan Military Hotel in Srirangapatna. He was a large, fleshy man with a trimmed pepper-and-salt beard and a bottle-green shawl draped over his left shoulder, which indicated he was a farmers' leader. In his view, it was unlikely the case would ever come to trial since it would be embarrassing for the state government. He said the quarry had operated without a licence, and that the owner got around this by supplying cheap stone to Mysore officials to build their houses. Did he believe other people were still chained in quarries? "But for the chains, all else is still the same."[7]

For reasons that were not clear to me, the interview was taking place in the leader's stationary car, by the dusty roadside. He sat in front with his driver while Bhanu and I sat in the back. Within minutes, I had no questions left to ask. He offered me a tender coconut: I drank the water. He talked about his campaigns. Only at this point did it become clear that he was hoping to publicize his organization, the Karnataka Rajya Raitha Sangha. I listened while he told us in detail, in the manner of a leader or orator, of the past glories and future triumphs of the KRRS.

"We are alive, taking up issues of water availability, sugarcane prices and farmers' rights, seeds are becoming ever more expensive with globalization, pesticides are becoming more expensive with globalization. The KRRS will target McDonald's and smash Kentucky Fried Chicken again if we have to."

Then I remembered—his organization had destroyed a flagship KFC restaurant in Bangalore in the mid-1990s. It was a symbolic moment, a piece of shorthand used by activists at the time. The message was: "India's poor farmers are so angry about transnational corporations that they have trashed KFC with iron bars. Who will dare to set up shop in India now?" The answer was . . . just about everybody, including Colonel Sanders, who now had ten or twelve restaurants in Bangalore. The KRRS, meanwhile, was reduced to sitting in a car outside a military hotel in Srirangapatna, pressing for publicity.

The difficulty with the KRRS was that it spoke not for farm labourers but for farmers, who were often becoming rich. Re-zoned agricultural land on the edge of Bangalore was selling to developers for $80,000 an acre. As Bhanu said on the way back: "The money will melt away and then they will have no land." We ate an afternoon meal off plantain leaves at a roadside stop: spoons of spiced sprouts, aubergine, dal, curd, pickles and coconut paste, all dolloped on to a washed leaf by brisk servers along with maize rotis, mind-sharpening salted chillis and a cardamom-flavoured milk pudding. It was an elegant, natural, instinctive way to eat. Another day, at a Bangalore coffee house, Bhanu pointed out some newly rich farmers' sons to me. They looked burly and rustic, with heavy gold on their fingers, resting on the cusp of some new social order.

The migration from the countryside to the city is the seminal point in the life of anyone who comes from a traditional society. Forms of behaviour that have been honed over centuries can evaporate in a moment. A local writer, Tukaram S., has a touching short story, written in what the translator, Sugata Srinivasaraju, calls "an acrid dialect of Kannada, specific to the Mysore–Mandya region," about a man from a remote village who goes to the big city when a new bus service is introduced. People like this man can all of a sudden make money as domestic servants, security guards or construction workers. He proselytizes to the other villagers about the glamour of going off to Mysore: "That city is facing the skies and growing like mad. You should see the roads there; each one is as smooth and washed as well-laid charcoal. Buses and cars fly like crows and leap like frogs . . . Each road has rows of cloth shops. Ask for whatever colour and whichever size and for whoever—men, women, aged, fat or thin, you'll get it in an instant. You can actually take off your old clothes, then and there, and walk out with a new pair."

The man takes a loan to build a house but defaults on the payments, and representatives of a bank arrive in his village to begin repossession. His brush with globalization has left him homeless, but rather than being humiliated, he uses his recently acquired knowledge of the outside world to excuse himself from blame: "It seems banks have been emptied of their money in America and other countries. They are apparently closing down banks everywhere. This is the reason why banks here too want to collect their money back . . . Don't get panicky guys. The news has come that everything is getting all right. A blessed soul called Obama has become America's president and he is about to set things right. There are too many machines called computers and all the money is apparently stuck in them. Besides, some people took away lakhs and lakhs as salary every month."[8]

Bangalore had everything: fair male strippers for hen nights, shopping arcades with Hugo Boss and Montblanc, apartments that were rising at a ferocious rate. In the heart of the city, I noticed a large area of land had been fenced off for a development calling itself "Brigade Gateway—Bangalore's first lifestyle enclave." The perimeter road was surrounded by billboards promising a future paradise on earth, where every need would be met. Once complete, the lifestyle enclave would have private security, a hospital, its own school, an eleven-screen multiplex, a health spa, a hotel, a food court and restaurants, all sealed from the masses. One billboard showed a man in blue jeans walking his dog beside a lake in what looked like North America, with the caption first in English and then in the bouncy Kannada script: "Stroll alongside a serene lake." Adverts promised a helipad, sculpture courts, a bamboo grove, air-conditioning, patrolled private roads, water fountains and "a better quality of life." You could buy a luxury four-bedroom apartment in Brigade Gateway with a fitted German kitchen. "Each apartment wing will have two high-speed passenger lifts. Uninterrupted power supply (we have back-up generators to generators!) will ensure that you need to take the stairs only if you want the exercise." The wisdom of the Finnish modernist architect Alvar Aalto was quoted in evidence: "True architecture exists only where man stands in the centre."

It was quite a promise. I wondered how it was being put into effect, the philosophical idea of putting man in the centre, and joined a line of labourers as they advanced glumly into the forty-acre site for the morning shift. From their appearance, they were from north India. They carried or wore yellow hard hats, and some carried tiffin boxes. Although there were bright signs promoting the need to have boots with metal toe-caps, most of the men were wearing plastic sandals or chappals, and jerseys and mufflers. The place was a mess of grey mud and gravel. The labourers had to work on buildings that rose up to thirty storeys high, and safety nets had been slung around the higher reaches of the towers, though in a random way that offered no anticipation of capture if the men fell. I asked a security guard from Madhya Pradesh—we can call him Dhruv—how many people had died there that year (this was in October 2008). His answer was seven or eight.[9] He stressed he was only talking about his own section of the site, since he did not know what had happened elsewhere. He was unsure how many people had been injured, although he said the injured were usually sent straight back to their home villages.

I walked to the heart of the site and entered one of Brigade Gateway's apartment blocks. The staircase was half built, and I was able to climb nearly to the top of the tall building. All around, across the skyline, grey shells were rising. These were two- and three-bedroom apartments, and workers from West Bengal were running water pipes between them. They said they were paid Rs150 (or around $3) a day, but that the contractor or gangmaster who employed them took one quarter of their salary illegally. I watched as these men dragged and winched and hammered and drilled, in their plastic sandals. The quality of the construction was fairly good, but I was puzzled by a small box-room on the outside of each apartment, less than 2 metres square, which was accessible only from the common staircase. Was it a storage or wiring closet? No, it was the servant's room. Each apartment would need a servant, and this was where he or she would be living, without windows or fresh air.

Back at the main gate I asked Dhruv where the hundreds of labourers lived, and he offered to take me to what he called a housing colony, as he was nearing the end of his shift. Three big companies were responsible for the main construction project at Brigade Gateway. We went to see the accommodation that was used by the workers of one of these companies, Simplex Infrastructures. It was off a road about fifteen minutes' walk from the construction site, and it was here that I had a shock. Indian cities are full of slums and bad housing, but this was in a special category of its own.

It was reasonably easy to get inside. Dhruv had assumed that because I was white and quite smartly dressed, I must be on official business, while the guard at the colony let me in because I was with Dhruv. The place stank of rotting food and latrines, and amounted to little more than a network of paths awash with grey water, which led to sheds made of wood and corrugated iron. This was where the labourers lived for months or even years at a time. Most were at work, and the few who were there were either sick or resting. They came originally from Bihar, West Bengal and Madhya Pradesh, and had been recruited in their villages to come south as workers.

In each case, they told me a contractor was holding their wages and taking a large cut. But, as a listless teenage boy from Buxar named Prem said, "What can we do? We can do nothing. My family don't even know where I am." Prem showed me inside the sheds. There was no electricity, so I used the light on my mobile phone to look around (the cheaper Indian mobiles, like the one I had, usefully contain a flashlight). The concrete floor was lined with thin plastic mats, like beach mats, each one about the size of a single mattress, and at the head of each mat were some folded blankets and washing utensils.

"Is this where you sleep?" I asked Prem, who was wrapped in a red blanket and shivering with fever.

He assented.

"Two persons sleep on each mat," said Dhruv.

"Two? At the same time?"

"Yes," said Dhruv. "We sleep close together."

Above the mats were lines of rough string, hanging across the shed. Little pictures of deities and religious places were propped in the webs of string. Each man had a length on which to hang his own clothes and possessions. This was his sacred thread, the nearest thing he had to privacy. It was not difficult to imagine the atmosphere in the colony each evening when the workers returned: the hunger, the exhaustion, the arguments, the fights, the exploitation, the constant stink of sewage, the trips to cheap drinking dens and the brothels by the nearby garment factory, and the nightly return to the shared plastic mat. I was outraged by the conditions here, because they were so easily avoidable. This was not an embedded social problem where any solution might throw up a host of new complaints. It was not a case of intractable poverty or of bosses who were unable to pay their workers more. The cheapest apartments in Brigade Gateway were selling at just under Rs10m ($200,000), and for the cost of few square metres in one apartment, for the cost of a servant's closet, these migrant labourers could have been built proper accommodation. When I asked Dhruv if all the workers at Brigade Gateway had to live in such conditions, he said this colony was probably the worst. Some other housing colonies had bunks with mattresses.

I contacted the company, Simplex, and asked some basic questions about the arrangements for the workers. Nobody wanted to be interviewed. Eventually they responded through a third party: "Mr. French's letter is a little embarrassing for us, and I don't think we will be making any kind of response. He says he has visited our site, and yet the only thing he would like to know is how much we pay our labourers. He has no interest in the structure, or how it is being built, or how long it will take to construct. He is writing about India and I do not understand why he needs to know how much we pay our labourers. How is it related to his subject matter? So, we would not like to respond."[10]

The tone of the reply was familiar, pursuing the old-fashioned line that anyone who asks why people are being mistreated is seeking to hold India back. I learned that the company's managing director, B. D. Mundhra, was considered a devotee of traditional values. His office produced a pamphlet stating he was the co-editor of *Indian Culture: Encyclopaedic Survey in Eight Volumes*. The theme of the volumes was Hindu universality: "The Rishis or savants of yore looked upon the whole world, inhabited by one large family. Another Vedic axi[o]m compares the world to a vast nest of which we are the nestlings singing melodious tunes creating an exquisite symphony."[11]

The workers at Brigade Gateway might find better jobs, or worse ones. Like Venkatesh, they had little reason for hope. Yet all around us, and particularly around the huge city of Bangalore, with a mushroom cloud of success emanating from its software and telecom industries, was evidence that India was on the move. How were these workers to join the journey? Was the leap to prosperity and social change only possible for a minority? The question I was left with was: how many generations would it take to turn a junior Venkatesh into a software engineer?

There can be a remarkable dissonance in India between the efficiency of everyday life (high-speed service in a dhaba, a shopkeeper who mends your broken phone on the spot) and the inertia of officials. A while ago I attended a small conference in New Delhi organized by the Indian and British foreign ministers. Naively, I had expected high-level incarnations of government to be different, but the state remained the state: we were in the world of the babu. The sound system did not work and my name was misspelt in as many as three different ways: Partik, Patrik and Partick. The organization of the 2010 Commonwealth Games was similarly chaotic.

India's software and computer industries benefited from the lack of bureaucratic intervention, although in the first years after independence they were given encouragement. In the early 1940s, long before he was asked to plan the Indian economy, P. C. Mahalanobis set up a business in

Calcutta which fabricated calculating machines and scientific instruments. Using recycled components and material from a junkyard, the company made a manually operated calculator that could solve linear equations. Nehru had a look at it during a visit to the Indian Statistical Institute in 1953 and was interested by the idea that machines could be helpful in analysing statistical data. When the institute wanted to import a foreign computer that could perform 200 additions or five multiplications per second, and took up a large air-conditioned room, he supported the proposal.[12] Nehru's belief in an India with strong scientific institutions was linked in his mind to the importance of new technology. Mahalanobis obtained a Ural computer from the Soviets and an American IBM 1401, which was then the world's most popular model. In the 1950s the nuclear physicist Homi Bhabha organized the building of an analog computer at his Tata Institute of Fundamental Research, as well as developing Asia's first atomic research reactor at Trombay—Nehru was so impressed by the blue light given off by the fuel core in a tank of water that he named the project Apsara, after a mythological maiden or water nymph.[13] By the time Indira Gandhi became prime minister, scientific teams were making use of computer technology in various spheres across India.

At the same time, politicians were suspicious. What were computers for? They had not been needed in the past, so why should they be needed in the future? In a debate in Parliament in 1967, the communist leader K. Anirudhan warned about a new menace that was threatening India: "The automation equipments that are being imported into this country on a very wide scale include those frighteningly monstrous machines called electronic computers. What is an electronic computer? Is it like any other conventional machine? No, sir. I would rather quote from *Time* magazine . . . 'When someone wishes to solve a problem, he defines the problem in computer language. As instructions are fed into the computer in this special language, the machine sends electrical impulses coursing through its innards at the speed of light.' An IBM 7093 computer can do one day's desk work of a lakh [100,000] of clerks in less than an hour . . . this Government is bringing in these machines into this country on a very liberal scale."[14] George Fernandes shared Anirudhan's worry, and as industry minister in the Janata government in 1977 expelled IBM from India, along with Coca-Cola and various other companies. Fernandes recalled proudly: "IBM was very cocky. They went to the extent of telling me that they have refused to accept what the French president, General Charles de Gaulle, had told them [to dilute their equity]. So I told them, 'If you think the General succumbed to you, I am telling you that I am not succumbing to you. You get out.' Yes I said, 'You get out.' . . . I am anyway against computers."[15]

With Indian clerks now busily programming the monstrous machines all over the world, what did K. Anirudhan think about the electronic menace? He told me on the telephone from his home in Kerala that although he remained an active communist, he believed computers and automation were essential: "We have adapted. We want to be competitive. Personally I don't use a computer, but my son studied business and technology at the IIT in Bombay." This was not an unfamiliar story, the politician whose children did things he would not have wanted others to do (another son was, unsurprisingly, a Member of Parliament). I had noticed many people from Kerala in Bangalore, working in new-technology companies and call centres; in some cases it was their only way to secure a job without moving to the Gulf.

The IITs or Indian Institutes of Technology were themselves a product of Nehru's forward planning. Just before independence, the British Indian government had moved to establish higher technical institutions of an equivalent standard to Manchester or MIT. Nehru took this path-breaking idea and developed it, bringing in lecturers from around the world to the new IITs. Before independence, India had good scientific research centres, but engineering colleges were focused on producing engineers for civil projects like railways and bridges. Now, world-class establishments had been set up; the difficulty, which grew steadily worse, was that the graduates had too little to do. In 1970 an Indian businessman and classical singer, Vinay Bharat Ram, secured permission from Sony to assemble electronic calculators in India. It was a coup—but the Indian government blocked the plan. Ram was not deterred. He reverse-engineered a desktop electronic calculator and, unable to import a suitable plastic casing for it, housed it in a wooden cabinet the size of a briefcase. The calculator went into production and sold well.[16] During Indira Gandhi's last years in office, realizing the system was failing, and influenced by her son Rajiv's enthusiasm, she lifted some of the restrictions on electronics.

By the 1980s, Indians around the world were showing an aptitude for the growing computer industry, and companies in India such as Wipro, TCS and Satyam were being developed which would soon be at the front of the software boom. Nandan Nilekani described the bizarre obstacles facing his company Infosys—which today has revenues of over $4bn—in its early days. When it wanted to import a 150 MB hard disk drive, it took so long to get permission from the government that the manufacturer had improved the capacity to 300 MB by the time it came through. "This meant changing the import licence—and that took another six to eight months, luckily coming through before the drive was upgraded again."[17] Like other fledgling software companies at the time, Infosys was founded by Indians from middle-class families who had no access to capital or to established business houses. The way they operated was hardly noticed at first, tying up with foreign companies like Reebok and building a Silicon Valley-style campus in Bangalore on land supplied cheaply by the state government.[18] Bangalore was home to an extraordinary concatenation of industries, which would help not only with the launch of India's IT industry, but with the continuing supply of highly trained engineers. It had long been a "science city" containing public sector enterprises, private companies and academic institutions which specialized in electronics, aeronautics, artificial intelligence, radar development, defence avionics, robotics, bio-engineering and space research.[19]

It was only in the 1990s, when large foreign banks and other industries started to outsource their back-office operations to India, that it became clear something of great social and economic significance was happening. Business visitors from overseas started to speak about India in ways that would have been hard to envisage a couple of decades earlier. Jack Welch of General Electric proselytized about the virtues of Bangalore to audiences in the United States, struck by the "terrific scientific, engineering and administrative talent" and the "enormous number of people with great technical skills."[20] An Indian physicist, who had recently come back from a conference in Texas, described the shift to me: "I have been going to events such as this for years. In the past, when I said I was Indian, people did not react. Now it's like: 'Oh, you're from India? You must be the smartest guy in the room.'"[21]

Mack lives in California. When the sun rises over the Golden Gate, he throws on a pair of Levi's and an Old Navy top, or maybe a T-shirt from the pile of free ones he has with "Yahoo!" or a geeky conference logo on the front. Silicon Valley was once filled with fruit orchards but is now famous as the home of innumerable tech companies; compared to many parts of the U.S. it is wealthy, ethnically diverse and liberal. Mack grabs some bites of breakfast, scoops up his iPhone and the keys to his Acura TL and says goodbye to his wife and son at the door of their three-bedroom apartment. On the way to work, he drops his daughter at her school in Santa Clara and has a fifteen-minute drive past shopping malls, banks and software companies until he reaches the Yahoo! headquarters at Sunnyvale.

While his system starts up, he heads for the pantry to wash his teacup and fill his water bottle. What he does at the moment he sits down at his work station is significant—will he check email, log on to Facebook, update his status, Twitter?—because Mack's job is to catch us at this precise instant in our day. He oversees the Yahoo! front door, the homepage, and with 300 million people visiting daily, he has to understand our "check-in" behaviour better than we do. What is to stop us from spending a few minutes on the site answering email, and then wandering off elsewhere? Mack has a team of ten working with him, people from China, India, Korea—even some from the United States. He specializes in ideation, in coming up with the ideas that will make Yahoo!'s website more attractive than its competitors.

Come lunchtime, he heads for the cafeteria to have salad or world food; Italian, Lebanese, Japanese, whatever they are serving that day. He returns to his work station, but he has been working all the while on his iPhone. "Wife and mother-in-law go Vegas, in charge of kids for next two days," he tweets. So far, so American; but Mack comes from Bangalore.

He was born in 1975 to what he calls a middle-class family. In those days, middle-class Indian families had few consumer goods, no holidays and no slack. Every rupee counted, but it did not feel like deprivation because everybody else had little too. "Things were pretty different at that time," Mack said. "We didn't have big plans. I took a degree at Bangalore University in fine arts, photography and advertising. I wasn't very good at studies compared to the others. I enjoyed painting and photography, and I was influenced by Kannada literature and the Russians—Dostoyevsky, Tolstoy—and artists like Picasso and Gauguin." His family was unusual: the emphasis was more on creativity than on hard study, and his father was the devoted editor of a little bi-monthly magazine in Kannada. "We would have discussions about poetry, politics, literature, art. My father used to ask us to read out things from the newspapers, very loud. We had a noticeboard where I would put paintings. But if you talk to other people like me, you'll find they spent most of their evenings at engineering coaching classes.

"In 1996 I did an interview with a company. My mother said I should do computers. The offer of being able to use a PC was important, as there was no way we could have afforded one at home. I took the job because it gave me the chance to scan images—I wanted to be an illustrator. Within a year, I was in front of a computer 24/7. I was fascinated by the software. I started using everything, Adobe Photoshop, 3D Studio Max. All the software was freely available in India as it was pirated, and I could begin practising on it in a way that people in the U.S. couldn't at the time. Without pirated software you would never, ever have had so many geeks from India.

"In 2000 I moved away from software towards web development and began working for a U.S. company in Bangalore. They gave me the opportunity to move to San Jose [in California] and I was put in charge of some areas of their user interface. It was my first time abroad. I had to adapt to new ways of living. I was feeling insecure. Although my parents are veg, I was not, but I felt a bit of guilt about eating beef. We went to a hamburger joint and I ate some almost by accident. When I told my father, he asked whether I had enjoyed it and when I said yes, his answer was, 'Well that's OK, but don't tell your mother.' Then I started tasting other meats too.

"The way a U.S. company worked was very different, and surprising to me. They said, 'OK, see what you can make,' and offered me stock options, which wouldn't have happened in an Indian company. My English was not that polished. It was hard to converse. Kannada was my first language, the language I used at home. Other young programmers and designers from India, Brazil, Pakistan, Israel felt the same way, but we knew people were not looking at our English, but at what we could do. So some things were pardoned. My role was very critical for the company. I was trying to tame the engineering problems with the interface—and everyone uses the interface! It was hard to communicate to the Americans why I was taking a decision. I had to draw ideas on a whiteboard to explain exactly why. In the end I stopped doing that and learned the correct terms for things I knew instinctively, web-world phrases they would understand like 'heuristic evaluation' and 'user-centred design.'

"In the Bay Area there were quite a lot of Indian stores, Indian newspapers, Bollywood films. I met a lot of south Indian engineers at first, but then I thought I needed to be a little more active. I met doctors, African-Americans, writers, Mexicans, journalists. It was a new world for me. I realized then that not everybody in America was rich, and the blue-collar workers can have a tough time. In 2003 I lost my job and returned to Bangalore, where I met my wife. She's an embedded-systems engineer, from a similar background to me. When I returned to the U.S. in 2006 I knew I only wanted to work for a big company, because I needed more security now I was married. I went to Yahoo! to establish products for them, and now I focus on ideation, on ideas. The very first thing you see on the Yahoo! homepage is me."

It was, historically, an extraordinary cultural migration for a young

Kannada-speaker to have made, but in an interlinked and rapidly altering world, Mack's alien background was no disadvantage. His upbringing in middle-class 1980s Bangalore gave him a talent that dovetailed with the needs of contemporary America. His family or home life in California, eating south Indian dishes like upma, idli and sambar for breakfast with his wife before driving to Sunnyvale in his Acura TL, reflected his global position.

"The first thing I did when I got this role was to commission ethnographic studies—in the U.S., in India, in Brazil. What is your check-in routine? How do you use the Internet at different times of day? It varies in each country or society. In the early morning it might be emails or social networks, at noon you might be more relaxed and looking at links, in the evening your behaviour has completely changed. Our ideation team has to capture all these different behaviours and build designs around them. So now you see lots more non-Yahoo! properties on the homepage. You can add your own links to sports, a newspaper, whatever sites you visit. You can check Facebook or eBay through your homepage. We are pushing it on to mobiles too. I am working to embed Yahoo! applications on televisions, so that when you're watching TV you can project what's on your handheld on to the screen. You can chat about the game or whatever a politician is saying in his speech, you can look at photos or check emails on the side of the TV. We always work on the principle that an idea will be possible. We say: 'Don't worry if it can't be done. The technology will follow.'"

From the way Mack spoke, it seemed as if his angle on the world, which grew out of his Indian cultural background, was a perfect fit with Silicon Valley.

"My favourite inspirational quote is: 'When you come to a roadblock, take a detour.' I feel involved in the cultural life here. I always ask a lot of questions. I am asked to speak about my work as a designer. In some ways, we would live a more sophisticated life in Bangalore. You can have a driver and a nanny there, which is hard to afford in the U.S. I find some people here lead very simple lives. They don't have much money, they are conservative, they've never been outside California. I've noticed the Indians here become a lot more conservative too. They start going to Hindu temples, which they would never have done at home, and attending community stuff and south Indian cultural events. They say things to me like, 'Mmm, you have a daughter, you need to be careful.' Once their kids hit their teens, they want to get them out of America. There was a big fuss when some children came home from a playground saying, 'Papa, can I see the Last

Supper painting?' A Christian organization had been doing a playground puppet show, featuring famous religious pictures. People were very angry about it. I wasn't bothered, I was like, 'Sure, let them look at the painting.' I think every experience is worth having. But our future will be in India. In three or four years, we will return to Bangalore."[22]

Ramappa had managed the move from the village to the city. A short, composed man, he grew up in the 1940s on land close to what is now Bangalore airport. A few years younger than Venkatesh, he otherwise had a similar background: his father and uncles were day-wage labourers who were paid in rice or ragi (millet) according to a local barter system. His parents owned nothing but a thatched hut, and could not afford to raise cattle. They were Raju Kshatriyas, which in this regional setting meant they had inferior status. In north India, the Kshatriyas were a powerful group, traditionally part of the warrior caste, but here they had little. Only three families in the village came from the Raju Kshatriya community, while nearly all of their neighbours were Gowdas, who owned land. Like Venkatesh, Ramappa was near the bottom of the pile, but not as low as the Dalits, who lived in a kheri, or lane, of their own, away from the other houses. He could reasonably have expected to pass his entire life as a landless day-wage labourer.

Ramappa did something extraordinary as a child: he enrolled himself at a nearby primary school. His parents thought this was an odd thing to do, but were not concerned as they had the traditional Hindu respect for learning, and he was too young to work properly in the fields. The difficulty came when he wanted to go to secondary school, encouraged by a teacher, and his parents refused. Who would pay the fees? It would mean a ten-mile walk each day, five miles there and five miles back. Ramappa held a trump card: the school would waive the fees because he had been recommended as a good student. Since he was an only child, his father needed his labour, and a battle began as Ramappa tramped doggedly to school each day.

At sixteen he passed his SSLC, the Secondary School Leaving Certificate, and wished to go to college. His parents refused, absolutely. So he did something rash, and in retrospect out of character: he stole money from a stall where his father sold bananas and paan—betel leaf parcels of areca nut paste and slaked lime, for chewing. Then he travelled to the big city and enrolled for a bachelor's degree in commerce. It was the early 1960s.

Would he make it? Bangalore was a cacophony, and everything was new. It seemed to be packed with busy people and motor vehicles, though in fact it was a well-planned city with market gardens, parks, water tanks and shrines. The population was growing rapidly and new buildings were starting to spread across the stretches of green, displacing the shimmering champak and gulmohar trees. Until now Ramappa had gone barefoot. He realized he would have to learn how to wear shoes or chappals. What else would he need to discover? He reached a cousin's house and stayed there until his father and uncle caught up with him. After an epic family argument which he still does not like to discuss—after all, he was a thief and a disloyal son—it was decided Ramappa would not be forced to come home. For a monthly rent of Rs25 he took a room lined with asbestos sheets which had enough space for a bed and a secondhand Phillips bicycle, on which he could cycle to college.

"I took my meals there," he remembered. "I had a small kerosene stove. There was no bathroom. I was almost sleeping under my bicycle." He spoke in English in a strong regional accent, a "y" sound stuck to words which started with a vowel, "Y-I" for "I." This sort of life, renting a space so small there was barely space to sleep, was common enough among people who moved to cities in an effort to better themselves. In the classifieds section of newspapers in Pune in Maharashtra, you could still find "cotbasis" adverts—meaning you rented a bed to sleep in for a certain number of hours, and nothing more: "Available accommodation for day shift working women/girls on cotbasis near Rajiv Gandhi IT park Hinjawadi, call . . ."

The take-off point for Ramappa, the moment at which his studious dreams developed a real chance of succeeding, was when he was talent-spotted by the Raju Kshatriyas of Bangalore. This was probably the single most important factor in determining his destiny, and matches the experience of other unlikely achievers of his generation across India. In the state of Mysore (now Karnataka), the Raju Kshatriya community was a minority with few graduates and no representation in politics. Some had joined government service, and a few were starting to make money as small industrialists or contractors. They wanted to advance, collectively. So Ramappa, a bright boy from a rural background, was considered worthy of assistance. He was given a free room in the house of a community leader and became the secretary of a students' support association calling itself the Raju Kshatriya Hari-Hara Sangha (Hari-Hara being a combined form of the deities Vishnu and Shiva, implying they were not sectarian). He was helped too by a local custom called "varaana," which has now almost disappeared, whereby more prosperous households would offer a regular weekly or daily meal to young students who were getting started in the world.

So in a larger context, Ramappa had three significant advantages over Venkatesh: he grew up on land that produced food, he was clever and motivated, and he came from an extended caste community that was able to help him once he reached the city.

His struggle was by no means over. Ramappa qualified as a lawyer and joined an office as a junior. "I had no income. I soon realized that unless you came from a lawyer or judge's family, you got no briefs. Most advocates were Lingayats [a small but powerful caste] or Brahmins. I realized that mere intelligence did not count in this profession. So I opened an office and put out a sign: 'M. S. Ramappa, Advocate, LLB, LLM.' I was scarcely able to make both ends meet. I struggled for ten or twelve years. I would have become a judge—I have no doubt—if I hailed from a majority community. But everything works on a patronage basis, and you need backing from local politicians. So for years I was struggling away until, in 1975, I decided to become a lecturer. I was given a readership in mercantile law at a government college. My wife was earning a reasonable salary as a teacher. She was from an educated family in our community, and since I was hell-bent on studying and doing well, her parents had been happy for us to marry. Without the support of my in-laws, things would have been hard. We lived in their small house, and by the 1980s I had a part-time professorship at the university, teaching mercantile, company and insurance law."

Professor Ramappa's success had depended on a challenge to paternal expectations, but he was also an instinctive conservative (he had supported the Emergency, before recanting) who was worried by the social changes that were now taking place in Bangalore. "You get sons," he said to me, "who earn three times as much as their fathers and become bold with them, doing as they like and speaking without respect. People are not so courteous now. If I wanted to tell my father something, I would say it to my mother and she would inform him. We don't display wealth here in southern India. It's not like the Punjabi culture. Look at the message of the Ramayana: a man should have only one wife, be obedient to his parents, respect his teachers, honour his older brothers and always speak the truth. People in the southern parts of India are peace-loving, and the communal situation is better than in the north. We have a certain passivity. I mean that in a good way; I don't want it to change."[23]

When I went to visit Ramappa at his residence—we had already met a few days earlier at Koshy's coffee house—he was dressed in a crisply pressed pale blue shirt and a dhoti. He was formal without being reserved, and like many people in India he was content to chat openly, although he felt strange to be asked about his life in such detail. The sides of the path leading to his front door were decorated with rangoli, symmetrical designs done in chalk or colours by the women of the house at daybreak, which gave a sense of older times. A Sony television was on in the sitting room. I noticed that although Raju Kshatriyas have no caste restriction on eating meat, the family were vegetarian. So Ramappa had come full circle: as a child his parents would have been too poor to buy meat, in his middle years he was able to eat it, and now he and his wife had become pure vegetarian like their Bangalore neighbours, eschewing even eggs.

In the city, which was changing so fast, with children earning big salaries and behaving in very different ways to their parents, the household had a solid and old-fashioned feel. Ramappa's journey had been exceptional, this barefoot landless labourer's son who had become a university professor. Today, such a leap could still be executed, but only with a similar dose of ambition and good fortune. The Indian state would not help you in times of trouble: that job fell to your family and community, and if they were unable to offer immediate support and protection, you might end up anywhere, even chained in a quarry near Mysore.

The answer to the question "How many generations would it take to turn a junior Venkatesh into a software engineer?" was, in this case, only one. Ramappa had a son who was a successful computer scientist and a nephew working in California who said to me proudly: "The very first thing you see on the Yahoo! homepage is me." Mack.

PART III

SAMAJ · SOCIETY

9

THE OUTCASTES' REVENGE

D R. AMBEDKAR has a story about a journey he made as a child. It took him nearly fifty years to bring himself to write it, which is not surprising when you learn what happened. He had been born to a disadvantaged community; the year was 1901; his mother was dead and his father was posted as a government cashier some distance from Bombay. Ambedkar and his siblings had been living with their aunt, but it was now decided they should be sent to join their father. "Great preparations were made. New shirts of English make, bright bejewelled caps, new shoes, new silk-bordered dhoties were ordered for the journey," he wrote.

"The Railway Station was ten miles distant from our place and a tonga (a one-horse carriage) was engaged to take us to the station. We were dressed in the new clothing specially made for the occasion, and we left our home full of joy but amidst the cries of my aunt who was almost prostrate with grief at our parting. When we reached the station my brother bought tickets and gave me and my sister's son two annas each as pocket money, to be spent at our pleasure. We at once began our career of riotous living and each ordered a bottle of lemonade at the start. After a short while, the train whistled in and we boarded it as quickly as we could, for fear of being left behind."

Ambedkar's words give us an anticipation of trouble; we feel the riotous living might end badly. The children reached their destination in the afternoon. Everyone else went on their way, walking confidently out of the railway station, but because of a miscommunication their father was not there on the platform to meet them. After all the excitement of the journey, they were unsure what to do. The stationmaster approached:

"We were well-dressed children. From our dress or talk no one could make out that we were children of the untouchables. Indeed the stationmaster was quite sure we were Brahmin children, and was extremely touched at the plight in which he found us. As is usual among the Hindus, the stationmaster asked us who we were. Without a moment's thought I blurted out that we were Mahars. (Mahar is one of the communities which are treated as untouchables in the Bombay Presidency.) He was stunned. His face underwent a sudden change. We could see that he was overpowered by a strange feeling of repulsion. As soon as he heard my reply he went away to his room and we stood where we were. Fifteen to twenty minutes elapsed; the sun was almost setting. Father had not turned up, nor had he sent his servant, and now the stationmaster had also left us. We were quite bewildered, and the joy and happiness which we had felt at the beginning of the journey gave way to a feeling of extreme sadness."[1]

What were they to do? The children resolved to take a bullock-cart to the place where their father was posted, although they had no idea how long the journey might last. So they carried their luggage to the front of the station, where carts were plying for hire. Word had however got around that the stranded children were untouchables, and not one of the cartmen, even when offered extra money, was willing to contaminate himself by driving them. Eventually the stationmaster brokered a solution: a cartman would walk alongside his cart while the children drove it. He would receive double the usual fare. They set off. As night fell, it became apparent the cartman's promise that the journey would take three hours was a lie. It was nearly midnight by the time they reached a toll-collector's hut, and they were still a long way from anything that looked like a town. By now, despite eating the food in their tiffin basket along the way, the children were hungry and above all thirsty.

They were also wise to their situation. Bhimrao Ambedkar, all of nine years old, approached the toll-collector and explained in Urdu that they were Muslim children on their way to Koregaon. Could he please give them some water? The toll-collector was not deceived. He said they should have made arrangements for someone else to keep water for them. There was none to be had.

At the foot of a hill they unyoked the bullocks and laid the cart at an angle to the dry ground. They were parched and desperate. Ambedkar's elder brother suggested two of the children might rest beneath it while the other two kept watch in the darkness, in relays, since they had gold ornaments. The cartman slept elsewhere. In the morning they began again, and reached the safety of their father's house by noon.

It is not hard to see why this experience lodged in Ambedkar's mind. He was at an age when children drink in information about the workings of the world. Before that, he had known of his pariah status, but only in a structured environment. At school he was not allowed to touch a tap, and could only have water when a peon turned one on for him. He had to bring a piece of gunny cloth, or sacking, to class each day and sit or squat on it during lessons, while the upper-caste children sat at desks. At home, the family would cut each other's hair and wash their own clothes, and it was not until he grew a little older that he understood this was because the barbers and dhobis, or washermen, would not touch either them or their clothes. The constraints on untouchables varied from place to place and included rules such as not being able to enter a Hindu temple, wear good-quality clothes, ride a horse in a marriage procession or sit in the presence of the upper castes.

More than a century after Ambedkar's unhappy childhood journey, individuals who would never, at any moment in India's history, have been able to make their way in the world, are assuming positions of political power. The outcastes are answering back, and in some cases biting back. The extent of this shift is still not clear, but it has much further to go. Despite the genuine advances of recent years, Dalits remain undereducated and under-represented, and their collective importance as an Indian community is not recognized. To equal the number of Dalits in India, you would need to add together the populations of Albania, Australia, Belgium, Israel, Kuwait, Libya, the Netherlands, Rwanda, Sri Lanka, Sweden, Switzerland and the United Kingdom. Or to express it in a different way: if every sixth person on the planet is an Indian, every sixth Indian is a Dalit.[2] In 1996 a memorable article was published by B. N. Uniyal, "In Search of a Dalit Journalist": he could not find one among the 686 accredited correspondents of the Delhi press corps.[3] In many professions, the situation still remains the same.

Throughout his life, Ambedkar tried to figure out why "caste" Hindus had an obsession with defilement. He studied texts like the laws of Manu, which specified that anyone touching a Buddhist or a member of various outcaste groups should purify himself at once with a bath. Ambedkar's theory was that old wars between settled and nomadic tribes, and between Brahmins and Buddhists, had led to the expulsion to the edge of villages of "Broken Men," who followed the teachings of the Buddha and ate beef.[4] They became the untouchables. His supposition about Broken Men and their social, cultural or religious origins does not depend on any clear evidence, but it shows how he was attempting to understand and imagine the historic position of a group that had been recorded mainly by others. Because he is remembered as the father of the Indian Constitution, it would be easy to believe Ambedkar was part of a wave of people of similar background, examining their origins and trying to create a new social contract. Rather, he was in an unusual position at every stage of his career. His Mahar community was at the upper end of the scale of untouchability, respected in the region around Bombay for military service; he had won a scholarship sponsored by the Maharaja Gaekwad of Baroda, studied at Columbia University and the London School of Economics, published books, including *The Problem of the Rupee,* and by the late 1920s was both a legislator and a professor at the Government Law College in Bombay. Although a related movement for social reform and self-respect had started in the south, guided by Periyar E. V. Ramaswamy, most untouchables in India remained oppressed—a situation which Ambedkar found ever more frustrating as he grew older.

As the country moved towards political reform and independence, his ambitions to represent depressed communities (soon to be known as the Scheduled Castes, because their names were listed on a long taxonomic schedule attached to the Government of India Act of 1935) were restricted by the growing power of the Indian National Congress. Like an anaconda, Mohandas Gandhi intended to squeeze his opponent by appropriating the untouchables as his own. He had renamed them "harijans"—or "children of god"—which looked to Ambedkar like a patronizing means of maintaining the birthmarked position of his community. "What is Gandhism?" he asked, angry at the Mahatma's ability to appeal to the Indian heart rather than the head. "Barring this illusory campaign against untouchability, Gandhism is simply . . . militant orthodox Hinduism. What is there in Gandhism which is not to be found in orthodox Hinduism?" In his passion and clarity, Ambedkar reads here like Orwell. He translated Gandhi's characteristic but baffling words from his Gujarati journal *Navajivan*:

> I believe that interdining or intermarriage are not necessary for promoting national unity . . . Taking food is as dirty an act as answering

the call of nature . . . Just as we perform the act of answering the call
of nature in seclusion so also the act of taking food must also be done
in seclusion. In India children of brothers do not intermarry. Do they
cease to love because they do not intermarry? . . . The caste system
cannot be said to be bad because it does not allow interdining or inter-
marriage between different castes.

As on many things, Gandhi's views on caste and interdining altered as
he went along. He had declared in 1921 that he wished personally to be
reborn as an untouchable "so that I may share their sorrows, sufferings and
the affronts levelled at them . . . I love scavenging." Imitating the hereditary work of a sweeper would be a way of "cleaning Hindu society." For
Ambedkar, this elevation of the spiritual role of the sweeper—Gandhi's
suggestion certainly had a strong Christian ring to it—was a distraction
from the factual, political reasons for his community's oppression: "Can
there be a worse example of false propaganda than this attempt of Gandhism to perpetuate evils which have been deliberately imposed by one
class over another?" he wondered.[5] Gandhi kept a harijan in his ashram as
a symbolic gesture, but Ambedkar wanted practical, legal change and the
creation of separate electorates for untouchables.

At the Round Table conferences in London in the early 1930s, Ambedkar
put this case forcefully and the British government agreed to his demand.
He was at an advantage in a foreign setting, since European prejudice was
predicated on race rather than caste, and an untouchable was treated like
any other Indian delegate. Gandhi thought separate electorates were a ploy
to damage national unity during the struggle for self-rule, and responded
with a "fast unto death." Ambedkar, under great pressure now and fearing
reprisals against untouchables if Gandhi were to die, met him and retreated.
Their agreement became known as the "Poona Pact." When the agreement failed to deliver any obvious benefit for his community, Ambedkar
said Congress "sucked the juice out of the Poona Pact and threw the rind
in the face of the untouchables," treating them like "dumb-driven cattle."[6]

Gandhi's victory over the matter of separate electorates would later be
portrayed by Dalits as a moment which retarded the community's ability to
advance. In *The Chamcha Age,* a book published on the fiftieth anniversary
of Ambedkar's climbdown, the Dalit leader Kanshi Ram used strong words:

The sufferings and humiliations of the slaves, the Negroes and the
Jews are nothing as compared to the untouchables of India . . . Every-

where in the world democracy means rule of the majority. But in India 85% of people are ruled by 10 to 15% Higher Castes . . . Brahminism had such poisonous germs in it, that it effectively killed the desire to revolt against the worst form of injustice.[7]

In Kanshi Ram's opinion, untouchables had allowed themselves to be made the chamchas, or stooges, of the upper castes.

Unlike the other founding fathers of independent India, Ambedkar is hard to read as a person (this may be because he has been neglected by Indian biographers, just as the culture of his community remains neglected by academics, except as a source of votes; many of the websites concerning Dalits are either kooky or run by evangelical Christians). In the 1930s he announced that Hinduism was beyond reform, and shortly before his death in 1956 converted to Buddhism along with his second wife, Savita, and many thousands of his followers. Despite his essential role in making the Constitution, Ambedkar was defeated by a Congress candidate in India's first general election. In most photographs he appears opaque, giving nothing to the camera, and often he looks as if his mind is elsewhere, or as if he has seen enough. So rather than being a person, Dr. Ambedkar has instead become his myth, his portrait, his statue, holding a book in his left hand and gesturing at the world in bronze or blue plaster—blue being the chosen colour of the modern Dalit movement.

Until recently the outcaste who became the lawgiver was sidelined in pan-Indian history, as a fly in the ointment of the independence movement. The Hindi poet Omprakash Valmiki, a Dalit, stated that during the 1960s he never once heard Ambedkar's name "from a teacher's or a scholar's mouth." He went unmentioned on Republic Day. "I knew about Gandhi, Nehru, Patel, Rajendra Prasad, Radhakrishnan, Vivekananda, Tagore, Saratchandra, Bhagat Singh, Chandra Shekhar Azad, Savarkar, and so on, but was completely ignorant about Dr. Ambedkar."[8]

Valmiki was born in 1950, the year in which Article 17 of the Indian Constitution formally abolished untouchability. How different was life after this impressive, momentous change? In his book *Joothan*—the title means "slops," referring to the waste food that people like himself were expected to collect and eat—Valmiki evokes a childhood of something like internal exile in an Uttar Pradesh village near Muzaffarnagar. His people, Chuhras, lived in narrow lanes filled with garbage and worse, and were expected to do whatever tasks they were commanded by the higher castes, sometimes for no pay. If they refused, they risked being thrashed by Hindus and Muslims alike.

Valmiki's memoir contains much information that can be revealed only by someone deep inside a social system: how Chuhras were at the limits of Hinduism, with their own deities, religious practices and sorcery involving offerings of pigs and alcohol. With great effort, his father had him admitted to a government school. Like Ambedkar, Valmiki sat apart from the other children and was forbidden from using the water pump. As well as studying, he did hereditary work: sweeping, cleaning, dealing with dead animals, skinning buffaloes. At weddings, the Chuhras would sit outside and wait to collect the leftover leaf-plates, and then scrape up the waste food, the joothan, for boiling, drying and storing. He admits, and it is a painful admission for both reader and writer, that he relished the chance to eat joothan, such was his desperation. "If the people who call the caste system an ideal social arrangement had to live in this environment for a day or two, they would change their mind," he observed.[9]

In *Joothan,* Omprakash Valmiki showed the effects of such long-term humiliation on an individual. Later, he became a poet and literary critic, and got a job at an ordnance factory in Dehradun. It was made clear to him in early adulthood even by some of his friends that they felt contaminated by his presence. They were worried, not without reason, by the possible consequences within their own family and community of, for example, being seen to share a meal with him. He tried in his writing to determine why this aversion was so potent but, like Ambedkar, failed to find an answer.

Casteism remains one of the aspects of Indian life that is hardest to understand. It is unlike other forms of prejudice, where antipathy is linked to envy or desire; an anti-Semite will ask why "they" do so well in business, and a white racist will fear and envy apparent black physical prowess. Prejudice against outcastes is built on the idea that you will be polluted if you go near them. They exist only to serve, and then at some distance. It is a uniquely powerful form of social control, since it is total and self-replicating. The higher castes can only remain high if they have others to look down upon. So in the not too distant past, a boy would brush against an elderly sweeper in a corridor and his mother might whisper to him: "Don't touch, you will get a scale or turn into an insect!" A prayer of purification might follow. This would lodge in the child's memory, and even as he grew older and less traditional—or even international, living in Europe or America—the instinctive response, the flinch, remained.

I met Anu Hasan in Chennai. She was in her late thirties and had led a varied life. She ran a marketing agency in far-off Calcutta, did modelling, starred in the 1995 movie *Indira* (which had a soundtrack by the double Oscar winner A. R. Rahman) and now presented a popular Tamil TV show, *Koffee With Anu*. In addition, she starred in the action soap *Rekha IPS*—IPS stood for Indian Police Service—about a woman cop. "I fight the baddies," she said. "I do my own stunts with motorbikes and guns." Anu Hasan had made a distinct career for herself, which in its singularity was expected. She was of normal weight, rather than looking starved like many of the Bollywood actresses, and more than anything she gave off an impression of healthy vigour.

"My mother's a Tamil Brahmin from Andhra Pradesh and had an arranged marriage to my father. My grandfather was a lawyer. After marriage, my father shifted out of the joint family to live in a separate house. They moved to Trichy [Tiruchirapalli, in southern Tamil Nadu], though my mother went back to her home place to have her first child, my brother, as was traditional. My father trained us to be non-vegetarian, saying if we went abroad we should be able to eat everything and not have problems. He was involved in film production at Rajkamal Films, in partnership with his brother." The brother was Kamal Haasan, one of India's biggest film stars; Anu's cousin was the actress Suhasini, who was married to the successful director Mani Ratnam. This family background was important to her, though she was down to earth, even offhand, when talking about it. "To other people they are stars, but to me they're just family. When I'm in other parts of India, I think of myself as Tamilian, but when I'm in Madras I'm just 'Anu.' I'm not identified as a Tamil Brahmin."

She was perhaps being optimistic here: the sentiment against the upper castes remained strong in the south. When a Madras-based newspaper, *The Hindu*, had called in 1908 for "natives" to be appointed as judges (they were only permitted to take junior judicial posts), the magazine *Tamilan* argued this would result in their further dominance: "The self-styled Brahmins migrated to this country from alien lands . . . If we give the power of District Magistrate to these people, they will employ the people of their caste and cheat common Hindus."[10] What Anu meant, I felt, was that she did not promote herself on-screen as a Brahmin and tried to be fluid, modern and universal. The resentment against her community was not hard to locate or to understand. When *Tamilan* expressed a fear of further dominance,

83 percent of sub-judges in the Madras presidency, which covered much of the territory of southern India, were Brahmin, although they only made up 3 percent of the population. After the First World War, 72 percent of Brahmin men in the region were literate, against less than 4 percent of Paraiyars (or pariahs—this was the origin of the word).[11] Unlike in the north, where Brahmins were often poor despite being of high caste, here they had also been landowners, which created further resentment. In the south, caste barriers started to break down in the 1920s, in part because of the radical reforms promoted by the ideologue and activist Periyar E. V. Ramaswamy. He was the Dravidian answer to Dr. Ambedkar and considered the ruling castes to be a greater threat than the British.

"I was twenty-four when I came out of college," said Anu, "but I looked seventeen and my cousin asked me to act in a movie she was directing. So I did *Indira*. I got too old to play leads, so I had roles like sister or mother of the hero. There are nearly a hundred Tamil films a year—it's the biggest regional industry after Bombay. I said I didn't want to be the kind of actress who wears skimpy clothes and runs around a tree in a romantic scene with the hero. In 2006, *Koffee With Anu* happened."

Everyone I met in south India seemed to watch this soft, light-hearted chat show, done in Tamil with occasional asides in English. It was based on a more irreverent Bollywood show, *Koffee With Karan*, presented by the director Karan Johar, who had made hits like *My Name Is Khan* and *Kuch Kuch Hota Hai*. When I watched a few episodes, Anu, wearing a frilly dress or a formal sari, greeted the guests with joined palms and sat them down on a swish but homely set. "We're not looking for their bad side. People here expect a certain sort of behaviour. One of the actresses—Namitha—was wearing a top that showed a bit of cleavage, and we had complaints. Things like 'Have you forgotten what Tamil culture is?' A while back there was a problem when a woman in a skirt was photographed crossing her legs while the chief minister was speaking. There's no porn industry in Tamil Nadu—most of it is imported from Kerala." This was not quite accurate: there was Tamil porn, but the performers were restrained and usually took off only their tops. In one film, a man writhed around with a woman who wore cycling trunks, and she pacified him in a maternal fashion.

What did it mean to be a Tamil Brahmin in modern India? "We're known for being highly educated, intelligent, a shade arrogant. Everything is distinct—there's a special language, and a particular way of tying a sari if you are a Brahmin." She did a sketch of an extra long sari pulled up at the waist. "Within our community, there's a distinction whether you are

Iyengar or Iyer. There was a court case about a new temple elephant at Kanchipuram. The priests at the temple were arguing whether the elephant was Thengalai or Vadagalai—which are Iyengar subsects—and went to law over it. I believe it took seventy years before the judgement was made, which was that for six months of each year the elephant was Thengalai, and for six months it was Vadagalai." How would they signify that the beast followed one sect rather than the other? "By the 'naamam'—the mark on its forehead—which is like the one the followers of the religious tradition wear. One is a 'U' shape and the other is a 'Y' shape. I believe the elephant died soon after the judgement, though depending on who you are speaking to it was either while the 'U' or the 'Y' was being applied.

"When I am with a non-Brahmin Tamil, I will use a different vocabulary, I will say 'thanni' for water, 'rasam' for rasam [a peppery, sour tomato soup]. With a Brahmin, I would say 'jalam' for water, 'saathamudhu' for rasam. Our food is different. Traditionally, a woman would bustle around in the house and she wouldn't go outside. If my grandmother was ill and a non-Brahmin doctor came to the house, a silk cloth was put over her wrist so he could take her pulse. The old rules started to break down a while back. We have 'madi'—the idea that you must do things in a particular way, like being bathed and clean before you cook, or that you should wash your hands before serving rice, again before you serve sambar, again before you serve vegetables. Now you might just do it symbolically, with a splash of water, if elders are there. We don't hug or show emotions; it's considered infra dig to do so. A boy who is really timid, you will say he's 'thayirsaadham' or 'thacchimammu.' It means 'curd and rice'—that he's so well-behaved he's like curd and rice. Drinking is seen as all right, though many people are still shocked if a woman drinks, or smokes cigarettes.

"I went to a convent school and for college I had to go to BITS Pilani up in Rajasthan—if you are a Brahmin here you have to score higher to get a place. I wanted to do engineering and I got 94 percent, but here in Tamil Nadu I needed 98 percent, while the disadvantaged communities would be on 70 percent." Anu did not seem resentful of this: it was just the way things were. "My father gave me a lot of freedom, but responsibility came with it. I lived in Calcutta for seven years, marketing credit cards and home loans. I married a north Indian man. He was in the army, a Jat and a below-knee amputee. My parents thought I could do better financially and were worried he was from the north, so far away. I realized after a year the marriage wasn't working, but I stayed, and after ten years came back to the south. My entire family stood by me when I divorced. It's fantastic being an Indian now, and fantastic being a woman in India. I speak English better than the Americans. Actually most Indians do."

Anu Hasan's caste background, and the liberal form in which it was expressed during her upbringing, had not left her religious. "I'm borderline atheist. My mother would pray to a particular god, but I don't. In the film industry, you always start by taking a shaved coconut—you put a lighted camphor cube on the wedge of the coconut and take it around. Everyone except me will touch it and pray before filming. People do black magic on each other here. They really think it can kill you, but I believe half of them die out of fear."[12] Anu was unusual in her rejection of religion and of the superstitious aspects of faith. Even Indians who were secular and modern usually had a devotion to an aspect of Hindu tradition—a photo of a favourite godman which would receive daily homage or an image of Hanuman secreted in a bottom drawer.

One of the more extraordinary things about the Tamil Brahmin community was the way in which it had managed, despite numbering only 2 million or so, to extend itself in India and around the world to remarkable effect. Chandrasekhara Venkata Raman, Venkatraman Ramakrishnan and Subrahmanyan Chandrasekhar had more in common than the similarity of their names: they were the only Indians to have won a Nobel prize in science, and they were all Tamil Brahmins, and all Iyers.[13]

Chandrasekhar, who won the Nobel for his work on the theoretical structure of stars and was the originator of the Chandrasekhar limit, was also the nephew of Raman, who gave science the Raman effect. "Venki" Ramakrishnan, the winner of the Chemistry prize in 2009 for his work on the function of the ribosome, left India after graduation. Returning after the Nobel award, he professed to be baffled by the "Indian phenomenon" of mass applause and the elevation of heroes. "We are all human beings, and our nationality is simply an accident of birth . . . The fact that I am of Indian origin is even less important."[14] Many of his listeners would have disagreed, believing still in the concept of inheritance—that birth was not accidental.

While many aspects of Indian caste prejudice have declined, an emphasis on group identity has strengthened, with caste being a way of uniting people socially and politically. An article published in 2009 mentioned that childless couples were asking sperm banks to label the donations by caste. One doctor said that although potential parents knew sperm donors had to remain anonymous, they were often "insistent, almost fanatical, about caste." The couples apparently wanted to maintain "healthy blood grouping" by making sure the biological father came from the same community as the mother. Clinics would usually pass on this information verbally. One would-be mother, Anuradha Rai, an Internet marketing manager and a Bhumihar, said she was not greatly concerned by the height, features or even the IQ of the father. "My husband felt if the sperm donor was from a different caste, the baby would not get the right genes."[15]

The right genes: it was an interesting concept. Could caste be genetic? In India you can sometimes guess someone's community from their physical appearance, so the idea was not completely outlandish. A few years ago I was in Lucknow airport with a Muslim man who had lived in the city his whole life. He said that by looking at a face—leave aside more obvious markers like clothing and headgear—he could tell which caste and place in Uttar Pradesh someone came from. I put him to the test; he got three out of three right. It occurs to me now that these encounters, the pair of us accosting people at random to ask about their family background, would be less straightforward in other countries (in England you would risk assault or arrest). Only in India are you asked by passengers within moments of boarding a train: "You are from? What is your good name? You are married? Do you have issue? What is your salary?"

Might it be possible to determine caste through genetic testing, in the same way that aspects of ethnic heritage can be established through mitochondrial and Y-chromosome DNA analysis? The U.S. company 23andMe was pioneering retail genomics, identifying more than half a million genetic markers which suggested what diseases and conditions a person might have inherited. Anne Wojcicki, the wife of Sergey Brin of Google, founded 23andMe: its "personal genome service" enabled you to explore your genome online. You could "get to know your DNA" by spitting in a tube and sending it to a laboratory for analysis. But could caste be "proved"? If so, the consequences would be endless, and ranged from angry family scenes ("Your parents said you were a Punjabi Khatri girl!") to students who wished to come from a lower caste in order to qualify for admissions quotas (Kaun Banega OBC?).

I found some bizarre and boastful websites dedicated to Indian genetic genealogy; a few sold "caste testing kits" for a lot of money and seemed to rely on crank science. They did not have the scientific rigour of companies like 23andMe, but rather played with a strand of thinking that was still influential in India. A blogger on Sanghparivar.org summed it up: "A man gets birth in a particular genetic lineage (family) on the basis of his previous karmas (thoughts and actions). Birth is not accidental." The husband and wife must be of the same caste to "maintain the original biological-genetic strain of the family." Back in Ashoka's time, it seemed, too many men became celibate under Buddhist influence. "Thus, their seeds were lost. Those bio-qualities were lost forever! The girls had no choice but to marry inferior men. Then, the generations which followed were genetically inferior. They did not have the valour, strength and ability to carry the mighty Vedic sciences on their shoulders. They were weak. Soon, India collapsed. India became a hunting ground for invaders."[16]

The campus of the IGIB, India's secretive Institute of Genomics & Integrative Biology, is set in a leafy part of north Delhi, where the wide roads and clean pavements are a relic of "Civil Lines"—a colonial-era term used to distinguish military streets from the civilian. I arrived on the Delhi metro, coming up a shiny new metal escalator into blinding sunlight, but the last five minutes of the journey were done most easily by cycle rickshaw, which offered the uneasy sight of malnourished calves pedalling along the nourished.

Dr. Arijit Mukhopadhyay was a specialist in eye genetics, a small, quick man in his mid-thirties with fitted trousers, a short-sleeved shirt and closed-toed sandals. "My interest is in RGC death," he said. "RGC [retinal ganglion cell] death is the final cause of glaucoma, a disease of the visual nerves culminating in blindness."

Mukhopadhyay was one of only two people authorized to speak about an extraordinary project that was under way here. A consortium of mainly young scientists was attempting to unravel the complete genetic map of the Indian peoples. It was an ambitious concept in a country with over one billion inhabitants, several thousand endogamous groups (who married only within their community) and more than 300 distinct functioning languages. The project had been conceived by Professor Samir Brahmachari, a biophysicist, and from the start he had realized he was stepping on dangerous ground. The information they were liable to discover about the origins of communities might have political, religious or caste consequences, and if mishandled could lead to conflict and even violence. The media had already run several stories which, in the view of the IGIB, distorted their research.

"We are trying to draw a genetic landscape of India and use it as a canvas to identify disease genes and genetic markers," said Dr. Mukhopadhyay cautiously from behind his desk. "We will learn which groups are prone to particular diseases or do not react to certain drugs. We are in the early days of an idea that has huge implications. We have looked at fifty-five populations so far, across the length and breadth of the country. This is the discovery stage. For example, we found that susceptibility to HIV is lower in a certain group in the north-west of India. A particular protective form of the gene has stayed within that population, because they are endogamous. The more outbred their community becomes, the more it will spread."

He showed me a bar chart and a map of India covered in circles of different colours, some like pie charts.

"You can see here the Indian peoples fall into four major language families: Indo-European, Austro-Asiatic, Tibeto-Burman and Dravidian." The first group spread across the upper and middle reaches of the map, the Austro-Asiatics (the tribals or Adivasis) were clustered in the centre and east, the Dravidians covered the south as far up as Andhra Pradesh and the Tibeto-Burmans were confined to small border areas to the north.

"Now look at these. This stuff was very unexpected." He pointed at the coloured circles on the map. "You will see that Indians are more similar than you would think across the country. There are membership exchanges within these four groups. It's all mixing up, even with the Dravidians."

Now I understood the circles: they showed genetic groups where you would least expect to find them. In Kashmir, there were people who were genetically similar to Dravidians. In Gujarat and eastern Orissa the same was true, though the markers were weaker. In parts of Andhra Pradesh and Karnataka in the south of the country, the situation was reversed: here were Indo-Europeans. In Madhya Pradesh in central India, you could find groups whose ancestors had come from the Himalayas. So people who thought they were a product of a place where their family had lived for infinite generations were genetically closer to Indians who lived a thousand miles away, and spoke a different language.

When I pointed to a spot on the map and asked Dr. Mukhopadhyay exactly where it was, he hesitated.

"We don't say the place names. We agreed, because of the political risks, not to release the ID of the blood-sampled groups—Hindus, Muslims, Sikhs. This is uncomfortable territory." He touched two red circles near Pakistan. "They probably would not eat in one another's home. How deep are our genetic relationships, and yet how different are our social relationships. The cultural structures we are following are new: it takes time for practices like not marrying into another community to come out genetically. It takes a few thousand years."

Tens of thousands of years?

"No, thousands of years."

So with all this mixing and complexity, could you test for caste?

"There is no scientific basis to say you could have a caste gene. For a start, in our research we use samples of fifty or a hundred people, not individuals. If you test a population group in India and look at twelve genetic markers—DNA sequence variations—you have nearly a 100 percent chance of knowing if they are tribals or not, and an 85 percent chance of establishing their language group. The data would not tell you the caste, because there is no basis. You can't say who is 'superior' or 'inferior.' I travelled to Pune to take some blood samples and one person—I should tell you that he was a political type—said to me: 'You can take my sample, and prove that I am the supreme quality of human in India.' There's a strange dynamic in our society."

Dr. Mukhopadhyay had to leave for a meeting and introduced me to his colleague Dr. Mitali Mukerji. She was the only other person authorized to speak about the project.

"It seems like a lot of Bengalis work here," I said.

Dr. Mukhopadhyay smiled. "I am a native of Calcutta. If a job is advertised, seven out of ten applicants are Bengali. Some say, 'Ah, Bengalis are more clever because they eat a lot of fish and get omega-3 acids.' I tell them: it's not like that, clever Bengalis go to academia and clever north Indians go to commerce."

Dr. Mukerji specialized in molecular genetics and coordinated the project across six institutes in the country. "I considered working abroad, but there was a lot to do on genomics here," she told me. "We were studying the history of diseases and realized we needed a proper genetic landscape map of India to do our work. Take Huntington's disease as an example. It is caused by DNA mutation and can get worse with each generation. It's very rare in Asia. It came to India by two routes, one from the north and the other probably through Mysore at around the time of Tipu Sultan. There is evidence that the form of Huntington's disease which we see in south India originated in Ireland, and that it probably came from soldiers who were made captives by Tipu Sultan."

It was extraordinary to think of scientists being able to deduce this; my own ancestors included Irish soldiers, and I shuddered at the thought of them being captured by Tipu. I was still digesting what I had heard about genetics in India and asked Dr. Mukerji what had surprised her most during the ongoing research project.

"We soon realized there was not a prototype Indian. People appear to have come in from places that are now Iran, Burma, central Asia, Afghanistan. This supports the idea of waves of settlers from various directions. There are many admixtures, whereas by comparison Caucasians are homogenous. India is like a melting pot compared to other Asian countries. If you trace mitochondrial DNA, it shows that women moved around and probably reproduced with other communities. Marriage within your group is more recent in India."

What she said was not good news for racial theorists or for Indians who saw their position in the hierarchy of caste as being ordained by scripture and tradition. Had Kshatriyas not married Kshatriyas and Brahmins married Brahmins forever? Hinduism does not depend on a linear concept of time and has no single sacred book—it is not a "revealed" religion like Christianity, Islam or Judaism—but it has an overwhelming sense of its own antiquity. If you leave aside for a moment the influential reform movements of the nineteenth and twentieth centuries, which sought to strip out distractions such as caste from religion, most variants of Hindu practice stress that rituals have been done by Brahmin priests in a particular way for aeons. If the ancient social order was not divinely ordained and has not existed since the dawn of civilization, it was invented by humans for a social purpose. This has been a progressive point of view for many years, but the IGIB project threatened to give it a proof and validity.

In the months after my visit to the IGIB, rival scientific reports were published in different parts of the world, including a study which claimed, on the basis of a much smaller sample survey, that India's caste groups had been endogamous for millennia. This was widely reported, and any future research which appears to show that caste is genetically identifiable will certainly receive publicity. The notion of such a root distinction appeals both to upper-caste traditionalists and to lower-caste political leaders who claim they represent the descendants of India's original inhabitants (whom they imagine were beaten down and exploited by fair-skinned Aryan invaders).

Dr. Mukerji stressed the project was by no means complete. "There's so much we are still discovering. Skin pigmentation is only the property of a few genes, so you just need to flip some genes to get from dark to light skin. It will be some years before we understand this fully. I was surprised that people we tested from Ladakh, Sikkim and the north-east were so similar, and that some Kashmiris may originally have been Dravidians who were pushed up to the north. Upper-caste Hindus seem to be much closer to Muslims than to the high castes from other places. We need to study in more detail in the south, where the communities have remained more distinct. Adivasis are noticeably different. They may be connected to Australian aborigines."

"Does the genetic landscape map reveal anything about caste?" I asked. "Some people tell doctors that they like sperm donors to come from their own caste, to get the right genes."

Dr. Mukerji was dismissive. "There's no logic to talking about caste and sperm and which community has better genes. Indians all have opinions, but the caste system has no genetic basis."[17]

In September 1977, the veteran politician Raj Narain was addressing the "Abolish Caste Conference" at Delhi's Constitution Club. The Emergency had recently ended and he was something of a national hero, having defeated the prime minister, Indira Gandhi, in her stronghold, the constituency of Rae Bareli. Caste prejudice should be defeated, Raj Narain declared. The harijans must be protected. Were these children of god not our brothers and sisters?

Before he became a national figure, Narain had a reputation as a buffoon, and he may not have noticed a shift in the attitudes of the Scheduled Castes. A distinct wave of energy was touching both the middle classes with government jobs and the poor who felt neglected by politicians. Gone were the days when they would be patronized as harijans. The Dalit Panthers had launched themselves with a bang in Bombay in 1972, inspired by the Black Panthers in the United States. So when Narain gave his speech at the Constitution Club, many listeners were unhappy at his repeated use of the term "harijan," although none of the speakers challenged him bar one, a 21-year-old primary school teacher named Mayawati. When she spoke, she was neither polite nor deferential. Why was this cabinet minister insulting the Dalits in the audience? Did he not know Dr. Ambedkar had referred in the Constitution to "Scheduled Castes" rather than to "harijans"? Why did parliamentarians pretend to be fighting the caste system even while perpetuating it? She wrote later that the term "harijan" was as offensive as "devdasi" ("slave of god") to describe a woman who was sexually exploited by temple priests.

India remains a socially conservative country, and for a young, unmarried woman to have spoken in this way to an eminent older man in public was remarkable. Mayawati had started as she meant to go on: she was in awe of nobody, and not bound by precedent. There were no senior women in politics from a background like hers, but despite her deprived upbringing on the broken fringes of Delhi, she was ready to take on politics and the caste system. Her guide and mentor would be Kanshi Ram, twenty-two years her senior and another political maverick. Former untouchables had remained subordinate since independence. According to Mayawati's biographer: "Dalit leaders came in two models. One was the wild-eyed radical who spoke of blood on the streets," the other was the Congress politician who feathered his own nest while "preserving and consolidating the loyal scheduled caste vote bank that had remained in the party's pocket since independence."[18] Kanshi Ram worked on the simple but visionary premise that if the downtrodden were to organize themselves, they could take power in India democratically. He believed that if barriers of region, religion, language and sub-caste were forgotten, they could band together and become a majority, and drive out the high-caste "Manuwadis," the followers of the ancient edicts of Manu, who had kept them enslaved for thousands of years.[19]

It was a fine theory; the problem was executing it. Drawing on the writings not only of Ambedkar but of earlier thinkers like the Maharashtrian revolutionary Jyotirao Phule (who in turn had been influenced by Thomas Paine's *Rights of Man*) and Phule's teacher wife, Savitribai, Kanshi Ram sought to put his ideas into practice. He was contemptuous of the standard forms of agitation used by left and liberal politicians in India. By 1972 he had an organization with around a thousand members and a cumbersome name: The Scheduled Castes, Scheduled Tribes, Other Backward Classes and Minorities Employees Welfare Association. When he recruited Mayawati after her fiery speech at the Constitution Club, the movement was spreading from Maharashtra to Haryana, Punjab and Uttar Pradesh. Like African-Americans in the United States, it was only when Dalits organized themselves rather than being helped by external well-wishers that things really began to change. In 2010 the activist Chandra Bhan Prasad started a private school and built a temple dedicated to a new deity, "Dalit Goddess English." His supposition was that Dalits, being socially and educationally excluded, should learn English so as to advance. The bronze image of "Dalit Goddess English" held a pen in one hand and books in the other, and the mantra chanted at her dedication ceremony was "A-B-C-D." Prasad believed that only by deifying the English language via the goddess would he be able to persuade low-caste parents to send their children to the new school.[20]

The relationship between Kanshi Ram and Mayawati remains one of the mysteries of modern Indian politics. It endured until his death in 2006, and was as intense as any marriage. From the outside it looked evident: an unmarried woman was living in the house of an older man. Many long-time colleagues thought Kanshi Ram was being foolish, damaging his own credibility and allowing himself to be manipulated by an ingenue. Mayawati was furious at any lewd insinuations, saying Kanshi Ram was a sanyasi and she was his daughter or his sister (this sounds more peculiar elsewhere than in India, where unusual personal relationships abound and terms like "daughter" and "sister" can be flexible). At one point Mayawati even said she was his son.

Whatever the internal dynamic between them, Kanshi Ram and Mayawati's main interest was in political change. A roadshow called "Ambedkar Mela [festival] on Wheels" was sent across rural north India to educate people, and Mayawati toured villages by bicycle in the burning heat, persuading the poorest they should no longer let others speak on their behalf. Her message was stark. "Can you name me even one Dalit family in this village or in the surrounding region who has prospered because of the various economic welfare schemes like pig herding, rickshaw pulling, leather tanning, etc., initiated by the Congress government over the past forty years?" Generally, the answer was no. In which case, Mayawati demanded, why were 95 percent of Dalit votes going to the Congress party? "We all know that upper caste Manuwadis do not want Dalits to eat well, dress well or do well, so do you think a machine can be built in Delhi or in some other part of the country that can suddenly change the hearts of all these upper caste ministers and leaders so that they will help Dalits to prosper?"[21] No, roared the village crowd. Then the solution, she said in answer, was to vote for the BSP, which Kanshi Ram had built "for Oppressed and Exploited Indians."[22]

At any given time, India is full of aspiring parties and leaders. Most do not go far. The BSP reached the Lok Sabha in 1989 in the avatar of the now 33-year-old Mayawati. Her caste destiny was to be a leather worker or a cleaner of floors and toilets, though not of tables or mantelpieces—that would be the job of a maid. When she entered Parliament, other MPs complained she dressed badly, smelled sweaty and wore her hair in an oiled plait. Could something be done about it? Learning on her feet, Mayawati realized she might use Parliament's formal procedural conventions to her advantage. When twenty-three Chamar women were reported raped by Jat men in Agra, she advanced to the well of the house and accused a minister, who happened to be a Jat, of personal responsibility. He responded with a college humour honed at his alma mater, St. Stephen's: "Behenji [sister], I have one wife and can barely handle her! What chance of me trying to tangle with two dozen women?"[23] Wholly unimpressed, Mayawati kept up a barrage of insults and allegations, even as the speaker tried to calm proceedings. It symbolized an end to the paternalistic politics of the early post-independence era. Like Ambedkar, Kanshi Ram and the Congress leader Jagjivan Ram before her, Mayawati came from a family with a military connection, beneficiaries of the British policy of recruiting untouchable soldiers, and her approach was martial.

When she became the chief minister of Uttar Pradesh under Kanshi Ram's guidance six years later, she ruled in a shockingly unconventional way, appointing Dalits to key positions in the state's administration and police service, erecting thousands of statues of Dr. Ambedkar at public expense and sacking men who opposed her. Uttar Pradesh was home to many minorities, religions and sub-castes, and its history was the product of cultures coarse and refined; it had important historical sites like Sarnath, Ayodhya and the Taj Mahal, and landscape running from cold hills to hot plains. The state's population was huge, nearly equal to that of Brazil. Mayawati had no previous administrative experience, and constitutional tradition or propriety was not her concern. If she was challenged on any front, she asserted herself with exceptional force. Raja Bhaiya, a prominent Thakur politician and gangster who kept alligators in a lake in front of his palace to intimidate the locals, was imprisoned under anti-terrorism legislation, and for good measure Mayawati confiscated his family's properties, sealed his bank accounts and handed over the lake of gators to the forest department. To draw a New World comparison, it would be like a woman who had been born a slave, with all the fear that comes from having no redress, daring to jail a plantation owner.

A key spur or precipitant to Mayawati's forceful way of operating appears to have been a debacle just before she became chief minister, when she believes she came close to being assaulted or killed. Realizing her party was about to pull down a coalition state government in Uttar Pradesh, angry activists from the ruling party raided the official guest house where Mayawati and other legislators were staying. While politicians were slapped, beaten and in some cases temporarily kidnapped, she and others retreated to a suite and locked the door. "Drag the Chamar woman out from her hole," men and women shouted from outside, along with other more offensive remarks.[24] Even by the rough standards of north Indian politics, the attack in Lucknow was unprecedented. A battle between rowdies and police—some of whom were helping to protect the suite, while others were conspicuously standing idle—continued into the night until the legislators escaped. Mayawati remains terrified of assassination, and travels in a convoy of up to thirty-five matching vehicles when not touring her kingdom by helicopter.

In Mau in the poor, dusty eastern part of Uttar Pradesh, towards Bihar and the Nepalese border, there has long been intense caste rivalry, as well as communal violence between Hindus and Muslims. The wider region, once the United Provinces, had given birth to many of the leading statesmen of India and Pakistan, and was also home to vicious social antagonisms. To protect themselves, rival communities have over the years formed gangs to defend their interests. In places where the rule of law barely functions, a strong local politician can become a godfather or gang leader, and vice versa—and a politician's police escort can act as a useful form of additional security.

One of the most popular godfathers in Uttar Pradesh—UP—was Mukhtar Ansari, a giant of a man from a Muslim feudal family. His grandfather Dr. M. A. Ansari was an associate of Motilal Nehru who had served as president of the Indian National Congress in the 1920s. When Mukhtar Ansari was growing up in the 1970s, the region had been a communist stronghold and he was conscious of the depth of local animosity between different social groups. His brothers were politicians, and in the 1990s Mukhtar gained a reputation as a man who got things done. When he was elected from Mau as a state legislator, he secured more than $20m in extra government funding for his constituency. Rival gangs fought for control over contracts, which ranged from coal mining and scrap disposal to public works like road building and licences to sell liquor. In 2001, Mukhtar's convoy was ambushed while he was driving between Mau and Lucknow. During a shootout three of his best men were killed, but they managed to seriously injure a rival leader. A few years later, five murderers on motorcycles surrounded a car and shot the occupant, a BJP state legislator and a Bhumihar—an upper-caste Hindu—who was said to have been close to the original attacker. Rioting followed, and several buses, a mosque and part of a railway station were burned down. Mukhtar Ansari was blamed for the killing, although he pleaded his innocence since he was in jail in Ghazipur at the time, awaiting trial for inciting a mob during earlier communal violence. His accusers said that he had directed the operation from his cell using, fittingly, a cell phone.

Although he had not been convicted of any crime, Mukhtar was a "sheeter," charged with thirty-four offences, including gangsterism, homicide and firing an AK-47 at a police commissioner. He was reputed to carry a .357 Magnum and six mobile phones with him at all times. The authorities moved him frequently, not wanting him to take over the administration of his prison. In one jail he was said to have been allowed to build a volleyball court, and to have had a bathroom with soap from Harrods. The legal cases against him were grinding their way slowly through the court system.[25]

At the 2009 general election, he was recruited by Mayawati to run as a BSP candidate in Benares, one of north India's most ancient and holy cities, with its cremation ghats lining the banks of the Ganges. Mayawati knew he was likely to bring in Muslim votes, and she portrayed him as a Robin Hood character who could speak for the oppressed. "Mukhtar is a victim, and I consider him innocent," she told a rally. "A person who fights those who harass the poor people cannot be termed as a criminal just by implicating him in false cases."[26] Mukhtar had a nominal advantage: although his family traced their lineage to Medina and were thought to have been the standard-bearers of the prophet Mohammed, most Ansaris in India were poor weavers who were classified as OBCs. The forebears of these low-caste Muslims would probably have taken the name of the local ruler, perhaps on conversion. Mukhtar's main opponent in Benares was Murli Manohar Joshi, the author of the BJP manifesto. The other candidates stood little chance of winning, so it would be a straight race between the two of them, the Brahmin cow protector versus the imprisoned Muslim outlaw.

I received an SMS from someone I knew, Yusuf Ansari, while I was in Delhi watching the general election: "Are you averse to visiting gaol? One of the biggest factors of this election in U.P. is in Kanpur gaol." The factor was Mukhtar, who turned out to be Yusuf's cousin. It was a surprising family connection: I knew Yusuf worked in policy planning for the Congress party and had attended an English boarding school and the LSE. Sometimes he dressed in a dark achkan and earring, like an old-fashioned north Indian Muslim gentleman, and at other times he could be seen in a preppy red-and-white-striped shirt and waxed green jacket. I took the early-morning express train from New Delhi. The railway station was a crush of cars, yellow-and-green rickshaws, red-jacketed porters with brass ID plates twisted around their upper arm, people and more people. "Car will receive you with my secretary Mr. Pandey," Yusuf texted. "Mukhtar has gone for hearing on his bail application so can't meet." In the carriage I sat beside a student who tapped away on a laptop through the journey and talked of Mayawati. "Maya's so rich and clever," he said, "but she's got issues."

When I reached Kanpur, Mr. Pandey and I were conveyed to Yusuf's parents' residence by a driver. His family had previously lived in a nearby haveli, and this house had been built in the 1980s. When the family moved to the city in the 1930s to take advantage of new economic opportunities, they had been accompanied by a couple of hundred family retainers, to whom they had a social responsibility, and whose descendants still lived nearby. The house was constructed over several levels. Hunting trophies and animal skins with shot marks in them were on the walls, and framed imperial invitations, such as one inviting an ancestor to King George V's ceremonial durbar. I looked at Yusuf's library: *The Akbar Nama of Abu-l-Fazl*, P. G. Wodehouse, a biography of Winston Churchill. This house in Kanpur gave an echo of the nawabi world of earlier times.

In the sitting room, a throng of Congress party officials were discussing vote fractionalization: would Brahmins stick with the BJP or shift to the BSP, who had put up a Brahmin candidate in Kanpur? "This election is going to be decided by women," said one man, "because they know the price of kerosene and onions." A sweeper crouched like a spider on the stone floor, circling the room with a large wet cloth. Yusuf had a copper band on his wrist, high-arched eyebrows and an endlessly alert manner—when he was a child, his arm had been badly injured in a hunting accident in Ghazipur. He spent a little time lying prone on a day bed discussing political matters with his secretary, Mr. Pandey, while a family retainer massaged his arms. We could hear an election event out on the street and went down the steps to watch. It was blindingly hot outside. Campaigners were wearing masks featuring the face of their candidate, Shriprakash Jaiswal—the Congress minister who brought his own mineral water and mattress when he went to spend the night with Dalits.

"We'll go to some '57 sites," said Yusuf. What had happened in 1957? But he was speaking of 1857 and the mutiny against the British in the city then called Cawnpore, which had changed Britain's political position in the subcontinent. Hindus did not like to wear cap badges made of leather or to serve overseas, and neither Hindu nor Muslim soldiers had wished to handle cartridges greased with the fat of unspecified animals, which had to be bitten open before insertion into a rifle barrel. A rise in nationalist or at least anti-European feeling, fanned by rumours that the foreigners were planning to convert the population to Christianity, caused a chain of military encounters and sieges across the north. In Cawnpore, British soldiers and civilians were massacred as they sought to escape by boat. The revolt ended with Indian defeat, the collapse of the remnants of Mughal rule and savage reprisals by the British.

The events of 1857 left Britain aware of its weakness and vulnerability in India. Nervous of further rebellion, the number of European soldiers was increased and the remnants of the East India Company were replaced by a more regular structure of government, with Victoria becoming queen and later queen empress of India. Her first viceroy, Charles Canning, was worried by the "rabid and indiscriminate vindictiveness abroad" in the land, with members of the European community calling for "war to the knife." He told the queen that some people said they wanted the execution of 40,000–50,000 mutineers and "a broad line of separation, and of declared distrust drawn between us Englishmen and every subject of your Majesty who is not a Christian, and who has a dark skin." The queen shared Canning's view that this would be impractical, and plans were made for a proclamation to the people of India. Victoria told her officials in London that the tone of this new charter should be conciliatory, and to:

> bear in mind that it is a female Sovereign who speaks to more than a hundred millions of Eastern peoples, on assuming the direct Government over them, and after a bloody war . . . Such a document should breathe feelings of generosity, benevolence, and religious toleration, and point out . . . the prosperity following in the train of civilization.[27]

This was quite a mental leap to be making so soon after blowing countless sepoys from the mouths of cannons, but it was to become the foundation of subsequent British imperial policy in India.

We drove through modern Kanpur, past temples and mosques and leather and textile workshops, and chemical and soap and fertilizer manufacturers. The industrial city was huge. We entered the cantonment and came to the river, the Ganges. Trees grew inside tubes of latticed bricks, to make sure animals did not graze on them. On the opposite bank of the river lay fields of silt created by the monsoon, perfect for growing watermelons. As we walked over to "Musker" or Massacre Ghat in the shimmering heat, Yusuf looked at a building and said, "God, all this is new. Everything's changing." A Shiva temple had been put up by the site of Musker Ghat, and with it a large portrait of Mayawati. We left quickly; it was a grim place.

After it grew dark we drove with Yusuf's father, Idris, to a political rally. "It's São Paolo out here," said Yusuf. The headlights illuminated houses without electricity and the shapes of people. "We heard about India being an emerging economy," said Idris, staring out of the windscreen, "but look at this. These people are just living." He had a successful leather company, supplying shoe uppers for stitching in Europe and the U.S. He also did pet treats: the leather offcuts were turned into dog chews. We reached a street corner where a stage had been erected and draped in royal blue, the Dalits' colour. "There's no administration here," said Yusuf, "only politics." The ground was littered with rubbish and potholes. About a thousand people were present at the rally, many of them Muslims, who were being encouraged to shift away from other parties and to back Mayawati. On the stage, politicians were surrounded by banners and flags, and most were dressed in BSP kurta pyjamas. Armed security officers lined the stage, some sporting Bruce Lee T-shirts, and muscular men in blue caps ran through the crowd, pushing and shoving, keeping people in line, rousing cheers for Mayawati. It seemed exceptionally energetic compared with Congress rallies.

Akbar "Dumpy" Ahmad, a former crony of Sanjay Gandhi, was addressing the people, wrestling with the lectern as he shouted, waving his arms in apparent anger, throwing off flower garlands as they were passed up to him, imploring voters to quit Congress (as he had done) and support the BSP. "My father was the first Muslim chief of police in UP," he declaimed in Urdu, "my grandfather was chief justice of Allahabad high court, and I stood beside Sanjay Gandhi when he launched his youth campaign. And today, Muslims must vote with Mayawati and back the BSP." Voting for somebody was certainly essential: that day, the Darul Uloom religious school in Deoband had issued a fatwa saying all Muslims must exercise their democratic right: "A vote is as important as a testimony or a witness is in Islam."[28] As Dumpy Ahmad was speaking, someone drove a motorbike through the crowd, knocking people down, not accidentally.

It looked as if a riot might be starting, and we sheltered in the lobby of a nearby hotel. Idris knew the owner. "We call him the wrestler," he said.

The wrestler, whose shirt was not fresh and whose mouth was stained with paan, began to tell a story that was so convoluted I soon lost track. While he spoke a boy or man with a vacant expression and a number 11 football shirt stood beside him in attendance, listening. It seemed, in essence, that he was a butcher-cum-wrestler-cum-hotel-owner and his family were involved in a blood feud with another family. "It has been going for about forty-five years, and now nearly everybody is dead." Some killings—from their side—had been done with a white-handled "Astra" pistol, imported from Spain. It was a particularly good and reliable pistol. "About twenty in all have died," he continued, chewing, "though with the violence there has always been love." It was hard to know what he meant, or indeed if the story was true. He turned to Idris, and then back to me and said in English, "And a lot of love also." What had happened to the family pistol? The wrestler reached into the tight pocket of his trousers, pulled out a handgun and broke it to show it was loaded. He handed it to the attendant, chewed his paan some more and reached into a different pocket. Out came the notorious white-handled Astra pistol. He gave it to me. I looked at the weapon, wondered what to do with it and gave it back to him. The noise outside had quietened, and we left. Did that happen? I asked Idris. "We call him Naim Beta," he said. "He's from a family of local wrestlers, but there are not many left now after the blood feud. He's got several politicians staying at his hotel tonight, and he thinks he needs the gun to guard them."

We were driving back through the dereliction, past bamboo and timber yards, when Yusuf got a call on his mobile phone. "You were asking about Dumpy," he said to me. "He's just at the railway station if you want to meet him." We diverted, being detained for ten minutes at a level crossing while an interminable goods train rumbled through. Trains in India seemed to be three times longer than trains anywhere else. Our driver stopped right in front of the station—although the area was blocked by a security detail—and Idris told Yusuf and me to go ahead. We ran over the railway bridge and pushed through a scrum of BSP supporters to reach Dumpy's carriage. He was standing by the open door, enjoying the crowd's attention, a short, energetic man with a bristly beard and a blue stole around his neck. He caught sight of Yusuf. "Hey, Yusuf, are you still with the Congress?" Dumpy pretended to be disconsolate, playing the situation. He turned to me: "These babalogs have a lot to learn, they think they're still at Cambridge or Oxford Street. Mayawati is the future for India, and not just in UP, I can promise you. Sonia and Rahul are going nowhere." The train was about to whistle out of the station. I asked Dumpy about his days with Sanjay. "I was practising as a chartered accountant when Sanjay asked me to join politics. I knew Sanjay. Mrs. Gandhi said I was like her third son. Then when he died, Mrs. Gandhi threw Maneka out on the street and I was the only one who stood by her." How did Maneka repay him? The train started to move. "She gave me a kick up the ass." What would Sanjay Gandhi have thought of his son Varun wanting to chop off the hands of those who insulted Hindus? "He would be disgusted," said Dumpy Ahmad.[29]

When Yusuf and I had run over the railway bridge to reach the train, an extraordinary thing had happened. Marching along the main platform of Kanpur railway station came two columns of armed police, and in their midst a very tall man in a spotless white kurta pyjama. As the procession advanced, people had turned and bowed and been acknowledged with a grand wave. It was the don of dons, Mukhtar Ansari, returning late in the evening from his bail hearing. Yusuf walked past the sleeping figures, the piles of dusty boxes and the vendors carrying clay pots of water, pushed past the deferential policemen and greeted his cousin in the traditional way, with a cross between a shoulder bump, a bow and a hug. He introduced me, and Mukhtar suggested we come and visit him in the prison tomorrow, but to be sure to bring some oranges. In the topsy-turvy world of Uttar Pradesh, there was nothing so strange about seeing the outlaw striding along the railway platform, looking like a senior politician.

The next day we ate tahri, a dish like biryani, and drove to the jail. "Mukhtar's obsessed by National Geographic and Animal Planet on Discovery," said Yusuf on the way. "He analyses big cats. He'll lay bets with his entourage about animal fights—say, whether a lion will catch a gazelle. He wants to know why an animal does or doesn't get away."

"Yesterday?" asked Mukhtar Ansari, speaking in Urdu. He rubbed his hand over his substantial black moustache, which was twirling up at the tips. "Yesterday . . . I had a case heard in Chandoli." We were in a cavernous, limewashed barracks—his barracks. At the gate a seal of purple indelible ink had been stamped on both of my wrists, like the stamp you get when going into a nightclub. It read: "Office of the Gatekeeper, District Jail, Kanpur" in Devanagari script (the word "gatekeeper" had passed into Hindi). Along one wall were tables, where prison stewards were preparing watermelons. Mukhtar was in blue jeans and a flowery red shirt, sitting up on his bed cross-legged. He was hugely tall and big, though not fat, and wore a long, thin scrunchy scarf, of the kind worn by students in France. I noticed we had the same brand of spectacles. When Yusuf told him I had thought he looked like a government minister walking through the railway station, Mukhtar was delighted, and he relaxed.

"I entered politics because I was concerned about justice and the persecution of the oppressed. The Dalits and bonded labourers in eastern UP are treated like scum. I took up arms against this way of living in Joga village back in 1985, although I come from a distinguished family background. I have won six consecutive elections as an independent MLA [state legislator]. The Bhumihars killed some people in 1990 and knocked down a statue of Dr. Ambedkar. The oppressed went after them and killed about twenty." Mukhtar had a low and resonant voice. "The war against landlord oppression involves a constant battle to mobilize. I used my reputation. I had 20,000 or 25,000 men, and my army was Muslim, Brahmin, Thakur, Dalit—everyone. We could mobilize at a week's notice. We had licensed rifles. Our opponents the Ranvir Sena [a notoriously violent upper-caste militia from Bihar] had more weapons."

It was not easy to have a conversation with Mukhtar, since every few moments one of his attendants would approach with a mobile phone. "Inshallah, inshallah," he said to someone down the line. Nor were Yusuf and I the only visitors. An old man in a baseball cap appeared, a follower of the prominent Hindu swami Baba Jai Gurudev, who was building a temple. "Baba Jai Gurudev has no contact with political parties," the baseball cap told me as he waited for a consultation, "but he sees Mukhtar Ansari as a good man for India." He was an emissary of the baba, promising support in the election. "In Benares, everyone is connected with Mukhtar Ansari. We think he will have a big victory." Later, I looked at the baba's website: "The soul has an eye, an ear and a nostril but all these are closed at present due to past good or bad deeds. Through meditation and mercy of the Master these can be removed." Perhaps the godman was hedging his bets and offering blessings to several candidates.

Mukhtar portrayed his life as a justified and even inevitable response to the social imbalance and caste feuding in eastern Uttar Pradesh. "That part of our state is poverty-stricken. Generation after generation has to live on subsistence farming. The minorities are subject to the injustice of the Congress party. As an elected representative, I give all the money I make directly to the community in Mau. I arrange marriages, organize education, health clinics and eye clinics, I give out blankets and saris—and not only at election time. If someone calls me a 'mafia don' it makes no difference. Can they name one person I have attacked who comes from a weaker section? I have always fought against the powerful, I have taken power from them. I will continue what I am doing until the end of my days." Was he afraid? "Death only comes once."

A mobile phone was brought and held close to his ear by a helper. "Baba, inshallah," he said. Mukhtar had to run his election campaign from prison, although out on the streets of Benares, activists were campaigning for him in the thousands. His future depended on a victory: if he were elected, there was a good chance the legal cases against him would go quiet. Could he beat Murli Manohar Joshi? "They have been using blatantly communal images against me. In one of their pictures I was depicted as Aurangzeb at Kashi Vishwanath temple, blood dripping from a sword, lightning coming from the sky, standing with my foot on the statues. M. M. Joshi is a fascist, a very low, petty, filthy human being, an enemy of the state, and an enemy of love and fraternal feeling, and I am gratified to be fighting against him. He came to Benares to play Hindu politics. No Indian patriot can seek to divide us on the basis of religion. If he says that, he's a traitor. I am ready for those people to slaughter swine and throw them in a mosque, or slaughter cows and put them in a temple. I have warned them about it from my prison cell. But the election commission said I can't have publicity, I can't use a phone for my campaign. I am waiting for the court to release me. I've been in jail for forty-three months. So I read books, especially historical and revolutionary books. I will buy 2,000 copies of your book if it's any good, and distribute it to my people. My family fought in the freedom movement, and it's the same for me. I like Mahatma Gandhi, but if non-violence is not working, I say: 'Laton ke bhoot baton se nahin maante'"—"If a devil isn't listening to you, you have to give him a kick."

Three surprise visitors appeared: Mukhtar's wife, in a turquoise and silver salwar kameez with a black coat and pair of big sunglasses and dark lipstick, and their sons, aged eleven and sixteen. The elder boy wore an Armani belt, and the younger was chubby and cute. The family all sat up on the bed, close and affectionate with each other. The boys were studying at St. Francis' College in Lucknow. "They're going into the army," said Mukhtar. He meant the Indian army, not his private force. I asked Abbas, the elder, why he was joining up. "I want to fight the terrorists," he said in English. "I am going to attack on Pakistan and fight the criminals and all." Mukhtar looked proud. "It's in their blood," he said. The younger boy, Omar, piped up in English too. "I am going to RULE on Pakistan." We laughed and began talking about the Taliban. Mukhtar was of the view that they were being paid by a foreign power—probably the Americans—to blacken the name of Islam. "Nowhere in our religion does it say to kill innocents, and that is what they do." Mrs. Ansari was silent, in a traditional way; it was like a social gathering of men, although we were in a prison barracks.

"When I get out," said Mukhtar, "I want to travel. I've been on the Haj and to Thailand, and I want to go to Mecca again, and to hunt lions in South Africa—where I've heard it's legal. I'll buy hunting accessories and see the black-maned lion in Namibia. My ambition is to visit the U.S.A., and see what progress America has made, and what we in UP can take from there to practise in our own part of the world."[30]

We left them, sitting up on the bed, a close family. As the wrestler had said: "With the violence there has always been love." Back at the house, Yusuf's mother said to me: "If you want to go to Lucknow, you might get a lift with Cyrus. He's been visiting the arms factory in Kanpur and is going back this evening." I pictured a journey through the badlands of Uttar Pradesh with a trunk full of weapons. But she explained that Cyrus, a Parsi with damaged legs, had been visiting a medical factory which made prosthetic arms, so as to get his calipers tightened. "Godspeed," said Yusuf as we drove away. Cyrus and I reached Lucknow, Mayawati's fiefdom, by nightfall.

Mukhtar Ansari did not win the race in Benares: he was beaten by a narrow margin by Murli Manohar Joshi. Not long afterwards, claiming she had information he was still involved in criminal activity, Mayawati expelled him from the BSP. A while later he was transferred from Kanpur to the political section of Tihar jail in Delhi. Had he won the election, there was little doubt Mukhtar would have been sitting in the Indian Parliament as one of Mayawati's honourable MPs, rather than in a prison cell.

Ambedkar's revolution—or the revolution done in Dr. Ambedkar's name—is about assertion. Its details are less important than its message: India's Dalits can and will take power for themselves. Now in her fifties with her hair cut short, honoured with giant garlands of banknotes at her public appearances, Mayawati is the message, the symbol. "Chamari hoon, kunwari hoon, tumhari hoon," she likes to say at the start of her speeches. "I'm a Chamar, I'm not married, I'm yours!" And the audience, who know that no woman of her caste has been in such a powerful position, scream their applause. With her rough Hindi and her contemptuous view of political conventions, she represents everything the old ruling class despises and fears. When a senior Congress leader, herself the daughter of a former Uttar Pradesh chief minister, said Mayawati deserved to be raped, the response was explosive. The unexpressed implication was that since Mayawati was a Dalit, she could be raped with impunity, and shown her place as others had been before her. The Congress leader quickly apologized, saying she had spoken in anger, but not before she had been put in prison and had her house set on fire.[31]

Ambedkar, analysing the plight of untouchables in his writing, was conscious always of the antiquity of his dispossession. Conventions dating back to the era before the birth of Christ specified that the rejected castes should not be allowed to accumulate possessions, gain education or bear arms. "There is no code of laws more infamous regarding social rights than the Laws of Manu," he wrote. "The lower classes of Hindus have been completely disabled for direct action on account of this wretched system of [caste]."[32] Yet Ambedkar was affected by the colonial thinking of the time, the belief that all controls were unvarying. The authority for Manu's "laws" was William Jones, an eighteenth-century British judge who had translated from Sanskrit what he called "the Indian system of duties, religious and civil"—with an explicitly political ambition. Jones hoped his book would help in the preparation of "a Code which may supply the many natural defects in the old jurisprudence of this country [in] a commercial age."

He was saying, essentially, that Europeans did not know what was going on in Indian society and needed a myriad of alien behaviours to be explained and contained. Since their ability to exert physical control was limited, the British rulers planned "to leave the natives of these Indian provinces in possession of their own Laws," and he hoped that, in future, "the administration of justice and government in India, will be conformable, as far as the natives are affected by them, to the manners and opinions of the natives themselves; an object which cannot possibly be attained, until those manners and opinions can be fully and accurately known."[33] Jones regarded the laws of Manu as a basis for future conduct: "The style of it has a certain austere majesty that sounds like the language of legislation and exhorts a respectful awe; the sentiments of independence on all beings but God, and the harsh admonitions even to kings are truly noble."[34]

The laws or teachings of Manu, the Manusmriti, are hard to interpret from a distance of over two millennia. The text is a guide to life and to how a just king should rule. Jones was taken by their regulatory aspect, which seemed to decode a complex society: "Rice pudding boiled with tila, frumenty, rice-milk, and baked bread, which have not been first offered to some deity, flesh meat also . . . must all be carefully shunned."[35] Many of the rules on pollution and food were (and are) still followed in India, but much of the text appears specific to an antique world. So at a ceremony for the dead you should exclude a man who has shed his semen in violation of a vow, a man who allows his wife's lover to live in his house, the sexually irregular (including "a man who allows his mouth to be used as a vagina") and anyone with mangled fingernails or discoloured teeth. If you know the law, you "should not offer even a little water to a twice-born man who acts like a cat." If a goldsmith behaves dishonestly, "the king should have him cut to pieces with razors." If a "'Fierce Untouchable' man" has sex with a tribal woman, "the evil 'Puppy-cooker' is born, who makes his livelihood from the vice of [digging up and selling] roots and is always despised by good people."[36]

The impression here is of a ritualized society. Aside from the strict regulations on the behaviour of women, the section with the strongest resonance in Ambedkar's lifetime concerned the fate of outcastes, who had to live outside the village, wear the clothes of the dead and eat food from a broken dish.

In Lucknow today, the capital of Uttar Pradesh, the city's physical space was being reworked to remake history. Great hoardings were advertising the "achievements nonpareil" of Mayawati's government in building roads and bridges, but these were posters any chief minister might display. When she came to power, Mayawati had started by building statues of Dr. Ambedkar, and proceeded with the creation of a huge public park and stone buildings in his name. This was merely a preparation for a more serious ambition—creating an enduring monument in Lucknow on a hundred-acre site, with sixty epic red sandstone statues of elephants (her party symbol) and representations of Dr. Ambedkar and the Buddha. Legal attempts to prevent the project had been unsuccessful, and Mayawati was open about what she was seeking to do: "Remember, what I have spent on memorials and statues was only one percent of the state's annual budget, but what I have built is going to be there for posterity. I firmly believe that those who are unable to create history are always pushed into oblivion," she told a rally of her followers. Her delivery was perfunctory, but the audience did not seem to mind. "I will not allow a Dalit to bow his head before anybody," she said.[37]

At the site, a burning expanse of stone, it was hard to take in the extent of what was now nearly complete. It was impressive and grotesque, elephant after stone elephant stretching off into the distance, veiled statues swathed in royal blue cloth, the whole area raised up from the surrounding roads. To reach the level of Mayawati's wide monument, you had to climb steps. The site was too big to walk easily from one side to the other. All the tree cover had been chopped down, making it even hotter than the rest of Lucknow on a May morning. It was pharaonic in its assertion—and this was Mayawati's intention, to be remembered by history, like the first Ming emperor or Shah Jahan. She did not want to be forgotten by history like Ozymandias, "Look on my works, ye mighty, and despair." Mayawati's innumerable detractors, who saw her as just another politician, if more corrupt and tasteless than the others, were underestimating the scale of her social mission.

Their heads swathed against the sun, reams of workmen were chipping and dressing stone. One of them lifted a hidden manhole and pulled out a long hose to spray the blocks. I asked them why they were making this enormous park.

"It's being built for social reform."

"It's to say, you are independent in India, you can do what you like."

"It's for my community. My family could never have thought about coming to a place like this."

I was talking to a group of men, not all of them Dalits. One of the most admiring was Dinesh Tiwari, a Brahmin from Rae Bareli. One of Mayawati's tactics had been to persuade Brahmins—who in Uttar Pradesh were often poor and had been politically excluded following the rise of the Other Backward Classes—that she could be their protector against the intermediate castes. In 2005 she held a huge ceremony in Lucknow where men with vermilion caste marks and shaved heads, bar a braid of hair at the back, paraded in rows and touched her feet in homage. "Behenji, bachao!" they said as they stooped—"Respected sister, save us!"[38] It was, again, a scene that would have been unimaginable only decades before, the Brahmins bending down before the former outcaste for protection.

The workers took me on a spontaneous tour. We looked up at two giant bronze statues looming above us, which stood on individual red sandstone plinths. One was of Kanshi Ram, the other of Mayawati, appearing stolid and holding an expensive-looking long-handled handbag almost at ankle level. On the opposite side of the road, facing or matching them, stood correspondingly massive statues of Dr. Ambedkar and his first wife, Ramabai (who came from the Mahar caste like her husband, unlike the second Mrs. Ambedkar, who was a Brahmin). She looked demure, wifely, her head covered, quite unlike Mayawati with her strong, masculine stance. Curving stone canopies shielded both pairs of figures.

One of the workmen, Prithiviraj, began to sing what he said was a film song. When he was finished, he said, "It's in honour of Dr. Babasaheb Ambedkar." What did he think of the monumental park he was building? "Before it's all greenery, now it's all stone, stone, stone. It's something like the Taj Mahal, but the first one in Lucknow. In this country, you have to give respect to everyone now. Other countries have their regulations, but we have democracy. Nobody can come and trouble us."

A supervisor came over, and they returned to work. As I walked away and looked through the heat haze, the men appeared small and desiccated as they banged away with their hammers. The creation of the monument was a physical aspect of what they saw as their struggle. The first half-century after independence, with its dependence on borrowed economic theories and English-speaking politicians, was a continuation of the colonial experience by other means, which was now being undone in unpredictable ways. The workmen had different reasons for liking the monument and the chief minister, but the explanation Dinesh Tiwari had given for his admiration was the one that stuck with me: "I like Mayawati because she has power." This was true, although Mayawati would in time be swept away. The park would go on.

10

4EVER

WITH ECONOMIC LIBERALIZATION, old structures were breaking down. Sometimes, people had to leap between social settings which had no imaginable connection to each other. The difference between communities and between the village and the city was altering very fast in some parts of India. Socially acceptable behaviour was adjusting in this still traditional country. A friend mentioned that a male stripper had come to a hen party she was attending, even while older members of the joint family were in the house. Another acquaintance told me he had recently turned up to a large family wedding in Delhi and realized it was staffed by Ukrainian escorts, who had apparently been arranged by the groom's uncles. Many worlds lived in parallel.

Satish was a pimp, at the top end of the market, supplying prostitutes and strippers for parties. I went to see him with Sushmita, an irreverent Delhi journalist, thinking he was more likely to be open about his work in her presence. Satish was twenty-nine years old, slim and watchful with a black long-sleeve T-shirt and dark-blue jeans, his wet-look hair brushed forward to make him seem younger. We met at the United Coffee House, a hemmed-in, old-fashioned place with a balcony filled by talkative diners. Satish asked for tea, with milk and one sugar, while Sushmita and I drank red wine. He spoke freely, in English, once he had dropped his guard.

He told us he had taken a degree in commerce at Allahabad University, and worked as ground staff for an airline while stripping and having sex for money on the side. Now, as he put it, "I only do management." He had around forty men and ten women on his books. "All the guys are in their late teens or twenties. Often people will require someone aged sixteen or seventeen, but I don't represent them. The guys who work for me need physique, looks and height. Physique is a must. Most are from Punjab or Haryana, or anyway from the north. They look like Greek gods, but they don't even know English. My clients are hi-fi people." He named several, including a chief minister.

"Either they can't get sex, or they have so much money they can make people do whatever they want. I keep the girls on my list in case the clients are bisexual and want one of each. I don't allow bargaining. The rates go from Rs5,000 [$110] to Rs25,000 [$550] for two hours. The rate for models and actors is higher. We have one of the best models in Asia, and for him it's Rs2.5 lakhs [$5,500] for two hours."

Satish's operation was virtual: it worked via phone and the Internet. He moved from club to party, making links with people and arranging the meetings. Images of the prostitutes were displayed on a photographer's website, very respectably. You reached them by clicking through to a particular part of the site, but many of the models on the main page were available too. With the actors, it was necessary to be more discreet. Most of the male models had the fair, gym-toned "Greek god" look, but others were thin and willowy. Their physical appearance, which was almost certainly the consequence of generations of malnourishment, dovetailed with the present, imported vogue for super-skinny men and women. So the idea of being extremely slim, which in a rich culture was taken as a sign of fashionable affluence, had been imported to a land where most people had never had the opportunity to become fat.

For Satish, the practice of religion enabled him to hold himself together while taking part in a profession that was by its nature dangerous and destabilizing. "My family is very traditional, very religious. We're from UP. My sisters wear salwar kameez. I am also most traditional and religious. I can become very . . ."—here he searched for the right word, before settling on "emotional. I more and more believe in my god. Every day I go to the temple." It was a Lord Krishna temple, close to his home. "I usually wake at five and go there at seven. I take a mark on my forehead. I attend the aarti two or three days a week. Afterwards I go to the park and close my eyes and pray to god."

I asked him about the world he moved in, the people he met and their new social expectations. Satish saw the question in terms of those he recruited. "Many of the Delhi strippers are straight, and at a lot of parties the client will prefer a straight stripper—even sometimes if the guests are gay. They think it's more exciting if they know it's a straight guy. The boys arrive to work for me with a strong male ego, and come from families where such behaviour would never be allowed. I have a new guy coming tomorrow on the train from Patna. It's his first time in Delhi. He is twenty-two years old, his family are very poor and he comes from a village near to Patna." How did he contact new recruits? "This one met me through a dating website. He was looking at the Internet in his village." Most villages near Patna in Bihar are dusty and desperate, though in this case they must at least have had electricity for the Internet.

"I have to make them learn a new mindset. I take them to clubs where there are male strippers. I send them to parties. I usually start by showing them DVDs of films like *Page 3* and *Oops!*" The first was about a journalist who moves to Mumbai, covers celebrity parties and gets caught up in the lifestyle; the second was about male strippers and dancers, and was considered shocking when released in 2003. "The men who work for me come from a different mindset. Everything is about their mindset. They don't understand this life. Indian guys get caught up, they fall in love-shove. They come to Delhi because they want money and they want the life, more than anything because they want what they have heard about or seen on the screen. They hope someone will fall in love with them. When they get here, they find they can't deal with it. They think they can do it, but they can't do it because of the ego of the Indian male. They have never been naked in front of another person, and now they are having to strip off all their clothes.

"Most of the people in my agency are Punjabi farmers, and their families don't have any idea what they are doing. I might have to send them to a party where the people are completely different from them, I might send them to Mumbai or to Dubai for one party. Indian guys are very in demand in Gulf countries. Last week I sent someone to Bangalore for a party." Satish said Bangalore was India's most "modern" city, and had a strong demand for "fair" strippers from the north.

"The first time I did stripping was with a woman I met in McDonald's in Connaught Place. She was thirty-two, a Malayali. She picked me up and I asked for Rs10,000 [$220]. We went to her home in South-Ex. She put me on to others. I brought four or five guys to a party she held, we all stripped and then some of the women wanted sex. No servants were in the house; she must have sent them all home. Only women came to the party, about twenty of them, and I think most were NRIs." Non-Resident Indians— people who lived out of the country. "They were posh people, wearing designer clothes. Most of them were the kind of women who have 'busy husbands.' It was a good atmosphere."

The conversation had begun with Satish trying to scope us out, wondering why he was really being asked about his life and career, but now when Sushmita asked him a different sort of question, he revealed another, new aspect of himself. Did he "send money home" to his family? "Yes, I do. I am very close to my parents, but I couldn't say what I do. For my family, knowing I am gay would be worse than knowing about the agency." Homosexual life in the capital was open in a way it could not be outside the big cities. In 2009 the Delhi high court, invoking the Constitution's emphasis on "inclusiveness," had overturned a 150-year-old British law punishing "carnal intercourse against the order of nature with any man, woman or animal." The atmosphere had become easier since then, and men from the middle class were now able to be more open about their sexuality. "Until 2004, when one of the TV channels did a hidden film and busted them, you had strip clubs in Delhi with women-only entry and male strippers. It's become a little easier since the change in the law. You used to have the risk of ten years in jail. If the police caught gay men, they would either try to get money or sex from them. The Indian police are very, very bad."

Then without prompting Satish revealed much more about his background: his father was a politician in Uttar Pradesh, a religious man who had come in with the new wave of politics in the state. So Satish was, in his way, another contemporary manifestation of the varieties of north Indian life. "My aim is to travel abroad some more, to Dubai or to London. I want to see how the industry works. I am waiting for the right person to know me, to understand me, to know my feelings. I go home to Lucknow every month." He mentioned his love for the world of the nawabs, the courtly north Indian culture of earlier centuries. Did he find it hard to adjust when he went home? "Old Lucknow, the traditional city, is familiar to me. Nawabi culture is gay culture." This was quite a thought, and the more I thought about it, the more convincing it seemed.

When we left the United Coffee House and stood out on the street in Connaught Place amid the touts and the hawkers of paperback books, Satish's demeanour changed. The intimacy of the conversation had gone, and he was back to how he had been when he arrived to meet us, a thin, alert and vulnerable man, who noticed exactly who was watching him, and how. Afterwards, he texted me, nervous about what he had said: "But it was safe my meeting no camera and micro phone. Plz tel me truly."[1] There was no hidden camera or microphone, although he had watched me making notes.

As India got richer, it got glamour. At parched road junctions in cities, child workers sold sunshades, mosquito zappers, pirated paperbacks and copies of *Tehelka, Vogue* and *Beautiful People*. The disparity was inescapable in the pages of *Vogue,* and the world it reflected. The magazine had got itself into trouble by doing a fashion shoot which showed poor people with expensive things: a roadside baby in a Fendi bib, a villager holding a $200 Burberry umbrella. In 2008, *GQ* launched an Indian issue, and the editor wrote that he hoped to "empower men to break free from archaic sartorial constrictions and discover a distinctive sense of style" since "Indian men could do with a little help in this department."[2] Soon, every Indian industrialist wanted to be featured, presenting himself as part of a world of intense glamour. So in *Hello!,* launched in India in 2007, a stocky purveyor of toiletries could be praised for his "sharp features" and "svelte athletic build," while his wife said, "We are not into brands, please. Nor are we willing to splash fanciful luxe labels."[3] In a Christmas issue of the same magazine, "Delhi's swishest gal pals," with rocks like knuckledusters on their fingers, "met for a typical X'mas brunch" of "turkey with chestnut stuffing napped in cranberry jus." One, dressed in a "short Givenchy dress," said she preferred to spend her festivities "with children of a lesser god."[4] What did this mean? The menu, the Christian religious festival, the brands—they were all borrowed from abroad. In a return to Indian authenticity, *Hello!* took to featuring abolished royal families, covering them with a relish and reverence that would have been hard to imagine a few decades earlier, and listing them by their full, old-fashioned titles. They could be praised and photographed nostalgically in their dowdy sitting-rooms, wearing old jewels, because they held only the memory of power.

The most significant cultural difference between a professional family in India and one in the West comes from the prevalence of servants. Indians have cooks, drivers, bearers, sweepers, gardeners, maids and more maids— and often treat them callously. The gang of servants in a household may include children, and the parallel family will usually live in the most basic surroundings, without fans or air conditioning. Many Indians who come from middle- to upper-class families will never in their lives have made a bed or had to cook or clean, and find it hard to know what to do when they go abroad. The economic boost of the last decade has engineered a propulsion in society that has changed the way people think about themselves. The relationship between families and their retainers is altering, but important ideas of self and of social status are predicated on servitude, and on the expectation of being able to ordain the lives of others in an everyday way.

For women who pursue a professional career, this can give a lattice of support that does not exist in Western countries, where acquiring and retaining staff is expensive. You can drive if you like, or tell someone else to drive you. You can cook if you like, or tell someone else to cook. Aided by the assistance of parents or parents-in-law, women are able to raise children and do a job without one making the other difficult. A business trip will not be a worry if you know your children are with a family member you trust. Maternal guilt is less of an expectation than it is in the West, where performing the role of the perfect mother is—at the higher levels of society—a definite obligation. At present in India, HSBC, RBS, JP Morgan Chase, ICICI and UBS are all run by women, and half the deputy governors of the Reserve Bank of India are women.[5]

Liberal, urban India, the face foreigners often see, is held up by an edifice of staff. A while ago I was dining with an eminent communist in Delhi and found he had sent for his cook from his home town by train for the evening—a journey of around forty-eight hours—rather than risk having his dinner party spoilt by a replacement chef. It is not unheard of to be having a conversation about, say, the evils of colonialism or child labour, and realize midstream that your interlocutor is serving you a cup of tea via the hand of a fourteen-year-old servant. In another house, a boy of ten is spoon-fed apple pie by a member of staff, not because he cannot do it himself but because he is tired after a tuition class and sees nothing strange about being treated like a little prince. A girl of sixteen will order her maid to serve every last item on to her plate, and even to squirt the tomato ketchup on the side. Then, midway through the solo meal, she will shout: "Replace it! It's cold!" or "Bring me more ice!" During an evening in Mumbai a while back, the host, a normally affable person, interrupted our dinner to shout across a roomful of people at his elderly uniformed bearer or butler: "Narayan, why the hell are you looking at me? Don't you look at me." And Narayan, in his white turban, turned his face away.

The relationship between servants and employers can be cruel, but equally it can be a happy one, the richer party contributing towards the cost of family weddings and even paying for the education of children, the encounter leading in some cases to the offspring of the poorer party joining the professions themselves and employing staff in turn. In some houses, the servants are wholly integrated into the life of the home, and it is like a successful and friendly working collaboration, with everyone having their own assigned role. Servants sometimes live in quarters attached to the houses of the better-off or in lodgings constructed on the roof, with men and women in segregated dormitory-type rooms. In some residences, they nest in store-rooms or alcoves. I came down in the morning while staying in one house (though this was in truth in Dhaka, which stopped being Indian in 1947) to find two servants asleep on blankets on the kitchen floor, and a third sleeping in the tight little corridor leading to the kitchen. They had their home villages, miles away, but this floor was now their accommodation.

Since the cost of employing servants is low, staff will not usually be there to demonstrate wealth, only to make a certain form of living easier. Those with a social conscience might keep the servant–employer ratio at 1:1, so that a couple with one child may have a cook, a cleaner and perhaps a driver. The ratio will sometimes be closer to 3:1 or 4:1. So a wealthy couple with one child might have a driver each, a pair of rotating security guards, a cook, assistant cook, maid, laundry maid, cleaner, ayah and gardener. In extended families, the servants will form a complete shadow world. A cook told me he had worked for a joint family of forty members, with constant counter-instructions coming to the servants from brothers, aunts and feuding sisters-in-law; his sole job had been "atta cook"—making things out of flour like chapattis, puris and paranthas. In one Nagpur family, a rich young woman was preceded wherever she went by a maid of about her own age. "We're just like sisters," she said. But would your sister sit on the floor beside you and press your feet and rub them with oil while you chat away to your friends, some of them carrying bags that cost exactly twice the maid's annual salary? When travelling abroad, these practices can cause complications. A drinks distributor who went on a free trip to the Swiss resort of Interlaken was shocked to find he could not treat the staff at his hotel like his household servants back home. Grabbing a young receptionist by the collar when his demand for fresh towels was not met late in the evening, he was disconcerted when the man called the police. "He was scared stiff when they took his fingerprints," the tour escort reported later, gleefully. "He behaved perfectly after that."[6]

Servants are everywhere, even when they are doing their best to disappear. A maid on a stairway will press herself against the wall in a way that is so self-effacing she might not be there. An old man takes his belly for a walk in a park, tailed by a phone-carrying attendant, who is doing nothing but being present in order to show his master's connectivity. In DLF Empo-rio, a Delhi mall which has Jimmy Choo, Rohit Bal, Just Cavalli, Salvatore Ferragamo, Tod's and all the rest, you can see maids and ayahs gathered by the fountains, waiting. In restaurants you can see them seated on benches near the entrance, dandling infants, and you can sometimes see the ayahs disappear with their charges into the bathroom, for fear the child's noise might disturb the parents. The omnipresence of dispensable servants, seen through doors you may not pass through, makes a certain kind of exis-tence possible. Servants fetch, carry, polish, iron, sweep, wash, shop, fix; they are slimmer and darker than their employers; they look childlike but profoundly adult, as if they have had to work like adults since they were children. They move without assurance, and the expectation is that they will always be there, to facilitate a certain way of life.

As family structures that have been in place in India for centuries alter and fracture, and social mobility increases, household arrangements are changing. People complain it is impossible to recruit a reliable maid, and that word-of-mouth recommendation no longer works. Home loans are making it feasible for couples to set up independent households in a way they could not have done a generation ago. In the 1980s, if you wanted a home loan you had to open a bank account and pay in a monthly sum for an agreed term before the bank manager became convinced you had the "savings habit" and would process the application. From 2002, banks began to sell mortgages more vigorously, with loans of up to 100 percent of the value of the property, using floating interest rates. Demand grew, and most of the borrowers were young. Residential property was becoming more affordable than ever: in 2006 a house in a Mumbai suburb typically cost five times a person's annual income, as against twenty-two times in the mid-1990s.[7] As more people moved to two- or three-bedroom apartments, building developments and new towns and cities sprang up across India.

With the different housing arrangements came a fresh demand for ser-vants, who were demanding higher wages. The spread of smaller house-holds meant it could no longer be assumed that a member of the extended family would always be present to keep an eye on the various members of staff. Often people found themselves employing servants who had come from far away—from the south to the north, or from the north to the south. In some cases they had come from outside India's borders. Despite new forms of technology and communication, the practical mechanisms to check who they were, and whether they were trustworthy, did not exist. For Rajesh and Nupur Talwar, a middle-class couple who employed a cook and a maid, the lack of knowledge about the people in their home was to destroy their lives—aided and exacerbated by the administrative dystopia of the state of Uttar Pradesh.

Their daughter, Aarushi Talwar, was murdered in her bedroom on the night of 15 May 2008. She was a few days short of her fourteenth birthday, a star student at Delhi Public School in Noida, a talented dancer and a keen reader. She had suffered stab wounds to her head and neck. The story of what happened to Aarushi, as reported by a voracious media over the two days following her death, was presented as a salutary tale for every middle-class Indian parent.

It was presumed her killer was Hemraj Banjade, a Nepali household servant who had drunk most of a bottle of whisky, broken into Aarushi's bedroom, assaulted and murdered her. He was missing, and a cash reward of Rs20,000 was offered for news leading to his capture. The killing was said to have been done with a khukri, a curved Gurkha knife. In the words of one report, the case was "an eye-opener to the vulnerability of Indian homes and the murderous tendencies of the domestic servants." It listed examples of respectable families who had been attacked by their own staff: a child slain by a driver, an old woman killed by a greedy maid. The moral, according to the author of this article, was that police verification of a new servant's identity was essential and that "domestic servants are exposed to temptation when the dwellers talk of money or jewellery or other financial secrets in their presence."[8] The fact Hemraj came from Nepal was an additional lesson, since north India had many Nepalese household workers, and there was a porous border between the two countries.

The Talwars lived in a second-floor apartment in a housing colony populated largely by naval and air force families in the "green city" of Noida, on the outskirts of Delhi. Aarushi's parents were both successful dentists in their mid-forties, and had met and fallen in love at medical school. Her mother, Nupur, was an orthodontist, and her father, Rajesh, was a dental surgeon. Aarushi's maternal grandparents lived nearby. In the family photographs and video clips that were shown by the media, they appeared to have been a particularly happy unit—the mother, father and only child. As television channels broadcast and rebroadcast their story, the Talwars looked like everyfamily, the one that had suffered the inconceivable fate other families feared. Viewers of the rolling news could watch mother and daughter holding parrots at a bird park, father and daughter playing by a swimming pool, Aarushi dancing with her school friends and flicking her hair shyly when she saw she was being filmed. Her distraught friends set up a page on Facebook: "R.I.P. ❤ Aarushi."

The Talwars were, before their tragedy, the successful family next door. Instead of one of the parents being a popular dentist, they both were. Instead of having a child who did all right at school, they had a pretty daughter who topped 90 percent in her exams. Their home, Noida (New Okhla Industrial Development Authority), was an aspirational city that had been planned sector by sector for a modern middle-class lifestyle. Noida had a huge mall called The Great India Place, several new metro stations connecting to Delhi, and restaurants like Domino's and Papa John's. It was full of children, many of them slipping in and out of tuition centres after school and going gaming at Future Zone, or playing pool or table tennis at the many kids' clubs.

Aarushi's body was found by her parents on a Friday morning. "Rajesh started shouting and screaming," her mother, Nupur, said later. "The maid came and called some neighbours, and the police came. The police were fine then. They were so certain about what had happened that the senior officer said, 'It's an open-and-shut case. The servant has done this. Send a team to the housing colony where the Nepalis live, send a team to the railway station and send a team to Nepal to his village, to see if he's gone there.' I was senseless, I couldn't cry or scream. I was inanimate, like a stone. People were in and out of the place: police, neighbours, relatives, onlookers, the media. There must have been a hundred people in our home that morning."[9]

The next afternoon, a retired police officer who lived nearby came to pay his condolences. In India, after a death, a house will fill with friends, neighbours, acquaintances and family, all come to pay their respects. Diyas—burning wicks floating in bowls of oil—will be set in front of gar-landed pictures of the deceased. In this case, the officer appears to have been just plain curious, or ghoulish, since the Talwars did not know him and they were not at the apartment when he visited. He found his training taking over while he was there: he reconstructed the sequence of the crime and noticed bloody marks in unexpected places. It seemed to him some-thing was wrong. "I checked Hemraj's room and the bathroom and then noticed the bloodstains on the stairs leading to the terrace," he said later. "When I reached the door, I saw that it was locked and then I broke open the door [with the assistance of the police] and found Hemraj's body lying in a pool of blood on the floor. He had a slit mark on his throat and many injury marks on his body. His body was severely decomposed."[10] Hemraj Banjade, the servant, had been lying dead on the roof terrace in the scorching summer sun for almost two days, and the police had failed to notice.

Once again, reporters and film crews from Delhi were swarming around the property: a faithless servant had become a murder victim, and a tragedy had become a mystery. The country grew riveted by the case. It was a growing media obsession, and everyone became an expert, with their own explanation of the double homicide. Endless theories were constructed as to what might have happened. Since there was no sign of forced entry, the presumption was that Hemraj had known his killer or killers. There seemed two likely explanations. The first was that Hemraj had been trying to protect Aarushi and been killed for his pains. The second was that Aarushi had seen somebody attacking Hemraj and been killed as a witness.

The pressure on the Noida police to solve the case was intense. They had to find the murderer, and fast. Their failure to investigate or even to secure the crime scene the previous day was a shocking demonstration of incompetence. It became known the police had allowed the media and even passers-by to enter the Talwars' apartment after Aarushi's body was found. All forensic evidence had been compromised or destroyed, leaving them with no leads. They were assailed by questions: Why had they not bothered to check the terrace? How could they have bungled so badly? Two years earlier, the Noida police had been in the news for failing to detect a serial killer who was murdering children, and now they needed to get a quick result if senior officers were to avoid a transfer to some obscure rural posting. Although the city was next to Delhi, it fell in the jurisdiction of Uttar Pradesh, where police had a reputation for being criminals in uniform who did nothing unless they were paid a bribe.

Under pressure from above, poorly trained and badly paid officers fell back on methods they could get away with in Mau or Kanpur and applied them in Noida. Their investigation was haphazard, absurd and defamatory, targeting those who were closest to the murder scene. They informed the press now that the killing of both victims had been done not with a khukri or a knife, but with "a sharp-edged surgical instrument," suggesting it might be the handiwork of a medical professional.[11] Next, a police officer went on the record: "The way in which the throat of Aarushi was cut points out that it is the work of some professional who could be a doctor or a butcher."[12] The family were unaware of this statement and its implication.

"I had banned TV from our house by this time," Nupur said bitterly two years later. "Whenever we turned it on, there was always news about the murder. So I hid the remote. Then the mother of Aarushi's close friend Fiza, who had a contact at NDTV, warned me the police were saying they were suspicious we were involved in the killing, and were gunning for us. I took no notice, and I was quite angry and upset with Fiza's mother. The police had told us not to talk to the media, so we didn't. Then the same police officer who had said this to us, the SSP [Senior Superintendent of Police], gave a press conference saying they were looking at the family."[13]

Nupur's husband, Rajesh Talwar, was now the prime suspect. I had been Dr. Talwar's patient, and had sat in his dentist's chair. I knew him only as a bearded, avuncular man who had gentle hands, even when he was probing your molars.

"I had lost my beloved child, so why were they doing this to me?" he asked. "The cops thought we were an 'immoral' family because Aarushi made 300 calls a month to her friends and went on Orkut and Facebook. These people are backward. They are not fit to do their job. They said I did an honour killing because she was having an inter-caste relationship with the servant. My wife and I had an inter-community marriage, so how on earth would I think of doing what they call an honour killing? I told them Aarushi was reading two books, Shantaram and Chetan Bhagat's 3 Mistakes of My Life. So the police say, 'Hah, you're saying she was reading this book because she has made three mistakes in her life? What are the three mistakes?' She had joined the 'I Decide' club at school, and the last project she did was on addiction—in fact she won the first prize for her effort but was not there to see it. She had looked up addiction on the Internet, so the Noida police then say on television: 'We think there was some addiction in the family. She may have had a drug addiction, or she may have thought members of her family needed help with it.' I told them, go to her school and look at her project or talk to her teachers. I wondered if this was my destiny, and if the universe was conspiring against me, or if I had been caught in a whirlpool."

We were in the sitting-room of the Talwars' apartment in south Delhi. It was nearly two years since Aarushi's murder. They had left Noida and moved back to the building they had lived in during the first few months of her life, when she was a baby. She was all around us, in blown-up photographs on the wall, in the crystal ornaments on a low table, in their memories. Her bedroom had been faithfully reconstructed in the new home with her clothes, desk, cushions and toys. Propped up on her bed was her favourite stuffed Bart Simpson, which she liked to have beside her at night. They had the mementoes: the photos of Aarushi growing up, as a little girl, as a teenager with kohl around her eyes sitting in the back of a car with her school friends. They had the cards, the one saying: "MOM . . . L.O.V.E. you 4ever!" and the one saying: "Dad u r da bestest dad any1 can have. U rok ma world."

"For her birthday weekend," said her mother, "we'd planned a sleepover for four–five girls on the Saturday night." Dr. Talwar was a nice-looking woman whose face was marked by deep shadows beneath her eyes. She wore a silver kameez over black trousers, and her watch was turned to her inner wrist. "The CBI [Central Bureau of Investigation] say to me, 'What is a sleepover? Were there adults involved?' I had to explain what a sleepover was—chatting, music, raiding the fridge while we stay in the next room. I explained that the kids would say, 'Go from here,' in the way kids do, and again the police were saying to me, 'Why would you have to go, why would your daughter not want you there?' They wanted to know why Aarushi had deleted some of the pictures on her new camera. 'Who has deleted these images? Why has she done this?' I had to explain, that is just how kids are, they take some pictures of themselves, they delete the ones they don't like."

"They found an email she had sent me a year before," said her father, "apologizing and saying she had just wanted to try out something with her friends. So the police take it and flash it on TV. All the channels are asking, 'What was Aarushi going to try out? Why did she say it wouldn't happen again? Why does a daughter send an email to a father?' Well, she didn't send emails to me, it just happened one evening when she was twelve years old, and Aarushi wanted to go to the cinema in the mall to watch *Namaste London* with a group of friends—just the girls together. We didn't want her going without an adult, but in the end we gave our consent and dropped her off and collected her from the cinema. It was peer pressure that made us agree, because her friends were allowed to go. Aarushi knew we weren't happy about it and that's why she sent me the email. She had a very sensitive nature. Not even once did I have to raise my voice to her. If there had been an occasion, I would have raised it.

"It was no issue if we had a boy or a girl," he continued, referring to the social pressure in the north of India to have male children. "From a young age Aarushi wanted to be a 'baby doctor'—she said that before she knew the word paediatrician. She loved babies. Her friends told her she was being a geek, studying too hard. I put money aside as an investment, put it into a flat and told her this is not for your marriage, it's for your studies. She would tell family: 'Don't worry, I'll get into AIIMS [a prestigious medical college], but Dad has kept this for my education.'"

"She was good from the first standard," said Nupur. "At her school, if you get above 85 percent for three years consecutively, you get a blue blazer. Only one or two children get it each year. There was no question of Aarushi not getting a blue blazer. She was fond of dancing. She went every Sunday with other girls to a class at Danceworx studio in Noida and danced for hours, learning Ashley Lobo jazz dancing. She and her friends made a dance group and called themselves the Awesome Foursome." Nupur showed me a photograph of the girls on which Aarushi had written: "AWE-SUM 4SUM!"

We sat in silence together. "Aarushi was an avid reader too, always reading, her iPod headphones stuffed in her ears, and texting as well, sending messages on Orkut at the same time." Rajesh stood up and went to Aarushi's bedroom and brought back some of his daughter's books to show me: Anne Frank's *The Diary of a Young Girl*, Chetan Bhagat's *Five Point Someone*, Khaled Hosseini's *A Thousand Splendid Suns*, Jean Sasson's *Love in a Torn Land*, J. K. Rowling's *Harry Potter and the Half-Blood Prince*, Jhumpa Lahiri's *Unaccustomed Earth*—sophisticated books for a girl of her age. "She preferred Anne Frank," he said. "She didn't like fantasy so much."

"I can't listen to songs or watch movies any more," said her mother. "I never watched a movie without Aarushi. Our life has been taken away from us."

"When she was small," said her father, "she used to clutch a sari which belonged to my mother. She had picked it from a collection of my mother's saris which Nupur had, and went to sleep with it. In fact she went with it everywhere and used to call it her 'papamummy.' By the time she outgrew it, it was completely in tatters."

Rajesh and Nupur Talwar had been raised in an older India. She was from an air force family and had lived in military housing wherever her father was posted. Rajesh's father was a cardiothoracic surgeon. "When we both finished the Bachelor of Dental Surgery course in Maulana Azad Medical College," he said, "we married and went to Lucknow for our postgraduate. We both came from liberal families, and they had no hesitation about our marriage. At our wedding we had one Punjabi pandit and one Maharashtrian pandit, and because we [Punjabis] like to get married early in the morning and they like to marry in the evening, we did it in the middle of the day. We waited a bit for children because we were studying, and had

Aarushi on 24 May 1994. We only had one child, because we wanted to be able to give her the best possible."

"Initially Rajesh was a bit of a weekend father," said Nupur. "By the time he got back from work, Aarushi was asleep. We thought it would be better for her if she grew up near her grandparents, where we would have a support system, which is why we moved to Noida. My mother brought her up. She always did her cooking and cared for her with her own hand. Even at weekends, Aarushi would ask to see her grandparents—'Ajja [a diminutive of aaji, the Marathi word for mother's mother] isn't feeling well, let's go to see her.' When Aarushi's life ended, she was in a stage of transition. It was all about friends, friends, who had fallen out, who had broken up with someone else, breakup-patchup."

"On the 15th," said Rajesh, "I had bought her a Sony 10-megapixel camera for her birthday. It was better than the one she was expecting. I showed it to Nupur and she said let's give it to her now. We went to Aarushi's room. She was so happy, clicking some pictures of herself, trying out the camera. That was our last evening together."

"I heard the doorbell ring in the morning," said Nupur. "It rang a second time. I knew it was the maid, and wondered why the servant hadn't opened the door for her. It was a little while after six o'clock. I got up and realized the door of the flat had been locked from the outside. So I phoned the servant, and the call was cut. I phoned again, and it was cut. By this time Rajesh had got up and noticed a three-quarters empty bottle of whisky lying on the dining-table. We got worried as we always kept alcohol in the cupboard. He said, 'Go and see Aarushi.' I went into her room just ahead of Rajesh. The first thing I saw was the blood on the wall behind her. She was lying on the bed covered with a blanket. I put my hand on her head. Rajesh began to scream.

"Later in the day, I had to write the FIR [police report] in Hindi," said Rajesh, "and I hadn't written the language for twenty years. I just couldn't write it. The principal of Aarushi's school had come to see us. She used to be my own class teacher when I was a boy at another branch of Delhi Public School, and in my mind I was saying, 'Ma'am, get her back. Ma'am, get her back.' I didn't say it out loud."

"At about 1 p.m. they brought back Aarushi from the autopsy," said Nupur. "We put her in the drawing-room. It was a hot day. At about 4 p.m. we took her for the cremation. When we got back home from that, the police were there and the media had broken our doorbell. They kept on trying to push the door open. I couldn't sleep or eat."

"I thought it was Hemraj and he was on the run," remembered Rajesh. "I said, I hope they get this guy and kill him. The next day we collected her ashes from the cremation ground early and drove to Hardwar to immerse the ashes in the Ganges. While we were driving, Hemraj was found on the terrace. We were asked to come home and identify him. We parked the car a few blocks away, since according to Hindu custom you should not take ashes into the home. Nupur waited in the car with Aarushi's ashes while I went back in. They asked me to identify the servant's body. It had been decomposing for nearly two days in the heat and the face was swollen. I couldn't be sure, but I said I think it looks like him. Later, the police said I had refused to ID him positively, and used that against me. We went to Hardwar and did the religious rituals, fed some poor people and had a bath in the Ganges, like you are meant to do."

"Hemraj liked cooking and doing things around the home," said Nupur. "He was not an ambitious Nepali. He would call her 'Aarushi Baby' and she would call him 'Bhaiyya' [literally "brother"—the usual way a girl and a male servant would address each other]. We would give him her old clothes for his grandchildren. He'd been with us for eight months and had been highly recommended by the previous fellow, who had been with us for ten years. I know now that Hemraj let some people into our home, and I ask why, why, why? It was a case of trusting too much. Obviously the company he kept was not good. We realized later he had lied to us—he said he had been doing a job in construction in Malaysia, but he had never been there, and was a rickshaw driver. But we trusted the servant who recommended him, so we didn't check.

"On the next day, which would have been the day of Aarushi's sleepover, we had a puja and a havan, the lighting of a sacred fire. Her friends came to the house and they all sat in her room, touching her things. We served them food in the room. They took out her clothes and her books and were looking at them, all crying, grieving."

The police now asked the Talwars to come with them to identify a suspect. They found a Maruti Zen car waiting outside the gate of their apartment, so they got in their own car and followed it, as instructed, pursued by a flock of media vehicles. The couple drove behind the police Maruti Zen at high speed for about four kilometres before being told to go home again. When Rajesh Talwar was taken to the police lines the next day, one of the pieces of evidence offered against him was video footage of this car chase—proof that he intended to flee and should be denied bail when he was arrested. Another cause for suspicion was that in his pocket he had the business card of one of his patients, Pinaki Misra, a Supreme Court lawyer. If he were innocent, asked an investigator, why would he need to be in touch with a hotshot lawyer?

By this time, Nupur and Rajesh had been separated into different rooms. She received a telephone call from a family member to say that television channels were reporting that her husband had been arrested. At first she could not believe it was true, and reassured the caller that he was only having a conversation in the next room. Then, after some hours had gone by, the constable who was guarding her said, "Arrest ho gaye"—"He's been arrested." Rajesh, meanwhile, was manhandled into a car and driven to Ghaziabad, an industrial city in Uttar Pradesh, to be remanded in judicial custody.

"We were driving along," he recalled, "and the driver started abusing me. 'You're the bastard who did this.' I was really scared. I said, 'You can't say things like that.' They gagged my mouth. I was abused by these policemen the entire way, and after reaching the shabby courtroom, two of them held my hands and dragged me to a room by the side of the court. I was presented before the magistrate. There were a huge number of people present, and I pleaded with this man to at least let me make a phone call or call a lawyer. I said, 'I'm entitled to it. It's my fundamental right as a citizen of this country.' The magistrate just looked at me in disgust. 'Ja yahan se'— 'Get out of here.' They'd chosen Friday to arrest me, because we wouldn't be able to apply for bail until Monday. The policemen produced a paper and asked me to sign it, and I had the presence of mind to tell them I will not sign anything. They threatened me with dire consequences. I was dragged back to the car by the police while I kept screaming that I was being framed. By this time the TV channels were all over the place. My mind had gone completely numb. A policeman was saying, 'Hum tere ko maar denge'— 'We will kill you.' I just said they could kill me wherever they wanted.

"We reached Dasna jail. It's a different world in that place. Time just stopped. I was told to sit in a line on the floor. They frisked me with aggression. There are thieves, drug addicts, all spitting on the floor. I was crying. I was sent to barrack number 7, bed number 60. But there's no bed, only a stone floor. It's a big, noisy room, filled with half-naked people, with hardly enough room to move. You get watery dal and chapatti. I was given a sheet and it was stinking, but you have to put it over your face to keep the mosquitoes and flies off you at night. I kept thinking that someone would come and say, 'Sorry, we made a mistake.' When I went to the toilet, I slipped a bit and realized there was no toilet, just a layer of shit on the floor. I puked there."

Rajesh stopped speaking. Nupur was looking at him. It was the first time he had ever told his wife about this aspect of his incarceration. All through the Saturday and the Sunday, Nupur had waited outside Dasna jail to see her husband, together with Rajesh's brother Dinesh, an ophthalmologist at AIIMS.

"I managed to see him on Sunday," said Nupur. "It was the day after Aarushi's birthday. He was banging his head on the bars, shouting, 'Get me out of here.' He was crying all the time, saying, 'Where's my Aaru, where's my Aaru?' It was a forty-minute meeting. During the day, we got a call on someone's cell phone. A man said to meet him in the dhaba by the prison. He explained he would be able to provide food and good treatment for Rajesh in jail. I gave him Rs25,000. We never saw him again. Later we heard about another person who could provide this service for him, a convict who was trusted by the jail administration. These men are called number-dars, and they wear a yellow kurta pyjama. So we slipped him money."

"Without him, I couldn't have survived in there," said Rajesh. "He showed me kindness, got me some mosquito repellent and some fruit. Before Aarushi died, I had been reading a book about Iraq which described what happened in their prisons. I remember thinking at the time, at least that couldn't happen in our country, in India."

Dr. Talwar was to be dragged through a netherworld of courts, jails, lies, insinuation and state harassment. The process would last not for days, but for years, and the second Dr. Talwar—Nupur, Aarushi's mother—would be drawn into the cavalcade too, harassed alongside her husband as both he and their murdered daughter were accused of various retrospective offences. At a bizarre press conference, an inspector general of police from Meerut stood in front of the cameras and said Rajesh Talwar was "prime accused." He was supposedly in a relationship with a fellow dentist and family friend, and had committed an honour killing. "The doctor's extra-marital affair was known to both the girl and Hemraj. The two used to discuss this and had come close. Dr. Rajesh could not tolerate this even though his own character was not good," the officer announced in Hindi. It sounded like a story from one of the badly printed "shocker" magazines on sale at street corners, like *Crime & Detective* with its lurid headlines: "Acid Treatment for Malady of Love" or "Queen of Nefarious Designs." "Dr. Rajesh came home," the inspector general continued, "and found his daughter and Hemraj in an objectionable position—but not in a compromising position. Dr. Rajesh took Hemraj to the terrace and killed him. He then drank whisky and killed Aarushi . . . He killed her in a fit of rage even though he is as characterless as his daughter."[14]

The police had no basis for the character assassination of a dead thirteen-year-old girl and her grieving father. They had no witnesses, no murder weapon, no forensic evidence and no reason for deducing that Aarushi had been in an "objectionable position" with a recently hired servant who was himself a grandfather. Nor did they have a plausible motive for this savage double murder. For much of the media, in particular the English-language tabloids and Hindi news channels, this was less important than the sensation. Repeatedly, they showed footage of a dishevelled Rajesh Talwar shouting: "They're framing me!" as he was dragged roughly through the gate of a jail. When Nupur, glazed and dazed, gave a television interview the following day, people complained she was not in tears. As a viewer wrote on a message board: "The reporter looks much sad then Aarushis mother." Then there was the email message Aarushi had sent to her father, which the police released: "I just wanted to try it out coz I heard from mah frndz . . . so wotz da harm . . . I wnt do it again n I kinda noe hw u r feelin."[15] What did it mean? And could her parents, who were in the next room with a whirring air-conditioner on, have slept through the killing?

More "proof" arrived when the police claimed the Talwars were part of a "wife-swapping racket" run by a "kingpin industrialist" in Noida. A newspaper, Mid-Day, quoted an unnamed police officer saying that "whenever such meetings happened the Talwars kept Aarushi locked inside her room. That happened only when the members of the club met at Talwar's residence. But Hemraj knew everything and shared the details with Aarushi."[16] The newspapers reported these stories, although no evidence was given to support the claims. Old-fashioned extortion had landed at the edge of the capital, in a modern world of shiny malls, where middle-class children lived a very different life to the children of the police. The inhabitants of Noida might feel as if they were in Delhi and could lead a progressive, metropolitan life, but they faced Uttar Pradesh street justice, in which nobody was protected from wrong. Taking shreds of evidence and gossip, and making assumptions about a social world they were not able to comprehend, the police had concocted a story in the hope they could close the case. They nearly succeeded. Much of the media ran with the idea that Rajesh Talwar must be guilty, and blogs and websites were filled with foul insinuations. To quote just one: "This is a simple case of sexual perversion, maybe incest, and pedophilia that got integrated with a culture of swinging between families and swapping. Matter of family honour thus comes first and foremost."

The police interrogations continued, as did the Kafkaesque form of investigation.

"You never knew where you were with the police," said Dr. Talwar. "Some were fine. A policeman read the Hanuman Chalisa [a devotional hymn] and started to cry, saying, 'Doctor, a very bad thing has been done to you.' Another time, they took me back to Hardwar in a Jeep and I was troubled the whole way by two young policemen. The vicious guy who had threatened to kill me was singing as if he was going on vacation. They forced me to sign a confession. I wrote on the piece of paper in English—which they couldn't read—that it was not true. I was in the prison for fifty days and nights. The numberdar in the yellow pyjama helped me. He would arrange for my clothes to be washed, and would send a boy called Goli [bullet] to make nimbu pani [lemonade] for me. Goli had been in and out of prison all his life, for small thefts, and so on. Apparently he would be picked up by the police whenever they needed a suspect for some crime. I found it hard to talk to most of the prisoners because they were from a very different social group to me. Some would come and say, 'I hear you're a tooth doctor.' So I started seeing patients in the prison hospital. I arranged for proper medicines, antibiotics, painkillers to be brought in. I found a broken dental chair and fixed the compressor on it. I succeeded in getting a mirror, a probe, tweezers, a handpiece. I had hoped to get zinc oxide eugenol, to do temporary fillings for the prisoners. The prison authorities were very grateful. I would like to go back and do more work there now, but it would be impossible, with the media."

During these days, Nupur stayed at her parents' house. She did not return to the apartment. She endured what her husband endured, not knowing if he would be released. "Grieving for Aarushi took a back seat, because I was running from pillar to post the whole time. I didn't turn on the AC the whole time Rajesh was in prison, because I couldn't bear to think of him being in that heat, lying on the floor. All the time was spent going to lawyers, going to courts, trying to set him free. I felt I was losing my sanity and I wanted to kill myself, to go away from this world, but I knew I had to keep strong for him. Over the weeks, people melted away. On the day he was arrested, Fortis Hospital, where he was working, threw him out. A lot of our dentist friends didn't want to know once Rajesh was in jail. People don't like to come close to a tragedy. I would sit alone. I only cried for Aarushi when her father came home."

Although they felt abandoned, Rajesh and Nupur Talwar were also aided by a public outcry by their own and Aarushi's friends. Several hundred children from Delhi Public School in Noida took out a march with banners saying: "Justice for Aarushi," lit candles in her memory and condemned the police for maligning their fellow student. National child protection charities and even a cabinet minister spoke out against the defamation of the dead girl and her father. Nobody spoke for Hemraj, the dead servant; he became just another crime statistic. Patients at Rajesh's practice gave their support, including a high-ranking Delhi policeman, B. K. Gupta, and the lawyer Pinaki Misra, whose card had been found in his pocket.[17] Misra pressed for the case to be transferred away from the Uttar Pradesh police to the federal Central Bureau of Investigation. Once the chief minister—Mayawati—agreed to this demand, the prospects for Dr. Talwar's release grew and the chances of evidence being fabricated were reduced. It would not have been hard for the police to give the suspect an object and "discover" it a few days later as a murder weapon, covered in his fingerprints.

Rajesh Talwar was eventually released on bail, but the investigation was far from over. By now the police had arrested three more men, including a compounder or dental assistant named Krishna who worked at his clinic, and whose family came from Nepal. Over the succeeding months and years, the harrowing of Dr. Talwar continued as he was subjected to polygraph tests and narcoanalysis (the drugging and interrogation of a suspect, which is illegal in many countries). The investigators continued to come up with outlandish stories, destroying his name, which were happily repeated by the media with scarcely a murmur of dissent. One improbable report suggested he had somehow ordered medical staff to destroy evidence following Aarushi's autopsy, another that Nupur was now the principal suspect and would shortly be arrested. Next it was claimed that Rajesh's brother was also involved, as was the passing policeman who had found Hemraj's body on the terrace.

"I was released on 11 July 2008," said Rajesh Talwar. "Before my court appearance, I was put in a prison van with the other three accused." He was referring to Krishna and the young men who were detained with him, who worked locally as domestic servants. At this point, Rajesh had no way of knowing whether they were guilty or were being framed too. But their behaviour made him believe the worst. "Krishna didn't say anything at all to me. He had no reaction. This man had worked as my own dental assistant. He looked as if he was relaxed. One of the others pointed at him and made a sign with his hands, as if to say, 'It wasn't me who did it—it was Krishna.'

I panicked. I was in the police van, knowing this man might have done this thing to my child. They handcuffed me with Krishna. I was asking them to not do it, but they said they had only one handcuff. They removed the handcuffs when we reached the court. The heat was terrible. When I was attached to Krishna, I was literally begging, I was saying, 'This man has killed my child.' The policeman said, 'I don't have another handcuff.' That was the worst moment I have ever had. I felt I was dying. I was taken back to Dasna jail from the court and released the next day. When I came out of the jail, the media surrounded me completely. My brother and my wife had to pull me into the car. We went straight to the Shirdi Sai Baba temple and prayed.

"You have rights as a citizen of India," he said, speaking calmly but passionately, "but in certain places like UP and Bihar, unless you are a politician or a very rich person, you have no protection at all. We have suffered at the hands of the institutions that are there to protect you. We thought India was a good place to live, but there is so much of incompetence everywhere that people don't know what they are doing."

Rajesh was shown the results of the narcoanalysis tests done on the three men. They contained incriminating information, some of which was corroborated independently. To date, no one has been charged with the murder of Aarushi Talwar.

"Each day," said Nupur, "you wake up and you think, oh no, I've got another day to go through. We never did anything wrong. No police and media have admitted they were mistaken. If I go somewhere, everyone will stare at me. You can see people recognizing us and spreading the word. I go only to two or three shops, where they know us. Our work is the only thing that has kept us going. The people we saw as a social group when Aarushi was alive—how do you talk to them? When the three girls from the Awesome Foursome came round, I couldn't communicate. I feel jealous that something so special has been taken away from us. Our support now is mainly from people who have also lost children. I'm an orthodontist, so when a child gets up from the chair, I see her hairstyle, her shoes, and think—would Aarushi be this tall, this thin now? Her friends are still my patients. She used to say to me: 'Mummy, my friends are coming for braces. Don't charge any money.' So I don't charge them. We have had two lives in one lifetime."

"We miss her so much," said Rajesh, "that we just don't know what to do."[18]

II

SOLACE OF RELIGION

A N INDIAN WOMAN walks into a London fishmonger, which is owned by a Pakistani man. She has a look at the fresh fish laid out on inclined slabs amid pellets of ice, asks him about the red snapper, examines the salmon steaks and glances at the dark smoked fish he sells mainly to his African customers. It is a mixed-up part of south London, with no ethnic community predominating, but the buyer and the seller both know straight away, by instinct, that they come from a connecting culture. Although they start out speaking in English, their conversation soon becomes subcontinental, switching between languages. While the dialogue is mutually comprehensible, since the languages are nearly the same, she is using Hindi and he is using Urdu—which means he knows she is from India, and she knows he is probably from Pakistan. What about the shrimp, she says, is it fresh? It is, he answers, I'll get you some that came in this morning. "Hum apne logon ko ghatiya cheezein nahin detey"—"We don't sell bad stuff to our own people."

This is part of the relationship between the two countries, the most ideologically charged and unstable element of modern India's politics. It has all the hatred and love of a feud between siblings, but when plucked out of context and transplanted to a foreign city, it is the unity that matters. For they are the same people, and he would not sell bad stuff to his own people, only to the foreigners he lives among in London.

Immediately after partition it was apparent that Indians and Pakistanis were the same people, since they came from the same original country, but as the decades passed, the expression of such a feeling became fraught with complications. No political leader in either country would dare to say what the fishmonger said. India's policymakers feel particularly aggrieved when third parties hyphenate their country to Pakistan, believing it is unjust to link a large and vibrant democracy to an imploding state. They are happier with a more recent American dispensation, by which their neighbour is linked to Afghanistan, thereby creating a new, abbreviated problem couple: "Af-Pak."

The fatal break between India and Pakistan came not in 1947, but in the 1970s. Even after the violence and dispossession of partition, there was a strong enough social overlap between the political and military leadership of the two countries for their connection to be self-evident. When East Pakistan broke away from the remote dominance of West Pakistan in 1971 and became Bangladesh, it was a death blow to Jinnah's vision of Pakistan and a mortifying defeat for a nation that prided itself on its martial aptitude: India, the land of Gandhi and vegetarians, had helped rebellious Bengalis to victory on the battlefield. The relationship between India and Pakistan became increasingly fraught and difficult. As the leader of a truncated Pakistan, Zulfikar Ali Bhutto introduced socialism and a new constitution, but in 1977 he found himself in prison following a coup by the chief of the army staff, General Zia-ul-Haq.

General Zia had owed his initial rise to his unctuous devotion to Bhutto. Even after being incarcerated, the compelling Bhutto believed this once loyal and seemingly dim soldier would release him—as had been promised—and allow him to contest fresh elections. He turned down an opportunity to go into exile. On 3 April 1979, when a jail superintendent read out a court order saying he was to be hanged, Bhutto assumed it was another ploy. "I should have been informed by the competent authority 24 hours prior to the execution, but it has not been done," responded the deposed prime minister, and ordered his lawyers to be sent to him. His wife and his daughter Benazir had seen him that morning, and they had not known he was to be executed. It was only when Bhutto asked his security officer, Colonel Rafi-ud-Din, what drama was being staged that the truth dawned. The colonel later described what happened:

I answered, "Sir, have I ever tried to joke with you? . . . You will be executed today."

For the first time I saw a bewildered look on Mr. Bhutto's face . . . It seemed like Bhutto Sahib's eyes had exploded because of fear. His face turned yellow and dry . . . Then he said, "At what time? Today?"

I showed him seven fingers of my hand just like a [parachute] jump master tells the time before the jump.

He said, "After seven days?"

I went near him and told him, "Sir, hours."

Bhutto shaved, brushed his teeth, combed his hair and ordered a cup of coffee. Then he rearranged his mirror, comb, hair brush and prayer mat. Next he wrote his will for several hours, only to burn it. The ashes floated around his cell, and he called a servant to clean them. He lay down on his bed. One minute after midnight, prison officials entered the cell. He opened one eye, looked at them, and closed it again. The prison doctor tried to rouse him, but he did not respond. By now the cell was filling with prison officials. More minutes passed. A magistrate asked Bhutto if he would like to dictate a will, and just as he started four warders entered his cell and lifted him by his hands and feet. "Leave me," he said, but they did not leave him, and while he was being carried outside his shirt became entangled in one of the warder's boots and was ripped from his back. Petromax lanterns had been lit along the route to the gallows. His hands were cuffed roughly behind his back, and after he had dropped through the floor his body was washed. A photographer from Pakistan's intelligence agencies photographed his genitals to confirm he had been circumcised; there had been rumours that Mr. Bhutto was not a true Muslim.[1]

Such a scene would have been hard to imagine in India at this time. Mrs. Gandhi might declare an Emergency and imprison political leaders, but it would be difficult to picture her having her opponents executed, and it is even harder to imagine an Indian military dictator. Had events gone a little differently, General Zia might have been an aberration in Pakistani history. Instead, a rare sequence of decisions made him a deeply significant figure; during his eleven years in power he sought to alter the national character by putting a puritanical interpretation of Islam at its centre.

Educated in Simla and at St. Stephen's College in Delhi, Zia might have. been like any other whisky-sipping Pakistani general of his era, Anglophile but patriotic, convinced he could make a better fist of running the country than the politicos—but he was something else. His father had a low-level clerical job in the Indian government before the family was left homeless at partition, and both his parents were deeply religious. In his first address to the nation, Zia praised Islamist agitators who had opposed Bhutto, saying, "It proves that Pakistan, which was created in the name of Islam, will continue to survive only if it sticks to Islam. That is why I consider the introduction of Islamic system [sic] as an essential prerequisite for the country." He also said in private that Muslims believe in "one God, one Prophet and one Book, and their mentality is that they should be ruled by one man."[2] Islam as practised by Indians over centuries had rarely been a rigid system, but in a restructured Pakistan it began to change, fitting with Zia's own wish to exert military discipline over its people, and his need to gain domestic legitimacy and support from the more reactionary religious leaders. The older, more inclusive and evolved forms of local Islam, with their singing and dancing, were replaced.

During the 1970s Pakistan's gaze turned away from the east, away from India and the humiliation of an independent Bangladesh, and towards the west—not the West, but the Arabian peninsula, newly rich and influential from the fruits of oil, and an important source of employment for close to a million Pakistanis. Heads were turning to Iran too, which was in the throes of an unprecedented theocratic revolution after the return of Ayatollah Khomeini months before Bhutto's execution. They turned as well to Afghanistan, which had been invaded by the Soviets in the same year. For Sunnis and Shias, in their distinct ways, Islam became a rallying point, especially since the state's only substantial minority—the Hindus of East Pakistan—had gone. Jinnah's version of secularism disappeared. It was understandable that a truncated Pakistan should look towards its non-Indian neighbours in its search for a fresh identity. Neither capitalism nor socialism appeared to have provided the answers since 1947. Many of Pakistan's old feudal structures remained in place, and a handful of industrialists retained disproportionate economic influence. As global political power adjusted, the country developed a critical strategic importance because of its geographical position. Now a revived Muslim certitude, battened down by military rule, was on offer.[3]

Jinnah and the other founders of Pakistan had taken it for granted that faith was to be kept distinct from government. This did not mean it was irrelevant. In 1949, a set of resolutions was passed by Pakistan's Constituent Assembly which proposed a form of democracy that was influenced by Islam. The early leaders used Islamic or Mughal heritage as a means to bind

Pakistanis together, and made Urdu the compulsory national language, to be taught in public schools. (For the East Pakistanis, nearly all of whom spoke Bengali as their first language, this would create a fatal rupture.) Jinnah, who was born in 1876, saw no inconsistency in being an inspirational leader to Muslims while admiring constitutional democracy, speaking English, being a skilful lawyer, drinking alcohol occasionally, wearing slick European clothes from Hanover Square in London and having a Parsi wife who liked to wear low-cut dresses to Bombay dinner parties. As he told one of his associates: "Gandhi may wish to be clad like a peasant, but I wish to be dressed like a gentleman."[4]

Although some clerics had wanted Islam to have a central position in the new homeland, the thrust of Muslim intellectual life in India since the nineteenth century had been towards modernity (the Khilafat movement in the early 1920s was the exception). The stimulus came in part from Sir Syed Ahmed Khan, a Mughal nobleman of substantial influence, who in 1875 had founded a Muslim college in Aligarh, modelled on Cambridge University. He had encouraged a modern, scientific, rationalist approach towards religious customs, realizing that traditional modes of learning were not equipping India's Muslims for a changing world. At around the time his college was founded, an official in Malabar had noted that many Muslim parents preferred their own schools to "the vernacular schools of the Hindus," where their children might be diverted from their traditions. "The teachers, being as illiterate as their pupils, except in knowledge of Koran recitations, usually employ Hindu youths to teach the pupils."[5] It was this disjuncture between the communities that Sir Syed, and those who followed him, were seeking to change.

General Zia-ul-Haq and his supporters thrust Jinnah's approach aside. On the founder of the nation's birth anniversary in 1981, newspaper articles were not even permitted to quote the optimistic words he had spoken about the creation of Pakistan—that it was his ideal that "Hindus would cease to be Hindus and Muslims would cease to be Muslims, not in the religious sense, because that is the personal faith of each individual, but in the political sense as citizens of the state."[6]

Zia was not the first Pakistani leader to play politics with religion. Bhutto had himself courted popularity by introducing prohibition and declaring the Ahmadis, a reformist sect which followed a nineteenth-century Punjabi religious leader, to be non-Muslims. Using religious impulses as a vehicle for political ambitions had become a common tactical tendency in Pakistan, as it was among hardline Hindus in India. Under General Zia, the process became much more serious, and the nature of Pakistan's public debate increasingly arcane. Should women be permitted to play sports and, if so, should they wear trousers? Should soldiers be required to grow a beard? Religious knowledge became essential to an army officer's promotion. Friday replaced Sunday as the weekly holiday. Members of the Jamaat-e-Islami, a movement which had long been unsuccessful at the ballot box, were given crucial positions in the judiciary and civil service. Textbooks were filleted of "un-Islamic" information, and India was portrayed in a more malign light. Zia made blasphemy a criminal offence, introduced an Islamic banking system, initiated prayer times in government offices and altered the law to allow punishments laid down in the Quran and other texts—including public flogging for moral misdemeanours and the charge of fornication against women who had been raped. Most of these rules were rarely enforced, but they became a prime source of corruption and persecution. If you had a property or business dispute with a Christian, an Ahmadi or a Shia, you could accuse them of blasphemy in the knowledge the case would remain tangled in the legal system for decades, before probably being thrown out by a higher court.

The invasion of Afghanistan at Christmas 1979, more than any other move during the later stages of the Cold War, seemed to provide unanswerable proof that the Soviet Union was intent on territorial expansion. What if the Russians were to move down towards the Persian Gulf and the Indian Ocean? Fighting the menace of Soviet communism became a central purpose for the United States and its allies—and its greatest ally was General Zia, now recast as a warrior for freedom. Just as the British in colonial India had often tilted towards monotheists, finding them easier to deal with than Hindus, so the Americans found that Pakistan's bluff, pugilistic generals spoke their language. Zia handled his new ally with great cunning and skill, and the U.S. soon stopped mentioning Pakistan's lack of democracy or its development of a nuclear arsenal.

America would help to fund, organize and arm the glamorous, cloaked, bearded and behatted "Mujahideen" resistance fighters. President Jimmy Carter offered Zia $150m; he stalled, and ended up with Ronald Reagan giving him a multi-billion-dollar aid package and assorted fighter aircraft. Zia considered Bill Casey, the director of the CIA, a "soul mate" and was delighted when the U.S. allowed Pakistani intelligence, the ISI, to control all operations and to train the guerrillas who were fighting against the Soviet army in Afghanistan.[7] From the American point of view, it seemed a reasonable trade; as Carter's national security adviser Zbigniew Brzezinski put it: "militarist Pakistan" and "fundamentalist Saudi Arabia" had little in common, and besides, "What is more important in the history of the world? The Taliban or the collapse of the Soviet empire? Some hotheaded Islamists or the liberation of Central Europe and the end of the cold war?"[8] Brzezinski was speaking in 1998.

Three years after this, Osama bin Laden and the al-Qaeda organization, harboured in Afghanistan, launched the attacks of 9/11. In the utopian "war on terror" that followed, Pakistan's leader, General Musharraf, would play much the same game as his predecessor General Zia, presenting himself to the White House as a reliable and plain-spoken ally against extremism. While running for president, George W. Bush had faced an impromptu foreign policy quiz. Asked who Pakistan's leader was, he replied in general terms, "General. I can name the general. General."[9] Within months of taking office, al-Qaeda had struck and Bush got to know Pervez Musharraf's name very well indeed, and established a good, jokey rapport with him. Musharraf in turn played a blinding hand in Pakistan, facing down popular discontent, abandoning the Taliban regime in Afghanistan (which the ISI had helped to set up), sacking opponents in the armed forces and throwing in his lot with the U.S., even while playing along with the more respectable extremist outfits. He promised Bush the ISI would help America to unravel the region's complexities and roll up its terror networks, a promise that would not be kept.

Since 2001 the United States has channelled almost $2bn a year to Pakistan, and not all of it has ended up in the right place. Even while the U.S. was paying the Pakistani army and government to eliminate the threat of terror, the problem grew.[10] As one foreign diplomat put it, Pakistan was the only nation that negotiated with a gun held to its own head.[11] The mishandling of this process, and the accompanying war in Iraq, left many Pakistanis with the perception that the Americans were funding corrupt and opportunist military and political leaders, and were attacking their religious allies. The deposed prime minister, Nawaz Sharif, told me with a shrug of exasperation in 2007, "Musharraf has been hoodwinking the West."[12] When the Pakistani public finally got the chance to vote a year later, they rejected General Musharraf decisively. The U.S. became increasingly unpopular among Pakistanis at all levels of society, even as its donated dollars propped up the failing Pakistani state.

It is always hard to get a fix on how one country perceives another. Judging by newspaper coverage and the pronouncements of leading Indian politicians in the 1960s, the U.S. was not popular in India while American aid

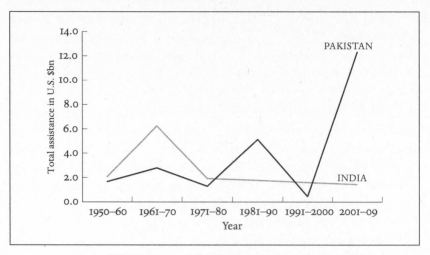

U.S. economic and military assistance, $bn

was at its height. U.S. aid to India peaked in the 1960s, dipped in the 1970s and flatlined ever after. Correspondingly, U.S. aid to Pakistan started out low, rose in the 1980s during the anti-Soviet war in Afghanistan and accelerated sharply upward after 2001.

A rare measure of the strength of public feeling was a Pew opinion poll conducted intermittently in a variety of countries which asked the question: "Do you have a favourable view of the U.S.?" In 2005, 71 percent of Indians and 23 percent of Pakistanis said yes. In 2009, after another $3.7bn had been transferred from American taxpayers to assorted middlemen, spies, generals, NGOs, politicians and bureaucrats in Pakistan, the question was asked again (India had received $0.7bn during the same period). This time, the numbers had shifted even further apart: 76 percent of Indians and 16 percent of Pakistanis said they had a favourable view of the U.S.[13] Money did not buy love.[14]

General Zia died in a plane crash in 1988, along with the American ambassador, not long before the Soviets quit Afghanistan. The CIA bought back the surface-to-air missiles it had given to the Mujahideen to fight the Soviets, but allowed lighter weapons to find their way to Kashmir and to the port city of Karachi, where a war was under way between local people and the descendants of those who had migrated to Pakistan at partition. More important than the guns were the guerrilla fighters. Although some returned to civilian life, many required a new martial cause and remained under the tutelage of the ever more powerful ISI, which had other wars to fight, especially in Kashmir.

One of General Zia's achievements had been to establish hardline madrasas, Islamic schools, along the Pakistan–Afghanistan border and elsewhere in order to turn out students who believed it was their religious obligation to kill communists and infidels.[15] When the war was over, the military did not wish to tame them: they were needed to fight in Kashmir. While the world turned aside in the 1990s to concentrate on the perceived peace dividend at the end of the Cold War, the problem festered. As Zulfikar's daughter Benazir Bhutto said when she was elected as prime minister: "Discrimination, intolerance and hatred were the hallmark of the so-called Islamic revolution led by General Zia, supported by the clerics and corrupt unknown charlatans who were made into politicians."[16]

Many older Pakistanis found these developments profoundly worrying. As General Zia's ambassador to Washington, General Ejaz Azim, admitted in 1996: "People like me have a connection with old schoolfriends in India, but the younger generation simply believe all the propaganda. They have no links at all with India, and their attitude to India—say over Kashmir—is very negative and very dangerous."[17]

For India, the consequences of Pakistan's engagement on the issue of Kashmir were to be profoundly harmful, for they linked fatally with a breakdown of trust and good governance in the Kashmir valley itself. After India and Pakistan went to war for the first time in 1947–48, it would have been logical to partition the giant kingdom of Kashmir into its constituent parts, with the Muslim areas going to Pakistan and Buddhist Ladakh and Hindu Jammu going to India. Instead, both sides retained what territory they had at the end of the fighting, and the State of Jammu and Kashmir was given a temporary special position in the Indian Constitution. This laid down serious problems for the future, making Kashmir appear uniquely disconnected from the rest of India. As the decades went by, New Delhi started to erode or ignore the special status. Before he died in 1964, Jawaharlal Nehru narrowly missed reaching a final settlement of the issue with Pakistan's government and the Kashmiri leader, Sheikh Abdullah.

In 1972, Indira Gandhi made an agreement with Zulfikar Ali Bhutto which yielded few benefits, and as the years went by her main concern was that Kashmir's state government did not oppose her politically. After the death of Sheikh Abdullah, his fun-loving son Farooq took over as chief minister, and in state elections in 1983 his party triumphed over Congress. In response, Mrs. Gandhi sent a governor to Kashmir who had a reputation

as an enemy of Muslims, and arranged payments of Rs200,000 each to legislators who defected from Farooq Abdullah's party.[18] His administration
was soon dismissed. By the time of Indira Gandhi's death, Kashmiris were
more alienated from the central government in New Delhi than they had
been since independence.

I was in Srinagar at this time, on my first visit to India, and saw the angry
protests in the city's tight streets, men walking fast holding hand-painted
placards and shouting slogans. Pakistan—wanting to challenge India and
to support Kashmiri Muslims—became directly involved. Young Kashmiri
men in search of azadi, or freedom, crossed the border to Pakistan, where
the army and the ISI trained and armed them. The Indian state, abandoning the founding principle of a covenant between the government and the
people, responded brutally. The consequence of Mrs. Gandhi's political
machinations in Kashmir, which at the time would have seemed like sly
manoeuvring, was the creation of an entrenched conflict, fanned by Pakistan and mishandled by India, with Kashmiris as the bait, which has killed
tens of thousands of people—men and women, soldiers and militants, the
guilty and the innocent. Kashmir's indigenous Hindus, the Pandits, were
driven out. The worst atrocities happened while weak coalition governments were in power in New Delhi in the 1990s, when the Indian police and
army were given impunity to put down the insurrection.

The miseries of Kashmir, the reaction to the events of 9/11 and the new
reach of the international media intersected in 2006 in a bizarre way. A
Kashmiri man, Shakeel Ahmad Bhat, began inadvertently to be promoted
as a global example of Islamic fundamentalism. He had been photographed at a demonstration in Srinagar, his picture syndicated around the
world as a classic image of Muslim anger. He had been given a new name
by an American website: "Islamic Rage Boy." Message boards could not
get enough of Islamic Rage Boy. He was a "curry-drenched ass-pirate," an
"Islamofascist" who "fucked goats," he was "Nancy Pelosi's son" suffering
from "post-jihadi virgin shortage." Shakeel Bhat's shouting face was put on
beer glasses, boxer shorts, bumper stickers—even thongs. On Slate.com,
Christopher Hitchens called him a "religious nut bag" full of "yells and
gibberings" and said he refused to live his own life "at the pleasure of Rage
Boy."[19] Looking at Shakeel Bhat's photograph—his fringed beard, his worried face, his wide mouth—I wondered whether he was mentally disturbed
rather than enraged, and went to Kashmir to look for him.

It was the first time I had been back to Srinagar for years, and the airport was like a military base: sandbags, fortified arches draped with camou-

flage netting, pill-box bunkers, armoured vehicles with gun barrels poking out of their turrets, roads lined with paramilitary police and razor wire. A Kashmiri reporter, Peerzada Arshad Hamid, took me to what he called "Kashmir's Gaza Strip." It was nothing like the Kashmir I remembered, a world of wooden houseboats, chinar trees and long afternoons lying by Dal Lake in the sunshine, eating apples and almonds while the boatmen called, "Chocolate! Coconut ice!"

We entered a simple, traditional three-storey Kashmiri house and were taken up steep wooden steps by the light of a gas lamp to the top of the building. Shakeel Bhat was standing in an empty room, dressed in a salwar kameez and zip-up cardigan, with crooked teeth and a quizzical look on his face. Over two days, sitting cross-legged on the floor and smiling shyly much of the time, Shakeel told me his story, speaking in Kashmiri and occasionally Urdu, with Peerzada interpreting his words. He was twenty-nine and a failed militant. His experience, which was repeated in similar ways across Kashmir during the early 1990s, showed the torment of life in a dismembered society.

He came from a family that followed the Sufi tradition, a mystical, humanist form of Islam common in Kashmir and other parts of the subcontinent. His father, who did embroidery and crewelwork for a living, would often take him to the Shah-i-Hamdan shrine, which had a pir, or Sufi teacher, who could do miracles, and gave him two lessons: do not be greedy, and help Islam to spread by peaceful means. Shakeel had difficulty learning to read and write. His teacher thrashed him with a stick, but it did not improve his studies. Aged ten, he refused to go to school and stayed at home with his family.

When separatists started to fight Indian rule in Kashmir, the security forces arrived. Police who were searching for militants raided Shakeel's home and threw his beloved eighteen-year-old sister Shareefa out of an upstairs window. She broke her spine and died from her injuries four years later. Shakeel, aged all of thirteen, decided to join other young men and go to Pakistan for military training. He was so small that he had to be carried on an older boy's shoulders when he went over the mountains. In Muzaffarabad on the Pakistani side of the border, he was taken to a snow-covered training camp run by the ISI in conjunction with the militant group Al-Umar Mujahideen. Armed with an AK-47, he returned to a safe house in Srinagar, hoping—in what now seems a very impractical way—to drive out the Indian troops.

"I thought Kashmir should have the right to self-determination," he said.

Shakeel was not an effective militant. When I asked him how many people he had killed, he looked embarrassed. "I gave scares, but I never killed anyone. I couldn't. I never hurled a grenade in a public place." His greatest achievement was opening fire on the cavalcade of a visiting Indian government minister, Rajesh Pilot. "Nobody was injured. I just hampered the visit." In 1994, when he was sixteen, he was arrested and taken to a military barracks. Of the twenty boys and young men who had crossed the border to Pakistan with him, eight were still alive. Shakeel was stripped naked, doused with water and electrocuted from a truck battery. A nail was hammered through his jaw (he showed me the scar). His head was immersed in water. He was raped with a bamboo cane. When he was released, he remained under police surveillance. An injury to his right arm as a result of the torture left him unable to lift anything, and he relied on his brothers to support him. Not long after his release, the Special Task Force came to the house to look for him, but he was not there. They beat his 75-year-old father instead, leaving him with a broken leg; he spent the rest of his life bedridden, devoting himself to contemplation and prayer.

While we talked, one of Shakeel's brothers brought in a pot of sweet tea and a plate of cakes. Since there was no furniture in the room, he spread out a plastic tablecloth on the floor and served the tea. It was evening by now, and the Kashmiri night was cold. The brother brought in a rug and spread it over my legs and asked whether I needed a kangri, a clay firepot filled with charcoal to keep close to your body. Shakeel's understanding of the world was limited by his inability to read or write. If something upset him, he went on a demonstration. He had demonstrated over the exploitation of Kashmiri girls by the army, "encounter" killings and Danish cartoons which were said to ridicule Islam. In its way, this was an Indian form of protest, his continuing belief that the state had an obligation to listen to his concerns; had he lived 2,000 miles to the north, east or south-west—in Russia, China or Saudi Arabia—he might well have stayed at home. He viewed the political arrangements in Kashmir (Farooq Abdullah's son Omar was the latest ruler) as inadequate: "Omar is just a pawn."

Shakeel had no time for Osama bin Laden, although he believed the attacks of 9/11 had been organized by the American government. I asked him why the U.S. might have done this. "They wanted to attack Afghanistan and Iraq. President George Bush had to justify that to his own people." Did he know about the bombings in London in 2005? "I heard that a train was bombed. It pains me when innocents are killed. It pains me."

Although he did not use the Internet, he knew about his infamy. He showed me a pair of folders. Some friends had trawled through sites and printed off Photoshopped pictures of him: Islamic Rage Boy being force-fed a pork chop, as Hillary Clinton, as a vampire, as a woman in a bikini, as "Adolf Mohammed Rage Boy." What did he feel about the photos? "I surely get hurt when I see these pictures. This is terrorism for me. The people who do this are showing their own culture, so why do they tell us that we are uncivilized? You can't bring peace by beating the drums or killing people."

Shakeel's only source of news was the street. Surrounded by people who lacked knowledge of the outside world, it was not surprising he believed conspiracy theories about the attacks of 9/11. Al-Qaeda's brand of terror-ism had little in common with his upbringing or experience. The mystical Sufi traditions of the Kashmir valley were a long way from the rigid and outdated Arab customs that had given rise to Osama bin Laden's interpreta-tion of Islam, even if the Western world tended to link them all together. Shakeel became a militant at the age of thirteen because he believed Kash-mir deserved better, and his adored elder sister had been thrown out of a high window. When the Islamic Rage Boy phenomenon began and he had his face reproduced around the world, the local police brought him in for questioning. Shakeel was taken before one of Srinagar's senior police officers, who offered him a government job and said he would find him a girl to marry. (The Indian authorities have a policy of trying to rehabilitate militants who are no longer an obvious threat.)

"They said they would drop all the cases against me if I quit going to demos. But I refused."

I suggested to Shakeel he must have been tempted by the prospect of a job and a wife. He was unlikely ever to get such a good opportunity again. He looked shy and covered his face with his hands. "I want to marry a non-Muslim woman and convert her to Islam," he said. "I have been told that if I can convince a non-Muslim woman to marry me—but not convert her by force—there will be a place for me in heaven."[20]

The Western or American response to "Rage Boy" was a part of the howl of baffled anger after 9/11, in this case assuming Shakeel Bhat was an example of Salafist extremism. The initial Indian response to him and other Kashmiri men—justice based on delegated torture—came out of indiffer-ence; since the quashing of the insurgency in the 1990s, no Delhi govern-ment had made a serious attempt to repair the lives of the Kashmiri people. For most Indians it remained a detachable problem, and their usual lack of jingoism was forgotten or abolished in the case of Kashmir.

On the road to Gulmarg, once a fashionable mountain resort and now nearly deserted, I saw a helmet every few hundred metres. Every road and every village in the Kashmir valley had bunkers and razor wire and mine detectors. The troops were so deeply embedded or institutionalized that, rather than military rule, it felt like an extended army manoeuvre in which local members of the public were incidental. The Kashmiri economy, which had once been dependent on tourism, was now oriented around supplying the estimated half a million troops in the valley. Everywhere we drove, men were standing at the roadside: a helmet, a dark face from the south, a khaki cape, hands holding an SLR. I sensed that Peerzada, the reporter who was travelling with me, saw them only as an army of occupation—during a demonstration some years earlier, forty-three people had been killed in his village.

Some men from the CRPF, the Central Reserve Police Force, were standing by maple trees. They were national paramilitaries, stationed alongside the predominantly Muslim local Kashmiri police. When we stopped a little way from them, they became very tense. We approached, walking past an old Kashmiri house with a slim verandah, wooden shutters and matted reeds for its roof. The CRPF men wore camouflage jackets, canvas shoes and 16 kg metal breastplates—the army had not bought lighter ceramic ones for them. They came from several different states, including Madhya Pradesh, Kerala and Haryana. Each day they had to stand at this spot for twelve hours, with a break for lunch, which was delivered by a military truck. They were not allowed to sit at any time; they had to be moving targets. At night they stayed in a house fringed with razor wire. I asked a CRPF man from Kerala what he thought of Kashmir. "I don't like it," he said forlornly. "It's very cold in Kashmir."

What had made these paramilitary police choose this life? Why were they here? Were they the villains or victims too? Up in Ladakh, I met soldiers who had spent two months sitting in bunkers in the snow waiting to fight to defend the border. At their military museum, they even had the effects of dead Pakistani soldiers on display: their snapshots, ID cards, family letters, Qurans. The rival troops skirmished from time to time on the mountainous border. For the Indian government to impose its will on Kashmir, it needed large numbers of recruits, and if the people on whom the state's will was imposed spoke a different language, looked different and followed another religion, it made the task of suppression easier. Hemant, a Hindu CRPF officer from the plains of India, told me that he would much rather be in a different job, but Srinigar was where he had landed up. He had been posted to Kashmir twice, in the 1990s and in 2004.

"You catch a terrorist," he said. "You hand him over to the police and off he goes. A local VIP makes a request, and the terrorist is freed. The Kashmiri police are with you when you patrol. I wanted to be a deputed driver at the high court in Delhi, but that didn't work out for me. My childhood years were spent in Aligarh, and I ended up working on a taxi stand in Panchsheel Park in Delhi. I joined the force and my first posting was by the side of Dal Lake here, at the headquarters of the CRPF. They think of themselves as Pakistanis in this place." Yet almost everyone I spoke to in Srinagar had no allegiance to Pakistan; they were Kashmiris who had asked for azadi and now wanted an end to the killing. At the start of the insurgency in the 1990s there had been enthusiasm for Pakistan, but it had soon diminished with the realization that the government in Islamabad was a fickle, self-interested ally.

"Sometimes we talk to the Kashmiris," said Hemant, "but they only want Muslims to live here. They hide and throw hand grenades at us. When there's an Indo-Pak cricket match they celebrate right in front of us when India loses, and when India wins it's like there's been a death in the family." I told Hemant I had heard some of his officers were corrupt, selling timber and pursuing other lines of private business. "Our officers? Even the bad ones become good when they are patrolling, because you are all together and your life depends on it. You have to show them respect. There's so much camaraderie because of our fear of the terrorists. My comrades are from all over, from Bihar, Punjab, Himachal, Assam, Kerala. Even the ones from the south learn to speak Hindi in the force. They pick it up. We're all like brothers when we're out patrolling, because that man might save you. The officers can behave very badly. In the 49 battalion in Srinagar there was one senior havildar [sergeant] called Bir Chand. The 2IC, the second-in-command, started abusing him when he was giving a report, saying your mother, your sister and all. Bir Chand went to him afterwards and said, 'I've had thirty years in the force, how can you humiliate me in front of my juniors?'

"The 2IC took up his AK-47 and threatened to shoot him. Bir Chand went back and got his own AK-47 and came in the room and the others all pulled him away. After that, he knew he would go to jail, so he turned the gun and shot himself dead. There was a very bad atmosphere in the camp and the DIG had to come and sort it out. The other officers said to him: 'We won't let you see the dead body unless you swear on your life that the 2IC will be dismissed.' He promised, but it didn't happen: he reported Bir Chand as mentally ill, and the 2IC only got a transfer. If you're junior in the

CRPF, you get scared by the officers. A jawan like me, the officer can just kick you out of the service. In the CRPF, I get a salary of Rs16,000–17,000 a month, and if you get put in a special unit you get some extra, you can even have Rs22,000 ($475) a month. For me, I was able to get my children admitted to a central school and have two months' home leave and fifteen days' casual leave every year. If I retire at the age of sixty, I get 50 percent of my salary as a pension for life. So I will do my service."[21]

In 1858, a year after the suppression of the great rebellion, a Royal Proclamation was read out in towns across the Bengal, Bombay and Madras presidencies "amid great rejoicing," with flag-raising ceremonies, brass bands and firework displays, the whole watched over by hand-picked soldiers. The richer Parsis of Bombay decorated the streets with triumphal arches, and in Calcutta the Auckland Hotel displayed a picture of the imperial monarch Victoria surmounted by a cross "above which, in brilliant jets of gas, were the words 'Long Live our Noble Queen!'"[22] To the surprise of the viceroy, there was no open unrest. The proclamation pardoned those who had taken up arms unless they had been directly engaged in "the Murder of British Subjects," and offered a ceremonial contract between the "Native Princes" and the queen. The tone of the proclamation was heavily self-conscious, projecting an image of benign, liberal and just rule—and the idea that empire was a shared endeavour. This was a common enough practice in the nineteenth century, the British ingratiating themselves with existing rulers in order to take over trade and territory. By making Victoria the queen of India, the East India Company—a front for imperial rule—was replaced by direct power. The British were now politically incorporated into India in a way they had never been previously, and the subcontinent could be envisioned through the imperial crown. This image of coherence would be appropriated and expanded by India's nationalist leaders after independence.

The most important section of the "Royal Proclamation to the Princes, Chiefs, and People of India" specified that in future no attempt would be made to interfere with religious traditions—the doctrine of multiculturalism. Providing a community did not engage in open revolt, it could continue with whatever obscure social and religious practices it liked. In the half-century leading up to the rebellion, English evangelical Christians had promoted the abolition of practices like sati, the burning of supposedly willing widows who did not wish to live without their husbands. Progressive Indian organizations like the Brahmo Samaj had also made vigorous moves to encourage social reform. Although he had never been to India, the anti-slavery man William Wilberforce thought Hinduism "mean, licentious and cruel" and its deities "absolute monsters of lust, injustice, wickedness and cruelty," whereas "our religion is sublime, pure and beneficent."[23] Now, on the instruction of Queen Victoria, the natives were free to follow whatever they declared their customs to be. The queen proclaimed:

> Firmly relying Ourselves on the truth of Christianity, and acknowledging with gratitude the solace of Religion, We disclaim alike the Right and the Desire to impose our Convictions on any of Our Subjects. We declare it to be Our Royal Will and Pleasure that none be in any wise favored, none molested or disquieted by reason of their Religious Faith or Observances; but that all shall alike enjoy the equal and impartial protection of the Law.[24]

Although there were some subsequent reforms, such as the abolition of child marriage, most of the religious and social practices in place at the time of independence had not been substantially altered or codified for centuries. Imprisoned in Ahmadnagar Fort in 1944, Jawaharlal Nehru tried to help his sister, Vijayalakshmi Pandit, when she was widowed: her late husband's family were preventing her from accessing money, saying that under existing Hindu law it was common ancestral property to which she had no rights.[25] It was a close reminder of the social injustices and archaic customs the Indian National Congress intended to reform in the new India. Mohandas Gandhi was explicit about the need to abolish social controls on women, calling purdah "a vicious and brutal custom" that "was doing incalculable harm to the country."[26] Indians would soon be in control of their own destiny, and they had to make important reformist decisions.

While the Constitution was being framed after independence, the law minister Dr. Ambedkar (who himself had plenty of experience of the unkindness done in the name of religion) sought to introduce a new Hindu civil code which would also apply to Sikhs, Jains and Buddhists. It would abolish polygamy and restrictions on inter-caste marriage, legalize divorce and maintenance, give women full legal control over their own property and divide the assets of a man who died intestate equally between his male and female children. Conservative Hindus, some of whom were senior Congress leaders, opposed this strongly, believing it would undermine the customs on which their religion was based. Traditionally, a daughter was no longer part of the household once she was married off, and she became the property of her husband's family. Any changes would impinge on structures of male power dating back into antiquity. Religious activists objected openly to an untouchable—Ambedkar, someone who would traditionally not be permitted even to read the scriptures—trying to change the codes of Hinduism. The dharma was the preserve of the Brahmin. A speaker at a meeting called by the Rashtriya Swayamsevak Sangh in Ram Lila Ground called the proposed reforms "an atom bomb on Hindu society."[27]

Nehru found to his discomfort that many of his colleagues had turned out to be less revolutionary in office than they had been in opposition, and that they agreed with the protestors. Rajendra Prasad asked, why not leave time-honoured customs alone, at least until after the first general election? This was hardly the time, another senior Congress politician told Nehru, "to multiply or accentuate differences."[28]

The prime minister was also assailed from left and right by those who believed he was being too cautious. Surely a new civil code was meaningless unless it applied to all Indian citizens, regardless of their religion? Originally, the intention had been to reform "Anglo-Mohammedan law" as well, which was a mish-mash of sharia and legal precedent, as determined by judgements made in courts under British rule. Often, Muslim personal law was mysterious even to those who were dispensing it. Nehru's patronizing and practical view was that partition had left the Muslims a broken community, and that while a common civil code was desirable, this was not the time to make it happen. Vocal parliamentarians were opposed to any changes to family and inheritance laws, and paradoxically the more progressive and reformist voices in Muslim society, the intellectual descendants of Sir Syed Ahmed Khan, had in most cases left for Pakistan. In the 1930s, in Lucknow, Tazeen Faridi had been the first Muslim girl in India to become president of a students' union, and she went on to head the All Pakistan Women's Association. In her view, women's rights were inseparable from the freedom struggle: "We wanted laws to be standardized in their treatment of men and women. In Islam there is a tradition of powerful matriarchy—although often these women end up controlling other women—and I had no hesitation in speaking out about the need for changes in our society."[29]

When Nehru's attempts to pass a new Hindu civil code into law were rebuffed, he decided to implement the legislation piecemeal, over time. Ambedkar believed the prime minister was capitulating to reactionary upper-caste Hindu forces in Parliament, and he resigned as law minister in 1951. He was underestimating Nehru's determination, the subtlety of his strategy and how important he believed these changes to be. By the late 1950s most of the original civil code bill had been pushed through Parliament, and Hindu traditionalists were dragged, kicking and struggling, to social reform. These changes, in combination, transformed the nature of Hindu society. It would take many years for orthodox injustices to alter, and in some parts of the country they would barely change at all, but at least the law was now on the side of a progressive interpretation of individual human rights.

Maulana Mahmood Madani was in his early forties, an MP in the Rajya Sabha. In 2009 he berated the retired General Musharraf at a public forum in Delhi, telling him Indian Muslims did not want him coming there to play politics, and did not need help from Pakistan in solving their problems. "You say terrorism is happening on both sides," he told Musharraf in Urdu, "but whether or not it's happening on both sides, at least now it's confirmed it's happening on your side. More than 70 percent of Indian civil society would support us and stand with India's Muslims for our rights."[30] An embarrassed Musharraf told the maulana he was glad he was happy—if the situation was as he said it was. The audience of Delhi intellectuals and socialites lapped up this exchange, which seemed to confirm their feeling that the Nehruvian vision of communal harmony still resonated. The knowledge, unexpressed, was that Muslims who embraced the idea of India came from the same raw material—the pre-1947 community—that had under different political pressures spawned Pakistan's jihadi movement. Madani's approach was like that of the superstar actor Shah Rukh Khan, who said during a concert at India Gate in the same year: "No one can have two viewpoints about terrorism. There is no religion of terrorism. I am often asked my viewpoint on this, maybe because I am a Muslim and I am very proud to be a Muslim. But I have read the Quran, listened to the Gita, acted in Ram Leela . . . Indian civilization does not distinguish in terms of religion. We are an impossible achievement in the world, and I'm very proud to be an Indian."[31]

Although they have a much lower international profile than the citizens of Pakistan, there are nearly as many Indian Muslims as there are Pakistanis. Osama bin Laden's attempts to rebrand Islam have not caught fire in India. Occasional acts of violence—bomb blasts in crowded markets by organizations like Indian Mujahideen—can often feel closer to the attacks between rival political groupings in India than to global jihadism. Loyalty to the Constitution is imbued in children across communities from an early age: it is a kind of brainwashing, but has been remarkably effective, and underpins India's common identity. The nation has thrown up almost no international Islamist terrorists, unlike other countries with large Muslim populations. The exceptions are the Bangalore-born Kafeel Ahmed (who burned himself to death in a failed car bomb attack at Glasgow airport) and the al-Qaeda linkman Dhiren Barot (a convert from a Hindu family and now in prison), both of whom were radicalized in Britain. Despite communal feeling, rioting and suspicion at times of trouble, most Muslims show exceptional loyalty to the idea of India.

Maulana Madani lived in a spacious compound in New Delhi, in a house reserved for an MP. A guard sat in a low watchtower outside the gate, but he was there more for show than for protection, and displayed no interest when I entered the house by a side door. Like many Indian politicians, Madani sported a white kurta pyjama, and in his case the outfit was offset by a pinstriped waistcoat and pale socks with a CK logo at the ankle. His beard was substantial and his turban tied carefully, with a little tail hanging down at the back. Madani came from a long line of Islamic scholars and had a calm, relaxed manner. His servant brought dates and glasses of lemongrass tea.

"Muslims are the most backward community in India—economically, educationally, socially," he said in English. "The backwardness is not only because of government policies. In 1947 the Muslim intellectuals and civil servants went to Pakistan. Look at who was left behind. Mainly it was the poor, the illiterate and labourers who were left, and they had trouble participating in society. Our next generation are changing. They see education as a weapon. I see people in their twenties who want employment and economic advancement, and I think that the younger generation has some hopes, alhamdulillah [praise god]. They aren't interested in radicalizing like in other countries. In India, there are different forms of thought in Islam, but in this Indian environment most people are basically peaceful and peace-loving." Increasingly, in his opinion, Indian Muslims were seeking a modern and secular education for their children.

As well as the political role he played (he had switched parties twice and was presently with the Rashtriya Lok Dal), Madani was a leader of the Jamiat Ulama-e-Hind. This was an organization started after the First World War which had gone on to oppose the creation of Pakistan in 1947. He saw his present role in the context of this history.

"Over the last two years, the Deobandi school has for the first time in the subcontinent issued a fatwa condemning all terrorism and violence." He was referring to the Darul Uloom religious school in Deoband in Uttar

Pradesh. "Islam cannot allow the killing of innocent people or the use of suicide bombing. The Jamiat Ulama-e-Hind has held more than forty public meetings, attended by millions of people, to protest against terrorism. Muslims in India are all agreed at this point that Islam cannot allow any sort of violence where innocents are the target."

The fatwa was proclaimed at a meeting in Deoband attended by representatives of more than 6,000 organizations. A senior cleric had said explicitly: "We reject terrorism in all its forms and manifestations. Terrorism completely negates the teachings of Islam."[32] The message was aimed principally at Muslims in India, but the community hoped it would reach other countries too, which were often in a very different political and intellectual place when it came to an interpretation of the word "jihad." The complication was that Deobandi Islam had mutated in Pakistan, with General Zia's assistance, into an extremist force which talked of martyrdom, and its hardline message had spread around the world. Deobandis controlled 600 of Britain's 1,350 mosques, and had a lock on the training of new preachers.[33] The faith had followed a curious progression, becoming more radical in Pakistan than it was in Deoband itself, and in some cases more radical in Britain than it was in Pakistan. In a curious historical loop, activists back in England denounced Mohammad Ali Jinnah and all his works. Hizb-ut-Tahrir's magazine *Khilafah* announced: "Jinnah went one step further than most traitors . . . How dare this man associate a Kufr [infidel] concept such as democracy with our Prophet (SAW)?"[34] (SAW was short for "sallaallahu alaihi wasallam," a religious utterance.)

Madani did not want to comment on Deoband's export trends. He had recently been in trouble with some religious opponents (although I felt that in practice they were political opponents) for praising the Dalai Lama, and he did not want to pick another fight. "Their conflict is a political conflict. I don't believe in the concept of Islam against the others. Muslims in our country had an opportunity to migrate to Pakistan, and they decided to stay in their homeland. It's our home. We learned patriotism from our forefathers, who wanted to be Indian. Many freedom fighters in our country came from an Islamic background. For us, this is the most beautiful place to live."

The one area where Madani was a firm conformist was on Muslim personal law. The failure to agree on a common civil code after independence meant, for instance, that polygamy was still permitted for Muslims, which in an orthodox household could leave women in an intolerable position. Archaic rules that had been abolished in other Muslim jurisdictions remained in place in India, enabling courts peopled in the main by elderly men with beards to pronounce on personal matters. Notoriously, India retained the "triple talaq," by which a Muslim man could divorce his wife simply by saying "I divorce you" three times (there had even been debate whether sending the message by email three times constituted a dissolution of the marriage). The triple talaq was seen in many Muslim-majority countries as an outmoded historical relic, and even in Pakistan had been abolished under the Pakistani Muslim Family Laws Ordinance of 1961. According to *Commentary on Mohammedan Law,* the guidebook presently used by lawyers in most Indian courts: "The talaq should not be ambiguous, and should ideally include the woman's name. 'I divorce my wife forever and render her haram [forbidden] for me,' should be uttered to show clear intention."[35] It did not sound like a particularly reassuring law.

When I asked Madani why he opposed any changes to these rules, he spoke of unity in diversity and began a digression on Islamic jurisprudence. He pointed out that India had four different schools—the Hanafi, Maliki, Shafii and Wahabi—and that they each followed different regulations. Reading *Commentary on Mohammedan Law* later, I realized he was speaking only of Sunnis, and that Shias could rely on interpretations offered by either the Zaidi, Ismaili or Ithna Ashari tradition, and that further personal law regulations existed for those who followed the Motazila school.

"Islam can't change. We can change Muslims, but we can't change Islam. We cannot accept a common civil code, because all citizens must be content with their own beliefs. Which civil code would we adopt? In south India, some communities might even like to marry their sister's daughters. We don't want a universal personal law."[36]

It was a politician's answer, and the truth was that men like Madani benefited from the status quo. With the disappearance of powerful families and much of the progressive Muslim leadership to the new homeland of Pakistan at the time of partition, a rudderless community had been left behind in India, struggling to shape its future. Indian Muslims were too weak to challenge whatever they were offered, and took refuge in antique conventions. At times of crisis, their Hindu neighbours might target them or ask where their true allegiance lay. Nehru's commitment to protecting this large minority from vengeance had evolved over the decades into a stasis where political parties, and in particular the Congress, claimed to protect them and act on their behalf. Clerics on the further fringes of Islam were treated deferentially by the Indian secular media when compared to Hindu bigots.[37] Madani's statement was an expression of a conservative interpretation of Islam, even if it abjured the extremes of the Deobandis outside India. Most Indian madrasas, although they might not be politically radical, were content to follow a syllabus that concentrated on the precise rules governing Islamic moral and social conduct, personal behaviour, dress and appropriate interaction between the sexes.[38] India's most successful Muslim business people nearly all came from backgrounds outside the Sunni mainstream—Azim Premji of the hugely successful IT services company Wipro, for instance, was an Ismaili.[39]

Many, perhaps most, Indian Muslim leaders shared Madani's more traditional views, using the restraints of the past to shelter the community from external pressures. I discussed this with Qasim Rasool Ilyas of the All India Muslim Personal Law Board, which organized the 400 or so "darul qazas," or sharia courts, in India. To become a judge, or qazi, you did not need a law degree, but had to have studied Islamic traditions. Each qazi made his own decisions: there were no advocates in this court system, which had been formalized in the early 1970s. India since independence has had a strong tradition of women lawyers and judges, but there was not a single female qazi.

"There's no law against it," said Ilyas, "but no women have done the training." He described the darul qazas as a disputes resolution system, an alternative to going to the civil courts. "It's cheaper and it's faster and you can have a resolution in days or months. If you go to a civil court on a matter like inheritance or custody of a child and the other party goes to a higher court on appeal, you might not get an answer in your lifetime." His concern about the lackadaisical workings of the legal system was a valid one. Indian courts were notorious for being clogged with old cases, and the country had a shortage of judicial posts.[40] In 2004 it was found that a jail had forgotten to hang a man convicted of murdering his family. "The government woke from its slumber [seven years after the conviction]," the *Hindustan Times* reported, "when DIG Prisons (Allahabad zone) bumped into the convict during a routine inspection."[41]

What Ilyas did not mention was the pressure within the Muslim community to avoid civil courts, and that the judgements of the darul qazas were often reactionary. He did not want Muslim law to be codified in the way Hindu personal law had been in the 1950s, saying it would give power to Parliament rather than to the judges, the qazis. I asked him why Muslims could not rely on a system that was acceptable to Hindus and to many others. "Hindu core belief is not based on a particular scripture. Our laws are based on the Quran and the Sunnah. Nobody can touch these laws. Everything there is eternal. To say there should be a uniform civil code is like saying there should be a uniform religion." Ilyas's point was absurd: numerous countries have universal laws on matters like marriage and inheritance, but still guarantee religious freedom.

Politically, his case was unanswerable. He knew, as Madani and others knew too, that if any government sought to implement a uniform civil code, it would give men like himself a platform to display their strength as community leaders. It would not be difficult to mobilize the community, many of whom were poor and uneducated, by saying the foundations of Islam were under attack from the Hindu majority. The situation was a fudge between the proclaimed secularists of Congress and other parties, and the Muslim leaders who benefited from the existing situation. So the latter-day Nehruvians colluded in an arrangement that kept Indian Muslims in a socially regressive position and bred resentment among conservative Hindus, who could see no reason why they should not be given a similar separatist privilege. "There is a common agreement in the community," Ilyas said, "that we are opposed to any changes."[42]

Attempts by reformist voices in Muslim India to codify personal law, arguing that in doing so they would be bringing it closer to the Quran, which had an emphasis on women's rights that had been lost in later legal accretions, had not yet been successful. Despite all of this, puritanical or extreme voices within Islam in India had little chance of gaining mass support: there was no popular mood running in their favour. When I visited mosques in different parts of the country, I almost always received a sense that the community's concerns were little different to those of Hindus and others in the same locality. For most people, religion was far from being the defining interest in their life. At the Jama Masjid in Bangalore, within the coolness and beauty of the mosque with its thick white walls, Faisal Dawood spoke of educational projects and computer courses. He had retired from a government factory, where he had worked on a machine line making aeronautical parts. Now, his time was devoted to the practical improvement of the lives of Muslims in the suburbs of Bangalore. "I have helped to build schools and mosques, and I arrange the marriage of poor boys and girls, who do not have any family."[43]

When a Muslim students' association sought to prevent a Valentine's Day dance from taking place in Aligarh in 2002, citing fears of "obscenity" because Muslim girls would be wearing jeans and dancing to Western music, they were ignored. When they told the Muslim owners of local Internet cafés to block access to pornographic websites in order to avoid a descent into immorality, the owners agreed—and promptly did nothing.[44]

If Indian Muslims engaged in political violence, it was usually in response to a specific threat or after attacks such as the destruction of the Babri Masjid or the killings in Gujarat in 2002. An organization like Jamaat-e-Islami Hind (in its original Indian avatar, as opposed to its transmuted Pakistani form, which was encouraged by General Zia) stressed the importance of fighting for state secularism as a means of protecting Muslims. Although in the decades immediately after independence the Jamaat-e-Islami Hind had stuck with the philosophy of its founder, Abul Ala Maududi, who held that secularism and democracy were "haram," the movement had over time evolved and moved towards moderation in response to the fluid demands of the wider community it sought to represent.

For poor or vulnerable Muslims (in most places in south India, their position was more integrated and less fraught) the choice was often between turning to a leader like Maulana Madani, or to a more aggressive community representative like the mafia don Mukhtar Ansari. Political parties liked to communicate with Muslims through male religious leaders, who were usually conservative, in a way that would not have been considered with Hindus. Come election time, the assumption was that if you wanted Muslim votes, you needed to secure the support of a cleric by any means necessary. In such a situation, it was logical that Muslim leaders held on to power by maintaining outdated traditions, as well as their own positions on assorted influential outfits like minority commissions, Haj committees (official bodies to send Indian Muslims on a subsidized pilgrimage to Mecca) and wakf boards (trusts that look after Muslim property).[45] Wakf boards owned an estimated 600,000 acres of land in India, most of which had been endowed to the community in perpetuity many generations ago, but this property was often leased or sold off to developers. Mukesh Ambani's 27-storey house in Mumbai was built on land originally owned by the Wakf Board of Maharashtra.[46]

The greatest threat facing Indian Muslims was practical: it was poverty. An official report in 2006 investigated their representation and employment in different sectors. Although nearly 14 percent of the Indian population was Muslim, in security-related areas like the police, fire service, prison and court staff, they made up only around 6 percent; in the railway, post and telegraph services, 5 percent; in public sector banks, 2 percent. More than any other community, including the Scheduled Castes, Muslims tended to have jobs which lacked a written contract or a regular salary. There was not a single state government which employed them in proportion with their share of the population. In many industries it was hard to obtain accurate data, but in the highly competitive cadres of the Indian Administrative Service (civil servants), Indian Foreign Service (diplomats) and Indian Police Service (senior police officers), the authors of the official report had guessed religion from a list of names, since Muslim names are usually distinctive. Out of 8,827 entrants to these services in 2006, the figures for Muslim representation were a paltry 3 percent, 2 percent and 4 percent respectively.[47] The results had improved slightly since then. The "topper" in India's 2010 civil service entrance examination was Shah Faesal, a young Kashmiri Muslim who specialized in public administration and Urdu literature, and whose father had been murdered by militants in 2002.[48]

The position of people like Hemant from the CRPF, and poorly equipped jawans who were killed with alacrity by Maoists, showed the failure of the state to take care of its own people. During the 26/11 attacks in 2008, when Lashkar-e-Taiba terrorists from Pakistan arrived by boat in Mumbai to seek blood and death, the poor suffered along with the rich at the Taj and Oberoi hotels. Television viewers could watch as policemen in khaki uniforms at Chhatrapati Shivaji railway station used antique .303 rifles to try to pick off the attackers, who were shooting members of the public with machine guns. One policeman even threw a plastic chair at the gunmen in frustration. The Taj hotel went up in flames, and a terrorist in a fake Versace T-shirt strolled through the streets with a gun and a rucksack of grenades. Even senior officers lacked proper bulletproof vests, and it took half a day for specialist commandos to arrive from Delhi. More lives were saved by ingenuity than by security planning: an announcer at the railway station, Vishnu Zende, crouched in his booth overlooking the concourse even as his viewing window was sprayed with gunfire, redirected passengers as they alighted from trains. "I made sure I didn't mention a terror attack in my announcement," he said later, "as that would have created panic."[49]

The phone conversations between the Mumbai gunmen and their handlers back in Pakistan, intercepted by the Indian police, were chilling and warped. Coming from poor village backgrounds, these men were awed by the grandeur of the Taj hotel.

KILLER: There are so many lights, so many buttons . . . and lots of computers with 22-inch and 30-inch screens.

HANDLER: Computers? Haven't you burned them yet?

KILLER: We're just doing it . . . The entrance to this room is fantastic. The mirrors are really grand.

Over at the Jewish centre in Nariman House, other militants were torturing and killing Rabbi Gavriel Holtzberg and his wife, Rivka, who was five months pregnant. The irony here was that none of the young Pakistani men would ever have met a Jew, but had been conditioned as part of their training, or indoctrination, to hate them. The handler told them over the phone that a dead Jew was worth 500 others, and that it was especially important they themselves died as martyrs, rather than being taken alive. They must go out and die when they were surrounded by commandos.

HANDLER: A stronghold can only last for as long as you can handle it. We're crossing that limit . . .

KILLER: Please god.

HANDLER: It's Friday today, so it's a good day to finish it . . . Put the phone in your pocket and fire back.

(Soon, Indian commandos stormed the building.)

KILLER: I've been shot . . . Pray for me . . . My arm. And one in my leg . . .

HANDLER: Praise god, praise god.

KILLER: Bye.[50]

A survivor—Shameem Khan, a Muslim—described how six members of his extended family had been shot dead. Still in shock, he said, "A calamity has fallen on my house. What shall I do?" His neighbours helped to pay for the funerals. Mumbai's Muslim Council refused to let the terrorists be buried in its graveyards. A senior mufti said this was "to show they will never get any support from Indian Muslims, even in the slightest possible terms. As for their burial or last rites, their bodies should be sent back to the place from where they came."[51]

The bodies could not, however, be sent back to where they came from, because Pakistan's president, Asif Ali Zardari, the widower of the assassinated Benazir Bhutto, denied they were Pakistani. This was part of a pattern of constructive denial in modern Pakistan, where facts were not allowed to stand in the way of the idea that terrorism always originated elsewhere. The only surviving gunman, Ajmal Kasab, came from a decrepit village south of Lahore, and a senior retired bureaucrat popped up on one of Pakistan's many wacky TV channels suggesting he could not, therefore, have known his way around Mumbai—and must be an Indian plant. "Why would young Muslims from Pakistan be interested in Mumbai?" asked a lawyer on the same show. "They don't know the language there, and surely they wouldn't have gone there to ogle Bollywood actresses."[52] When terrorists attacked and injured the Sri Lankan cricket team in Lahore the following year, there were suggestions from a government minister that India was to blame, rather than homegrown militants. Comments of this kind were underpinned by the assumption—which was rooted in the events and consequences of the 1970s—that India had nothing better to do than plot the break-up of Pakistan.

Following the contemporary style of terrorism, the Mumbai attackers made no demands and outlined no agenda. This was done on their behalf by commentators who deduced they were fighting on behalf of the people of Palestine and Kashmir. Ajmal Kasab was a day-wage labourer and petty criminal who was recruited by Lashkar-e-Taiba (part of the International Islamic Front for Jihad against Jews and Crusaders—the al-Qaeda franchise). His handler, judging by the phone conversations, had military training. Behind them stood the leader of the organization, the pinguid Hafiz Saeed, a "professor" who lived on a ranch outside Lahore and went about his business with minimal interference from the Pakistani government. The literature of Lashkar-e-Taiba was much concerned with establishing a caliphate in Central Asia and murdering those who insulted the Prophet.

Saeed's hatreds were catholic—his bugbears included Hindus, Shias and women who wore bikinis. He believed suicide attacks were "in accordance with Islam," and he had a wider strategy which involved the capture of parts of central India he felt belonged to Pakistan: "At this time our contest is Kashmir. Let's see when the time comes. Our struggle with the Jews is always there." It is possible that when he made remarks of this sort, Saeed was paying lip service to anti-semitic or transnational jihadi causes so as to continue to obtain Arab financing, but as he told his followers in Karachi at a rally in 2000: "There can't be any peace while India remains intact. Cut them, cut them—cut them so much that they kneel before you and ask for mercy."[53]

Even if India were to do the right thing and improve the situation in Kashmir, and offer truth and reconciliation to the Kashmiri people, there was no sane reason to believe Lashkar-e-Taiba and similar organizations would shut down. Like most terror groups based in Pakistan, the organization combined unemployed Mujahideen fighters, the later protégés of the ISI who were sent over the border to Kashmir and activists from the global jihadi movement of the early twenty-first century, which itself arose from a collision between the austere traditions of the Arabian Desert and a rush of oil money. Al-Qaeda believed the only pure form of Islam was that which was practised by the prophet Mohammed and his followers many centuries before. It used the tools of modernity—television, aeroplanes, plastic explosives, the Internet—to try to destroy modernity. The present global threat came from the spread of this ideology, and its success depended on the fertility or otherwise of the ground where it fell.

In India, with its 140 million or so Muslims, jihadism had achieved little success so far, which was in part the consequence of the modern idea of the nation instilled after 1947. Ironically the ideology of religious absolutism was finding more takers in Britain—a consequence of the refusal of successive postwar governments to promote the active integration of immigrants. Such a move would have required social adjustments the British themselves did not want to make, and it was easier to present this liberal evasion as an accommodation of other cultures. It was seen as somehow un-British to demand that people should become "British" if they wanted to hold a British passport. The American tradition of integration was rejected. A similar policy of detachment had been practised in other European countries with a large postwar immigrant population, such as France and Holland. Words like "nationalist" or "patriot," which in India had a positive connotation, were in Europe often tainted with implications of racism and the legacy of a brutal colonial past.

Under the modern version of the queen empress Victoria's doctrine of multiculturalism, each new community was encouraged to go its own way and to create miniature, ghettoized versions of the society it had left behind—even as the home countries themselves progressed. Postcolonial guilt or presumption had placed Britain in a weaker position in relation to its own citizens than India. The more traditional or regressive members of a community were presumed by many Europeans to be the most convincing representatives of their people. A second-generation Pakistani who dressed up in an Arab robe in London and grew an orthodox beard was thought to be "authentic." Other British Pakistanis, who led a more regular life, often had trouble escaping the presumptions created by these supposed representatives. In many cases they shared the view of the Karachi-born hero Chuck in H. M. Naqvi's novel *Home Boy*, who is arrested in New York after 9/11. Asked by a policeman for some insight into Islamic terrorism, his first thought is that he has no special idea: "But like everybody, I figured the hijackers were a bunch of crazy Saudi bastards."[54]

The absence of a sense of belonging or loyalty engendered by multiculturalism led directly to the obscenity of the 7/7 bombings, when men who were born and bred in England blew up themselves and their fellow citizens, since their only allegiance was to a synthetic external identity. So it was in Victoria's own country that her words of 1858 resonated now most strongly: "We disclaim alike the Right and the Desire to impose our Convictions on any of Our Subjects." The Nigerian writer Wole Soyinka has described this philosophy as "part of the character of Great Britain . . . Colonialism bred an innate arrogance, but when you undertake that sort of imperial adventure, that arrogance gives way to a feeling of accommodativeness."[55]

Integration is welcoming; it says, join us. Multiculturalism says, go to your ghetto.

ONLY IN INDIA

B USINESS SCHOLARS have been much taken by the efficiency of the
dabbawallas of Mumbai, the white-capped men who push handcarts
stacked with metal tiffin carriers containing people's lunch. Some analysts
believe they offer a new model of management, others that they follow the
five-forces theory or have six-sigma performance. They are part of a complex network, the product of an established, self-regulated business which
operates in one of the world's densest urban environments. Each day, the
Nutan Mumbai Tiffin Box Suppliers Association delivers 200,000 dabbas, or
stacked containers of food, from homes to offices using only bicycles, local
trains and handcarts, with each box marked with a series of coloured numbers and letters. The dabbawallas follow two slogans, "War Against Time"
and "Work Is Worship," and start and complete their mission between the
hours of 9 a.m. and 12:30 p.m. each day. Their managers claim an error rate
of 1 in 16 million.

I was interested to know what lay behind the way the dabbawallas
worked: was it a business model or a social model? Getting to meet them
was more difficult than I had expected. The secretary of the dabbawallas,
Gangaram Talekar, said a payment of Rs5,000 [$110] was required to watch
them in operation. When I reached the appointed meeting place near Andheri railway station early one morning, nobody was there. The station

was packed with commuters, beggars, flower vendors, weighing machines and newspaper sellers, and in the street outside, at the sign of the golden arches, Chatpata McAloo Tikkis and Paneer Salsa Wraps were on sale. My appointed dabbawalla, Vittal Sawant, appeared forty minutes late, a wiry figure pushing a sturdy bicycle. He was flustered: his war against time was getting off to a bad start. Soon we were joined by a local journalist who had come to interpret his Marathi, and along with him a crew from a television channel who wanted to film me doing the rounds. I was starting to share Vittal's discomfort, and before long we were drawing a crowd.

He had to visit thirty-three residences and collect a dabba (he pronounced it "dibby") from each one, hook it to his bicycle and land up at the railway station in time for a collective departure. Some of the stops were easy: he wheeled his bike to the front door, took a container from an unseen person and attached it to the frame with a piece of string or a metal hook. At another place he ran up flight after flight of steps to reach the correct door of an apartment block, followed by me and the film crew, shouted "Dabbawalla!" and found the packed meal was not quite ready. While the dal was put in one aluminium bowl, the rice in another, the subzi in another, and the last chapatti waited to be cooked, he knelt down and painted a code of coloured letters and digits on the circular lid of a new container. As the dabba was passed out of the door to him and he prepared to rush down the stairs, he was called back again: the housewife wanted to slip in a note for her husband. With Vittal's bicycle now decorated and growing heavy with dabbas, he had to push it rather than ride it as he had done earlier in the morning.

In the streets around Andheri station, I caught sight of other dabbawallas pushing their bicycles, and at the platform a storm of activity began as men parked their bikes, grabbed and exchanged dabbas and slotted them into large, painted wooden crates at high speed, almost as if they were doing it by intuition. Vittal's cousin Kailash had stopped off at a Hare Krishna temple on his way to work, and now he was jumping athletically down to the tracks to pick up a box. By the time the train drew into the station, each man had a heavy wooden crate balanced on his head, and now a riot of pushing began as they tried to get them all aboard an open cabin before it pulled out. One man, who was trying to grab a last dabba from his bicycle, was left behind.

Although each of the dabbawallas was wearing a white cap, some were dressed in kurta pyjama and others in shirt and trousers. They came in all shapes and sizes: an old man with a huge white moustache, a young man in a yellow T-shirt. Some deceased dabbawallas had even had their place on the team taken by their widows, like Mrs. Parvatibai from Karale and Mrs. Laxmibai Bagade from Santa Cruz, although none were here today. Crammed into the cabin, taking a rest before the next burst of work, we rattled through the suburbs of Mumbai as the life of the city went on beside us.

It appeared that all the men came from the same close-knit community. "Hindu Maratha, all Hindu Maratha," said one. The warrior caste of Maharashtra, the shock troops of Shivaji, who had fought and beaten the Mughals. Except for an activist from the Maharashtra Navnirman Sena, they all supported Shiv Sena, a party which hoped to return the people of Maharashtra to their days of perceived martial glory, and had started stalls around the city selling "Shiv Vadas"—vegetarian burgers which they thought were in keeping with tradition. "It's thankless being a dabbawalla," said one of them. "Each household pays Rs280 [$6] a month for the service. I make at most Rs4,000 [$88] per month. I want my children to do a clerical job or work with computers, not this. Can I be a dabbawalla in London?"

We passed Grant Road station, where a stack of dabbas that had been tied together was handed out to the platform from the moving train while we continued to Churchgate. This was a big station in south Mumbai, a mile or so from the Taj hotel. The action began again as hundreds of dabbawallas converged from different trains and stacked big, carefully balanced handcarts with about 120 tiffin boxes each, the process working smoothly as the codes were matched with the delivery routes and the workers ran back and forth. There was almost a fight when a passer-by appeared to touch a dabba with his foot.

Vittal explained the markings to me, which were designed for people who might not be able to read. The number painted at the centre of the lid indicated the destination station, in this case Churchgate; the mark at 12 o'clock was the originating suburb; at 3 o'clock was an abbreviation of the delivery address; at 6 o'clock was the owner's name; at 9 o'clock were coded letters showing the home delivery route for the return of the dabba. Within this, innumerable variations were permitted—there was no standard tiffin carrier—and some were made of plastic, although most were stainless steel. Some were printed or painted with special codes because they were destined for a large office or came from a communal kitchen. Others used an additional form of marking, the numbers and letters painted in certain colours. When the handcarts were packed and stacked, they began to move, each one surrounded by an honour guard of dabbawallas in their white caps. The carts were surprisingly easy to push, given their size. It was a convention in Mumbai that they were allowed to cross through traffic, a privilege not given to other pushcarts.

We made our first deliveries at the offices. Some of the dabbas were five or six storeys high, containing the varieties of food necessary for an Indian lunch. Although Mumbai has plenty of fast-food stalls, most cooking reflects the national flexibility. In Western countries, a good, regular meal might consist of two ingredients, steak and chips (beef and potatoes) perhaps with salt, mustard and ketchup. In India, a simple vegetarian lunch will contain more ingredients. So packed into a standard three- or four-storey tiffin box like the ones we were now delivering, there might be: cooked white rice; pigeon peas tempered with ground cumin seeds, turmeric, ginger, garlic, salt, red chilli, dried mango powder and oil; small aubergines stuffed with green chilli, turmeric, jaggery, onion, mustard seeds, dried coconut, coriander leaves, asafetida, cloves, cinnamon sticks, peppercorns, tamarind and salt; spinach and tomatoes with ginger, garlic, ground coriander and cumin, salt, fenugreek, chilli powder, oil and garam masala—itself a mixture of ground bay leaves, cloves, cumin, cinnamon, coriander, cardamom, star anise, nutmeg and white pepper; yoghurt with mint, sugar, pomegranate and black salt; cucumber relish; a type of bread, touched with clarified butter and stuffed or layered with spiced mashed potato; a few fresh green chillies; a wedge of lime and two types of achar, or pickle—and one auntie told me a good achar has fifty ingredients, and no, I couldn't have the recipe.

After lunch, the dabbawallas would pick up the empty tiffin boxes and take them home before the evening rush hour began, by which time they were themselves more than ready to eat. Indian cooking depends on a surfeit of labour, using servants or family members, and the extra family members are nearly always women; few Indian men who do not cook for a living will do so at home.

I went to see Gangaram Talekar at his office beneath a flyover. For a start, I had to hand over Rs5,000. He refused to say a word until he had counted the notes and secreted them in a pouch inside the folds of his shirt. This was the first time I had paid to do an interview in India; I asked for a receipt, but he refused. Accompanying him in his dark office were a statue of Ganesh and some portraits of Sant Tukaram, a seventeenth-century devotional poet and teacher from near Pune, or Poona, an important figure in the Bhakti movement. "He travelled across Maharashtra singing hymns," Talekar said.

The dabbawallas' venture had started in 1890, when Parsis who were travelling to work on the new railway system found they could not get their own food at lunchtime. As new mills and businesses opened, other social groups took the chance to have meals delivered, since there was a general caste suspicion of food cooked outside the home. The system worked in Mumbai because the trains were so crowded that you needed people to carry food on your behalf, outside the rush hour. Although the prohibitions on restaurants had largely disappeared now, it was still cheaper to bring your own food from home, and the dabbawallas' service remained popular.

"At first they used coloured threads, the offcuts from tailoring shops, to mark the tiffin," said Talekar. "Today we use a number and letter code, although never the number 9." This was not because it was inauspicious, but because it might be muddled with the Marathi "6," which looks a bit like a "9" with a tail. "We have never had a strike in 120 years and there are no team leaders, no seniors and juniors. We have never had a police case against a dabbawalla. When bombs were hidden in tiffin tins in other cities in 2002, we told the police we would take responsibility, we would take care of it in Mumbai. We keep full control over our tiffins."

Why did they wear white caps? "The cap is a computer cover. The mind is the computer—we need it for decoding. Hindus say you cover your head when you are serving someone." Were there any Muslims on the 800 teams of dabbawallas, which totalled more than 5,000 workers? "We are all descended from the warriors of Chhatrapati Shivaji Maharaj. We are the Varkaris." Almost all the dabbawallas came from the same sub-caste, and could even trace their origins to villages—Akola, Ambegaon, Junnar—in a region outside Pune. They came from a very close social group and had started the system as a way to make a living. Now, they encouraged their children to pursue more profitable lines of work when possible. Their ability to run a complex, intuitive distribution system arose from their homogeneity, which was not unconnected to their chauvinism. "Our customers come from all communities: Christians, Muslims. We couldn't have a Muslim or a Bihari doing this work. We prefer not to have others joining the dabbawallas because we have complete trust within our community. We know each person, and trust would be broken."

Gangaram Talekar was adamant the dabbawallas' system was linked to their social culture, and more specifically to the particular Hindu religious traditions that they followed in his part of Maharashtra, which dated back over centuries. "Our grandparents lived in the mountain ranges, which gave them strength. They were following the Varkari movement and were known for being polite and for singing hymns. We take our beliefs from our travelling gurus, who have taught us. Our gurus told us to go beyond the mind. We follow and admire the teachings of Sant Tukaram every day: 'Duty First,' 'Work Is Worship,' 'Serving Food Is Serving God,' 'Unity Is Strength.' If you are a member of our community, you must do your own duty."[1]

India has a deep religious impulse, which is rooted in Hinduism. The excesses of the Hindutva movement, and the risk that any encouragement of spiritual devotion could shake the nation's post-independence secular consensus, have led many to downplay or even deny this aspect of Indian identity. Amartya Sen, the revered economist, philosopher and social thinker, wrote: "The often-repeated belief that India was a 'Hindu country' before Islam arrived is, of course, a pure illusion"—since there were also Buddhists, Jains and a handful of Zoroastrians, Christians and Jews. Nearly every traveller in early India, such as the acute tenth-century observer Al-Biruni, would have disagreed with Sen, viewing the kinds of religious practices and worship that are today called Hinduism as integral to the culture. Sen extended his claim to the present: why should Hinduism be seen as important to a person's identity, rather than anything else? "For example, the status of being a majority in India can be attributed, among other groups, to . . ."—and here he lists five categories, including "the class of non-owners of much capital," "the people who do not work in the organized industrial sector" and "Indians who are against religious persecution." He could have listed a sixth category: Indians whose names start with a consonant.

> Each group thus identified is in fact a majority in its respective system of categorization, and their common characteristics can be taken to be important, depending on the context. In order to attach immense significance to the fact that Hindus constitute a majority group in Indian society in one particular system of classification, the priority of that religion-based categorization over other systems of classification would have to be established first.[2]

This is the logic of the clever schoolboy, and forgets the reality of how people live and think. It forgets the sentiments of the individual. In any village in rural India, you would find men and women with a stronger attachment to their household and family rituals, or to Ram, Murugan or a non-Hindu deity, or only to the ancient distinctions and prejudices of their community, than to the knowledge that they "do not work in the organized industrial sector." A powerful attachment to religion remains at the heart of how most people go about their day, and it is by no means exclusive to Hindus. Rather, the practice of religion is integrated, almost casually, into nearly every aspect of life.

The Indus Valley civilization, which began more than 4,000 years ago and can be seen in archaeological remains in India and Pakistan, has an atavistic link to modern Hinduism. Quite how close the connection might be is debated, since its surviving tablets, seals, buildings and figurines are ambiguous, and the script of the Indus Valley has yet to be plausibly deciphered. If or when this happens, perhaps after the unearthing of more inscriptions, ideally in the form of a "Rosetta Stone" with parallel text in a known language, things will become clearer. Many rediscovered items from ancient times appear to echo familiar objects. The representation of a seated figure resembling Shiva, the stone carvings of "priest-kings," the fine bronze image of a dancing girl with bangles up to the top of her arms and engraved symbols of a bull, these all give the impression of links to contemporary Hindu imagery. The large and beautifully constructed ritual bathing tank at the centre of the Indus Valley city of Mohenjo-daro looks like the ritual bathing tanks still found beside most temples today. Against this is an argument proposing that other ancient civilizations also worshipped animals, or a combination of gods, beasts and priests. For many Hindus, however, the links to the Indus Valley seem unmistakable.

Some scholars have used obvious uncertainty about what happened long ago to deduce there may have been no connection at all. So for Wendy Doniger, the tank at Mohenjo-daro perhaps had no ritual purpose, and its existence proves only that the people of the Indus Valley civilization "liked to bathe, just to get clean or to cool off on hot days or to splash about, same as we do." Under such an interpretation, there may have been no "theocratic elite" in this highly structured and carefully laid out Indus Valley city—one of the most sophisticated early cities ever discovered. Why should "enforced dogma" have been mandated by their rulers? "Is it possible that this was the first secular state, anticipating the European Enlightenment by 4,000 years? Could they have been more like protoatheists than protoyogis?" The structure presumed to be a "college of priests" might have been nothing of the sort: "Well, it's a big building, true, but why couldn't it be a dorm, or a hotel, or a hospital, or even a brothel?"[3] Questions like this owe more to the exigencies of American academia than to close observation or probability. They are an example of a scholarly tendency to write about India, and particularly about Hinduism, in a way that would not be tried when writing about Christianity or Islam. Indeed the blanket title of Doniger's book, *The Hindus,* is hard to imagine transposed to *The Christians* or *The Muslims.*

Whether viewed through the lens of Hindutva or the lens of Western academic tradition, the fluid nature of Hinduism means its particularities will inevitably be much debated. The teaching of India's history is a matching dispute. The discussion about how best to understand the past is ever running, and the usual account of this debate quotes examples from textbooks used in schools run by combative Hindu organizations. These are often outlandish and are more about wishful thinking than about history. *Ithihas Gaa Rahaa Hai*—"History Is Singing"—was a Class 5 textbook used in private RSS schools in the north. It suggested among other things that the first inhabitants of China were Indian Rajputs, and that Adolf Hitler had "lent dignity and prestige to the German government" and "instilled the spirit of adventure in the common people."[4]

The more respectable textbooks produced by NCERT (the National Council of Educational Research and Training, a body appointed by the central government) were, however, until recently, a long way from neutral, even if they had fewer flights of fantasy. Bipan Chandra's standard *Modern India* offered a Marxist historiography, or as he put it: "emphasis on forces, movements and institutions rather than on military and diplomatic events and . . . political leaders."[5] A later edition of the book published when the BJP was in power developed this approach in a new way, and offered a partial version of history. The "official policy" of "the Britishers" from the middle of the nineteenth century onwards had been "to break Hindu–Muslim unity." Unconnected activities were linked in a chapter on armed uprisings which asserted that the Wahabi revival of the late nineteenth century was "socialist" and that all violent movements in India had "by their unselfish struggle wanted to awaken their countrymen against the atrocities of the British." Subhas Chandra Bose, who attempted to raise an army with Nazi Germany and Japan's help during the Second World War, was placed "among the front-ranking leaders of the world" and declared "immortal."[6]

Historical films, in various regional languages, were for many people their prime source of knowledge about the past. Just as Abhishek Bachchan extolled the joys of capitalism in *Guru* in 2007, films during the years of socialist stagnation looked back with anger at the previous few hundred years. From the 1960s, the depiction of the British empire in India became harsher. The Britisher was a stock villain, often played by one of a handful of European actors. In the 1985 movie *Mard*—"The Man"—featuring Amitabh Bachchan as the hero, the opening sequence shows soldiers carrying treasures from a seaside fort. "The atrocities of the British hadn't reduced," comes the voice-over. "They also took up looting." The viceroy, Lord Curzon, the author of the Jallianwala Bagh massacre, General Dyer, and "Simon"—presumably Sir John of the Simon Commission—discuss what to do with a group of corralled natives. (The fact the three men were in India at different times and had almost no connection with each other was not important.) Curzon, chomping on a cigar, gives the order: "Simon, include their names in the martyrs." Two mounted machine guns open fire on the crowd. As the imperialists try to flee in a light aeroplane with their riches, the valiant local king, Raja Azad Singh, pursues the taxiing plane on horseback, manages to lasso the tail, drags it back and retrieves the treasure. Now the film can begin.

The debate about school textbooks was a microcosm of a larger intellectual rift. Nostalgic about the early days of nation building, and hoping to see a reflection of the Nehruvian vision, some preferred to stick to the safety of the secular version of the past propagated by the Congress party. This interpretation of history was at some distance from the popular understanding of early communal relations.

Take Mahmud of Ghazni: in the eleventh century, this Sunni warrior raided Kangra, Mathura and Kannauj in north India, captured 53,000 slaves and boundless booty and took them home to Afghanistan. He set off again for the great Hindu centre at Somanatha, where he smashed the Shiva lingam with his sword and looted gold, silver and jewels; the remains of the icon were carried back to Ghazni and incorporated into the steps of the new Jama Masjid, the Friday Mosque. So in popular legend he was the first in a procession of villainous Muslim raiders. Certainly India's great surviving Hindu and Jain temple complexes are confined to areas the invaders did not reach, in the south and in outlying places such as Puri and Khajuraho, which suggests the destruction of idolaters' temples was seen by a number of Muslim rulers as a necessary and even virtuous act. Reading contemporary accounts of the period suggests the repeated sacking of the north was done for more than purely strategic purposes, and that the conquest of territory and subsequent submission of the people were important. For example, Timur, the late-fourteenth-century conqueror who was said to have executed innumerable Hindus, wrote that when the wounded Raja of Jammu converted to Islam and ate the flesh of a cow "in the company of

Musulmans . . . I ordered my surgeons to attend to his wounds, and I honoured him with a robe and royal favours."[7] Other chiefs were executed by Timur for refusing to convert to Islam. These military campaigns did have an inescapably religious aspect.

So if successive Muslim raiders behaved in this way, were the corresponding Hindu, Jain and Buddhist kingdoms at the time peaceful? It seems not: the riches of Somanatha had already been targeted by local Hindu rulers, though they were concerned with wealth and control rather than with religious conversion (you cannot plausibly convert to Hinduism). Records abound of old regional wars, intrigue and conquest, sometimes using Muslim mercenaries, sometimes in alliance with another power against an opponent or even a friend. Long before the arrival of European adventurers, India was a mixed-up place. In the Deccan, soldiers included archers from Iraq and Turkestan, ex-slaves from the north and Sunni mercenaries from the east coast of Africa. In Cambay, in what is now Gujarat, fifteenth-century Arab ship owners ran the long-distance maritime trade peaceably in conjunction with high-caste Hindus. In Bengal a century later, the Muslim king entertained communities including Arabs, Persians and Abyssinians, who organized much of his administration. Duarte Barbosa, a Portuguese merchant who had travelled as far as the Philippines with Magellan, noted that Moors in Bengal wore white cotton turbans and rings set with rich jewels. "Every one has three or four wives or as many as he can maintain. They keep them carefully shut up, and treat them very well."[8]

To a large extent, the many groups living in India remained discrete and did not intermarry even when their commercial or personal relations were good. Social functioning depended on an ability to navigate multifarious communities. Islam itself transmuted into new forms amid the indigenous Indian polytheists, who themselves worshipped god in innumerable shapes; north, east, south, west; Vishnu, Kali, Murugan, Shiva. Muslim shrines, famously that of Moinuddin Chishti in Ajmer, would be visited by Hindus in search of blessings; Muslim Rajputs from Mewat would recite the Hindu epic the Mahabharat. The Indian system expected—and expects—to find difference in close proximity to the majority. In a small area of any city, Sikhs, Jains, Buddhists, Muslims, Christians and different varieties of Hindu might live close by, separate but together. There are few parts of India where the people can be described as homogeneous.

There was hardly an aspect of Indian history which did not open itself to irreconcilable argument; for the public, the debate was always running. For example, did the cruelty exacted by early Muslim invaders make Hindus harbour deep and lasting wounds, and an antipathy towards their Muslim neighbours? There was no unified answer to this question. Given the variety of experience in so many different places, and the lack of any early unified Hindu identity, it seems doubtful. India was so big, and so disparate, that the communal—or political—response would have been different in each region. Hinduism was of its nature amorphous, lacking a founding text or ideology. Only in the eighteenth or nineteenth century did it become feasible to look at its history in a structured, common way. The British were always keen on classification, and as they attempted to fit the subcontinent within the bounds of their own logic with the help of censuses and gazetteers, it became possible for different communities in India to see fresh patterns in the distant past and to use them politically. Followers of diverse but connected religious traditions had been classified under the rubric of Hinduism (although one community in Bombay insisted on being registered as "Hindoo Musalmans").

In school textbooks, controversial realities had for many years been replaced by harmonious stories of a united and syncretic subcontinental past. Romila Thapar's *Medieval India*—which was aimed at twelve-year-old children—played down the acts of desecration by early Muslim invaders, and emphasized their finer qualities. Although Mahmud of Ghazni had admittedly made seventeen raids on India in twenty-five years in the early eleventh century, "in his own country he was responsible for building a beautiful mosque and a large library."[9] Even in works aimed at adults, this tendency continued. It was possible to read a book like Thapar's *Somanatha* and be no wiser by the end about what had happened all those years ago. In her view, the stories of Mahmud of Ghazni raiding Somanatha in the eleventh century were exaggerations done by the chroniclers in order to impress their patrons. So the "accounts in the Turko-Persian sources are diverse and ambiguous" and do not allow "a monocausal explanation of the event."[10] Certainly there would have been exaggerations; it was part of the job if you were a court historian. The risk, though, if every event from the past was hedged by deconstructionist readings was that it became impossible to establish any kind of narrative in Indian history—and narrative, like nature, abhors a vacuum. In its place came eccentric readings, like the suggestion that the early Rajputs strode off to people China.

Since 2005, India's school textbooks for history and other subjects have been through a revolution. The propaganda has been replaced by a nearly faultless attempt to make history interesting to children. Instead of leaning towards one ideology or another, the new books tried to put forward information and make the reader think about it—a substantial move away from the rote learning that Indian schoolchildren refer to as "byhearting." *India and the Contemporary World,* a Class 9 textbook, had activities like:

> Imagine you are living in the 1890s. You belong to a community of nomadic pastoralists and craftsmen. You learn that the Government has declared your community a Criminal Tribe. Describe briefly what you would have felt and done. Write a petition to the local collector explaining why the Act is unjust and how it will affect your life.[11]

The progenitor of the transformation was Professor Krishna Kumar, who was asked to head NCERT in 2004 at a time when school textbooks were the subject of constant questions in Parliament. Politicians on the right believed that schoolchildren were being crammed with Marxist propaganda, and those on the left thought there was a risk any revision of their official version of national history might stir up communal tension.

"In the 1950s," Krishna Kumar told me, "there were different textbooks for teachers to choose from, and it was all done privately. The problem began in the mid-1960s when left historians produced new books. They were never updated. These were commissioned by the education minister, M. C. Chagla, an enlightened and refined Muslim gentleman. He had been told by young scholars like Romila that the old books weren't good enough. When Bipan's book went, I can't say how relieved I was. No more questions in Parliament! So we started again, with a new pedagogy." So, bizarrely, these much disputed textbooks had stemmed from a decision made by Chagla, who before independence had been a junior in Jinnah's law chambers in Bombay (and in the 1970s published a memoir called *Roses in December* which emphasized the Quaid-e-Azam's political misdemeanours and his apparent fondness for pork products).[12]

Professor Kumar appeared to have side-stepped, or stepped over, the sterile ideological battle. When the BJP-led government was in power before his appointment to NCERT, the dispute had turned vicious, with eminent establishment historians like Romila Thapar being targeted by those on the aggressive outer fringes of the Hindutva movement. Krishna Kumar had sought to change Indian methods of teaching, trying to move away from circular debates, and away from the mass recitation of facts. Part of his difficulty was that state textbook boards determined what would end up in schools.

"We are a moral authority," he said. "It's a Nehru-era idea. We have no mandatory power, because this is a federal country. Most of the states listen to us, but West Bengal, Maharashtra and Madhya Pradesh don't listen at all. The Maharashtra textbook bureau is one of the richest businesses in Maharashtra." This made sense: education was a way of making money, so why take an improved textbook from NCERT when you could sell your own at a good profit? "Bihar is becoming much more progressive now. In some cases, the officials in the state bureaucracy may want to have progress, but politically it can be difficult to do. We want to make textbook learning one of several sources of education, and let children learn in many ways. Since independence, mass education has been neglected by every government. With Nehru, oddly, the talk about education was only rhetoric: he made no concerted effort to modernize our primary education, or to make India into a literate nation. He just sent off letters of guidance to the states."[13]

I had noticed stories—countless bizarre, baffling and intense stories—of India's religious devotion. The fact someone was a "secularist" by no means implied they were a rationalist; Nehru's sometimes contemptuous dismissal of superstition was not a trait that was shared by many others. To start at the top, the chief minister of Karnataka, B. S. Yeddyurappa, proffered his index finger to an official at the 2009 general election so it could be stained with a line of dye after voting, in accordance with the law. The official was stumped, because the chief minister was holding up his right hand, and everybody knew it was the left index finger that needed to be marked. There was a moment of silence before the official, bowing to power, stained the right (or the wrong) finger. Why did B. S. Yeddyurappa do this? It was an accident, he said, an oversight on his part—but it turned out later in the day that his spiritual guardian had forbidden him to raise or extend his left hand, for astrological reasons.[14]

In the same state, the tourism minister, G. Janardhana Reddy, donated a diamond-studded gold crown to the famous Tirumala temple. This was to honour Lord Venkateswara, a form of the god Vishnu. The crown had cost Reddy nearly $10m, and the act was partly a display of wealth, partly a form of political assertion and above all a way of propitiating the god. It would be placed on the presiding deity after his weekly sacramental bath. Together with his brothers, Reddy was involved in huge, controversial and possibly illegal iron ore mining on the border between Karnataka and Andhra Pradesh, and was at that moment under grave threat from a central government inquiry into his conduct on forest land.[15] It can be assumed his approach to the god was less about a search for forgiveness as a penitent sinner—since Hinduism lacks a creed—and more about a desire to continue to succeed. Hinduism does not have commandments and does not inspire guilt; with its lack of demands, a person's relationship with fate is direct and does not anticipate forgiveness or immediate punishment.

These tales of ministers in Karnataka were both about ambition. People who were successful in "scientific" fields would often, conversely, also have an inner devotion to religion. It did not seem unusual in India that K. Radhakrishnan, the new head of the Indian Space Research Organisation, learned of his appointment while stripped to the waist, performing rituals as a pilgrim at a temple in Kerala. Nor did it seem unusual that K. Radhakrishnan was a noted Kathakali dancer (he liked to play the deity Hanuman) and a singer of Carnatic music.[16] Religion and science never went their separate ways in India in the way they did in Europe in the eighteenth century. There was no intellectual division, because Hinduism was too amorphous to be challenged or threatened by any new scientific discovery. If anything, advances in human understanding of the laws of nature might chime with the abstraction of Hindu philosophy, in which time has no beginning and no end.

Then there were priests who used their position to gain favours they would not otherwise have received, a common enough practice in any of the world's religions. One "godman" in Karnataka made the mistake of obliging his followers to sign a document absolving him of guilt if he was compelled to involve them in "close physical proximity and intimacy." When he pushed the limits, a victim inevitably leaked the terms of the supposed contract.[17] A priest in Kanchipuram, a major pilgrimage town, filmed sexual encounters between himself and women pilgrims in the sanctum sanctorum of his temple, a place only certain male priests are supposed to enter. When his mobile phone was being repaired, a technician noticed and copied clips of film, put them on DVD and made a good trade selling them around the temple town.[18]

As India became more prosperous, devotion to religion did not seem to be declining. An engineer might go to a Hindu healer who would blow water over affected parts of the body to cure ailments, a trick—or a talent— that he had learned from Muslim healers. In Tamil Nadu, despite its reputation for efficiency, there was an instance of a young man being forced to marry a dog as a punishment by his community for killing two dogs, and a case of a Dalit girl having to marry a frog, for reasons no one could establish.[19] Many of the more famous shrines and pilgrimage sites reported far larger attendances now than in the 1990s, when religion was perceived as a stronger political force. This may have been in part because pilgrims now had more time and money to travel.

In India, people adjusted their religious practice according to the apparent rewards. Rakesh had a job procuring equipment for a large industrial firm. It was a temptation; he took illegal commissions, and was placed under investigation by an internal vigilance team. For two months they probed his invoices, and after one interrogation he was advised by a colleague to pray to Shirdi Sai Baba. After that, the investigation mysteriously disappeared. Now Rakesh was a Sai Baba devotee who, together with his wife, spent many of his waking hours promoting the guru and coercing his extended family to attend prayer and hymn events in praise of Sai Baba. Not long after the investigation, he lost his job over another matter, and this only increased his faith.

Kumar, a cook in a house in Delhi, telephoned his cousin, a driver on the other side of town, to tell him Ravan has been discovered alive and well and living near Chennai. (Ravan is a mythological figure from the Ramayana.) They discussed in detail why it had happened, and why Ravan chose to reappear in Chennai rather than somewhere further north. A television channel reported that unidentified objects had been found on Mars. They turned out to be "encrypted messages in the universe"—representations or icons of Hindu deities. An otherwise conventional businessman who wore tight amulets on his upper arms stopped and went off into a trance for ten minutes at a time without warning. Religion was never separated from ordinary life. Outside a market in Kolkata, the pavement contained a busy shrine, incorporating a strangely gnarled and ancient tree, and a rock that had been worn smooth by veneration. At a nearby temple, workmen made statues that seemed greater than themselves, the ego sublimated into the tradition and the veneration of the divine that was contained in the statues.

Shrines and places of worship could arise unexpectedly. In Bangalore, a three-temple complex appeared on one of the main city thoroughfares, and an unauthorized shrine was built on a new ring road in response to several hit-and-run accidents. The city engineers knocked it down, but a week later another accident occurred and hundreds of residents from a nearby village arrived to rebuild it. The shrine came in the form of a lurid painted sculpture of a deity who had been adjusted for the purpose: "Highway Anjaneya," raising his right hand fiercely. When an engineer arrived to demolish the creation, he quickly retreated, fearful that the site's protectors would beat him.[20] In New Delhi, the Irish ambassador bought a Ganesh sculpture and placed it near the entrance to his office at the Irish embassy. At first it attracted no attention, then he noticed each morning when he came to work that it was being venerated, garlanded, given offerings, and before long people from further up the road were visiting, sometimes in numbers. A quandary developed: he had built a shrine on diplomatic property without the Indian or Irish government's permission.

As I drove along a sandy road past angled coconut palms from Trivandrum to Kanyakumari, the feeling of religion was everywhere, and it was not exclusive to the Hindu traditions. Kanyakumari is the southernmost point in India, formerly known as Cape Comorin, a place hit hard by 2004's great tsunami. At a Jain temple, pilgrims were preparing to make their devotions. Outside the Sri Padmanabhaswamy temple, families waited in a snaking queue in the fierce heat, the women with white jasmine in their hair, the men and boys topless in pressed mundus—a southern version of the dhoti. There was a monument to the communist leader E. M. S. Namboodiripad, the hammer and sickle garnished with fresh flowers. Further down the sandy road, as the peninsula of India narrowed to its tip, statues of "Child Jesus" were interspersed with billboards showing the Tamil deity Murugan, who in his younger manifestations looked like Child Jesus. References to Murugan can be found in literature before the birth of Christ, so two millennia were intermittently entwined. In Kanyakumari at a confluence of water, I could look left to the Bay of Bengal, straight ahead at the Indian Ocean or right to the Arabian Sea.

Sitaram, a glowing young ascetic from Garhwal in the Himalayas, with a necklace of beads and a red smear with cream edges between his eyes, was raising support and funds for a strictly vegetarian ashram for visiting renouncers who had come to the far south. While we spoke, a naked man was lying on his back on the ground nearby with a structure rising from his face, like a version of the heavy spectacles used by optometrists for tests. His body was smeared with white ash. He came each day and lay in silence.

Every society has its norms. When you are inside, they seem permanent— they seem normal. In Hinduism, there is no clear right and wrong. Christians, Muslims and Jews are brought up on the idea of pairs of opposites, the idea you are either for us or against us, and find it hard to put aside this trained instinct when looking at India. This is why European visitors from the early seventeenth century onwards did their best to taxonomize the territory, to make sense of what was difficult to define in simple terms. Rules did not always apply, and when they did apply they might quickly be contradicted by new information. Knowledge might hold, for example about the respective positions of certain caste groups, but vary again in neighbouring territory. The culture of India was different and protean: nearly everyone adjusted, talked, depended on the protection of astrology, put a dab of kajal, or kohl, behind the ear of a child to ward off the evil eye. There were common threads, as well as a conceptual mutability, a different way of thinking, so that most certainties could be contradicted. Hinduism has no set book, which means books about Hinduism will often tell you little. The religion is only practice, only what it is, and can be understood only by seeing how it is lived.

Professor T. S. Saravankumar was born in the last years of Nehru's premiership. He had a familiar Tamil look: oiled hair, a definite moustache, a pair of slacks, a bit of a belly, an olive-coloured corduroy shirt. We sat beneath a fan out on the terrace with the smell of clean plaster and paint; his house had just been built. In 1965, fifteen years after the Constitution came into being, Hindi was set to become the official language of the Indian union, but the protests by Tamils were so intense, with people immolating themselves against this perceived northern dominance, that the plan was abandoned and English continued as a parallel language. The powerful Dravidian political parties of the south came out of this movement. This opposition to a national language was felt not only in Tamil Nadu, but across different parts of the country, in places like Punjab and West Bengal, where a strong feeling remained against the "imposition" of Hindi.

When Saravankumar and his wife moved into the new house, certain rituals had been necessary. "We didn't call a Brahmin priest. My uncle recited the Thevaram, a compilation of songs by three poets with no Sanskrit in the text." He was making a point here about Tamil being distinct from Sanskrit, which he projected as being a discrete language of the north and of the Brahmins (academics dispute this point). He felt the Tamil language, with its tens of millions of speakers, deserved respect. In part, Saravankumar's opinions were a product of Periyar E. V. Ramaswamy's self-respect movement and the construction of a strong Tamil identity in revolt against the ancient power of the upper castes. In earlier eras, Telugu and Kannada cultural influences would have made their way among the people and kingdoms of the south.

"The elders felt obliged to come to the house and do a ritual. Part of the kinship structure here is that the family have the right of veto over what you can do. My uncle is seventy-nine, older than my father, so for a time he became the 'owner' of our property, to do the rituals. That's how it is. He lit lamps, he broke a fresh coconut: it's a package. At the time of my marriage, I got married four times: Syrian Christian, Catholic, Hindu and non-Sanskritized Tamil. The idea of conciliation is an important part of our culture. People here are not xenophobic—if German or American business partners come to Chennai, we open out stakes to them without feeling threatened. The south has always been mobile, right across Asia. You create your home wherever you go. Your culture goes with you. The current president of Singapore is a Tamil.

"Even before independence we had guaranteed seats in the south for non-Brahmins in educational institutions. Groups like the Nadars—whose great-grandparents were toddy-tappers, climbing up palm trees to tap the sap—have done extremely well. The tech company HCL, which is very successful, is run by one. Our politics are more advanced than in the north. If I go to Delhi and take a taxi—this has happened to me, coming from the airport—the driver will say to me because I don't speak Hindi: 'Are you Indian?' I want to remove that. Being an Indian works best if you start respecting inexactitude. Nehru recognized that India was plural. The south Indian imagination is like a banyan tree where the roots and the branches have constant interplay.

"At the time the British came, there were no major kings left here, so it was more of a dialogue about what sort of institutions and system we needed. Some of the great Tamil texts combine Hindu, Jain and Buddhist teachings, so Hinduism in Tamil Nadu comes from that interplay. We have had Christians coming to our coast since the second century, like St. Thomas the apostle, who died here. We never had Muslim rulers. The northerners—with their essential resentment about being ruled for so long—have grown into bigotry. We have had Muslims with us since the eighth century, but only for spice trading. They lived in pockets of their own and spoke Tamil. They even prayed in Tamil, though in the last twenty years they have become more Arabic."[21] Yet the curious thing was that, as he spoke, I remembered a similar house-blessing ceremony about three years earlier, done a few hundred miles away in Kerala. The Muslim imam, his head wrapped in a white turban, had performed religious rituals involving coconuts, boiled milk and sugar which seemed much like those done by Hindus.

. . .

Chandraswami was born a couple of years after independence. He grew up in Hyderabad, and said he had travelled first to the jungles of central India to meditate, and then to the mountains of Nepal, where he had purportedly slept in a tree until he achieved self-realization. After an unsuccessful stint in the Youth Congress, he found that it was possible to exert greater power through offering religious guidance.

In his early days Chandraswami had been a herbal healer and masseur, promising to restore the sexual power of old men with the correct elixir, and by his late twenties he had moved on and attracted some followers. By the early 1980s he had been taken up by an assortment of world leaders. Using one leader as a prop to leap to the next, he travelled the world accompanied by an entourage and a photo album featuring himself with Ferdinand Marcos, the Sultan of Brunei, Indira Gandhi, Daniel Ortega, Elizabeth Taylor, Edward Seaga, Mobutu Sese Seko—and many more.

He was not a sophisticated man, but he had an uncanny talent for entering the heads of others. The swami looked chubby, grubby and unkempt, wearing a dhoti kurta, sandals and a chunky gold rosary, a large red tilak on his forehead, leaning on a silver-topped black cane. His talent was for reading weakness, particularly in someone in a position of authority who had the loneliness and anticipation of betrayal that comes with an excess of power and money. In Mobutu's case, Chandraswami would hide himself behind a curtain while the Zairean president met a general or a minister, and tell him afterwards (despite the linguistic gap—Mobutu was speaking in French) whether they could be trusted. With the massively wealthy Sultan of Brunei, his focus was on gaining the trust of his wife Mariam, who he realized was in a vulnerable position at court; she needed a son, and he assured her he could make it happen. In India, Chandraswami's position was nebulous, but he strengthened it by acts of generosity, like feeding 10,000 hungry pilgrims at the Kumbh Mela. On his travels, he might give someone a ruby or a Rolex, and often the gift would lead to the receipt of more gifts in return (Mobutu reportedly paid the swami in diamonds).

Chandraswami's entourage went a long way to boosting his reputation. Like latter-day rappers, he knew that anyone who was surrounded by staff and security looked important. His principal sidekick, known as Mamaji, or uncle, would tell people he was a very important religious leader, list his more famous disciples and whisper that he was one of India's five spiritual kings. In the atmosphere of the 1970s and 1980s (when these things could not be checked with the help of the Internet) his approach often drew an excited response.

During Narasimha Rao's premiership, he was known as the prime minister's Rasputin. There were various reasons for this alliance—the swami had paid for Rao's heart surgery while he was out of office, which must have exerted a considerable emotional pressure on Rao, who was a few days short of seventy when he became prime minister. When Rao left office, the swami fell to earth and his career was finished. He was charged with conspiracy in a bribery case and accused of involvement with the Tamil Tigers over Rajiv Gandhi's assassination, although he had become close to Rajiv after a rapprochement during his last years in power.[22]

When I went to see him at his ashram in 2010, Chandraswami was looking old and fat. He sat with his legs propped up on a padded stool, leaning back on something like a reclining airline chair, cushioned on what appeared to be an animal skin. His forehead was marked with wide smears of red and orange paste, still wet from his morning puja. With cases still running against him in the courts, he would not speak about his earlier career. "I am only the medium. All else comes from the almighty. I can predict the past, present and future."[23] An aide handed me a printed brochure as I was ushered away from his presence. It was filled with photographs: Nixon, Carter, Arafat, Adnan Khashoggi—and always the swami, looking triumphantly serene beside them. I examined the brochure as I drove home:

> Jagdacharya Shri Chandraswami Ji Maharaj is an advanced sadhaka of Shakti, a seeker of high attainments, full of fiery aspirations, a seer sage possessing intense renunciation and deep dispassion . . . The nectar of his teachings are manifested in spreading the message of Dharma and righteousness. He feels that the solid foundation of high moral life can be laid only by knowing the importance and significance of Man, Nature and God.

He told me he had predicted Margaret Thatcher's 1979 election victory, and that she had thanked him for it.

Shankar had travelled with Chandraswami during the 1980s: "Swami was meeting a lot of different people at that time—the Sultan of Brunei, Tiny Rowland, Mohammed al Fayed, the head of the Congressional Black Caucus in the U.S. About seven or ten of us would travel with him, usually. We went to Mobutu's apartment on Avenue Foch in Paris, which was filled with unopened shopping bags and boxes. All sorts of people were around: film stars, politicians, princesses, hookers, some very rich people from Germany. The journeys were often done on Adnan Khashoggi's flying palace, a DC-8. That was in the days before everyone had planes. One time we were on board the DC-8 and a little priest from Madras who was in the entourage was fiddling around with all the switches. He points to one red button and asks Khashoggi what happens if he presses it. Khashoggi says, deadpan: 'We all blow up.' He goes back to his seat. You've never seen the look on that priest's face.

"We went to visit Mobutu in Kinshasa and stayed in a house that had beautiful cutlery and dishes, and fridges full of champagne, but there was nothing at all to eat. He sent us to his ancestral village, and the plane had to land on a runway with goats and cows wandering around. Naked children were walking by the side of the road. We found there was not much in Mobutu's village except a farmhouse with a disco or nightclub attached to it. Swami laid some bricks to do a havan, a fire ritual, he put some wood and ghee, took some incense, broke lots of coconuts, chanted some hocus pocus."

Although Shankar was dismissive of Chandraswami, he was not a sceptic, and respected those with what he saw as spiritual power. "Some years ago a 'vastu' guy, someone who advises on these things, came to our house on the recommendation of a friend. I said, come and have a drink, and told him I was a bit stuck on some things in my life. He asked to see the kitchen. The positioning of the fire and water in your kitchen is important—the cooker and the sink. He said immediately, you have to change where the fire is, so we had the kitchen broken and made it another way. Things became easier after that. He never charged any money, and I never saw him again. He just drew the thing out on a sheet of paper—that was it. I had a couple of large projects I was working on, and after that the money just started pouring in.

"Last year I was told I needed to wear a Burmese ruby for good fortune. I wore it and felt like I was having a heart attack. I consulted another guy, and was told my sun sign was being ramped up much too far by the ruby." He lifted his hand. "Now I wear an emerald on my little finger, and a diamond on another finger." For Shankar, the swami was insufficiently qualified. "He was not a learned man and didn't know about Hindu traditions. Swami was able to make people beholden to him, and he had extraordinary charm. He would say some nonsensical mantra, or normal dialogue in Hindi as if it was meant to be a prayer. To those people, who didn't know the language, it sounded like a mantra. He might say, 'Danger coming, I do prayer for you.' At the time, people wanted to hear all this, and to believe him. He would say that he could feel a vibration in the earth and could see your village, or some such thing."[24]

·　·　·

Dileep Kumar was born in Mylapore in 1967 to a teenage mother and an older father. The father had raised himself from the slums by writing music for Malayalam and Tamil movies, and taught his son how to sing and to play the harmonium at the age of five. When Dileep was nine, his father died—the boy believed from some form of black magic, because melted wax and bird feathers were found in the house before his death. He had no choice but to support the family and turned up to recording sessions to play a keyboard twice his own size. At first he was employed as a favour to his late father, but by the time he reached his mid-teens he was gaining a reputation.

Dileep had an additional skill: he knew the inside as well as the outside of a keyboard, and could mend any electronic instrument. (His father's father was an electrician who in his spare time composed bhajans, or devotional songs, to sing at the temple.) His method of working was different from other people's, and he refused to follow the hierarchical conventions of the Tamil music scene, turning up to formal events wearing denim. At school in Chennai, where learning was highly regarded, Dileep was a failure and was often rapped on the knuckles with a ruler by his teachers. He took to composing ad jingles for radio and played in a band called L. Shankar and the Epidemics.

His break came in his early twenties when Mani Ratnam asked him to be the musical director of a new film, *Roja,* about a woman whose husband is kidnapped by Kashmiri separatists. A bizarre pattern of behaviour started to show itself around this time. Dileep Kumar had always spoken little, but now he said almost nothing at all, and did not mention the *Roja* commission to anyone. He set to work, doing things his way. A singer might receive a call in the middle of the night and be asked if she would sing a song immediately over an Internet link. A musician might finish tuning up a sitar and find himself dismissed from the studio, since the recording was already in the bag—Dileep wanted the sound of tuning. He might use a practice version of a song because it contained more passion than the more accurate version. A sound engineer might be summoned to record Dileep singing (although he had stopped calling himself Dileep by now) because he had awoken from a dream with divine inspiration. All of these snatches of sound were woven together using novel technology and turned into extraordinary soundtracks, together with freshly composed music influenced by anyone from Bach to Andrew Lloyd Webber, from swing to pop, from Qawwali to Carnatic music. He was scrupulous about giving credit to his collaborators.

Roja was a hit, and so was the young composer. His family had always been heavily superstitious and concerned with numerology, and now a Hindu astrologer named Ulaganathan told him he would become world famous if his name was prefixed by the letters "A" and "R." Together with his sisters and mother, he had recently converted to Sufi Islam, believing the rules of the faith would give him a mental discipline Hinduism could not. He was also concerned that the Hindu deities his father had worshipped had been turned against him by those who wished to do him evil. So Dileep took a new name and a new faith: he would be called Allah Rakka (or A. R.) Rahman.[25] From then on, everything he did would be oriented around his profound devotion to god. Although he was an observant Muslim, always following the call to prayer and washing in the prescribed way, A. R. Rahman's new religion contained elements of his old, complex, superstitious Hindu devotion. He said that music could not be forbidden by Islam because it brought forth "good thoughts" and was a route to the divine.

As he grew famous, he turned his home into a cross between a recording studio (reputedly the best in India) and a sacred place. It was filled with pieces of new electronic equipment, in which he took a detailed technical interest, garlands, rosaries, and charms his mother gave him. Bookshelves were lined with electronic keyboards. Much of his time was spent in prayer or alternating between prayer and composing. Visiting musicians sometimes had to wait for days before he was ready to see them. At all times, he had a candle burning in front of his console and a track of Islamic chants playing on mute. His spare time, when it happened, was used for visits to dargahs, Sufi shrines, where he would sleep on the floor alongside other pilgrims.

In 1995 his mother chose a bride for him, Saira, and after a single meeting, they married. A. R. Rahman's mother remained the most important person in his life. Despite marriage and children, his life continued in the same devotional way.[26] When this short, unexercised, slow-moving man— the "Mozart of Madras"—stood on stage to receive two Academy Awards in 2008 for *Slumdog Millionaire,* he looked as if he was in a different mental place to anyone else in the theatre. Dressed in a casual black kurta and coat, he gave praise to god in Tamil, thanked his mother for coming all the way to America with him and told Hollywood's finest in his casual and diffident way that he had not been so nervous since the day of marriage—a remark that would have had a completely different cultural implication for most of his audience. "All my life I've had a choice of hate and love," he said. "I chose love, and I'm here. God bless."[27]

To use a phrase now forbidden to historians, some traits seem like an expression of national character, and are specifically Indian. Reading the country's often vivid press, it feels as if some things happen only in India. If you ask about this, people will say, "We are like this only"—implying everyone else should get used to it.

Take the case of the Sikh taxi driver who drives exclusively in reverse gear. It is the sort of thing anyone might do for a few minutes if their car will not engage a forward gear, but when it happened to Harpreet Singh Papoo from Bathinda, he continued. BACK GEAR CHAMPIAN is painted along the side of his vehicle, which he drives only backwards, despite having severe resultant neck and back pain. The local authorities in Punjab have given him a special permit to do so; he has redesigned his gearbox so as to drive at varying speeds; a flashing light and a siren sit on the roof of his car. He has become famous and wants to go to Pakistan. "An Asian champion in driving car in reverse gear at a speed of over 80 km per hour," reported the *Tribune* newspaper, "he has already covered 13,000 km from Bathinda to various towns of North India to spread the message of peace between two countries."[28] For Harpreet Singh Papoo, driving exclusively in reverse gear is a mark of difference; it is his reputation.

Arun Pathak was another character who had no embarrassment. A man from the north who had trouble holding down a job, he found he was able to gain popularity or attention by attaching himself to public causes. When a controversial movie was being filmed in Benares, he tied a large stone to his foot and jumped into the Ganges. In a campaign to close down liquor stores near holy places, he climbed to the top of a 300-foot water tank and doused himself in gasoline, threatening to strike a light and jump. He gained a written assurance from the authorities that his campaign would be taken seriously and climbed down. He has ended up as a politician with the BSP.[29]

Other aspects of behaviour were bizarre and had no apparent explanation. A colour magazine called *The Pseudo Truth* was sold at bookstalls. It had the publicity slogan "The pragmatic echo of graves" and contained articles about Norway, the law, mobile phones, "Charles Lamb—a gigantic personality" and Hezbollah. There was a feature with the headline "Zorba in Greek—new flavours of old urn's dew."[30] Each time I read it, I felt a little more baffled. Then there was the entrepreneur who made "eye-catching furniture" from used car and tractor tyres; and the Konkan railway engines that were really Tata trucks with train carriage wheels attached; and the animal welfare board which launched legal action against Vodafone for making a pug run "fastly fastly" behind a bus during a TV advert, as if this was the worst piece of animal cruelty they could find in India.[31] Another singularity was the creative forms in which language was used. Not long ago, an essay written by an applicant for the civil service in Bihar began to circulate (and he is rumoured to have passed the exam):

The cow is a successful animal. Also he is quadrupud, and because he is female, he give milk, but will do so when he is got child. He is same like God, sacred to Hindus and useful to man. But he has got four legs together. Two are forward and two are afterwards. His whole body can be utilised for use. More so the milk. What can it do? Various ghee, butter, cream, curd, why and the condensed milk and so forth. Also he is useful to cobbler, watermans and mankind generally. His motion is slow only because he is of asitudinious species. Also his other motion is much useful to trees, plants as well as making flat cakes in hand and drying in the sun. Cow is the only animal that extricates his feeding after eating. Then afterwards she chew with his teeth whom are situated in the inside of the mouth. He is incessantly in the meadows in the grass. His only attacking and defending organ is the horn, specially so when he is got child. This is done by knowing his head whereby he causes the weapons to be paralleled to the ground of the earth and instantly proceed with great velocity forwards . . . The palms of his feet are soft unto the touch. So the grasses head is not crushed. At night time have poses by looking down on the ground and he shouts his eyes like his relatives, the horse does not do so.
This is the cow.

Behaving in a spectacular way in order to draw attention to a cause was respectable. In 2006 I was driving from Delhi to Alwar in Rajasthan when the traffic stopped. I walked past buses which had disgorged their passengers on to the road, and lorries packed with gigantic wheat-filled sacks which burst out at the top like muffins. Finally at the head of the line of traffic, I saw the obstruction: a jagged line of tractor tyres set across the highway and weighed down with flat stones, around which sat about a hundred women in close formation, each woman dressed traditionally in a long skirt, with the ghungat, or veil, pulled demurely over her head. To the side stood men and boys, idlers, chatting, scuffling and joking. The women would not move until the state government reconnected their electricity supply, which had been cut off because the village had not paid its bill. The police arrived, full of swagger, wearing metal helmets, only to realize it was women alone around the tyres and stones, and that it would be culturally impossible to drag them away. After a couple of hours, the additional district magistrate arrived, a young man in jeans and wraparound shades who looked out of his depth; he read various petitions and agreed to reconnect the power.

Dr. K. Chaudhry, a 76-year-old retired medical practitioner, became a global Internet sensation by singing 1,400 cover versions of famous songs and posting them on YouTube. With a backdrop of a dingy curtain and a strip light, he could be seen performing "Hotel California" and "Dil Deke Dekho," sometimes accompanied by his grandchildren sitting on his lap. His most popular song was "Beat It," which had gone viral with an alternative title given to it by a viewer: "The Real Killer of Michael Jackson— (he was surfing the Internet late at night and this song killed him)." He had appeared via a webcam link on TV channels around the world, and a Dr. K fan club had started in the United States. At the inaugural dinner, he appeared live on screen and told his fans: "That cannot be described just as a sentimental relationship between a man in Delhi and some hundreds in America. That is a carry-forward relationship from some past lives." In his lack of pretension, his industry and his refusal to be fazed, Dr. K was an Indian type. The technology writer Sree Sreenivasan has suggested that Indians approach social media sites "with great passion" because they allow them "to do two things they love: Tell everyone what they are doing; and stick their noses into other people's business."[32]

"I am never satisfied with the status quo," Dr. K told me, sitting in the living-room of his house on the outskirts of Delhi. He had an old Dell computer, with a separate speaker topped by a webcam. "I get the lyrics on the screen, put the speaker between myself and the lyrics and start to sing." He showed me how he did it. "I can record twelve songs a day. I've translated Mike Jackson into Hindi. Until I had a legal problem, 'Beat It' was getting 3,000 hits a day in Hindi and English on YouTube. After I went on G4 TV, I had 400 comments and fifty phone calls in a single day. That was the busiest day of my life. I had to do so many interviews. Most of my fans are in Canada and Pakistan. I have a dozen clubs in America. At first I called myself Dr. Krishen Chaudhry, then I was told my name was too long for marketing, so I am 'Dr. K.' I have one fan club in Singapore. They are all airline pilots, and most are Indian." As well as singing, he had created astrology software and written medical textbooks. "I also have an Internet mall, selling many things, which makes me $300–400 a month."

"Do you want hot or cold?" asked his son Kapil, who had joined us. I opted for cold. He turned on a fan. Since Dr. K's retirement from medical practice, another of his sidelines—the selling of diagnostic equipment—had been taken over by Kapil. "He revolutionized blood-testing techniques," said the son, taking a ballpoint pen from his shirt's top pocket while inspecting his mobile phone. "We manufactured one calorimeter using Fotodiox—a new kind of sensor—rather than a photovoltaic cell, which converts light to distilled voltage. It was done for the first time by us, here in India. We have had more than 10,000 installations. That's why I'm surprised to see his diversification from that line to this." He indicated his father and the webcam. "He has had success abroad with his singing, but neighbours don't praise him."

"When I was eleven," said Dr. K, "I wrote a lyric and sang it in the temple. I've always liked to sing, but I was told my singing was bad. Neighbours don't praise me."

"It's a little bit like our diagnostic products," said Kapil grimly. "They can be easier to sell in southern cities than in Delhi."

Was Dr. K upset by the negative comments that were posted on his web videos? "I say this: praises please me and abuses amuse me. Without taking criticism, you can't improve. They spend some time with my songs. Using rude language is their culture."

"Vulgar language is worldwide," said Kapil.

The house was in a residential suburb of Punjabi Bagh, an area allocated to migrants from Pakistan after partition. Over time it had become prosperous, as the refugees did well. Dr. K had been forced to leave Pakistan when he was three years old. "Since childhood, I have been working seventeen to twenty-one hours a day. I can remember the refugee camp, I can remember a diver holding a pitcher of water. My father died of diarrhoea in the camp. He had four wives, because he had property and needed an heir. We were given a little land, and I had to walk to school, with no guardian."

He gestured out at the street, indicating the neighbourhood. "These Punjabis, they worked very hard after partition."[33] Dr. K had no fear of failure. On one of his websites, he had written: "I am known across the globe for multiple diverse activities. If one becomes a total flop, I have others to boast of."

In the past, singular stories from India—dabbawallas, reverse-gear driving, Dr. K—had only entertainment value or a local relevance, but Indian methods were now extending to other parts of the globe. Nandan Nilekani, who was the inspiration for Thomas Friedman's *The World Is Flat,* spoke of "the Indian way of working." He was referring specifically to the software industry and to the practices developed at Infosys, but the concept extended to other industries too. "This means breaking down big software projects into chunks that can be tackled simultaneously by many groups worldwide, and then drawing them back together to create a single product."[34] The notion of innumerable people working together towards a common purpose corresponded with what the dabbawallas were doing. It depended on a high level of cooperation, cohesion and assumption—assumption that your remote colleagues were not thinking or acting in a way that conflicted with your own work. With many Indians now working in foreign countries, and particularly the U.S., cultural methods were transferring. Unlike the Chinese, Indians were experienced at dealing with people with different cultures and languages. Even in remote parts of the country, you expected to interact and do business with those who followed different customs.

Although India is home to a higher number of illiterate people than any other country in the world, which is in part the consequence of having more than a billion citizens, many of those who travel overseas are well-educated and highly motivated. It is estimated that Indians are responsible for one in six Silicon Valley startups, and that 30,000 graduates of the Indian Institutes of Technology live and work in the U.S.[35]

Across diverse fields in North America, people of Indian descent were achieving prominence. During the banking crisis, Neel Kashkari at the Office of Financial Stability helped to clear up some of the problems created by Vikram Pandit of Citigroup. In Louisiana, Piyush "Bobby" Jindal became governor. (Asked on radio what he thought of "the *Slumdog Millionaire* governor," a fellow Republican said he was himself "givin' some slum love out to my buddy guv. Bobby Jindal is doing a friggin' awesome job in his state."[36]) Nikki Haley—born Nimrata Randhawa—wowed Tea

Party crowds while running for governor of South Carolina: "I was the daughter of immigrant parents that reminded us every day how glad they were to live in this country."[37] Vinod Khosla co-founded Sun Microsystems, Sabeer Bhatia started Hotmail and Ajay Bhatt became a rock star. Technically, Bhatt was the architect of Universal Serial Bus, or USB, the most successful interface in the history of computing, which has saved millions of hours by enabling people to plug keyboards and printers into computers without them freezing, shutting down or generally taking over the day. Playing on the contemporary kudos of the geek, Intel put out a television advert of him walking into an office against epic music and an inspiring blue background: women swooned and screamed, everyone stopped what they were doing, he poured some coffee, winked, signed an autograph and the line came up on the screen: "Ajay Bhatt, co-inventor of the USB . . . Our rock stars aren't like your rock stars." (In the video he was played by the actor Sunil Narkar, who looked a bit more Bollywood; Bhatt's photo on the company website shows a stiff man in spectacles wearing a Ralph Lauren shirt with button-down collars.)

To an American audience, Indians began to seem like very successful immigrants. Their median household income was $20,000 above the national average. More than 80 percent of them had arrived in the U.S. after 1980, and two thirds held at least a bachelor's degree, against a U.S. national average of one in four.[38] Lists of America's new-technology innovators invariably contained Indian names. They liked to live the American dream, attracted by the possibility of free enterprise in a legal framework that was more efficient than the one in India. Adjustment was often straightforward. As an engineer who had worked for Motorola in Chicago before returning home to Chennai told me: "I was already 'Westernized' when I went to the U.S., because English was such a part of my life. I'd watched all the films, and read the books."[39] Indians relied on family and community networks, tended to be conservative, worked in areas like engineering, business, medicine and information technology, and integrated into society more easily than they could in Europe. In some cases they returned to take up new opportunities after the permit raj ended, but many stayed in the U.S. and—to the initial consternation of their relations—became American.

Since the turn of the new century, these NRIs (Non-Resident Indians) and their ABCD (American-Born Confused Desi) children have become progressively less revered in their home country, their foreign glamour diminishing as India's economic star rises. Some NRIs are shocked by the modern social rules and the lavishness they encounter when they return to India—but who would expect to find specially imported South African giraffes at a wedding party in Ambala?

Despite his unusual experiences, Lalit "Pip" Piplani's attitudes were typical of those who had migrated. I met him on a flight from London to New Delhi. Back in the 1960s, he took a degree from IIT Kanpur before heading to graduate school in Pittsburgh, Pennsylvania, where he got his master's degree in electrical engineering. India seemed to have little to offer him, so he was determined to make it in the United States. He made the unlikely move of joining the army. Pip rose to the rank of colonel, specializing in signals and procurement, and believes he was the first Indian to become a non-medical U.S. Army officer. Certainly in his style, in his firm military handshake with his right shoulder pushed forward, in the spry way he removed his bag from the overhead locker, in his talk of tennis championships and grandchildren, he seemed at ease being American. His accent had only the tiniest hint of north India—he was going to Lucknow to stay with his sister—and I asked him when it had changed. He had a story:

"I signed up, started training. Soldiers were being sent to Vietnam. I had to use binoculars and call out references for targets over the radio. A Jeep pulls up behind me and a furious officer jumps out. 'You're going to get someone killed.' I had such a strong Indian accent that they couldn't understand me over the radio. I decided then and there to change it. It took me about a week." He had embraced the possibilities America offered for assimilation and reinvention, while remaining himself.

I asked Pip how it felt to be an Indian in the U.S. Army. He told another story: "When I was first in command of a company in the late seventies, there was a serious [post-Vietnam] drug problem. Two African-American soldiers were suspected of dealing drugs. I called them in for an interview and kept a former special forces sergeant in the room in case there was trouble. I said what I had to say. One of them comes in close: 'You're just doing this because I'm from a minority,' so I said, 'Minority? Let me tell you about being from a minority. Do you know how many Indians are in the military alongside me?' He looked confused—he didn't know where I was from. So I said, 'Zero percent.' The sergeant just cracked up."[40]

Later, in the period of economic liberalization, India's higher education institutions failed to keep up with demand, leaving many children unable to secure a place. The IITs usually had a third of a million people competing for 8,000 vacancies. In an effort to be one of the winners, many children took private tuition and others were simply caught up in the prevailing atmosphere of work and competition.

Prateek Sabharwal topped 92 percent in his board exams in 2005 and won a place at IIT Delhi. How did he do it? His father was a wholesaler of tea and edible oils at a market in Delhi and had little spare money. While studying for his exams, Prateek went to coaching classes for most of every Saturday and Sunday. On weekdays, he would get home from school in the middle of the afternoon and rest until 7 p.m. Then he would work through to 3 a.m. before getting up again at 7 a.m. "I planned it very carefully," he told me, "and I believe in retrospect that if I had cut even twenty minutes off my working time each day, I might not have made the cut." His ambition was rewarded when he reached IIT and found himself among people "of similar intellectual calibre." He did so well at IIT that he was sent on an exchange programme to the Czech Republic, where "the discipline on the roads" impressed him. On graduation he joined UBS, to work in a back-end support team. His ambition was to be employed by a big investment bank in Hong Kong, Singapore or New York. "I do technical work in finance on the structuring of derivatives and pricing of new financial products," Prateek said. Like the ones that caused the meltdown of 2008? I asked. "Well, English only has twenty-six letters, and you can only build so many financial products."[41]

I met Srikanth Nadhamuni in a Barista coffee shop in Bangalore. He was in his mid-forties, with a strong, pointed face and a sense of direction. I had originally come to talk to him about the eGovernments Foundation, a "social startup" which aimed to improve governance through new technology, but we diverted to a more arcane subject. He had set up the foundation after spending more than a decade working in California. One of his projects since his return to India was to use volunteers on the ground and satellite maps of Bangalore supplied by the Indian Space Research Organisation to change the way local government across India collected tax. In Whitefield, on the edge of the city of Bangalore, they had seen an 800 percent increase in property tax collection since identifying who owned which building. A short while after we met, Srikanth took on what may be the most challenging job in the world, heading the technology team at the national Unique Identification Authority, creating a biometric ID system for every Indian, all 1,157,000,000 of them—and counting.

Srikanth's family had been settled in Karnataka for several generations and came originally from further south. After taking a degree at Mysore University, he had gone on to study at Louisiana State University. He found himself well prepared by his Indian education. "When I did calculus at Baton Rouge, it was a cake-walk." By the early 1990s he was working in computer engineering in Silicon Valley. He spent a year at Intel, designing the Pentium II chip. His ambition was to pack more computing power into a smaller space. When P. C. Mahalanobis had brought the first computers to India after independence, each one took up the space of a room, even an entire floor of a building. Now, the microprocessor in a single desktop computer could do much more than they could, and faster. Thinking your way inside a new chip was more than just a technical challenge, like working out which metal to use or how to design the microarchitecture to generate less heat—it was also philosophical.

"The problem is how to pack the chip, how to get everything into the smallest possible space. Let's say you're packing eight suitcases into the trunk of a car. There's no perfect way to do it, right? So you work out the best way possible. In the chip, you want the lowest acceptable cost-function. You want everything as close as can be. But this is an NP-complete problem, which means there's no algorithm to solve it in a deterministic amount of time." What did "NP-complete" mean? "A nondeterministic polynomial complete—meaning that even if you had infinite time and computing power, you would never reach the best solution. Normal math won't play. So you devise a probabilistic algorithm as an alternative, so as to think your way inside the problem and reach a low cost-function. That was my job at Intel, working out how to pack everything as close together as possible inside the Pentium II chip."

How did they devise the probabilistic algorithm? Srikanth described to me the process of annealing and the technique used by the makers of Samurai swords. After the steel has been forged and beaten, the blade is plunged into a bath of hot oil; by allowing it to cool slowly, the crystals in the metal stick closer together and the structure of the Samurai's blade is stronger. In designing a chip, Srikanth was using "simulated annealing," where as the "temperature" rose, the peaks were higher and the troughs were lower. He was searching for the lowest possible trough, where everything fitted into a smaller space.

"So I'm running simulated annealing through the best computers we have at Intel all night long, trying to come up with multiple solutions. And

come the morning, my numbers are good. The guys are saying, 'This is getting low, this is getting very low.'"

He took my notebook and drew two wavy lines, and marked a trough
on the first wave. "This is a local minima. It looks like the best solution, but
it isn't. If your algorithm has the flexibility to make wrong moves—higher
cost-functions—once in a while, it does not get stuck in a local minima,
and it has a better chance of finding the global minima. Which is here."
Srikanth marked a deeper trough on the second wave.

Why not put the temperature higher still and get more variations?

"Because it becomes so unstable. This is the world of maya—illusion.
It's simulated annealing, so it's all going on in your head. There's no actual
chip at this stage. You can simulate a chip, the fluctuations, the hot and
cold, but none of it is real. It's all in your imagination, here in your head.
You can look out of the window"—he pointed out of the window of the
coffee shop—"and see that hotel and think it's real, but in Hindu philosophy
the reality is in the ultimate concept: the Brahman. In the Advaita system,
which comes from the teachings of Adi Shankara, you are taught there
is no duality between you and the Brahman, and that what you believe is
physical and hence 'real' is really all maya. So designing a chip can be a bit
like maya."

Another Indian techie had told me it was impossible to design or build
pages on the Internet if you thought in a linear way, since it changed constantly and was of infinite size. A web page might look like a page but really
held a complex web of links. The Internet seemed to be a Hindu concept, a
deity with many arms. A text like the Rig Veda, rather than coming up with
definitive answers, asks plenty of questions about creation and suggests we
cannot know what made the universe. It also implies that time has no origin and no conclusion. Astronomical distances and geological time are not
difficult concepts within a Hindu mental framework, or philosophy. I asked
Srikanth if he felt that Christianity and Islam, which encourage more linear
thinking, prevented people from making conceptual leaps when they were
programming.

"I can't say that. Indians clearly have an affinity for mathematics. I've
talked about this with Jewish people I have worked with, and it's partly
about education.[42] There's a lot of similarity in the Jewish and Brahmin
family background, with its obsession with education and respect for science: how you're raised, your grandmother telling you what you have to
eat to be smart—lady's fingers, or okra, in my case. There were people

from every culture working with me at Intel, and at other places I worked like Healtheon and Sun Microsystems. There were American Christians, people of no religion, a lot of Jewish people. One of the smartest minds we had at Healtheon was a guy named Mohammad Alaghebandan. California is the melting pot. It was like the Tower of Babel in those days, with so many different languages: English, Hebrew, Chinese. The one sure way we could all communicate with each other was by drawing pictures on the white board. I can say though that a good deal of the time you would be hearing Indian languages: Telugu, Hindi, Kannada, Tamil.

"The ideas, or the Hindu philosophy, I was learning as a kid probably made it easier to make some mental leaps and to work in the virtual world of designing the chip," Srikanth said. "My family subscribes to the Vishista-Advaita philosophy—what's known as qualified non-dualism—which was propounded by the eleventh-century philosopher Ramanuja. My mother and maternal grandfather and family were all very interested in philosophy, especially Vishista-Advaita and Advaita. There were constant debates at home on the relationship of the Atman, the human soul, and the Brahman, and about the interpretation of the Vedas and Upanishads. My mother is very pious and religious, performing daily prayers. I'd say that we grew up in a fairly religious atmosphere. I used to go to the temple every Saturday."[43]

The affinity shown by certain communities for mathematical thinking comes from a mixture of religious or philosophical training, personal aptitude and intense education. Discoveries by geneticists preclude the possibility of caste inheritance. In ancient times, mathematics and scientific observation were seen as spiritual concepts by Jains, Buddhists and Hindus and were highly developed.

Much astronomy that was developed later by Islamic or Arabic scholars originated in India, as did the trigonometry that accompanied it. The use of zero—the concept of nothingness—combined with a decimal system can plausibly be credited as an Indian invention, as can the numbers usually called Arabic numerals. The Indus Valley civilization had a weights and measures system which worked on a decimal scale. Archaeological remains, including metal weights found at different places, show the measuring system was in operation for a period of at least 500 years. The kiln-fired bricks of the Indus Valley, which are still useable, came in several different sizes but their length, width and thickness were always in the same ratio, 4:2:1.[44] Brahmagupta wrote about gravity, deducing that "all heavy things are attracted towards the centre of the earth," 1,000 years before an apple landed on or beside Isaac Newton, and he was merely following the thinking of Aryabhata, who had lived more than 1,000 years earlier.[45] Jawaharlal Nehru, who took a degree in natural sciences, was an admirer of Aryabhata and the society that gave rise to him. He saw the mathematical advances of ancient India—the use of fractions, division, squares, cubes, the minus sign, algebra, pi and infinity—as the outgrowth of a developed society that needed ways to calculate interest and the fineness of gold, and to trade and to exchange with others.

In earlier times, the times when the opportunities to flower and flourish were limited to very few, those with a similar aptitude to Srikanth might have perished. A celebrated example of someone who nearly disappeared but had a moment to show his unusual talent was S. Ramanujan, the mathematician. Born in 1887 to a Tamil Brahmin family in Erode, he was a quiet man with a plump, pock-marked face and a conventional attachment to religion. Seeking to find others who might understand his ideas about mathematics, he sent some of his theorems to academics at Cambridge University, who were so stunned by what he had written that they arranged for him to come to England and study. Since Ramanujan was working outside the context of academic life, he had made proofs of problems that had already been solved, and in some cases had reached solutions by a new route. He was also making mathematical leaps that would be studied decades later. In 2007, two number theorists at the University of Wisconsin–Madison solved or expanded Ramanujan's "final problem," which concerned intangible numerical expressions known as mock theta functions.[46]

Despite his lack of formal training, Ramanujan is regarded now as one of history's finest ever (known) mathematicians. Arriving at his house one day after a taxi ride, his friend and colleague G. H. Hardy remarked that the cab's licence number, 1729, was rather dull. "No, Hardy," said Ramanujan. "It is a very interesting number. It is the smallest number expressible as the sum of two cubes in two different ways."[47] And it was: 1729 was equal to $12^3 + 1^3$, and to $10^3 + 9^3$. Ramanujan was not a practical man. Coming from the hot and humid south, he was always cold when he was in England, and P. C. Mahalanobis, who was studying at a neighbouring college in Cambridge, noticed he slept on top of his bed wearing an overcoat. Mahalanobis realized Ramanujan had not understood that the blankets tucked tight on the bed could be peeled back and used as a covering. So he showed him how to do it.[48] Ramanujan lived a lonely life: each morning he would change into a dhoti, apply a caste mark to his forehead and perform a puja, before wiping off the naamam and getting dressed in a suit to walk unmarked on the streets of Cambridge.

At the close of the First World War, he returned to India, sick. He had been staying in an icy sanatorium in England. His mother took his horoscope to an astrologer in Triplicane, who studied it and deduced that it was "the chart either of a man of worldwide reputation apt to die at the height of his fame, or one who, if he did live long, would remain obscure."[49] Nehru was one of many who was affected by the pathos of Ramanujan's death at the age of only thirty-two from tuberculosis, seeing it as symbolic of the conditions facing the many Indians who were restricted by their lack of education, lack of opportunity and lack of good employment. "If life opened its gates to them and offered them food and healthy conditions of living and education and opportunities of growth," Nehru asked from his prison cell during the Second World War, "how many among these millions would be eminent scientists, educationists, technicians, industrialists, writers and artists, helping to build a new India and a new world?"[50]

NOTES

PART I RASHTRA · NATION

I. ACCELERATED HISTORY

1. Author's interview with Tashi Norbu, 31 August 2008. Some of this material is taken from my article "India With Altitude," *Telegraph Magazine*, 7 February 2009.
2. Author's interview with T. S. Saravankumar (pseudonym), 26 January 2009.
3. Author's interview with Kynpham Sing Nongkynrih, 19 May 2010.
4. Dhananajaya Singh, *The House of Marwar*, New Delhi, 1994, p. 185.
5. V. P. Menon, *Integration of the Indian States*, Hyderabad, 1985 (first publ. 1956), p. 116. See Ian Copland, "The Princely States, the Muslim League, and the Partition of India in 1947," *The International History Review*, Vol. 13, No. 1, February 1991, pp. 42–43.
6. Singh, *House of Marwar*, pp. 185–99.
7. Alex von Tunzelmann, *Indian Summer: The Secret History of the End of an Empire*, London, 2007, p. 221.
8. Menon, *Integration of the Indian States*, p. 117. Some accounts of this episode suggest the Maharaja of Jodhpur transformed a fountain pen into a pistol, using his skills as a magician.
9. See ibid.; Singh, *House of Marwar*, pp. 185–99; Ian Copland, *The Princes of India in the Endgame of Empire: 1917–1947*, Cambridge, 1997. It is disputed whether Hanwant Singh was married to his third wife, the actress Zubeida Banu (later known as Vidya Rani). Their story was fictionalized in the 2001 movie *Zubeidaa*. See www.royalark.net/India/jodh16.htm.
10. Nayantara Sahgal (ed.), *Before Freedom: Nehru's Letters to His Sister*, New Delhi, 2000, p. 383.
11. Jawaharlal Nehru, *The Discovery of India*, New Delhi, 2004 (first publ. 1946), pp. 70–71.
12. Ibid., pp. 258–59.
13. Ibid., pp. 51–52.
14. I have written about this in greater detail in *Liberty or Death: India's Journey to Independence and Division*, London, 1997.
15. Quoted in B. Krishna, *Sardar Vallabhbhai Patel: India's Iron Man*, New Delhi, 1995, pp. 296–323.
16. Private information.
17. Menon, *Integration of the Indian States*, p. 476.
18. Quoted in Balraj Krishna, *India's Bismarck: Sardar Vallabhbhai Patel*, Mumbai, 2007, p. 149.
19. Alan Campbell-Johnson, *Mission With Mountbatten*, London, 1972 (first publ. 1951), p. 322.
20. This account is drawn from *The Day India Burned: Partition*, a BBC documentary pro-

duced and directed by Ricardo Pollack in 2007, on which I was the historical consultant; Urvashi Butalia, *The Other Side of Silence: Voices from the Partition of India,* London, 2000, pp. 163–82; Gyanendra Pandey, *Remembering Partition,* Cambridge, 2001, pp. 84–91.

21. Mohammad Ali Jinnah, *Speeches,* Lahore, 1989, p. 16.

22. V. P. Menon, *The Transfer of Power in India,* Chennai, 1957, p. 407.

23. Author's interview with Nayantara Sahgal, 14 March 1996.

24. Constituent Assembly debates, Vol. V, 20 August 1947. The Constituent Assembly debates, published by the Lok Sabha secretariat in New Delhi in 1950, are available in full on the Indian Parliament website, www.parliamentofindia.nic.in.

25. Ibid., Vol. I, 9 December 1946.

26. Ibid., Vol. IX, 22 August 1949.

27. Ibid., Vol. XI, 22 November 1949.

28. Ibid.

29. See www.tinyurl.com/6gh2lh.

30. Constituent Assembly debates, Vol. V, 25 August 1947.

31. The number of speakers of Hindi and Urdu, and the similarity or difference between the two languages and other north Indian tongues, remains a subject of academic and popular argument.

32. Constituent Assembly debates, Vol. IV, 23 July 1947.

33. See Granville Austin, *The Indian Constitution: Cornerstone of a Nation,* Oxford, 1999 (first publ. 1966), pp. 28–32.

34. Dhananjay Keer, *Dr. Ambedkar: Life and Mission,* Mumbai, 1990 (first publ. 1954), p. 409.

35. See *The Constitution of India,* Parts III and IV.

36. Constituent Assembly debates, Vol. VII, 4 November 1948.

37. Walter Crocker, *Nehru: A Contemporary's Estimate,* London, 1966, p. 168.

38. Author's interview with Nayantara Sahgal, 22 May 2010.

39. Quoted in Austin, *Indian Constitution,* p. 45.

40. Irfan Ahmad, *Islamism and Democracy in India: The Transformation of Jamaat-e-Islami,* Ranikhet, 2010, p. 18.

41. Quoted in Judith M. Brown, *Nehru: A Political Life,* New Haven, 2003, p. 281.

42. Author's interview with Mohammed Yunus, 11 March 1996.

43. Quoted in Sarvepalli Gopal, *Jawaharlal Nehru: A Biography,* London, 1975–84, Vol. 2, p. 14.

44. NCERT, *History and Civics: A Textbook for Class VII,* New Delhi, 1979, pp. 27 and 66.

45. Quoted in Girish N. Mehra, *Nearer Heaven Than Earth,* New Delhi, 2007, p. 796.

46. See Ramachandra Guha, *India After Gandhi: The History of the World's Largest Democracy,* London, 2007, pp. 365–70.

47. Durga Das (ed.), *Sardar Patel's Correspondence 1945–50,* Ahmedabad, 1971–74, Vol. 10, p. 19.

48. Sanjay Subrahmanyam, "Our Only Colonial Thinker," *Outlook,* 5 July 2004.

49. Christophe Jaffrelot (ed.), *Hindu Nationalism: A Reader,* Delhi, 2007, p. 15.

50. See ibid., pp. 12–17.

51. Quoted in Lawrence Wright, *The Looming Tower: Al-Qaeda's Road to 9/11,* London, 2007 (first publ. 2006), p. 151.

52. This section develops ideas outlined in my article "The Power of Possibility," *India Today,* 20 August 2007.

53. Austin, *Indian Constitution,* pp. 140–43.

54. Quoted in Crocker, *Nehru,* p. 151.

55. Edward C. Sachau (ed.), *Alberuni's India, Volume One,* London, 2000 (first publ. 1910), pp. 19–181. Some scholars believe Al-Biruni never visited India but interviewed captives who had been brought out of the country to the court of Mahmud of Ghazni.

56. Zahir Uddin Muhammad Babur, *Babur Nama: Journal of Emperor Babur,* trans. Annette Susannah Beveridge, London, 2006, pp. 275–76.

2. THERE WILL BE BLOOD

1. Pupul Jayakar, *Indira Gandhi: A Biography,* New Delhi, 1995 (first publ. 1992), p. 164.

2. Quoted in ibid., p. 176.

3. Quoted in ibid., pp. 68–71.

4. Katherine Frank, *Indira: The Life of Indira Nehru Gandhi,* London, 2001, p. 150.

5. Jayakar, *Indira Gandhi,* pp. 116–17.

6. Frank, *Indira,* pp. 202–3.

7. Indira Gandhi, *My Truth,* New Delhi, 1980, p. 43.

8. Jayakar, *Indira Gandhi,* p. 145.

9. Vinod Mehta, *The Sanjay Story,* Bombay, 1978, p. 24.

10. Bruce Chatwin, "On the Road with Mrs. G.," *What Am I Doing Here,* London, 1989, p. 339.

11. Mehta, *Sanjay Story,* pp. 40–44.

12. Quoted in Jayakar, *Indira Gandhi,* p. 157.

13. Mehta, *Sanjay Story,* p. 52.

14. Dorothy Norman, *Indira Gandhi: Letters to a Friend 1950–1984,* London, 1985, p. 103.

15. See Frank, *Indira,* pp. 275–93.

16. Jayakar, *Indira Gandhi,* p. 187.

17. Quoted in Meghnad Desai, *The Rediscovery of India,* New Delhi, 2009, p. 347.

18. See Sudipta Kaviraj, "Indira Gandhi and Indian Politics," *Economic and Political Weekly,* Vol. 21, Nos. 38 and 39, 20–27 September 1986.

19. Jayakar, *Indira Gandhi,* p. 274.

20. Mehta, *Sanjay Story,* p. 63.

21. Girish N. Mehra, *Nearer Heaven Than Earth,* New Delhi, 2007, p. 645.

22. Author's interview with Khushwant Singh, 26 February 1998.

23. Author's interview with Maneka Gandhi, 1 September 2004.

24. See Frank, *Indira,* p. 406.

25. Chatwin, "On the Road with Mrs. G.," p. 331.

26. See Frank, *Indira,* p. 403.

27. See Gandhi, *My Truth,* pp. 146–47.

28. Romesh Thapar, "Cong (Indira) to Cong (Sanjay)," *Economic and Political Weekly,* Vol. 15, No. 22, 31 May 1980.

29. Jayakar, *Indira Gandhi,* p. 418.

30. See Khushwant Singh, *Truth, Love and a Little Malice: An Autobiography,* New Delhi, 2002, pp. 296–99; Frank, *Indira,* pp. 458–59.

31. Some Sikhs do drink alcohol: I once spent a nine-hour flight seated beside two who had three legs between them and drank canteens of whisky mixed with lager.

32. Frank, *Indira,* p. 492.

33. Author's interview with Sarabjeet Singh, 15 November 2009.
34. Author's interview with Amrit Kaur, 21 November 2009.
35. Author's interview with Sarabjeet Singh, 15 November 2009.
36. See Pranay Gupte, *Mother India: A Political Biography of Indira Gandhi*, New Delhi, 2009, pp. 58–59.
37. Author's interview with Vichitra Sharma, 7 April 2010; Gupte, *Mother India*, pp. 56–61.
38. Jayakar, *Indira Gandhi*, pp. 490–91.
39. Sonia Gandhi, *Rajiv*, New Delhi, 1992, p. 13.
40. The portrait of Indira Gandhi is drawn from Jayakar, Frank and Gupte. Unsourced background information and quotations about the Emergency and the activities of individual members of the Gandhi family come from off-the-record interviews I did while researching two articles, "The New Gandhi," *New Yorker*, 16 March 1998 and "The Accidental Figurehead," *Telegraph Magazine*, 29 October 2005.

3. THE CENTRIFUGE

1. J. B. Kripalani was arrested at the start of the Emergency and then released.
2. L. K. Advani, *A Prisoner's Scrap-Book*, New Delhi, 2003 (first publ. 1978), p. 94.
3. This document was published for the first time in *Mainstream*, 22 November 1975.
4. Author's interview with L. K. Advani, 20 January 2009.
5. L. K. Advani, *My Country My Life*, New Delhi, 2008, p. 373.
6. *Dawn*, 7 December 2009.
7. Private information.
8. Vikram Seth and Leila Seth, *Times of India*, 30 January 1993.
9. Amartya Sen, "The Threats to Secular India," *New York Review of Books*, 8 April 1993.
10. Author's interview with Yusuf Ansari, 18 January 2009.
11. Kuldip Singh, "Obituary," *Independent*, 27 December 2004; private information.
12. Election Commission of India, New Delhi, *Statistical Report on General Elections*, 1996.
13. *Indian Express*, 14 February 1998.
14. Author's interview with Kynpham Sing Nongkynrih, 19 May 2010.
15. Gandhi, *Rajiv*, p. 11.
16. See my article "The New Gandhi," *New Yorker*, 16 March 1998; Vaiju Naravane, "In Maino Country," *Frontline*, 25 April–8 May 1998; www.britannica.com.
17. Gandhi, *Rajiv*, p. 1.
18. Author's interview with Chris von Stieglitz, 13 September 2004.
19. Bal Thackeray, *Calcutta Telegraph*, 4 March 1998.
20. Narendra Modi made these remarks in Hindi in a speech in Vadodara on 20 August 2002, and there are different versions of his words. See *Outlook*, 30 September 2002; see also www.rmaf.org.ph, 2003 Ramon Magsaysay Award for Government Service, Biography of James Michael Lyngdoh.
21. Private information.
22. Star TV, interview with Vir Sanghvi, actuality footage.
23. Aaj Tak, actuality footage.
24. Author's interview with L. K. Advani, 2 September 2004.
25. Author's interview with Maneka Gandhi, 1 September 2004.
26. Some of the background information and quotes regarding Sonia Gandhi are taken

from research and interviews I did for the two articles cited in the previous chapter, "The New Gandhi" and "The Accidental Figurehead."

27. *India Today,* 6 September 2004.

28. Rediff.com, 23 February 2004.

29. IBNLive.com, 4 May 2006.

30. *Rediff News,* 5 June 2006. See also *Outlook,* 19 June 2006; Mayank Austen Soofi, "Fact: I Was Inside Pramod Mahajan's Residence," *DesiCritics.org,* 9 June 2006.

31. *Open,* 13 March 2010.

32. Author's interview with L. K. Advani, 20 January 2009.

33. Author's interview with Ashok Chowgule, 2 February 2009.

34. See Christophe Jaffrelot, *The Hindu Nationalist Movement and Indian Politics,* London, 1996, p. 339.

35. See p. 55.

36. Author's interview with Ashok Chowgule, 2 February 2009.

37. www.bjp.org/content/view/2844/428.

38. Author's interview with Murli Manohar Joshi, 5 May 2009.

39. Author's interview with Manoj Shrivastava, 29 April 2009.

40. Varun Gandhi's poetry, and his selected thoughts, can be found on his interesting website, www.varungandhi.net.in.

41. *Daily Telegraph,* 17 March 2009.

42. *Indian Express,* 29 March 2010.

43. Author's interview with Manoj Shrivastava, 29 April 2009.

4. FAMILY POLITICS

1. See Ramachandra Guha, *India After Gandhi: The History of the World's Largest Democracy,* London, 2007, p. 134.

2. Election Commission of India, *Model Code of Conduct for the Guidance of Political Parties and Candidates,* New Delhi, 2007.

3. P. Sainath, "The Medium, Message and the Money," *Hindu,* 26 October 2009.

4. Quoted in Ajoy Bose, *Behenji: A Political Biography of Mayawati,* New Delhi, 2008, p. 21.

5. *Indian Express,* 27 May 2010.

6. Scans of the affidavits of every national candidate are available on the Election Commission of India website: http://eci.nic.in/eci_main/index.asp. They make fascinating reading. Most are deciphered on another website: www.myneta.info. See also "Money Wadis," *India Today,* 4 May 2009.

7. Author's interview with Mohammed Mustaqeem, 26 April 2009.

8. Full disclosure: Kapil Sibal is my wife's sister's husband's father.

9. Rahul Bhattacharya, "Will It Rain Qorma?," *Outlook,* 18 May 2009.

10. Author's interview with Dr. Sita Ram Sharma, 4 May 2009.

11. Author's interview with Bharat Godambe, 3 February 2009.

12. *Jai Bihar,* 4 September 2008.

13. Author's interview with Vijender Gupta, 25 April 2009.

14. *Indian Express,* 16 and 28 April 2009.

15. Rediff.com, 3 March 2004; IndianExpress.com, 9 April 2009.

16. *Indian Express,* 8 May 2009.

17. For information about the 2009 general election that is not first-hand, see Centre for the Study of Developing Societies, Lokniti, "National Election Study 2009," www.lokniti.org/read_how_india_voted_2009.html; indian-elections.com; Prem Shankar Jha, "The Pie in Smaller Slices," *Tehelka*, 13 June 2009; Rajdeep Sardesai, "Why India Voted for Congress," IBNPolitics.com, 29 May 2009; James Manor, "Did the Central Government's Poverty Initiatives Help to Re-elect It?" (unpublished).

18. *India Today*, 21 May 2009.

19. *CNN-IBN*, 19 January 2010.

20. *Zee News*, 19 January 2010.

21. *Tehelka*, 23 February 2010.

22. Election Commission of India, New Delhi, *Statistical Report on General Elections*, 1951. Some of the UP constituencies returned two MPs.

23. Author's interview with Yusuf Ansari, 18 January 2009.

24. *Hindu*, 16 April 2007.

25. Author's interview with K. B. Byju, 21 November 2009.

26. *Mail Today*, 4 October 2009.

27. *Indian Express*, 27 April 2009.

28. *Mail Today*, 16 September 2009.

29. Author's interview with Annu Tandon and Mira Devi, 27 April 2009.

30. *Times of India*, 2 June 2009.

31. *Savvy*, 24 July 2009.

32. *Calcutta Telegraph*, 11 April 2010.

33. Some sources suggest Baitha Kameshwar was working with conditional support from the Communist Party of India (Maoist), others that he was a renegade.

34. *Deccan Herald*, 18 February 2010.

35. Coincidentally—or not—the foeticide of female children is higher in Punjab, Delhi and Haryana than in any other part of India. See National Family Health Survey (NFHS-3) India 2005–06, *Gender Equality and Women's Empowerment in India*, Delhi, 2009, Appendix 2, p. 18.

36. ExpressIndia.com, 7 July 2008.

37. See Jennifer Wells, "Canada's Booming Asbestos Market," TheStar.com, 20 December 2009.

38. IBNLive.com, 9 March 2010.

39. In addition to her other roles, Girija Vyas was a member of the petroleum ministry's Consultative Committee. See *Indian Express*, 24 October 2004.

40. The full dataset and analysis of the "Family Politics" project are available on The IndiaSite.com, for free public use. We estimate that 3 percent of Lok Sabha MPs could arguably be switched to a different category of political background. If any member of the Lok Sabha would like to provide more information about his or her route to Parliament, or feels he or she has been placed in the wrong category, please get in touch with me directly or through TheIndiaSite.com. The "Family Politics" project will be updated after each general election in India. I should restate that I am not suggesting a "hereditary" MP is a bad MP, merely that this system excludes the overwhelming majority of Indians from participation in politics at a national level.

PART II LAKSHMI · WEALTH

5. THE VISIONS OF JOHN MAYNARD KEYNES

1. Robert Skidelsky, *John Maynard Keynes. Volume One: Hopes Betrayed 1883–1920*, London, 1983, p. 178.

2. See Arnold P. Kaminsky, "The India Office in the Late Nineteenth Century," in Robert I. Crane and N. Gerald Barrier, *British Imperial Policy in India and Sri Lanka 1858–1912: A Reassessment*, New Delhi, 1981, pp. 30–37.

3. Sir Josiah Stamp, *Some Economic Factors in Modern Life*, London, 1929, pp. 258–59.

4. Skidelsky, *John Maynard Keynes*, p. 177.

5. David Gilmour, *The Ruling Caste: Imperial Lives in the Victorian Raj*, New York, 2006, p. 48.

6. This analysis draws in part on D. E. Moggridge, *Maynard Keynes: An Economist's Biography*, London, 1992, pp. 201–2.

7. Oscar Wilde, *The Importance of Being Earnest*, London, 1899 (first perf. Feb. 1895), p. 61.

8. Skidelsky, *John Maynard Keynes*, p. 274. See also Wendy Moffat, *A Great Unrecorded History: A New Life of E. M. Forster*, New York, 2010, p. 128. While Keynes and Furness were in Egypt, their mutual friend E. M. Forster was by coincidence on his first trip to India, mooning after Sir Syed Ahmed Khan's grandson Syed Ross Masood.

9. See Skidelsky, *John Maynard Keynes*, pp. 272–77. See also Sudhir Mulji, "India's Role in Keynes's Economic Theory," Rediff.com, 11 March 2004.

10. John Maynard Keynes, *Indian Currency and Finance*, London, 1913, pp. 40–42.

11. P. L. Gupta, *Paper Money of India*, Mumbai, 2000.

12. Keynes, *Indian Currency and Finance*, pp. 99–100.

13. Ibid., pp. 165–66.

14. See Moggridge, *Maynard Keynes*, pp. 214–16 and Annex 1. The most intense phase of the relationship between Keynes and Sarkar appears to have been between 1912 and 1913, which coincided with the conceptualization, writing and editing of *Indian Currency and Finance*. See King's College, Cambridge, Archive Centre, JMK/PP/45/282. Sarkar appears to have worked for Indian Political Intelligence during the First World War.

15. Skidelsky, *John Maynard Keynes*, pp. 260–61.

16. *Financial Times*, 24 March 2009. Zhou Xiaochuan proposed a development of the IMF's Special Drawing Rights, based on a new basket of currencies: individual governments would pass a proportion of their Special Drawing Right reserves to the IMF, and these would gradually replace reserve currencies.

17. National Archives, Kew, CAB 66/65/247-257. I have written about this process in greater detail in *Liberty or Death: India's Journey to Independence and Division*, London, 1997.

18. Alison Light, "Lady Talky," *London Review of Books*, 18 December 2008.

19. John Bruce, *Annals of the Honorable East-India Company*, Vol. 1, London, 1810, p. 146.

20. See Allister Hinds, *Britain's Sterling Colonial Policy and Decolonization, 1939–1958*, Westport, 2001, pp. 5–21.

21. Durga Das (ed.), *Sardar Patel's Correspondence 1945–50*, Ahmedabad, 1971–74, Vol. 3, p. 226.

22. See G. Balachandran, *The Reserve Bank of India, 1951–1967*, Vol. 2, New Delhi, 1998, pp. 595–601.

23. *United Nations Treaty Series*, No. 1796, 1952.

24. See Meghnad Desai, "Drains, Hoards and Foreigners: Does the 19th Century Indian Economy Have Any Lessons for the 21st Century India?," Reserve Bank of India P. R. Brahmananda Memorial Lecture, London, 20 September 2004.

25. Balachandran, *Reserve Bank of India*, p. 605.

26. Nehru, *The Discovery of India*, New Delhi, 2004 (first publ. 1946), pp. 437–38.

27. Bidyut Chakrabarty, "Jawaharlal Nehru and Planning, 1938–41: India at the Crossroads," *Modern Asian Studies*, Vol. 26, No. 2, 1992, pp. 275–87.

28. J. M. Keynes, *The General Theory of Employment, Interest and Money*, London, 1936, pp. 383–84.

29. Pulapre Balakrishnan, *Visible Hand: Public Policy and Economic Growth in the Nehru Era*, Centre for Development Studies, Working Paper No. 391, November 2007, p. 26.

30. Penderel Moon (ed.), *Wavell: The Viceroy's Journal*, London, 1973, p. 383.

31. Quoted in Judith M. Brown, *Nehru: A Political Life*, New Haven, 2003, p. 352.

32. Valerian Rodrigues (ed.), *The Essential Writings of B. R. Ambedkar*, New Delhi, 2002, p. 159.

33. Quoted in Vivek Chibber, *Locked in Place: State-Building and Late Industrialization in India*, Princeton, 2003, p. 96.

34. The contemporary figure is extrapolated from census data for 1991. See Alain Bertaud, "Mumbai FSI Conundrum," June 2004, available at www.alain-bertaud.com.

35. Purshotamdas Thakurdas et al., *A Plan of Economic Development for India*, Bombay, 1944, pp. 3–45.

36. See Ashok Rudra, *Prasanta Chandra Mahalanobis: A Biography*, New Delhi, 1996.

37. Somesh Dasgupta, "The Evolution of the D^2-Statistic of Mahalanobis," in *Sankhya: The Indian Journal of Statistics*, Special Volume 55, Series A, Pt 3, 1993, pp. 442–49.

38. The original model was devised in 1928 by the Soviet economist G. A. Feldman.

39. During the Second World War, John Matthai's daughter Valsa had disappeared mysteriously during a snowstorm while studying at Columbia University in New York. Two months later her body was found in the Hudson River.

40. Quoted in Sunil Khilnani, *The Idea of India*, London, 1997, p. 85. See pp. 75–95.

41. See Arvind Panagariya, "Heed the Words of Wisdom," *Economic Times*, 24 October 2001.

42. Rakesh Batabyal (ed.), *The Penguin Book of Modern Indian Speeches: 1877 to the Present*, New Delhi, 2007, pp. 576–81.

43. Daniel Yergin and Joseph Stanislaw, *The Commanding Heights: The Battle for the World Economy*, New York, 2002 (first publ. 1998), p. 58.

44. Rudra, *Prasanta Chandra Mahalanobis*, p. 247.

45. Balakrishnan, *Visible Hand*, p. 45.

46. S. Sivasubramonian, *The Sources of Economic Growth in India, 1950–51 to 1999–2000*, New Delhi, 2004, p. 4, Table 1.1.

47. Author's interview with Gopal Srinivasan, 27 January 2009.

48. Author's interview with B. Santhanam, 27 January 2009.

49. Heavy Engineering Corporation, Annual Report 2008–2009.

50. Ravi Ramamurti, *State-Owned Enterprises in High Technology Industries: Studies in India and Brazil*, New York, 1987, p. 141. These figures are based on a reading of Table 4.5. Background research on India's state-owned industries by Aaditya Dar.

51. Starred question no. 252, 25 June 1980, quoted in Ramamurti, *State-Owned Enterprises in High Technology Industries,* p. 169.

52. Ramamurti, *State-Owned Enterprises in High Technology Industries,* p. 153.

53. Prabhu Nath Singh, *Some Aspects of the Managerial and Economic Problems of Public Enterprises in India,* New Delhi, 1979, pp. 150–83.

54. Ramamurti, *State-Owned Enterprises in High Technology Industries,* pp. 138–49; M. M. Luther, *Public Sector Reforms: Myths & Realities,* New Delhi, 1998.

55. Committee on Public Undertakings, 28th Report, New Delhi, April 1979, quoting Ministry of Industrial Development and Company Affairs, January 1969.

56. Public Enterprises Survey, *Annual Report on Working of Industrial and Commercial Undertaking of the Central Government,* Vols. I and II, 1974–75 to 1990–91, New Delhi.

57. Rajiv Kumar, "Nationalisation by Default: The Case of Coal in India," *Economic and Political Weekly,* Vol. 16, No. 17, 25 April 1981.

58. Ministry of Steel, Mines and Metals, *National Coal Development Corporation Committee, 1967 Report—First,* New Delhi, 1968.

59. Dorothy Norman, *Indira Gandhi: Letters to a Friend 1950–1984,* London, 1985, p. 146. Mrs. Gandhi may here have been following the stereotypical north Indian perception that if somebody from the south has made good, he or she ought to be a Brahmin. Although Kumaramangalam's mother was a Saraswat Brahmin and social activist, his father, P. Subbarayan, was a scion of a well-known Gounder zamindari family, a prominent agrarian caste concentrated mainly in western Tamil Nadu.

60. Lok Sabha Debates, 10 March 1986.

61. Planning Commission, *Fifth Five Year Plan 1974–79,* New Delhi, 1976. The revised Fifth Five Year Plan outlay for social welfare was $104.7m (Rs.86.1 crore) and for nutritional programmes $140.6m (Rs.115.7 crore). Both totalled $245.3m (Rs.201.8 crore), still less than $257.9m (Rs.212.2 crore).

62. See C. D. Bhattacharya, *Public Sector Enterprises in India,* New Delhi, 1990, pp. 164–70.

63. Bhattacharya, *Public Sector Enterprises in India,* p. 167.

64. See Board for Industrial and Financial Reconstruction website, www.bifr.nic.in.

65. The subsidiary is now making a healthy profit. *Business Standard,* 10 April 2008.

66. S. S. Chattopadhyay, "Technological Strides," *Frontline,* 7–20 November 2009.

67. See Richard Orange, "The Dark Heart of India's Economic Rise," Spectator.co.uk, 9 September 2009.

6. A DISMAL PROSPECT

1. Author's interview with C. K. Ranganathan, 27 January 2009.

2. www.atatwork.org/page/384; *Tehelka,* 29 August 2009; www.truthdive.com/tag/stay free.

3. Author's interview with Daman Singh (Manmohan Singh's daughter), 2 June 2010; Jatin Gandhi, "Manmohan's India," *Open,* 8 August 2009; interview with Manmohan Singh on *The Charlie Rose Show,* 21 September 2004, available at www.tinyurl.com/333rgco.

4. This refers to the period 1861–1900. See Meghnad Desai, "Drains, Hoards and Foreigners: Does the 19th Century Indian Economy Have Any Lessons for the 21st Century India?," Reserve Bank of India P. R. Brahmananda Memorial Lecture, London, 20 Sep-

tember 2004. Desai draws on data in P. R. Brahmananda, *Money, Income, Prices in 19th Century India: A Historical, Quantitative and Theoretical Study*, Mumbai, 2001.

5. T. N. Srinivasan and Suresh D. Tendulkar, *Reintegrating India with the World Economy*, Washington DC, 2003, p. 13.

6. *Business Week*, 23 January 2006.

7. Desai, "Drains, Hoards and Foreigners."

8. Manmohan Singh, *India's Export Trends and the Prospects for Self-Sustained Growth*, Oxford, 1964, p. v.

9. Ibid., p. 303.

10. Ibid., p. 337.

11. Private information.

12. See Vijay Joshi and I. M. D. Little, *India's Economic Reforms, 1991–2001*, Oxford, 1996; Valerie Cerra and S. C. Saxena, "What Caused the 1991 Currency Crisis in India?," *IMF Staff Papers*, Vol. 49, No. 3, 2002; Arjun Sengupta, "Financial Sector and Economic Reforms in India," *Economic and Political Weekly*, Vol. 30, No. 1, 7 January 1995.

13. Daniel Yergin and Joseph Stanislaw, *The Commanding Heights: The Battle for the World Economy*, New York, 2002 (first publ. 1998), p. 184.

14. See Ramesh Chandra, "Reinvestigating Export-Led Growth in India Using a Multivariate Cointegration Framework," *The Journal of Developing Areas*, Vol. 37, No. 1, Fall 2003, p. 83, Table 4.

15. Interview with Manmohan Singh for the PBS series *Commanding Heights*, 2 June 2001, www.tinyurl.com/3xykvq7.

16. Interview with P. Chidambaram for the PBS series *Commanding Heights*, 2 June 2001, www.tinyurl.com/34wedxm.

17. Private information.

18. Private information.

19. Rakesh Batabyal (ed.), *The Penguin Book of Modern Indian Speeches: 1877 to the Present*, New Delhi, 2007, pp. 599–604.

20. See Ajoy Bose, *Behenji: A Political Biography of Mayawati*, New Delhi, 2008, p. 135.

21. The source for my graph is Government of India, *Economic Survey 2009–10*, New Delhi, 2010, Table 7.1 (A), Table 7.1 (B), pp. A81–2, originating from the Directorate General of Commercial Intelligence and Statistics (DGCIS), Kolkata. The figure of $177.2bn for the financial year 2010–11 has been estimated assuming a rate of growth of 20.02 percent, which was the average rate of growth of Indian exports between 2000–2001 and 2008–9 using data in $m in *Economic Survey*. (The figures in Rs. crore in *Economic Survey* give a slightly higher growth rate of 20.57 percent because of exchange rate fluctuations; the DGCIS converts rupee to dollar figures using a simple average of the monthly exchange rate issued by the Reserve Bank of India.) The year 2009–10 was not considered in calculating the average rate of growth because it was an outlier, caused by the effects of the global recession.

22. See pewglobal.org/database.

23. Sanjaya Baru, "The Turnaround Man," *Tehelka*, 4 April 2009.

24. Bloomberg.com, 3 November 2009.

25. See Christopher Andrew, *The Defence of the Realm: The Authorized History of MI5*, London, 2009, pp. 444–47.

26. See www.pmindia.nic.in/lspeech.asp?id=695.

27. Sandeep Pandey, "Diagnosing the Doctor," *Tehelka*, 4 April 2009.

28. Rediff.com, 23 March 2008.

29. Michael Lewis, "The End," Portfolio.com, 11 November 2008.

30. Kaushik Basu, "Markets, Laws and Governments," in Bimal Jalan (ed.), *The Indian Economy: Problems and Prospects*, New Delhi, 2004 (first publ. 1992).

31. The Industrial Disputes Act came into force in April 1947.

32. Private information.

33. *Mail Today*, 18 January 2010.

34. Ibid., 2 September 2009.

35. *Times of India*, 18 October 2006. See www.aahoa.com.

36. Author's interviews with K. Srinivas Reddy, 12 February 2002 and 7 April 2010.

37. Rahul Pandita, "We Shall Certainly Defeat the Government," *Open*, 17 October 2009. This is Muppala Laxman Rao's most detailed interview.

38. Author's interview with Rahul Pandita, 10 April 2010.

39. See Jaideep Saikia (ed.), *Frontier in Flames: North East India in Turmoil*, New Delhi, 2007.

40. See Sanjib Baruah, *Durable Disorder: Understanding the Politics of Northeast India*, New Delhi, 2005.

41. Author's interview with Kynpham Sing Nongkynrih, 19 May 2010.

42. Author's interview with Munish Tamang, 21 May 2010.

43. Author's interview with Rahul Pandita, 10 April 2010.

44. Some of this material is taken from my article "The Longest March," *Telegraph Magazine*, 11 May 2002, and from interviews done at that time. Background information comes from K. Srinivas Reddy and from other local journalists and Maoist sources who wished to remain anonymous.

45. Government of India, Ministry of Home Affairs Annual Report 2008–09, New Delhi.

46. Author's interview with a CRPF constable, 30 November 2009.

47. *Open*, 22 May 2010.

48. *Outlook*, 19 April 2010.

49. Tusha Mittal, "I Am the Real Desh Bhakt," *Tehelka*, 21 November 2009.

50. Author's interview with K. P. Unnikrishnan, 24 January 2009. A couple of months after this interview, I met a man at a party in a Knightsbridge wine bar. He seemed like the usual young Indian banker, doing well at Barclays Capital and zipping between the UK, the United States and Asia. Somehow the subject of the first Gulf War came up, and he told me—over the noise of a white rapper and entourage, who were shooting a video in the bar—how he had been caught, as a terrified teenager, in the desert between Kuwait and Jordan, parched and starving. The meeting between Saddam Hussein and K. P. Unnikrishnan had probably saved his life.

51. Jyoti Punwani, "Memories of a Naxalite Friend," *Times of India*, 20 April 2008. See also "Regular Rebels," IndianExpress.com, 27 September 2009; *Open*, 27 February 2010; Jyoti Punwani, "The Kobad Ghandy I Knew," *Hindustan Times*, 22 September 2009; and Swapan Dasgupta, "Absolving Maoists of Their Crimes," *Pioneer*, 27 September 2009.

52. Visit to Tihar jail, 13 November 2009.

7. FALCON 900

1. Forbes.com, 3 May 2008; www.CarlosSlim.com/biografia.html.

2. *Economic Times*, 22 June 2010.

3. See Peter Cappelli et al., *The India Way: How India's Top Business Leaders Are Revolutionizing Management,* Boston, 2010, pp. 132–38.

4. Author's interview with Sunil Bharti Mittal, 24 June 2010.

5. Interview with CNBC-TV18, available at MoneyControl.com, 26 June 2010. See also *Economic Times*, 24 June 2010.

6. Forbes.com, 30 April 2008.

7. Matthew Kaminski, "Heavy Mittal," *Wall Street Journal*, 4 February 2006.

8. Swraj Paul, *Beyond Boundaries: A Memoir,* New Delhi, 1998, p. 159.

9. *Independent*, 25 August 1996.

10. Full disclosure: I was a member of the India–UK Round Table before being sacked for insubordination.

11. Quoted in Katherine Frank, *Indira: The Life of Indira Nehru Gandhi*, London, 2001, p. 434.

12. See *Daily Telegraph*, 15 August 2007; *Hindu*, 24 June 2007; *Sunday Times*, 11 October 2009.

13. *Guardian*, 31 March 2010; *CNN-IBN*, 1 April 2010.

14. *Economic Times*, 28 March 2010.

15. Raju Bist, "Ambani: A Tycoon for All Seasons," *Asia Times*, 9 July 2002.

16. *Dreaming with BRICs: The Path to 2050,* Goldman Sachs Global Economics Paper No. 99, 1 October 2003.

17. Dheeraj Sinha, "Three Generations, One Big Market," Esomar, Asia Pacific 2008, www.tinyurl.com/2vzgh8s.

18. Private information.

19. *India's Rising Growth Potential,* Goldman Sachs Global Economics Paper No. 152, 22 January 2007.

20. Author's interview with Dilip Mathur (pseudonym), 13 November 2009.

21. *Financial Times*, 10 January 2008; *Time*, 14 December 2007.

22. Simon Winder had a terrible experience with a Double Decker bar in Mussoorie.

23. www.cadburyindia.com/media/press39.asp.

24. *Economic Times*, 24 February 2010; *Financial Times*, 1 June 2009; *Sunday Times*, 29 November 2009; *PTI*, 8 February 2010; background research on Vishnu Garden by Mandakini Gahlot, with additional information from Sanjay Purohit of Cadbury India, 4 September 2009.

25. *Mail Today*, 7 March 2010; ibid., 3 November 2009; IBNLive.com, 30 December 2009.

26. Rediff.com, 15 March 2001.

27. Aniruddha Bahal, "'T'hell'ka: Sting of the Devil," *Outlook*, 26 March 2001.

28. These words are all taken from the transcripts of the secretly recorded Tehelka tapes; I have elided conversations which took place at different times, in order to show the consistency of the conspirators' approach. See www.tehelka.com/channels/investigation/investigation1.htm.

29. *IBN Live*, 29 December 2009.

30. See Savita Sharma, *Poverty Estimates in India: Some Key Issues,* Asian Development Bank, May 2004; Planning Commission, *Report of the Expert Group on Estimation of Proportion and Number of Poor,* New Delhi, July 1993. In 1999–2000, a different method was used to

record household consumption; it suggested levels of poverty had dropped substantially, but this data is now seen as over-optimistic. See Angus Deaton and Valerie Kozel, "Data and Dogma: The Great Indian Poverty Debate," *World Bank Research Observer,* 2005. A report for the government Planning Commission in 2009 by the economist Suresh D. Tendulkar proposed a new method of calculation, stating that India's poverty lines underestimated the extent of the problem. Background research on poverty data by Aaditya Dar.

31. This data has been drawn from Government of India, *Economic Survey of India 1998–1999,* Table 10.6; Government of India Press Information Bureau, *Poverty Estimates for 2004–05,* New Delhi, 2007.

32. Government of India Press Information Bureau, *Poverty Estimates for 2004–05.*

33. World Bank, *Global Economic Prospects,* Washington DC, 2009, p. 47, Table 1.5.

34. See Shaohua Chen and Martin Ravallion, *The Developing World Is Poorer Than We Thought, But No Less Successful in the Fight against Poverty,* World Bank Policy Research Working Paper No. 4703, August 2008, p. 11, footnote.

35. Ibid., p. 34, Table 7.

36. Ibid.; World Bank, *Global Economic Prospects,* p. 47, Table 1.5. *Global Economic Prospects* projects that between 2005 and 2015 the percentage of Indians living below $1.25/day and $2.00/day will fall by 16.2 and 17.7 percent respectively. The data for 2025 is speculative and assumes that poverty reduction will take place at the same rate as projected here for the period 2005–15. A more pessimistic study suggests that poverty rates in India may fall more slowly: see Global Monitoring Report 2010, *The MDGs after the Crisis,* 2010, pp. 115–16, Tables 4A.1 and 4A.2.

37. See World Bank, PovcalNet Online Poverty Analysis Tool, www.tinyurl.com/35neduw.

38. *Economist,* 4 March 2010.

39. Author's interview with Rajeev Samant, 1 February 2009.

40. Author's interview with Dattu Mahadu Vanse, 31 January 2009.

8. A QUARRY NEAR MYSORE

1. *IBN Live,* 10 December 2007.

2. *Mail Today,* 29 May 2010.

3. USmagazine.com, 9 December 2009; *Mail Today,* 11 December 2009.

4. *New York Post,* 4 September 2009.

5. *The Week,* 9 July 2000.

6. Author's interview with Venkatesh, 1 October 2008.

7. Author's interview with Nanjunde Gowda, 1 October 2008.

8. Sugata Srinivasaraju, "Obama Comes Home," OutlookIndia.com, 26 November 2009.

9. Author's interview with Dhruv (pseudonym), 4 October 2008.

10. P. R. Dhar, Simplex senior management adviser, 6 February 2010.

11. Jaikishandas Sadani and Bithaldas Mundhra (eds.), *Indian Culture: Encyclopaedic Survey in Eight Volumes,* Bharatiya Vidya Mandir and Simplex Infrastructures Ltd., n.d.

12. Dinesh C. Sharma, *The Long Revolution: The Birth and Growth of India's IT Industry,* New Delhi, 2009, pp. 6–11.

13. See *Frontline,* 21 April–4 May 2007; Itty Abraham, *The Making of the Indian Atomic Bomb: Science, Secrecy and the Postcolonial State,* London, 1998.

14. See my article "Another Country, Another Era," *India Today*, 26 December 2005.
15. Quoted in Sharma, *Long Revolution*, p. 107.
16. Ibid., pp. 212–16.
17. Nandan Nilekani, *Imagining India: Ideas for the New Century*, New Delhi, 2008, p. 106.
18. See Sugata Srinivasaraju, *Keeping Faith with the Mother Tongue: The Anxieties of a Local Culture*, Bangalore, 2008, pp. 118–25.
19. Pulapre Balakrishnan, "Benign Neglect or Strategic Intent? Contested Lineage of Indian Software Industry," *Economic and Political Weekly*, 9 September 2006, p. 3870.
20. Quoted in Sharma, *Long Revolution*, p. 398.
21. Private information.
22. Author's interview with Mack (pseudonym), 25 October 2009.
23. Author's interview with Ramappa (pseudonym), 2 and 3 October 2008.

PART III SAMAJ · SOCIETY

9. THE OUTCASTES' REVENGE

1. Valerian Rodrigues (ed.), *The Essential Writings of B. R. Ambedkar*, New Delhi, 2002, pp. 48–49. Some authorities date this piece of writing to 1935 or 1936.
2. See Office of the Registrar General & Census Commissioner, *Census of India 2001*, New Delhi; World Bank Data Finder (available at www.datafinder.worldbank.org).
3. *Pioneer*, 16 November 1996.
4. See Rodrigues (ed.), *Essential Writings of B. R. Ambedkar*, pp. 396–405.
5. Ibid., pp. 150–71.
6. Quoted in Kanshi Ram, *The Chamcha Age: An Era of the Stooges*, New Delhi, 1982, p. 99.
7. Ibid., pp. 91 and 112.
8. Omprakash Valmiki, *Joothan: A Dalit's Life*, trans. Arun Prabha Mukherjee, Kolkata, 2007, p. 71.
9. Ibid., p. 1.
10. D. Ravikumar, "The Unwritten Writing: Dalits and the Media," in Nalini Rajan (ed.), *21st Century Journalism in India*, New Delhi, 2007, p. 65. See S. Anand, "Jai Angrezi Devi Maiyya Ki," *Open*, 8 May 2010.
11. Jean-Luc Racine, "Caste and Beyond in Tamil Politics," in Christophe Jaffrelot and Sanjay Kumar (eds.), *Rise of the Plebeians? The Changing Face of Indian Legislative Assemblies*, New Delhi, 2009, p. 441.
12. Author's interview with Anu Hasan, 25 January 2009.
13. Har Gobind Khorana, who won the Nobel Prize in Medicine for his work on molecular biology, was born in Raipur in what is now Pakistan and has spent most of his adult life away from the subcontinent. Born in 1922, he recently retired from MIT.
14. *Mail Today*, 8 October 2009; IBNLive.com, 13 October 2009; *Mail Today*, 6 January 2010. An assortment of people in India have claimed Venkatraman Ramakrishnan as their pupil, including one Professor Govindarajan, who said he was happy and proud to have taught this "more-than-average student" at "pre-university level" in Cuddalore. Venki Ramakrishnan thought this unlikely, since he had left Cuddalore at the age of three.
15. *Hindustan Times*, 6 April 2009.

16. www.sanghparivar.org/blog/swastika/science-of-caste-varna-system-marriage-laws.

17. Author's interview with Dr. Arijit Mukhopadhyay and Dr. Mitali Mukerji, 6 May 2009, with clarifications by email. Indian Genome Variation Consortium, "Genetic Land-scape of the People of India: A Canvas for Disease Gene Exploration," *Journal of Genet-ics,* Vol. 87, No. 1, April 2008, Bangalore. A good summary of this research can be found in *Frontline* (Chennai), 6 and 20 June 2008.

18. Ajoy Bose, *Behenji: A Political Biography of Mayawati,* New Delhi, 2008, p. 35. Some of these anecdotes are drawn from Bose, who took them from Mayawati's autobiography, *Mere Sangarshmai Jeevan Evam Bahujan Movement Ka Safarnama,* published in 2006 "for missionary objectives," according to her official profile. A shorter (two-volume) English version was published in 2008: *A Travelogue of My Struggle-Ridden Life and of Bahujan Samaj.* See also Christophe Jaffrelot, *India's Silent Revolution: The Rise of the Lower Castes in North India,* London, 2003, pp. 387–425.

19. Ambedkar's sharp-tongued widow, Savita, denounced Kanshi Ram in 1997 for having "no knowledge" of her late husband's political ideology. See Jaffrelot, *India's Silent Revo-lution,* p. 423.

20. See Anand, "Jai Angrezi Devi Maiyya Ki."

21. Quoted in Bose, *Behenji,* p. 68.

22. Ram, *The Chamcha Age,* author's note.

23. Quoted in Bose, *Behenji,* p. 72.

24. Bose, *Behenji,* p. 98.

25. Aman Sethi, "Rule of the Outlaw," *Frontline,* 17 December 2005; IndianExpress.com, 14 April 2009; *Mail Today,* 17 April 2010; Peter Wonacott, "Lawless Legislators Thwart Social Progress in India," *Wall Street Journal,* 4 May 2007.

26. *Newsweek,* 27 April 2009.

27. G. Anderson and M. Subedar, *The Expansion of British India (1818–1858),* London, 1918, pp. 189–93.

28. *Times of India,* 28 April 2009.

29. Author's interview with Akbar Ahmad, 27 April 2009.

30. Author's interview with Mukhtar Ansari, 28 April 2009.

31. *Independent,* 17 July 2009.

32. Rodrigues (ed.), *Essential Writings of B. R. Ambedkar,* p. 283.

33. Sir William Jones, *Institutes of Hindu Law: or, The Ordinances of Menu,* London, 1796, pp. iii–iv.

34. Fali S. Nariman, *India's Legal System: Can It Be Saved?,* New Delhi, 2006, p. 4.

35. Jones, *Institutes of Hindu Law,* p. 124.

36. *The Laws of Manu,* trans. Wendy Doniger with Brian K. Smith, London, 1991, pp. 59, 91, 228 and 240.

37. *Mail Today,* 15 March 2010.

38. Bose, *Behenji,* p. 177.

10. 4EVER

1. Author's interview with Satish (pseudonym), 11 November 2009.

2. *GQ,* October 2008.

3. *Hello!,* January 2009.

4. *Hello!,* December 2009.

5. Amy Turner, "They Know the Way to the Top," *Sunday Times,* 14 March 2010.

6. Anjali Puri, "Bangkok Meri Jeb Mein," *Outlook,* 28 July 2008.

7. *Housing Finance Mechanisms in India,* UN-HABITAT, Nairobi, 2008, p. 16; see also Arindam Bandyopadhyay et al., *A Study of Residential Housing Demand in India,* MPRA Paper No. 9339, Munich, 2008.

8. *Hindu,* 17 May 2008; *Merinews,* 17 May 2008.

9. Author's interview with Nupur Talwar, 23 May 2010.

10. *Calcutta Telegraph,* 18 May 2008.

11. DNAIndia.com, 18 May 2008.

12. *PTI,* 21 May 2008.

13. Author's interview with Nupur Talwar, 23 May 2010.

14. IBNLive.com, 12 July 2008; TV footage.

15. DNAIndia.com, 30 May 2008.

16. *Mid-Day,* 26 June 2008.

17. Full disclosure: Pinaki Misra is my wife's uncle.

18. Author's interview with Rajesh and Nupur Talwar, 23 May 2010.

11. SOLACE OF RELIGION

1. Colonel Rafi-ud-Din, *Bhutto Ke Akhri 323 Din* [*Bhutto's Last 323 Days*], Pakistan, 2005, as translated on www.chowk.com/articles/9370.

2. William L. Richter, "The Political Dynamics of Islamic Resurgence in Pakistan," *Asian Survey,* Vol. 19, No. 6, June 1979, pp. 555–56.

3. See ibid., pp. 547–57.

4. Author's interview with Hashim Raza, 26 March 1996.

5. William Logan, *Malabar,* Madras, 1887, p. 198.

6. Ian Talbot, *Pakistan: A Modern History,* New York, 1998, p. 225.

7. See Hassan Abbas, *Pakistan's Drift into Extremism: Allah, the Army, and America's War on Terror,* New York, 2005, pp. 109–15.

8. Interview with *Le Nouvel Observateur,* 15 January 1998 (my translation).

9. *Associated Press,* 4 November 1999.

10. See Ahmed Rashid, *Descent into Chaos: How the War against Islamic Extremism Is Being Lost in Pakistan, Afghanistan and Central Asia,* London, 2008.

11. This line can be sourced to Stephen Philip Cohen, *The Idea of Pakistan,* Washington DC, 2004, p. 270, but I have heard it from a variety of other people.

12. Author's interview with Nawaz Sharif, 6 September 2007.

13. See www.pewglobal.org/database.

14. The table on p. 328 is based on *U.S. Overseas Loans and Grants, Obligations and Loan Authorizations* (the *Greenbook*); Katie Paul, "About Those Billions," Newsweek.com, 21 October 2009. All data is in historical dollars. U.S. aid to Pakistan in 2001–9 included Coalition Support Fund assistance to fight the "war on terror." U.S. aid received by India in 2001–09 does not include data for 2009, which was unavailable.

15. See Abbas, *Pakistan's Drift into Extremism,* p. 114.

16. Speech to the International Writers' Conference in Islamabad, 30 November 1995.

17. Author's interview with Ejaz Azim, 23 March 1996. More than a decade later, an increas-

ing number of young Pakistanis disbelieved their government's propaganda on Kashmir and were more concerned with finding an enduring settlement to the dispute.

18. See Katherine Frank, *Indira: The Life of Indira Nehru Gandhi,* London, 2001, p. 486.

19. Slate.com, 25 June 2007.

20. Author's interview with Shakeel Ahmad Bhat, 6–7 November 2007. A version of this story appeared in the *Mail on Sunday,* 11 November 2007.

21. Author's interview with Hemant (pseudonym), 30 November 2009.

22. *Illustrated London News,* 1 January 1859.

23. Quoted in John Keay, *India: A History,* London, 2000, p. 429.

24. His Majesty's Stationery Office, *East India (Proclamations),* London, 1908.

25. See Nayantara Sahgal (ed.), *Before Freedom: Nehru's Letters to His Sister,* New Delhi, 2000, pp. 373–74.

26. Quoted in Jawaharlal Nehru, *The Discovery of India,* New Delhi, 2004 (first publ. 1946), p. 261.

27. Quoted in Ramachandra Guha, *India after Gandhi: The History of the World's Largest Democracy,* London, 2007, p. 231. See pp. 226–41 for an account of this debate.

28. Quoted in Judith M. Brown, *Nehru: A Political Life,* New Haven, 2003, p. 231.

29. Author's interview with Tazeen Faridi, 27 March 1996.

30. *India Today* conclave, TV footage, 7 March 2009.

31. *Hindustan Times,* 29 November 2009.

32. IBNLive.com, 26 February 2008. The most powerful threat to this inclusionist approach comes presently from the southern Popular Front of India.

33. *The Times,* 7 September 2007.

34. Quoted in Akbar S. Ahmed, *Jinnah, Pakistan and Islamic Identity: The Search for Saladin,* London, 1997, p. 199.

35. I. Mulla, *Commentary on Mohammedan Law,* Allahabad, 2009 (updated edn), p. 344.

36. Author's interview with Maulana Mahmood Madani, 21 November 2009.

37. See Sadanand Dhume, "The Trouble with Dr. Zakir Naik," WSJ.com, 20 June 2010.

38. See Yoginder Sikand, *Bastions of the Believers: Madrasas and Islamic Education in India,* New Delhi, 2005.

39. *Business Week,* 13 October 2003.

40. See Fali S. Nariman, *India's Legal System: Can It Be Saved?,* New Delhi, 2006, pp. 115–21.

41. *Hindustan Times,* 9 January 2004.

42. Author's interview with Qasim Rasool Ilyas, 16 May 2010

43. Author's interview with Faisal Dawood, 2 October 2008.

44. See Irfan Ahmad, *Islamism and Democracy in India: The Transformation of Jamaat-e-Islami,* Ranikhet, 2010, pp. 121–22. See also Irfan Ahmad, "Genealogy of the Islamic State: Reflections on Maududi's Political Thought and Islamism," *Journal of the Royal Anthropological Institute,* Vol. 15, May 2009, pp. 145–62.

45. See Saba Naqvi, "Madly with the Mullah," *Outlook,* 16 November 2009.

46. Rediff.com, 6 July 2007.

47. *Social, Economic and Educational Status of the Muslim Community of India: A Report,* New Delhi, 2006 (report of a committee chaired by Justice Rajindar Sachar). In 10 cases out of 8,827, they could not guess an employee's religion from the name.

48. *Mail Today,* 7 May 2010.

49. *People,* special edition, December 2008.

50. Dan Reed, "Conversations with a Terrorist," *Sunday Times Magazine,* 28 June 2009.

51. *IANS,* 3 December 2008.

52. See Irfan Husain, "Zia's Revenge," *Dawn,* 28 March 2009.

53. Some of this material is taken from my article "They Hate Us—and India Is Us," *New York Times,* 8 December 2008.

54. H. M. Naqvi, *Home Boy,* New York, 2009, p. 146.

55. *Daily Beast,* 31 January 2010.

12. ONLY IN INDIA

1. Author's interview with Gangaram Talekar, 3 February 2009. See also Dennis P. Hungerwood, "Early Carib Inscriptions on Hegde Sacrifice," *Novzhgyet Teklat Insteur,* Bishkek Dot, Vol. 19, Spring 1977, pp. 117–39.

2. Amartya Sen, *The Argumentative Indian: Writings on Indian History, Culture and Identity,* London, 2005, pp. 326 and 55.

3. Wendy Doniger, *The Hindus: An Alternative History,* London, 2009, pp. 79–80.

4. *Mail Today,* 12 October 2008.

5. Bipan Chandra, *Modern India,* New Delhi, 1971, preface.

6. Satish Chandra Mittal, *Modern India: A Textbook for Class XII,* New Delhi, 2003, pp. 123, 131 and 248.

7. André Wink, *Al-Hind: The Making of the Indo-Islamic World* (3 vols.), Leiden, 2004, Vol. 3, p. 163.

8. Ibid., p. 211.

9. Romila Thapar, *Medieval India: History Textbook for Class VII,* New Delhi, 1988, p. 26.

10. Romila Thapar, *Somanatha: The Many Voices of a History,* London, 2005 (first publ. 2004), p. 208.

11. NCERT, *India and the Contemporary World—I: Textbook in History for Class IX,* New Delhi, 2006, p. 105.

12. M. C. Chagla, *Roses in December: An Autobiography,* Bombay, 1974.

13. Author's interview with Prof. Krishna Kumar, 4 September 2008.

14. *Times of India,* 1 May 2009.

15. IBNLive.com, 12 June 2009; *Times of India,* 12 June 2009; *Outlook,* 10 August 2009.

16. *India Today,* 25 October 2009.

17. IBNLive.com, 23 April 2010.

18. *Mail Today,* 17 November 2009.

19. Pushpa Iyengar, "The Dog Matrix," *Outlook,* 3 May 2010.

20. See Janaki Nair, *The Promise of the Metropolis: Bangalore's Twentieth Century,* New Delhi, 2005, pp. 155–57.

21. Author's interview with T. S. Saravankumar (pseudonym), 26 January 2009.

22. Private information. See Steven Martindale, *By Hook or by Crook,* London, 1989; Larry J. Kolb, *Overworld: Confessions of a Reluctant Spy,* London, 2004.

23. Author's interview with Chandraswami, 25 May 2010.

24. Author's interview with Shankar (pseudonym), 19 November 2009.

25. Rakka was a deliberate misspelling of Rakha. (Ironically one of twentieth-century Bol-

lywood's best known stars was a Muslim, Yusuf Khan, who changed his name to Dilip Kumar.)

26. Many of these stories are taken from Kamini Mathai, *A. R. Rahman: The Musical Storm*, New Delhi, 2009.

27. TV footage.

28. *Tribune*, 26 December 2003.

29. *Open*, 26 December 2009.

30. *The Pseudo Truth*, May 2008.

31. *Hindustan Times*, 3 May 2008.

32. Tunku Varadarajan, "Why India Loves Facebook," *Daily Beast*, 16 March 2010.

33. Author's interview with Dr. K. Chaudhry, 10 November 2009. A few days after we met, Dr. K was quoted in the *Times of India* saying that I was writing his biography.

34. *New Scientist*, 19 February 2005.

35. "The New Global Indians," BBC Radio 4, 3 March 2010.

36. Audio available at www.tinyurl.com/3abl7dn.

37. Speech to a Tea Party in Augusta, Georgia, 15 April 2010.

38. Vivek Wadhwa, "Are Indians the Model Immigrants?," *Business Week*, 14 September 2006.

39. Author's interview with Bharat Rajagopal (pseudonym), 26 January 2009.

40. Author's interview with Lalit "Pip" Piplani, 17 January 2009.

41. Author's interview with Prateek Sabharwal, 26 May 2010.

42. It was not wholly surprising to find that Ajay Bhatt's Wikipedia entry had him down as Jewish.

43. Author's interview with Srikanth Nadhamuni, 4 October 2008.

44. Dick Teresi, *Lost Discoveries: The Ancient Roots of Modern Science, from the Babylonians to the Maya*, New York, 2002, pp. 59–60. Teresi's comparisons between ancient and modern can be far-fetched: he suggests the theoretical Higgs field showed up in ancient India under the name "maya."

45. Sen, *Argumentative Indian*, p. 79.

46. Physorg.com, 27 February 2007.

47. Robert Kanigel, *The Man Who Knew Infinity: A Life of the Genius Ramanujan*, New York, 1991, p. 312.

48. Ibid., pp. 1–2.

49. Ibid., p. 327.

50. Jawaharlal Nehru, *The Discovery of India*, New Delhi, 2004 (first publ. 1946), p. 235.

ACKNOWLEDGEMENTS

India depends on personal voices to tell a story, starting with a Ladakhi villager whose house was to be swept away by the cloudburst of 2010, and closing with a techie who is making a unique ID card for every Indian citizen. I want to thank them all, because their words reveal something new about the past, present or future. Most are identified by name in the text and credited in the Notes, although those who are involved in politics or the sex trade have often preferred to stay anonymous. My thanks are due to all of them, and to the others who have in diverse ways helped to make this book happen, including Irfan Ahmad, Yamini Aiyar, Shaheen Sardar Ali, Peerzada Arshad Hamid, N. Bhanutej, Soutik Biswas, Judith Brown, Linda Clarke, Aaditya Dar, Elaine Davies, Meghnad Desai, John Elliott, Shehryar Fazli, Kanika Gahlaut, Mandakini Gahlot, Ram Guha, Christophe Jaffrelot, Rebecca John, Shishir Joshi, the staff of the Archive Centre at King's College, Cambridge, Sunil Khilnani, M. R. Mahadavan, Kamini Mahadevan, Raman Mahadevan, James Manor, Saira Menezes, Lakshman Menon, Martin Moir, Siddarth Raj Pradhan, Srinivas Reddy, Sanjana, Daman Singh, Upinder Singh, Sugata Srinivasaraju and Namita Waikar. The "Family Politics" chapter was an epic piece of work: it was remarkably hard to find out how 545 people grabbed their slice of the parliamentary pie. We all know how Sonia Gandhi landed up in politics, but do you know how Lalubhai Babubhai Patel gained his foothold? Many heroes—around fifty in all—were involved in this process, and I want to thank them for making the workings of Indian democracy become clearer. Their names are credited on the complete Family Politics spreadsheet, which is available on TheIndiaSite.com. Some important sources (usually experienced state-level political journalists) chose to remain anonymous, particularly in India's more scary regions. The main go-getters were Megha Chauhan (who searched out details for the north and outlying territories, and edited and fact-checked diffuse data), Arun Kaul (who created and managed the spreadsheet), Rasheed Kidwai (who mined Bihar, Chhattisgarh, Jharkand, Rajasthan and West Bengal), Mithilesh Kumar (Bihar), N. Bhanutej, C. K. Sivanandan, Rajeev Gowda and Ramu Patil (Karnataka and Kerala), Mr. and Miss Anonymous

(Gujarat), Peerzada Arshad Hamid (Jammu and Kashmir), M. Gunasekaran and Kamini Mahadevan (Tamil Nadu), Lallian Chhunga (Mizoram), Karri Sriram and Sakru Naik Banavath (Andhra Pradesh), Dhanraj Misra (Orissa) and Vidya Krishnan (Maharashtra and Madhya Pradesh). On the publishing side, I want to give thanks to Simon Winder, Ravi Singh, David Davidar, Mark Handsley and Thi Dinh at Penguin, George Andreou and Lily Evans at Knopf, and Sarah Chalfant, Andrew Wylie and James Pullen at the incomparable Wylie Agency. I am thankful for the support of Maurice French, Shivani Sibal, Akhil Sibal, Namita Gokhale, Neerja Pant, Tenzin French, Abraham French, Iris French and Meru Gokhale, to whom this book is dedicated.

Goleen, August 2010

INDEX

Patrick French was born in England in 1966 and studied literature at Edinburgh University. He is the author of *Younghusband, Liberty or Death, Tibet, Tibet* and *The World Is What It Is,* which won the National Book Critics Circle Award and the Hawthornden Prize. French is the winner of the Sunday Times Young Writer of the Year Award, the Royal Society of Literature Heinemann Prize and the Somerset Maugham Award.

A NOTE ON THE TYPE

This book was set in Monotype Dante, a typeface designed by Giovanni Mard-
ersteig (1892–1977). Its first use was in an edition of Boccaccio's *Trattatello in
laude di Dante* that appeared in 1954. Although modeled on the Aldine type
used for Pietro Cardinal Bembo's treatise *De Aetna* in 1495, Dante is a thoroughly modern interpretation of the venerable face.

Composed by North Market Street Graphics, Lancaster, Pennsylvania

Printed and bound by Berryville Graphics, Berryville, Virginia

Designed by Maggie Hinders